The Bentons

The Bentons

*How an American Father and Son
Changed the Printing Industry*

Patricia A. Cost

RIT CARY
GRAPHIC ARTS
PRESS

ROCHESTER, NEW YORK

The Bentons: How an American Father and Son Changed the Printing Industry

Portions of this book appeared in an article written by the author: "Linn Boyd
Benton, Morris Fuller Benton, and Typemaking at ATF," *Printing History* 31/32, vol.
16, nos. 1 & 2 (1994): 27–44.

Published and distributed by
Cary Graphic Arts Press
90 Lomb Memorial Drive
Rochester, New York 14623-5604
http://carypress.rit.edu

Designed by Marnie Soom

ISBN 978-1-933360-42-3

Library of Congress Cataloguing-in-Publication Data

Cost, Patricia.
    The Bentons : how an American father and son changed the printing industry / by
Patricia A. Cost.
        p. cm.
    Includes bibliographical references and index.
    ISBN 978-1-933360-42-3 (alk. paper)
    1. Benton, Linn Boyd, 1844–1932. 2. Benton, Morris Fuller. 3. Type designers—
United States—Biography. 4. American Type Founders Company—History. 5. Type
and type-founding—United States—History. I. Title.
    Z250.A2C76 2011
    686.2092'2—dc22
    [B]
                                                                        2010016546

to Frank

Contents

Acknowledgments

This story of the Bentons could never have been written without access to the complete set of *Inland Printer* magazines, beginning with the first issue of October 1883, and the myriad other resources held by the Melbert B. Cary Jr. Graphic Arts Collection at the Rochester Institute of Technology (RIT). Because these materials are not readily available to the average reader, they are quoted directly and often at length. RIT Professor David Pankow, who is also curator of the collection, shared its treasures with me and was unfailingly supportive. Thank you, David.

The earliest version of this book was a master's thesis for a degree from the School of Printing at RIT. I remain indebted to my original advisors, RIT Cary Professor Herbert H. Johnson and Professor Archibald Provan, for their encouragement and long hours of consultation in the early 1980s; and to the graduate program's coordinator at the time, Professor Joseph Noga. In 1984, Morris Benton's daughter Caroline Benton Gregg graciously invited me to Milwaukee to talk about her father and grandfather; much of the personal information about the Bentons in this book comes from the long conversations we had in her home, which I remember with fondness and gratitude. Her older sister, Elizabeth Benton Swain of Hingham, Massachusetts, also spoke with me at length over the phone. Rudolph Ellenbogen, curator of rare books at Columbia University's Rare Book and Manuscript Library, helped me navigate what was then Columbia University's ATF Collection.

I am grateful to many others who also helped with the initial research: fellow RIT students Joann Berg, Nancy Bittner, Malcolm (Tim) Coe, and Beth Lewis; RIT Professors Michael Peres and Frank Cost; RIT biomedical photography student Sheila Donnelley; RIT photographer James Castelein; Matthew Carter, then senior vice president at Bitstream, Inc.; printing historian Dr. James Eckman; George Gasparik, ATF's plant manager when I visited in 1984; type historian and retired RIT Professor Alexander Lawson; Richard C. Marder, proprietor of his phototypography business, Graftek, and grandson of John Marder, one of the founding members of the American Type Founders Company (ATF); type historian M. F. (Mac) McGrew; David Pankow, at that time curator of the Melbert B. Cary Jr. Graphic Arts Collection; Ralph Van Horn of the Little Falls (New York) Historical Society; Henry Weiland of Milwaukee, a type historian and collector of typographic artifacts; and type designer and RIT Professor Hermann Zapf.

Many individuals paved the way for this book by reading and commenting on the original thesis, and therefore deserve credit and certainly have my sincere thanks: Matthew Carter; private typefounder Paul H. Duensing; Dr. James Eckman; Professor Emeritus Clifford L. Helbert, former dean of the College of Journalism at Marquette University and a business partner of Henry Weiland; Richard L. Hopkins, president of the Pioneer Press of W. Va., Inc.; printing historian and author Richard E. Huss; my father, Roger F. Knittel; Richard C. Marder; M. F. McGrew; George Taenzer of Eastman Kodak Co.; and book publisher W. Thomas Taylor. In the mid-1990s I was fortunate to have had the help of several people in preparing an article about the Bentons for *Printing History*: Dan Carr, owner of Four Zoas Press; David Pankow; Theo Rehak, owner of the Dale Type Foundry; and my friend Karen Reimringer.

More recently, Caroline Benton Gregg's son Laurence Gregg generously shared personal remembrances, photographs, treasured artifacts and ideas for this project, sending me countless emails and small packages in the process. He also introduced me to his cousin Caroline (Kit) Clayton, who sent her personal remembrances. Theo Rehak's enthusiasm for the project continued unabated for years; he gave my son Roger and me a tour of his Dale Guild Type Foundry in New Jersey and donated many Benton artifacts to RIT's Cary Graphic Arts Collection, including original patents, a complete set of ATF cutting slips for Morris Benton's Freehand, and the ATF "Day Book."

In addition to these friends, I am indebted to many others for their help over the past three years: Matthew Carter, who so kindly wrote the foreword to this book; software engineer Raph Levien, who helped to bring the Benton legacy into focus with his perspective on the importance of optical scaling to digital typography (Appendix A); RIT Professor Charles Bigelow, who helped me broaden the scope of my research; Rare Book Librarian Jane Siegel, and Librarian for Public Services and Programs Jennifer Lee at Columbia University's Rare Book and Manuscript Library; designer Juliet Shen, who generously shared her University of Reading master's thesis with me; Gregory Walters, who updated his "Census of ATF Matrices" in January 2009 for inclusion in Appendix B; David Chan at the New York Public Library; Sam Hoff, who scanned my 1984 ATF pictures; Taro Abe and Toko Suzuki, who helped me understand the Japanese sources I used; and many friends who were willing to listen, including Virginia Clark, Diana Green, Peggy Lull and Joan Malley.

I am also extremely grateful to all those who read and commented on some or all of the revised manuscript: RIT Professor Charles Bigelow, Matthew Carter, Kit Clayton, RIT Professor Frank Cost, Laurence Gregg, RIT Professor David Pankow, Thomas Phinney of Adobe, Ann H. Stevens of East River Editorial, and Theo Rehak.

RIT really is a wonderful place, and so many in the community encouraged me that it would be impossible to name them all. However, I would like to acknowledge Dr. Joan Stone, former dean of RIT's College of Imaging Arts and Sciences, and Dr. Patricia Sorce, chair of RIT's School of Print Media and co-director of the Sloan Printing Industry Center at RIT, for their enthusiasm over the past several years. Thanks also go to RIT's Educational and Technology Center and to graduate students Jacquelyn Clements, Megan Miller, Candice Reese, and Mariela Rodriguez for digitizing the hundreds of illustrations included in this book. And for their diligence, advice, and kindness, I'm greatly indebted to everyone at the RIT Cary Graphic Arts Press: Molly Cort, Amelia Hugill-Fontanel, Marnie Soom, and David Pankow.

Finally, I am grateful that, throughout the long years of research and writing, my family has remained very patient with my preoccupation. Thanks to my parents, Roger and Anna Mary Knittel, to Mary Jo Knittel, O.P., to the families of Tom and Kathleen Knittel and Dr. Greg and Catherine Knittel; and to Emil J. and Elaine G. Cost, Emil C. Cost and family, James and Kathleen Cost and family, and Dean and Carolyn Mason and family. Frank Cost has always been an eager sounding board for my ideas. And Roger, Gus, and Elaine kept me motivated—the Bentons are certainly not obscure in their minds!

Foreword

THE AMERICAN TYPE FOUNDERS COMPANY, formed in 1892, was not the first to revive historical styles of type, nor the first to exploit type designs in large families of weights and widths, nor the first to reconcile the design with the technology of type, nor the first to understand the importance of marketing to the success of type. However, if it did not invent these things, it practiced them so well that the result amounted to ATF's real invention: the modern type business. In the history of type-making, ATF in its heyday came very close to the paradigm. It had a great boss in Robert W. Nelson, an engineer of genius in Lynn Boyd Benton, a fine and prolific type designer in Morris Fuller Benton, and a brilliant publicist in Henry Lewis Bullen, amasser of ATF's typographic library, the best historical resource ever housed at a type company. The legacy of ATF's business model, chiefly in the form of the typefaces designed wholly or partly by Morris Benton, survives to this day.

How ATF came to choose the typefaces it produced, sometimes following and sometimes leading typographic fashion, makes a fascinating study. It is not hard to understand how Morris Benton came to revive the type of the 15th-century Venetian printer Nicholas Jenson, as he did in Cloister Oldstyle: he was following the trail blazed by a great reformer, William Morris, whose Golden Type for the Kelmscott Press acknowledged a debt to Jenson. It is not hard either to see why Benton revived the type of Claude Garamond: the French Imprimerie Nationale had dusted off its Garamond types for the Paris Exposition of 1900, where they were much admired (although later found to be wrongly attributed). But in the case of Benton's first revival, Bodoni, there seems to be no obvious precedent. Bodoni was the antithesis of everything Kelmscott. It was against "modern" types, the degenerate 19th-century offspring of Bodoni, that William Morris rebelled. Bodoni was neoclassical elitism on the page. Morris, the medievalist socialist, spoke of "the sweltering hideousness of the Bodoni letter." The impetus to cut a Bodoni seems to have come not from outside the company but from ATF's own resources: the library, and the acumen of Henry Lewis Bullen as a typographic taste-maker. ATF's library had a copy—in fact it eventually had three—of the *Manuale Tipografico,* the massively comprehensive specimen of Giambattista Bodoni's foundry published in two folio volumes by his widow in 1818. For a type designer hunting for inspiration the *Manuale* is an embarrassment of riches. It took Benton three years of research, Bullen said, to design his interpretation. The result, ATF Bodoni, propagated over time into a large family and much copied, became a staple for American newspaper headlines, where its digital renditions are still in everyday use.

To have turned his hand to two apparently antithetical designs, a Jenson and a Bodoni, suggests a versatility in Morris Benton more than a strong personal style. Added over time to the range of his designs were an enhanced version of an existing typeface (Century Expanded), an exercise in legibility (Century Schoolbook), a face from an outside designer, the architect Bertram Goodhue (Cheltenham), a blackletter (Cloister Black), an Egyptian (Stymie), a Jazz Age titling (Broadway), and a sans-serif that culminated a tradition of sturdy 19th-century American gothics (Franklin Gothic). Benton, a man who graduated from Cornell with a degree in mechanical engineering in 1896, went immediately to work at ATF, was put in charge of the company's type-design department in 1900 and designed a typeface as good as Franklin Gothic in 1902, might be said to disprove William Morris's dictum that "The letters should be designed by an artist and not an engineer." It was no doubt the lack of an artistic temperament that explains Benton's adaptability as a designer. The picture of him that emerges is of a loyal employee more concerned with equipping the company to do its business than with his own self-expression. It would be hard to find two more different temperaments in the same line of work than Benton and the type designer Frederic Goudy, his contemporary: the one modest to a fault, the other extroverted and famously good at self-promotion. Benton's reputation has suffered by comparison with Goudy's, perhaps more from the disparity of their characters than from the quality or survival rate of their respective type designs.

The eclectic treasury of typefaces made by ATF was the beginning of the all-out pluralism that we take for granted in today's typography. In their day, as in ours, it was a new technology that allowed the expansion. Boyd Benton's invention of a pantographic machine that engraved punches or matrices accelerated the production of typefaces by replacing the hard-won manual skill of cutting letterforms at actual size in steel with the drafting of letterforms on paper at conveniently enlarged scale. The gain in productivity came from putting a single designer with the equivalent skill of a punch-cutter to supervise the work of a staff of letter-drawers, particularly by delegating the repetitive work of ATF's breeding program that multiplied a typeface design by adding new members to the family (11 Cloister Oldstyles, 15 Bodonis, and so on).

The physical properties of type have changed unrecognizably since ATF was formed: digital data has replaced lead-alloy as the material of type, software engineering has replaced mechanical engineering in making and setting fonts, and the Internet has largely replaced print as a means of marketing them. The last vestiges of ATF's foundry were sold by auction in 1993, mostly for scrap metal, but the qualities that the company fostered—good engineering, good design, good marketing—remain as vital to the type business today as they were at the height of ATF's success, and the professional standards to which the Bentons, father and son, dedicated themselves have never been surpassed.

Matthew Carter
June 25, 2007

A Note on Sources

Many type enthusiasts contributed to this study by correspondence, published articles, conversations, or all three. A few of them had strong opinions that are not necessarily apparent in their words as quoted. Some background knowledge may help to place their ideas in context.

Henry Lewis Bullen (1857–1938) spent 66 years in the printing industry, "as compositor, salesman, promoter, engineer, and without remuneration and because of his love for the graphic arts, as a librarian."[1] He held various positions in sales and management at the American Type Founders Company (ATF) between 1892 and 1936 and was a major figure in New York City's type community. He wrote an unsigned series of articles, "Discursions of a Retired Printer," for the *Inland Printer* magazine between 1906 and 1908, and many other signed articles before and after, over 400 in all, including extensive histories of those who had brought about recent changes in type founding. Bullen "was both a witness of and a participant in many of the dislocations and also advancements which followed the introduction of the machine in the craft of setting printers' types,"[2] wrote Dr. James Eckman, who compiled a list of Bullen's second extensive series of short articles for the *Inland Printer* between 1918 and 1931, "Collectanea Typographica."

Bullen established ATF's Typographic Library and Museum in 1908 and maintained it until 1934, a huge task that took many hours on holidays, weekends, and after regular business hours. He managed ATF's Engineering Department, which promoted production efficiency in printing plants and composing rooms, and received several patents for machines in ATF's line of "Cost Cut Equipment."[3] He was also involved in the planning and production of ATF specimen books and wrote articles for ATF's house organ, *The American Bulletin*.

Stevens Lewis Watts (see below), who also worked at ATF, wrote a tribute to Bullen that he gave as a lecture in March 1966 for the Heritage of the Graphic Arts series in New York City. Watts called Bullen a "resourceful and superior salesman," and "a many-sided man with multiple objectives, achieving successful results in nearly every undertaking."[4]

Bullen's historical writings must be read with his ATF connection in mind, because for all the years he was working at the company he was also, of course, promoting it and its products. He was known to stretch the truth in some cases, perhaps not deliberately but out of a rush of enthusiasm. According to David Walker Mallison's 1976 Columbia University dissertation, "[Bruce] Rogers … tried to encourage Bullen to restrain a propensity for hyperbole and occasional inaccuracy." And again, "D. B. Updike also indicated to Bullen that eagerness to establish an attractive point could misrepresent the blander truth of a situation."[5]

However, since Bullen was a colleague of the Bentons at ATF, his version of some stories may in fact be more accurate than later retellings.

Dr. James Russell Eckman (1908–1987), a cardiac surgeon, medical intelligence officer during World War II, and member of the Mayo Clinic's staff in Rochester, Minnesota, was also an avid printing historian. The Smithsonian Institution called on him regularly in his capacity as a type expert.[6] Eckman wrote a series of articles about printing history for *Printing Impressions* magazine that were later expanded into a book, *The Heritage of the Printer*. He was very helpful in my original research, and later sent six pages of detailed notes about the outcome, pointing out several instances where a Bullen quotation I had used that was flattering to one of the original founders of ATF was also either deceptive or completely false. Eckman painstakingly proved each of his points with quotations from documents in his own collection or the ATF Collection at Columbia University. In this revision, when certain Bullen "facts" were contradicted elsewhere, I included both versions of the story.

Theo Rehak is a type founder and the author of *Practical Typecasting*. He worked for 12 years at ATF in Elizabeth, New Jersey, until it closed in 1993, and now owns and operates two rebuilt and meticulously maintained Benton engraving machines at his Dale Guild Type Foundry in Howell, New Jersey. His foundry casts true foundry types, ornaments, borders, and initials.

In 2000, a Tokyo publishing house commissioned Rehak and Alan C. Waring to re-cut and cast the types needed to reproduce four pages of the Gutenberg 42-line Bible for the grand opening of the Tokyo Printing Museum. Working against an extremely tight deadline, they produced 160 characters of a blackletter type they named B-42, based on "photos, scans, a few revealing half-tones, and a complete facsimile reproduction"[7] of the type that Gutenberg used in his 42-line *Bibla Sacra*, circa 1455. Once the project was successfully completed, they tinkered with their work, re-cutting many of the characters and adding others as new and better examples revealed themselves.

On his Dale Guild Type Foundry website, Rehak explains his position on Linn Boyd Benton's inventions:

> The Benton system is perhaps the most thorough and accurate way of producing matrices for type designs that has ever been devised. The Engraving Machine itself is but one of five infinitely precise components. Properly adjusted and maintained, the measuring microscope, fitting machine, cutter grinding device, and the Barth Automatic Typecasting Machine, enhanced with many Benton-engineered patented improvements, combine to create the finest types in the world.[8]

Major Stevens Lewis Watts (1895–1966) served in both the Army and the Navy in peacetime as well as during the two World Wars.[9] He was a chief printer for the Navy during World War I, became an Army anti-aircraft artillery officer in 1943, and was reassigned in 1947 as a constabulary officer in Occupied West Germany.[10] Between the wars Watts began his long career with ATF at its Richmond, Virginia, branch. He worked as a Kelly press erector, traveling sales representative, branch and regional manager on the West Coast, and from 1948 until he retired in 1955, as manager of type sales and "auxiliary arbiter of the selection, design and production of new type faces"[11] at ATF's main plant in Elizabeth, New Jersey.

"If the full name and the Major rank which he carried from the Army sounded imposing and pretentious, it was an impression which was soon corrected by the briefest conversation or correspondence,"[12] one obituary reported. When Watts retired he founded the Privateer Press at his 110-acre Skyline Bend Farm in Front Royal, Virginia, "as a medium for his typographic tinkering."[13] He published *The Pastime Printer* there, an irregular, eclectic journal consisting of stories about his cats, recollections of his Army and Navy days, and essays on type and typography. Circulation grew to 2,000 copies. *The Pastime Printer* is one of the few private press publications about the graphic arts that was cataloged and preserved by the Newberry Library in Chicago.[14]

Dr. James Eckman wrote this about Watts in 1964:

> Those who knew him while he was at the vast plant in Elizabeth well remember how he would rummage through grimy matrix vaults and dusty stacks of old specimen books of vanished type foundries until he resurrected long-forgotten matrices and printed specimens that had escaped even the notice of Henry Lewis Bullen, the founder of the company's great typographic library. After Major Watts went to retirement he carried out a series

of impressive revivals of venerable type faces cast from the original matrices which he had found but which type fanciers had not known existed. Many a printing office today has fonts of elegant Nineteenth Century types only because of Major Watts' success in finding the matrices to cast them.[15]

M. F. (Mac) McGrew (1912–2007), author of the comprehensive and monumental 1993 book *American Metal Typefaces of the Twentieth Century*, was widely regarded as the leading authority on the history of metal type in America. He regularly received inquiries from around the world about the particulars of various typefaces.[16]

When he was 14 years old, McGrew bought a Kelsey Excelsior printing press. As a high school student, he made a typewriter typeface portrait of President Franklin D. Roosevelt that later appeared in Ripley's *Believe It or Not*. He worked at various printing companies in Pittsburgh while attending Carnegie Institute of Technology, now Carnegie Mellon University. After serving in the Army in World War II, he moved back to Pittsburgh and in 1950 became typographic director at Ketchum, MacLeod & Grove Inc. (now Ketchum Communications), from which he retired in 1977. Over the years he wrote hundreds of articles for various printing magazines and journals, including a regular column, "Let's Talk Type," for *Typo Graphic* magazine. McGrew also published a small periodical, *Let's Talk Type*, at his Press of the Licorice Cat.

1   Maurice Annenberg, *Type Foundries of America and their Catalogs*, 2nd ed. (New Castle, Del.: Oak Knoll Press, 1994), 13.

2   James Eckman, *The Collectanea Typographica of Henry Lewis Bullen 1857–1938 in The Inland Printer, 1918–1924, 1926, and 1928–1931* (Rochester, Minn.: Doomsday Press, 1960), iii.

3   Stevens Lewis Watts, *Henry Lewis Bullen and His Work* (Skyline Bend Farm, Va.: Privateer Press, 1966), 12–13.

4   Ibid., 4.

5   David Walker Mallison, "Henry Lewis Bullen and the Typographic Library and Museum of the American Type Founders Company," (Ph.D. diss., Columbia University, 1976): 220–221.

6   "Type Authority Dr. James Eckman Dies," *Type & Press*, Summer 1987.

7   Rehak, "Seizing Ordered Chaos: A Serious Attempt at Reproducing Gutenberg's B-42 Types, Part 2," Dale Guild Type Foundry website, http://www.daleguild.com/B-42_Story_02.html.

8   Ibid.

9   "Watts Had A Career Just As Colorful As It Was Typographic," *Printing News*, June 4, 1966, 7–8.

10 Eckman, "Taps for the Old Trooper: Steve L. Watts," *Printing Impressions* 9, no. 2 (July 1966): 19.

11 Ibid.

12 "Stevens Lewis Watts: Drillmaster of Little Leaden Soldiers," anonymous obituary, 1966.

13 Ibid.

14 Eckman, "The Many Talents of Stevens L. Watts," *Printing Impressions* 6, no. 9 (February 1964): 8.

15 Ibid., 7–8.

16 Mike Bucsko, "Obituary: M. F. 'Mac' McGrew/Foremost Authority on Metal Typefaces, Worked at Ketchum," *Pittsburgh Post-Gazette* March 4, 2007, http://www.postgazette.com/pg/07063/766709-122.stm.

Metal Type

"Type is something that you can pick up and hold in your hand."[1] So began the British typographer Harry Carter in a 1968 lecture series on the history of type at Oxford University. A few years later even Carter's opening statement became history as new technology began to push aside type's three-dimensionality, relegating metal type to museum status. Today, type is simply one of the many variables that we control electronically to produce documents. But in the late 19th- and early 20th-century world of Linn Boyd Benton and his son Morris Fuller Benton, type was still something to pick up and hold, as it had been since Johannes Gutenberg's day. The Bentons' working lives revolved around metal type, so this story begins with type itself and how it was made before they appeared on the scene.

Each individual piece of type was an oblong piece of metal slightly less than an inch high with a relief (raised) letter on one end in reverse, so that when it was inked and printed on paper it would appear "right-reading." The earliest description of how type was made appeared in a children's encyclopedia printed in 1567 by Christopher Plantin, *Dialogues Francois pour les jeunes enfans*.[2] In 1683 Joseph Moxon published a comprehensive account of the process in his famous *Mechanick Exercises on the Whole Art of Printing*,[3] and Pierre Simon Fournier's explanation in *Manuel Typographique* was completed in 1766.[4] Lucien Alphonse Legros and John Cameron Grant described how type was made in their 1916 classic *Typographical Printing-Surfaces*,[5] and another good source is Paul Koch's 1933 article, "The Making of Printing Types," printed in the first issue of the *Dolphin*, a journal on the making of books.[6] What follows is a simplified version of the process.

A piece of type

A punch

The Punch

The three preliminary steps in making type had to do with the "punch," the "matrix," and the "mold." Basically, a steel, hand-carved "wrong-reading" letter, or punch, was hammered into a piece of copper to create an indented cavity, or matrix, which in turn became the critical component of a mold assembly, into which a molten alloy of lead was poured to make an individual piece of type. The famous American printer, typographer, and type historian Theodore Low De Vinne defined the first step in the process, punch-cutting, as "the art of designing and engraving the model characters from which types are made."[7] Punches were cut by hand, in a profession that required a considerable amount of skill, precision, and patience. British typographer John Dreyfus explained that "punchcutting demands manual dexterity of a kind which can only be attained after many years of experience."[8]

The punch-cutter started with a bar of soft steel, usually about a quarter of an inch square by about two to three inches long. It had to be long enough to be held firmly in a clamp, and thick enough to avoid being bent when it was struck with a hammer. Until the middle of the 18th century these small pieces of steel had to be forged by the punch-cutter himself, which is why punches of that period are found in strange shapes and sizes.[9] The small bar of steel had to be made smooth at one end, called the "face." The punch-cutter filed and then ground the face on a stone until it was perfectly flat and at right angles to the length of the bar.

In some cases the punch-cutter was also the designer of the typeface he was about to cut, having envisioned it himself or having been inspired by letterforms he may have seen or by a previous typeface he wished to alter. Or perhaps the punch-cutter consulted a designer's precise drawing on a geometrical grid for each letter he was about to create. If so, he would etch fine lines corresponding to the grid on the face of the punch, and then transfer the letter, reversed left to right, within those lines.[10] He could also burnish a carefully drawn image right onto the face of the punch or perhaps draw the letter freehand on the steel, although Richard Southall, a contemporary

A 20th-century cutting of a typeface, Arrighi, done in the traditional fashion. From left, punch, matrix, piece of type.

The counter-counter punch and counter-punch used to cut a capital H, from a 1932 article in *The Colophon* by Rudolf Koch and Fritz Kredel

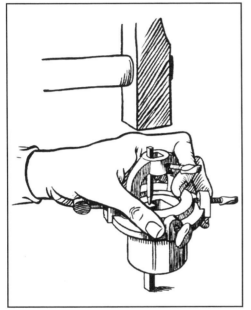

Driving the counterpunch into the punch with a hammer, from Paul Koch's 1933 article "The Making of Printing Types"

The punch-cutter's workspace

British type consultant, finds the last option hard to believe. "Defining the exact shape of a letter by scribing it freehand on a square of polished steel seems to me so difficult as to be almost impossible in the sizes used for setting normal text," he wrote, "… and quite impossible for the smallest sizes in which type was cut by hand."[11]

For letters that had a "counter" (such as a, b, and e), or recess within the letter's outline, most punch-cutters made and hardened a steel "counter-punch." They then drove the counter-punch into the face of the punch using a device that held both pieces in alignment. Certain letters required a counter-counter punch, such as a capital H. Some punch-cutters simply used gravers to manually carve out the counter of a letter.

Then the punch-cutter used a variety of hand-made files, scribers, and gravers to painstakingly cut away the excess metal from the perimeter of the letter. Legros and

Grant explained, "The production of the work requires the continued use of a magnifying eye-glass, combined with the artistic ability to produce the correct curves, and the accuracy to work to a limit of 0.0003 inch."[12] As he perfected the punch, the punch-cutter would stop to make "smoke-proofs" (trial prints) by holding the unfinished punch in the flame of a candle or gas-burner until its face became covered with soot. He then pressed the unfinished punch onto a piece of paper to obtain a sharp, right-reading impression of the letter that he could judge by eye. The punch-cutter repeated this process as necessary until he was satisfied with the design.

The punch determined the shape of the letter, not its spatial relationship to other letters. The lowercase m and cap H were usually the standards for a font, and were engraved first.[13] After a complete set of punches was cut, a proof was taken of the entire set to ensure that all the letterforms harmonized with each other. When the punch-cutter was satisfied, he polished the punches and hardened them by heating them red hot in a furnace and then cooling them in water or oil. This hardening process stressed the steel and made punches extremely brittle. In his *Manuale Typographique,* Fournier devoted an entire chapter to the hardening of punches and counter-punches.[14] A completed punch was slightly larger and longer than a piece of type. It sloped down to the face end, which would be exactly the size and shape of the printed letter.

It is generally agreed that punch-cutting was the most difficult work in early type founding. "No operation in typography requires more skill than this," De Vinne wrote, "and in none is error more disastrous."[15] S. L. Hartz of the Enschedé en Zonen type foundry in Holland wrote in 1958, "Anybody who has tried to cut punches knows that no ordinary jeweler or goldsmith can engrave anything remotely reminiscent of type."[16] P. H. Rädisch cut the punches for most of Jan van Krimpen's typefaces at Enschedé in the mid-20th century, averaging one punch per day.[17] When Henk Drost demonstrated hand punch-cutting at a 1985 workshop at the Enschedé foundry, he too said, "It takes a whole day, more or less, before a punch is ready."[18]

Good punch-cutters commanded relatively high wages—about £4 to £6 per week in England in 1900.[19] Twenty years earlier, the British punch-cutter Edward Philip Prince, working for the Kelmscott Press in London and also averaging one punch per day, had earned 8 to 10 shillings per punch, or about £3 a week (since at the time one British pound was equal to 20 shillings), while hand compositors working a 54-hour week were being paid only 36 shillings, or 60 percent of Prince's earnings. The national average wage of British male workers at that time was under 25 shillings a week.[20]

The quality of the punch depended as much on the artistic sense of the punch-cutter as it did on his skill and precision. If he worked from drawings, he would naturally interpret them as he cut each character. "Each punch was an individual work of art,"

Rudolf Koch's woodcut of a punch-cutter, from *The Typefoundry in Silhouette*.

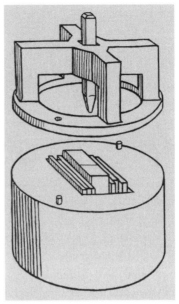

A striking fixture, for holding the punch as it struck the copper bar.

Frank Denman wrote in *The Shaping of Our Alphabet*. "If it broke, the punch that replaced it could never be quite the same."[21] Henry Lewis Bullen of the American Type Founders Company (ATF) exaggerated somewhat when he wrote in the *Inland Printer* magazine, "If the punch of a letter broke, the letter that replaced it was more or less a 'wrong font.'"[22] (A "wrong font" character, as the name suggests, is one that does not match the other characters in the "font" or style of letter.) While a hand-cut replacement punch could never be an identical copy of a broken one, most type-founders tried hard to insure that replacement punches were as accurate as possible.

In 1918, Paul Koch's father, Rudolf, a German type designer and lettering artist, realized that the craft of the hand punch-cutter would soon be obsolete. He cut a series of silhouettes by hand from black paper to provide an artistic tribute to the vanishing trade of traditional typefounding, and published them in *The Typefoundry in Silhouette*.[23]

The Matrix

Once a set of punches had been completed it was ready for the next step in the process: each hardened punch was used to make a "matrix." Matrices were small, polished bars of softer metal, usually copper (although later they were made of a combination of nickel and brass), about an inch long by a quarter of an inch thick. They varied in width according to the size of the letter or character that would be struck into them. A blank matrix was sometimes called a "planchet," after the term used for a flat disk of metal ready to be stamped as a coin.

The punch could simply be held by hand while being struck into copper, but elaborate striking fixtures were in evidence as early as the 1680s.[24] Rudolf Koch's son

A punch, an unjustified matrix, a justified matrix, an unfinished piece of type, and the finished type

Paul explained the use of one of these devices:

> Having cleaned the face of the punch with benzene and a fine brush, I screw the punch, face down, into the upper part of my striking fixture in such a position that, when the upper part is placed on the lower one, the distance between punch and copper bar is only 0.5 cm. On the brightly polished surface of the copper the image or the face of the punch is reflected; which enables me to move the matrix bar sidewise and lengthwise and finally fix its position so that the base line of the character on the punch touches (optically speaking) the line previously drawn across the copper bar; in other words, so that it is properly centered.[25]

Held securely in place, the punch was driven into the copper by a few blows with a heavy hammer to create an exact intaglio (sunken) duplicate of the letter, although reversed, and therefore right-reading. "Long experience teaches one the feeling of how deep the punch must be driven," Koch explained. At this early stage, the copper bar is known as a "drive," a "strike," or an "unjustified matrix." Multiple matrices could be made from one punch, but if the punch fell on the floor it might easily break, so the operation of striking the punch required great care.

Because the force of the blow would distort the copper bar out of square, causing the sides to bulge,[26] the strike (unjustified matrix) needed to be "fitted," i.e., leveled and squared-up. It took a keen eye and a high level of dexterity to properly fit a strike. "Matrix fitting represents one of the most crucial steps in preparing a new font for casting," type historian Stan Nelson wrote. "It is probably as important as punch cutting since a poorly cut design, well fitted, is useable, whereas a poorly fitted font of matrices will render a well-cut design useless."[27] The fitter filed down the strike to make the sunken surface of the letter parallel with the plane of the face in which it had been struck, to determine the amount of white space that would surround each printed character, and to ensure that the depth of drive was constant for every punch. Fitting required much time and patience. Trial casts were made of each letter for measuring, and when a strike was finally perfect it was called a matrix.

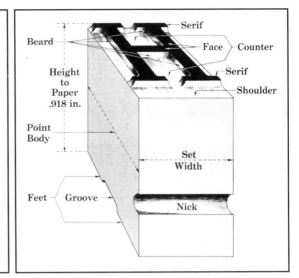

a. In these lines the e has too much space at the left, the a too much at the right; the t is too close at the right, the h too close at the left.

b. In these lines the letter o is too high ; the letter t is too low; the letter h is tilted out of perpendicular on one side.

c. In these lines the letter t leans to the right, and the letter e leans to the left.

Examples of badly fitted type, from De Vinne's *Plain Printing Types*

"The Anatomy of ATF Type." Note the "height-to-paper" indication.

The exact positioning of the letter on the matrix was critical to the look of the type on the page. For example, the bottom curves of letters like o and c need to extend slightly *below* the baseline of the type in order for them to appear to be sitting on it. De Vinne showed in *The Practice of Typography: Plain Printing Types* how a badly fitted matrix could cause the letters to lean slightly to the right or left (see example a), crowd each other or sit too far away from each other (b), or bounce up and down on the page (c).[28] Frank Denman explained in *The Shaping of Our Alphabet* that each letter "must be optically right, not mathematically right; for it to look right it must be in many respects mathematically wrong."[29] This detail had to be in the mind of the punch-cutter from the outset—letters extending below the baseline needed minutely larger x-heights to compensate. "In the traditional technology, achieving visually consistent horizontal alignment between characters is part of the work of justifying the matrices," Southall wrote. "However, the justifier cannot get the alignments right unless the punchcutter has first got the differences in caliber right, and these differences are not large."[30]

Another task of the fitter was to insure that the depth of impression of the letters in a set of matrices was uniform for the whole set. If the depths varied, the resulting individual pieces of type would have irregular "heights-to-paper," in turn causing an uneven printing surface when they were used to compose pages. "The difference of but one five-hundredth of an inch may be almost imperceptible when types … are printed together on damp paper against an elastic impression surface," De Vinne wrote, "but it is a fatal fault when these types are printed on dry paper against a hard surface. To bring up the low types the over-high types will be crushed."[31] The fitter used a "depth gauge" to determine the height-to-paper of the characters in a set of matrices.

The hand mold can be adjusted for different widths   The two parts of the hand mold

A set of matrices for one type style ("typeface") was justified as a unit so that the letters would work together to make a pleasing appearance on the printed page. The letters could be fitted tightly or with generous spacing around each character. "The difference between types cast from two differently justified sets of matrices struck from the same punches"[32] could be profound, as Nicholas Barker found in his research on 16th-century matrices. (Fitting is further discussed in Chapter 10.)

The Mold and Hand Casting

Once a set of matrices was properly fitted, individual pieces of type could be cast from them. Many individual pieces of type—thousands, actually—could be cast from one matrix, depending on the skill of the craftsman. In the earliest casting process, molten type metal was poured into a "hand mold," a small, hollow, adjustable chamber that held a matrix in place on one end. (As De Vinne explained, "The matrix [was] really the mould for the face of the letter."[33]) The adjustable hand mold was the critical component of Johannes Gutenberg's printing system. It was made of two L-shaped steel parts that fit closely together, with wooden end-pieces fixed to the sides to protect the caster's hands. The steel had to be able to withstand the heat of molten metal. By adjusting the two halves of the mold, a wider or narrower cavity would be formed, to accommodate the width of each matrix. The cavity changed only in width, so all the letters cast in one mold would have the exact same body size and height.[34]

Even though Moxon spent about 16 pages and two full-page diagrams describing the hand mold in his 1683 *Mechanick Exercises on the Whole Art of Printing*, the editors of a 1962 reprint of Moxon's book cautioned readers in a footnote: "No one who is unfamiliar with the typefounder's hand mould should try to understand it by reference to Moxon's plates."[35] Contemporary British historian John Man helped with this narrative:

> All you need to know is that the hand mould has two parts which slide together to grasp the matrix, with the imprinted letter facing upwards. With the matrix held firmly in place by a springy metal loop, the two parts leave a rectangular slot, at the bottom of which is the matrix with its imprinted letter. [The person casting type] takes a ladle, scoops up molten metal, pours an

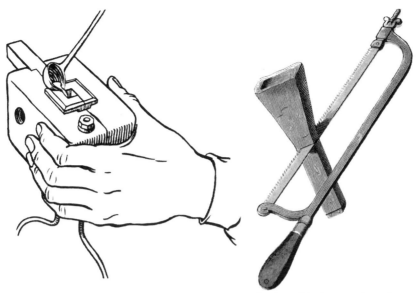

Hand casting   Sawing off the jet on a piece of type

egg cup's worth of it into the slot, lifts off the spring, slides the mould apart, and out falls a little silver rectangle, just over four centimeters long, already cool enough to hold … This is a piece of type, or 'sort,' with its letter standing proud at the top. The whole operation takes less than a minute.[36]

As the molten lead was being poured, the caster gave the mold a sharp jerk in order to let the metal "penetrate the finer lines of the matrix and give a good face to the type; for the metal cooled so rapidly that it otherwise would set before reaching its destination, and an imperfect type would result."[37]

The type casting process tended to destroy hand molds, so they were regularly repaired or replaced. Today the Plantin–Moretus Museum in Antwerp owns 62 original hand molds, dating from the 16th to the 18th centuries. Mike Parker explained in 1974:

A typefounder's hand mould sees hard use. In all its forms it is easily altered. With use and alteration it loses its close fit, grows shackly and in time is discarded. By contrast, the matrices with which it is used have an almost indefinite life, given reasonable and normal treatment.
The chance of finding early typefounders' moulds intact and unaltered, with the evidence to identify them precisely, has always been considered slight. The collection of moulds at the Plantin–Moretus Museum is one that contains, in the main, obviously altered, patched, and repaired examples showing heavy use.[38]

After casting, the type had to undergo additional minor operations before it could be used: the jet of excess metal attached to the center of the type's lower end was broken

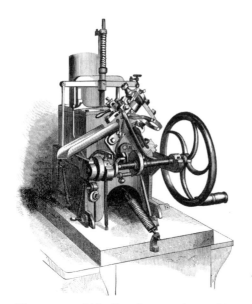

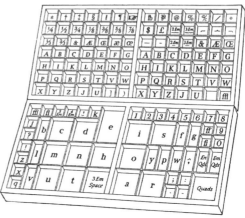

The patent model for Bruce's typecasting machine   A set of type cases

off and the sides were rubbed so as to produce clean surfaces.[39] The bottom end of the type was then grooved out with a plough to create the type's "feet."[40]

THE ADVENT OF MACHINE CASTING

While one piece of type took a relatively short time to cast, adjusting a hand mold for the unique widths of each character in a complete set of matrices and then hand-casting and finishing the types was time-consuming. Several Americans experimented with mechanizing the typecasting process (for example, in 1805 William Wing obtained a patent for a casting machine), but none of these early attempts caught on. In 1834, David Bruce Jr., a punch-cutter and partner in his uncle's type foundry in New York City, invented an attachment for the hand mold called a "squirt machine,"[41] and subsequently became, in his own words, "sorely afflicted with a mania for improvement."[42] He decided to withdraw from the type foundry partnership because his uncle and a third partner could not abide his experimenting at the foundry. The young Bruce studied previous inventions in the field and finally in 1838 received U.S. Patent No. 631 for a type-smoothing machine and No. 632 for his first typecasting machine.[43] According to Bruce, despite the prevailing attitude that type made by machine would be inferior to hand-cast type, his uncle George welcomed the invention:

> Throwing apparently aside his extreme caution, after an examination of the operation of the machine, & satisfied with the results of its practical working—the superior quality of the type, he became the purchaser in 1840 of the patent, & gradually adopted its use in his foundry. From this point the general successful introduction of machine cast type may be dated.[44]

Bruce continued to refine his invention, which eventually revolutionized the business of typecasting.[45] *The Chicago Specimen* (the house organ of the Chicago Type Foundry) for October 1875 explained in general terms how the Bruce typecasting machine worked:

> Mr. Mackellar gives the following description of their operation: "The metal is kept fluid by a little furnace underneath, and is projected into the mould by a pump, the spout of which ... is in front of the metal pot. The mould is movable, and at every revolution of the crank in the hand of the workman it comes up to the spout, receives a charge of metal, and flies back with fully formed type in its bosom; the upper half of the mold lifts, and out jumps a type as lively as a tadpole."[46]

Fonts of Type

Once the type was cast and rubbed down, it was assembled and sold to newspapers and printing shops in sets known as "fonts." A font was a complete collection of all the characters needed in a given type size and style, including upper case, lower case, figures, fractions (in some fonts), punctuation, spacing material, and "ligatures"—combinations of two or three letters on one piece of type, such as *ff* or *fi*. A font would contain a pre-determined number of types of each character—many more individual types of the letter *a*, for example, than the letter *x*.

For his 42-line Bible in 1455, Johannes Gutenberg had some 290 different characters cut and cast in type—47 capitals and 243 miniscules.[47] (The ligatures that Gutenberg used were holdovers from the manuscript practice of tying letters together, which allowed the scribes to limit the number of times they had to lift their pens from the page.) "This excessive number of variants on given letters was the result of Gutenberg's attempt to imitate the various nuances of ligatures ... and other special combinations in those contemporary manuscripts that were his models," Warren Chappell wrote in *A Short History of the Printed Word*.[48] Using ligatures also made it easier to justify the narrow columns of the Bible, producing the aesthetic effect that Gutenberg was seeking.

Another method that early type designers developed for fitting letters close together was to "kern" the characters. In metal type, a kern is a projection of part of the face of a letter beyond its body. A kerned letter had to be trimmed on a kerning machine to fit close enough to its neighbor, on which it relied for support.

Later, a typical font of type for book work was made up of 140 or more characters—capitals, lower case, figures, small capitals, accented letters, marks of punctuation, and marks of reference—not including spacing material.[49] Because each character required its own hand-cut punch, and because cutting steel punches by hand was so difficult, time-consuming, and therefore costly, new typefaces were infrequently

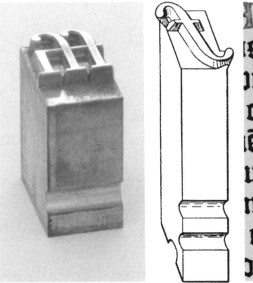

A ligature   A kern   From Gutenberg's 42-line Bible

issued.[50] The Italian type designer Giambattista Bodoni (1740–1813) was said to have been one of the most productive punch-cutters in history, completing more than one punch per day.[51] Even so, one font of type would have taken him two or three months to cut.

HAND COMPOSITION

In printing shops, "compositors" set individual pieces of type into lines of text by hand using "composing sticks." These compositors, or "comps" as they were called, inserted spaces (pieces of non-printing type) as needed to "justify" or fill out the lines of text, in other words, to make the text fit a predetermined line length.

Spacing material came in metal units of the same body size as the type, of course measuring less than "type high" so that they would not print.[52] Wider spaces were known as "quads." The "em quad" was the square of the body size (approximately the width of the capital M); the "en" quad, also called the "nut quad," was half as wide. Narrower spaces were frequently expressed as fractions of the em quad, i.e., three to the em space, four to the em, and thin spaces of five to the em.[53] To add space between lines of text, compositors inserted "leading"—thin strips of type metal typically two points in thickness,[54] again, measuring less than type high.

A typical 8½ by 5½-inch book page today has 30 to 40 lines, with about ten words per line. If a compositor set a 40-line page with approximately 60 characters (and spaces) on each line, he would have handled 2,400 individual pieces of metal for that page. When a page was completed, the compositor would tie it up with string to keep

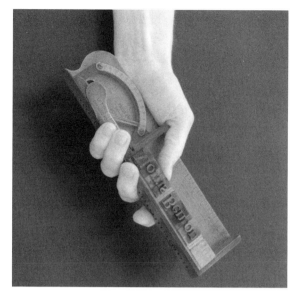

A composing stick

Rudolf Koch's woodcut of a compositor setting type

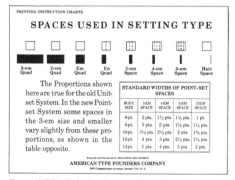

PRINTING INSTRUCTION CHARTS

SPACES USED IN SETTING TYPE

3-em Quad	2-em Quad	Em Quad	En Quad	3-em Space	4-em Space	5-em Space	Hair Space

The Proportions shown here are true for the old Unit-set System. In the new Point-set System some spaces in the 3-em size and smaller vary slightly from these proportions, as shown in the table opposite.

STANDARD WIDTHS OF POINT-SET SPACES				
BODY SIZE	3-EM SPACE	4-EM SPACE	5-EM SPACE	THIN SPACE
6-pt.	2 pts.	1½ pts.	1¼ pts.	1 pt.
8-pt.	3 pts.	2 pts.	1½ pts.	1¼ pts.
10-pt.	3½ pts.	2½ pts.	2 pts.	1¾ pts.
12-pt.	4 pts.	3 pts.	2½ pts.	1¾ pts.
14-pt.	5 pts.	4 pts.	3 pts.	2 pts.

Prepared and Distributed by EDUCATION DEPARTMENT

AMERICAN TYPE FOUNDERS COMPANY
200 Communipaw Avenue, Jersey City, N. J.

From ATF's Printing Instruction Chart

Tying up a form

it together. The individual pages were then made up into a "form," that is, "imposed" or arranged for printing. A typical form of type for a newspaper or book included all of the typeset pages for printing on one side of a press sheet. The form was locked up in a rectangular metal frame called a "chase" that could be moved and handled by the compositors and pressmen. The time-consuming method of hand composition for newspapers and books remained the printer's only option until the last few years of the 19th century. "Even after the availability, by 1870, of rotary presses capable of delivering 15,000 newspapers an hour, printing still required battalions of hand compositors."[55]

STEREOTYPING AND ELECTROTYPING

Harry Carter and George Buday suggested in a *Quaerendo* journal article that Joseph Athias of Amsterdam was perhaps the first printer to use a "stereotype" process, as early as 1673.[56] Other historians date the first stereotype to some time after 1700.[57] Stereotyping made it possible to preserve a replica of a completed type form for later use. First the form was pressed into soft material that could harden, such as plaster. After being separated from the original type, the hardened intaglio replica would then be used as a matrix to make a metal casting that would duplicate the entire form.[58] In the 1790s Firmin Didot experimented with the process in France, giving it a name from the Greek, "stereo," which means solid. Didot used alternate layers of tissue and blotting paper for the matrix material; in 1804 a method using plaster was devised, and by 1830 papier-mâché was being used in Paris.

Stereotype molds made of papier-mâché could faithfully duplicate type images, but were not sensitive enough to render the fine detail of wood engravings.[59] The galvanic battery, developed by Alessandro Volta in 1800, became the basis of an improved method of duplicating forms by the late 1830s, called "electrotyping," which became popular for reproducing and storing composed pages, illustrations, and advertisements. In this new process, a page of set type (and any relief engravings), locked in its form, was pressed into a waxy material that hardened and became the electrotype "mold." It was removed from the form, turned over and dusted with graphite, and then put in a galvanic bath where a thin shell of copper was deposited in every contour of the mold.[60] This copper shell was backed with type metal and mounted on wood to be made type-high, ready for printing.

As the electrotyping process further evolved, Thomas W. Starr of Philadelphia patented his brother Edwin's system for making individual type matrices in 1845 (U.S. Patent No. 4,130), a process that was to have a dramatic effect on the American typefounding industry. The first step was to "obtain a type of the character to be grown."[61] An already-cast type could be used, but for new type designs, each new character had to be engraved in relief on a bar made of the same ingredients used in type metal (lead, tin, and antimony) but in slightly different proportions so as to obtain a somewhat softer composition.[62] These letters in relief were called by various names: "originals," "models," "patterns," or "letter-punches." In 1885, Alfred Pye explained how the electrotyper converted these originals into matrices:

> A small brass plate, varying in thickness according to the size of the type to be made, with a hole punched near one end, is needed for each character, letter, figure, or point, and sometimes ornaments, in the font. These plates are laid upon a flat surface, the letters placed in the holes, face down, and fastened in position with quads or spaces, care being taken to get them as square as possible to the head and sides of the plate. Wax is poured over the portions not intended to be exposed to the action of the battery, and a number of these plates are fastened together, side by side, and placed in a battery, being connected with it and a copper plate by means of wires forming a complete circuit. The battery causes the copper to be deposited around the face of the type in the opening in the brass plates, filling up the opening, and becoming virtually a part of the plate. The time necessary for

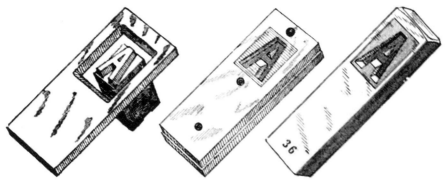

A hole in a plate of copper, with type positioned; a backing plate riveted to it; the matrix after being fitted

the accomplishment of this process varies according to the size of the letter, some of the larger sizes needing to be immersed twice or three times as long as the smaller. When sufficient copper has been deposited to fill the opening in each plate, they are taken out of the battery, the letters withdrawn, leaving their image deeply imbedded in the copper, the back of the plate filed smooth, and another brass plate firmly riveted thereto, making the whole of sufficient thickness for use as a matrix, and are then handed to the fitter.[63]

By the 1880s, many type founders routinely produced matrices with this messy but simple process since it was also less costly and more practical than traditional methods. "While almost every treatise on the history of printing mentions or describes the copper matrices struck from a punch," Carl Schraubstadter Jr. wrote in an 1887 *Inland Printer* article, "the electrotype matrices—which in this country probably exceed the other kind in a proportion of seven or eight to one—are barely mentioned, and where a few words are spoken of them, it is only to condemn their use."[64] Schraubstadter was no doubt referring to the common practice among type foundries of copying (stealing, actually) each other's original type designs by electrotyping them. Type historian and RIT Professor Alexander Lawson explained that the electrotype process "initiated the pirating of types on a large scale. It also contributed greatly to the difficulty of identifying a type, as the same design, reproduced by many foundries, frequently appeared under a dozen names."[65]

Foundries were of course reluctant to divulge their own peculiar electrotyping methods, which fostered competition between them. For example, Linn Boyd Benton explained in 1906 that he used nickel, not copper, to plate type metal originals.[66] According to Theo Rehak, proprietor of the Dale Type Foundry in Howell, New Jersey, "The electrotype matrix discipline for reproducing typefaces either from cast type or engraved models was one of the most zealously guarded mysteries of the old foundries."[67] Rehak's book *Practical Typecasting* divulges his own electrotyping protocols.

Despite the benefits of the electrotype process, producing a new typeface still required the tedious process of cutting letters by hand, whether in steel or in type metal. This remained an obstacle until Linn Boyd Benton discovered a simpler method in the 1880s in his own type foundry in Milwaukee. This, then, is where his story begins.

CHAPTER 1 ENDNOTES

1   Harry Carter, *A View of Early Typography Up to about 1600: The Lyell Lectures 1968* (Oxford: The Clarendon Press, 1969), 5.

2   Ray Nash, ed., *Calligraphy & Printing in the Sixteenth Century: Dialogue Attributed to Christopher Plantin in French and Flemish Facsimile* (Antwerp: Plantin-Moretus Museum, 1964).

3   Joseph Moxon, *Mechanick Exercises on the Whole Art of Printing*, eds. Herbert Davis and Harry Carter, 2nd ed. (London: Oxford University Press, 1962).

4   Carter, ed., *Fournier on Typefounding: The Text of the Manuel Typographique, 1764–1766* (New York: Burt Franklin, 1973).

5   Lucien A. Legros and John C. Grant, *Typographical Printing-Surfaces: The Technology and Mechanism of Their Production* (New York, London: Longmans, Green, 1916).

6   Paul Koch, "The Making of Printing Types," trans. Otto W. Fuhrmann, *Dolphin* 1 (1933): 24–57.

7   Theodore Low De Vinne, *The Practice of Typography: A Treatise on the Processes of Type-Making, the Point System, the Names, Sizes, Styles and Practices of Plain Printing Types* (New York: The Century Co., 1900), 10.

8   John Dreyfus, *The Work of Jan van Krimpen* (London: Sylvan Press, 1952), 21.

9   Carter, "Letter Design and Typecutting," *Journal of the Royal Society of Arts* 102, no. 4935 (Oct. 1, 1954): 881.

10   Koch, "Making," 31.

11   Richard Southall, *Printer's Type in the Twentieth Century* (London and New Castle, Del.: The British Library and Oak Knoll Press, 2005), 7–8.

12   Legros and Grant, *Typographical*, 194.

13   Fred C. Williams, "The Lost Art of Cutting Type Punches," *Type & Press* 82 (Fall 1994): 1.

14   Carter, ed., *Fournier*, 77–80.

15   De Vinne, *Plain Printing Types*, 11.

16   S. L. Hartz, "An Approach to Type Designing," *Penrose Annual* 52 (1958): 40.

17   Dreyfus, "Work," 21.

18   Henk Drost, "Punch Cutting Demonstration," *Visible Language* 19, no. 1 (Winter 1985): 104.

19   Legros and Grant, *Typographical*, 194.

20   F. C. Avis, *Edward Philip Prince: Type Punchcutter* (London: Glenview Press, 1967), 62.

21   Frank Denman, *The Shaping of Our Alphabet* (New York: Alfred A. Knopf, 1955), 214, 216.

22   Henry Lewis Bullen, "Origin and Development of the Linotype Machine, Part 2," *Inland Printer* 72, no. 6 (March 1924): 937.

23   Rudolf Koch, *The Typefoundry in Silhouette: A Portfolio of Twenty-Five Silhouettes* (Offenbach, Germany: Klingspor Bros. Type Foundry, 1918).

24   Stan Nelson, "Mould Making, Matrix Fitting, and Hand Casting," *Visible Language* 19, no. 1 (Winter 1985): 114.

25   Paul Koch, "Making," 47.

26   Dreyfus, "Work," 21.

27   Nelson, "Mould Making," 114.

28   De Vinne, *Plain Printing Types*, 45–46.

29   Denman, *Shaping*, 214.

30   Southall, *Printer's Type*, 9.

31   De Vinne, *Plain Printing Types*, 46.

32   Nicolas Barker, "The Aldine Roman in Paris, 1530–1534," *Library*, 5th ser., vol. 29, no. 1 (March 1974): 5.

33   De Vinne, *Plain Printing Types*, 17.

34   Nelson, "Mould Making," 107.

35   Moxon, *Mechanick*, 134.

36   John Man, *Gutenberg: How One Man Remade the World with Words* (New York: John Wiley & Sons, 2002), 130–31.

37   Alfred Pye, "Typefounding, No. III," *Inland Printer* 3, no. 3 (December 1885): 143.

38   Mike Parker, "Early Typefounders' Moulds at the Plantin–Moretus Museum," *Library*, 5th ser., vol. 29, no. 1 (March 1974): 93.

39   Vervliet, H. D. L., *Sixteenth-Century Printing Types of the Low Countries* (Amsterdam: Menno Hertzberger & Co., 1968), 8.

40   Jennifer B. Lee, "The Exhibition," in *The American Type Founders Company Collection* (New York: Rare Book and Manuscript Library, Columbia University, 2002), 67.

41   Legros and Grant, *Typographical*, 302.

42   David Bruce, *History of Typefounding in the United States*, ed. James Eckman (New York: The Typophiles, 1981), 58.

43   Legros and Grant, *Typographical*, 623.

44   Bruce, *History*, 63.

45   Lee, "Exhibition," 68.

46   "Type Making," *Chicago Specimen* 9, no. 4 (October 1875): 4. Book Arts Collection, Rare Book and Manuscript Library, Columbia University.

47   Aloys Ruppel, introduction to *The 500th Anniversary Pictorial Census of the Gutenberg Bible*, by Don Cleveland Norman (Chicago: Coverdale Press, 1961), 3.

48   Warren Chappell, *A Short History of the Printed Word* (New York: Alfred A. Knopf, 1970), 52.

49   Daniel Berkeley Updike, *Printing Types: Their History, Forms, and Use* (Cambridge: Harvard University Press, 1922), 1:17, 22n.

50   N. J. Werner, "Saint Louis' Place on the Type Founders' Map," *Inland Printer* 79, no. 5 (August 1927): 765.

51   Charles Bigelow, in conversation with the author, June 2007. In "A Bodoni Museum in Parma," *Linotype Matrix* 34 (December 1960): 6–7, author James Mosley noted that an inventory of items for sale from Bodoni's foundry (circa 1843) listed 25,491 punches. Assuming these were cut in the 45 years that Bodoni worked for the Duke of Parma, Bigelow reasoned, and assuming a six-day work week (Sun-

days off), that's 1.8 punches per day. Because Bodoni also printed, he didn't spend every day cutting punches, so his actual rate of output was greater than 1.8 punches a day—maybe 3 punches a day.

52   After dimensional standards for type in the U.S. were finally agreed upon in the late 1800s, type height was set at 0.918 inch and spaces were commonly 0.80 inch high.

53   Philip Gaskell, *A New Introduction to Bibliography* (New York and Oxford: Oxford University Press, 1972), 45–46.

54   The typographer's point is now almost universally standardized as 1/72 of an inch.

55   Walker Rumble, "A Time of Giants: Speed Composition in Nineteenth-Century America," *Printing History* 28, vol. 14, no. 2 (1992): 14.

56   Harry Carter and George Buday, "Stereotyping by Joseph Athias: The Evidence of Nicholas Kis," *Quaerendo* 5, no. 4 (October 1975): 312–320.

57   Ibid., 312–13.

58   Chappell, *Short History*, 176.

59   Clarence P. Hornung and Fridolf Johnson, *200 Years of American Graphic Art* (New York: George Braziller, 1976), 47.

60   Chappell, *Short History*, 177.

61   Roy Rice, "Matrix Making at the Oxford University Press, Part II," Atlanta: Recalcitrant Press, 1982, http://personal.lig.bellsouth.net/r/_/r_rice2/mmoup/part2.htm

62   Pye, "Typefounding, No. II," *Inland Printer* 3, no. 2 (November 1885): 84.

63   Ibid.

64   Carl Schraubstadter Jr., "Electrotype Matrices," *Inland Printer* 4, no. 6 (March 1887): 382.

65   Alexander Lawson, *Anatomy of a Typeface* (Boston: David R. Godine, 1990), 350.

66   Linn Boyd Benton, "The Making of Type," in *The Building of a Book*, ed. Frederick H. Hitchcock (New York: Grafton Press, 1906), 36.

67   Theo Rehak, *Practical Typecasting* (New Castle, Del.: Oak Knoll Books, 1993), 137.

Three Generations of Bentons

WHAT ENABLES SOME PEOPLE to accomplish amazing things? It can't be simply intelligence because many people have that gift. Desire and temperament are certainly critical ingredients, but early childhood experience may also be an important component. Facing difficulties, especially early in life, seems to trigger a set of responses that lead to achievement later on.

The Benton family raised several high achievers. Charles Swan Benton found opportunity where others would not have seen it. His son Linn Boyd was forced at an early age to rely on himself because his mother died before he was five years old and the family moved frequently. Linn Boyd's son Morris suffered from a childhood illness, which set him apart from his peers. Overcoming adversity gave each of the Bentons a strong character and played a part in shaping who they would become.

CHARLES SWAN BENTON

The Benton family's American history began when Andrew Benton, an Englishman, settled in Connecticut in 1638.[1] One of his descendants was Charles Swan Benton, born July 12, 1810, in Fryeburg, Maine, the youngest of the ten children of Dr. Joseph Benton and Catherine Britton Benton.[2] Charles's father, Dr. Benton, was a physician of the old school. He was competent and well-respected, traveling "day and night, through storm and sunshine, in season and out of season in a one-horse gig, to minister to the wants of the sick and suffering."[3] Charles admired his physician father, "of whom it was said that his scoldings cured more people than did his medicines."[4]

While still a boy his mother sent Charles to Little Falls, Herkimer County, New York, to be apprenticed to his uncle, a tanner. But after a short time Charles decided instead to attend Lowville Academy, paying his own tuition by doing chores. Later he studied law with his oldest brother, Nathaniel Seley Benton (1792–1869), also of Little Falls.[5] Nathaniel had been a soldier in the U.S. Army in the War of 1812, and later became a county surrogate, county judge, a member of the New York state senate, district attorney for northern New York,[6] and secretary of state from 1845 to 1847.[7] Nathaniel was the first "president" of Little Falls and the author of the first "History of Herkimer County."[8] Today there is a grade school in Little Falls named after him.

In 1832, when Charles Benton was 22 years old, he established the *Mohawk Courier & Little Falls Gazette*. Two years later, Josiah A. Noonan became publisher and Charles remained as editor,[9] bringing him prominence and a means for being vocal on political issues.[10] Charles was well liked: "by his kindly social qualities, with good principles and superior intelligence, [he] won his way to the esteem and confidence of the people in this village and county to a degree rarely equaled."[11] He was commonly known as "Colonel" Benton because of his connection with the New York militia, "having been commissioned, in 1833, as judge advocate of the first division of riflemen, with the grade of colonel."[12] Charles was admitted to the bar in 1835 but apparently was not destined to remain simply a lawyer since, as one hand-written eulogy pointed out many years later, "he possessed a warm feeling-ed, human friendly for right and truth glowing heart, and a man with one such heart, can as lawyer here not successful be."[13] In 1837, however, Charles was appointed surrogate judge of Herkimer County.

In 1840, he married Emeline Fuller of Little Falls. Two years later he was elected as a Democrat to Congress from the 17th Congressional District of New York State, and was reelected in 1844. In Washington, Charles met a congressman from Kentucky named Linn Boyd, who later became Speaker of the House of Representatives. The two became close friends and shared an interest in dueling. Linn Boyd trained Charles Benton by saying, "Never fight a duel; never be afraid to fight a duel; let them know you will fight and you will never have to fight."[14] Charles honored his friend by naming his first son Linn Boyd Benton, born in Little Falls on May 13, 1844.

Charles was elected as the first clerk of the Court of Appeals for New York State in 1847 and served for two terms. His wife Emeline died during this time, about three years after Linn Boyd was born. Boyd, as he came to be called, remained an only child and motherless for several years until 1853, when his father married Elizabeth Babcock Reynolds of Oswego, New York. She and Charles had one son in 1860, Charles R. Benton. At least for some time, Boyd was brought up by his maternal grandmother. He learned to rely on himself during those years, and became increasingly independent.[15]

At some point Charles S. Benton moved to Milwaukee, Wisconsin, and became the editor and part owner of the *Milwaukee Daily News*. In 1855, 11-year-old Boyd was introduced to type in the composing room of his father's newspaper.[16] Charles Benton's former publisher in Little Falls, Josiah A. Noonan, also moved to Milwaukee, whereupon he became a partner in a paper mill[17] and in 1863 bought the Northwestern Type Foundry, which had been established in 1856 by Edward Miller.[18] (Miller had sold his Albany, New York, type foundry, purchased another foundry's equipment, traveled to Chicago, and moved up to Milwaukee when he discovered that the Chicago Type Foundry was already well established.[19])

In 1856 Charles Benton was appointed registrar of the land office in La Crosse, Wisconsin, by President Franklin Pierce, and held that office until Abraham Lincoln became president in 1861. Charles was considered a potential presidential candidate at the 1860 Democratic convention, and if Stephan A. Douglas had not been nominated, Benton would have received some votes. In 1862 he was again a candidate for Congress on the Democratic ticket, and while he had no chance of winning the election in the highly Republican sixth district of Wisconsin, he did carry La Crosse County. After this Charles took up farming, first in West Salem, Wisconsin, and then, in Galesburg, Illinois, in 1865. In 1869 he returned to La Crosse, where he served as county judge from 1874 to 1881, when he resigned due to failing health.[20]

Apart from his many impressive offices and appointments, Charles remained a likeable man. The hand-written eulogy, apparently translated literally from German, affirms that "Ch. S. Benton was a good and decent person and also a man of great talents. He had a rich, sonny [sic] nature that ready was on a joke to enter and he possessed a non-lock-up-able treasure of anecdotes, which he in circle of acquaintances gladly to benefit gave …"[21] The 1907 book Memoirs of La Crosse County concludes its Charles S. Benton entry with this statement:

> Charles S. Benton was a strong character and a good lawyer—one who
> believed that the Sermon on the Mount was good law—with ideas of his
> own on the bringing up of boys, inherited, probably from that earlier time,
> when people did not believe in the present day method of removing all the
> difficulties from the path of the rising generation.[22]

If the successful careers of his elder son and grandson are the measure, Charles Swan Benton's child-rearing ideas were correct. His own diverse career path and subsequent family relocations encouraged his son Boyd to become resourceful and adept at handling new situations—characteristics that would serve him well in the future. Years later, Boyd's younger brother noted a similarity between their father and their grandfather the doctor, who had "cured" his patients with scoldings: "And father was proud of his own ability as a scold."[23]

Colonel Charles S. Benton died on May 4, 1882, and was buried at the Oak Grove Cemetery in La Crosse. His obituary from the Little Falls *Courier Journal* stated:

"He made friends wherever he lived and the short notice of his death [in La Crosse] adds that 'he was very popular.'"[24]

Linn Boyd Benton

Although Boyd Benton's early years were full of changes, he was a playful child who was fascinated by puzzles and mechanical things, overcame difficulties with enthusiasm, and learned to turn childhood problems into opportunities. For example, as a boy in Milwaukee, Boyd was sent to dancing school, much to his chagrin. He was always playing jokes, fooling around and not paying attention to the dance instructor, until he saw a reason to change his ways. Boyd became very fond of two girls in the class, Jessica Elizabeth Donaldson and Crosdella Fess. Good dancers were routinely promoted to the front of the line, and Jessie and Crosie, as he called them, were always up front. Before assigning partners after teaching a new step, the dance instructor would have each child come forward, starting at the top of the line, perform the new move, and be judged accordingly. One day Boyd turned his usual position at the very end of the line to his advantage: he had plenty of time to practice, and learned the new step perfectly. When his turn came he danced out and did it so well that he accomplished his goal—to be sent right up to the front between the two girls.[25] This charming example of Boyd's determination afterwards became a treasured family anecdote.

Since his grandfather was a doctor and his father a politician, it was perhaps logical for the precocious young Boyd Benton to seek out new territories for exploration. Because of the family's many relocations, Boyd's education was, as Henry Lewis Bullen later observed, "rather peripatetic."[26] After attending schools in Little Falls and Milwaukee, Boyd was sent to Galesville College in Galesville, Wisconsin (near La Crosse), and also studied Latin, Greek, and other advanced subjects for about two years in La Crosse with a private tutor. He was determined not to be taught from books all day, so Boyd arranged with his tutor to study in the mornings; if they finished his lessons, Boyd could do as he wished in the afternoons.

Boyd worked for a tombstone cutter in La Crosse during one of his vacations, first observing and then cutting roman letters into the tombstones. Evidently he was not particularly apt: his mistakes had to be chiseled off, the tombstone smoothed down, and the work started over, all paid for out of Boyd's salary. He later told his granddaughter that he never earned any cash money because he ruined so many tombstones, although he did learn a lot about letters.[27] Another vacation found Boyd working for a jeweler who had settled in La Crosse. Detail and accuracy became very important to young Boyd as he learned to remake watch parts. His mechanical aptitude became obvious when, according to his granddaughter, the jeweler gave him a piece of gold that Boyd incorporated into a tiny model steam engine that actually ran. But he didn't get to keep it because the jeweler, pleased with the project, put the little steam engine on display in the window of his shop.

Jessica Elizabeth Donaldson, May 20, 1866   Morris Fuller Benton, 1873

During his youth Boyd developed the theory that there would always be a way to solve any problem. "He went on that assumption, that there *was* a solution," his granddaughter said. "Maybe you wouldn't find it, but somebody would."[28] When he was 16, Boyd completed his formal education and began learning to set type in the office of Charles Seymour's *La Crosse Republican*,[29] while also working as a book-keeper for a leather house in La Crosse. In 1866 he was hired at Josiah A. Noonan's Northwestern Type Foundry in Milwaukee as its bookkeeper,[30] and soon after was promoted to buyer.

One summer night while out for a walk, Boyd heard the music of banjos and mando-lins being played by several young women as they sat on the steps outside one of their homes. Stopping to listen, he quickly recognized one of the young women as Jessie Elizabeth Donaldson, his friend from the Milwaukee dancing class whom he had not seen in years. She had been born in Milwaukee in 1849. Following a romantic court-ship, 27-year-old Boyd and 22-year-old Jessie were married in Milwaukee in 1871. Although they wanted to have a large family, Morris Fuller Benton, born in Milwaukee on November 30, 1872, was their only child. He was named after Boyd's maternal grandmother's brother, Morris E. Fuller.

MORRIS FULLER BENTON

As Boyd had learned to set type at age 11 with the help of his father, so also Morris spent time in his youth working in his own little printing workshop in the family's home in Milwaukee. He designed and printed admittance tickets for children's music classes and for neighborhood shows, receipts for work he did for his father, and booklets of riddles.[31] Although his father was apparently enamored of new technology,

RIDDLES.	ANSWERS.
1. Where is happiness found?	1. IN THE DICTIONARY.
2. Name me and you destroy me.	2. Silence.
3. What is the first thing a garden-er sets in his garden?	3. His foot.
4. What is the difference between a cat and a comma?	4. A cat has its claws at the end of its paws, a comma its pause at the end of a clause.
5. Why is a mouse like grass?	5. Because the cat'll (cattle) eat it.
6. What is the difference between a postage stamp and a bad boy?	6. One takes a lick to stick it, and the other a stick to lick it.
7. What is worse than raining "cats and dogs?"	7. Hailing street-cars.
8. What word is that which de-prived of a letter makes you sick?	8. Musick.
9. Which is the most ancient of the trees?	9. The elder-tree.
	10. When it has a hole in it.
	11. When it is adrift.
	12. Mice.

Pages from a printed book of riddles from Morris Fuller Benton's childhood workshop

Morris printed six stanzas of a seven-stanza parody of "Twinkle, Twinkle Little Star," deriding electric lighting. The entire poem had been published in *The Electrician* magazine for October 1888.[32] The first and last stanzas are given here:

> Twinkle, twinkle little arc,
> Sickly, blue, uncertain spark;
> Up above my head you swing,
> Ugly, strange, expensive thing.
> …
> Though your light perchance surpass
> Homely oil or vulgar gas,
> Still (I close with this remark)
> I detest you little arc![33]

Boyd Benton had a fine baritone voice and sang as a soloist at St. James and St. Paul Episcopal Churches in Milwaukee. He and Jessie belonged to a singing society in Milwaukee, the Arion Club (Boyd was president for some time),[34] and performed in a number of Gilbert and Sullivan productions as well as other light operas. An inter-est in music was also cultivated in young Morris, who sang as a choirboy until his voice changed and became "growly." Morris studied the violin and, like his mother, learned to play the mandolin. Morris was also an amateur magician, acting as propri-etor of neighborhood shows.[35] Morris's grandson Laurence Gregg remembers him performing tricks in New Jersey in the 1940s, and still has his grandfather's "black box" of tricks.

July 1889, in the backyard of the Benton's home

Linn Boyd and Jessie Benton, Wauwatosa, WI

Jessie E. Benton, circa 1889

Young Morris Benton

Like his father, Morris faced childhood difficulties that shaped his character; Morris was not a strong boy and suffered a variety of childhood ailments, including scarlet fever.[36] As a result of his poor health the doctor recommended that he be moved away from Lake Michigan. When the Bentons relocated a few miles west of Milwaukee to Wauwatosa, Morris again set up a printing workshop as well as a darkroom. An avid amateur photographer, Morris Benton documented many aspects of family life. "There are really tons of old Benton photos," Laurence Gregg wrote. "Morris was *the* snapbug!"[37] An identifying stamp with the word "Benton" appears on the back of many of his photographs.

One of the photographs from this period shows Jessie and Linn Boyd on either end of a group of people sitting on a hammock in a wooded area. The back of the photo has the familiar "Benton" stamp, and indicates that it was taken in July 1889 in the "back yard" of their Wauwatosa home, looking north to North Ave. There is also a boy in a tree in the background, to the left of the grouping. Is it Morris? He would have been 16 years old at that time, perhaps too old for the knee-length pants the boy is wearing. However, boys in upperclass families at that time "could be identified by their short or knee trousers and long stockings … In the 1880's on into the 1890's many teen-age youths went from grammar school to high school attired in them."[38] Morris was short and a few years older than his classmates in school because of the time he had lost due to his poor health; he might indeed be the boy in the tree.[39]

The temporary relocation to Wauwatosa took its toll on the social life that Boyd and Jessie had enjoyed so much in Milwaukee. The city was several hours away by horse and buggy, and the last train left Milwaukee too early in the evening for the Bentons to attend the theater. In keeping with his characteristic inventiveness, Boyd quickly found a solution to the problem. His granddaughter Caroline recalled, "My grandfather and two or three buddies decided to buy a train from the Milwaukee railroad,"[40] and set up their own passenger schedule. Running an engine and one car, the young entrepreneurs could take their friends to Milwaukee to see all the shows and other evening activities that interested them and leave the city just before midnight. The enterprise was so successful that they bought a second car, and then a third. At the end of the year, Caroline said, the railroad bought back the train.

A few years later the Bentons moved back to Milwaukee and had a house built on Wells Street, between 29th and 31st Streets and within a block of Boyd's patent attorney, Elias Huntington Bottum. Elias Bottum was a corporate lawyer who, according to his granddaughter Elizabeth, "had a hand in many local businesses and lived to be the head of a prominent law firm. He was an ardent Republican and president of the Republican club of Wisconsin for many years; it was said he could have had the governorship if he had desired."[41] Elias and his wife Caroline ("Kit") Melinda Bailey had one daughter, Mary Ethel Bottum, who had been born in Schuylerville, New York, in 1877. Morris met Ethel when she was about 13; although he was five years older, they belonged to the same neighborhood group of friends. They played tennis, bicycled, had picnics on the lake, and organized outings around Milwaukee. Morris never forgot his first sight of Ethel, "a plump little girl with pigtails."[42]

In September 1892, when he was almost 20 years old, Morris left Milwaukee for Cornell University in Ithaca, New York. He was older than most of his fellow students and open-minded about his future career.[43] After Christmas vacation during his freshman year at Cornell, Morris wrote to Ethel Bottum in Milwaukee to ask whether he might correspond with her. "Let me caution you against studying too hard," he wrote.

Self-portrait, Morris Benton, age 20   A professional portrait of Benton   Mary Ethel Bottum

> I know of girls who have spoiled their prospects of health and happiness
> for the rest of their lives, just for the sake of a little glory while in school,
> trying to be at the top of the heap, so to speak. It [doesn't] pay, what differ-
> ence will it make ten years from now anyhow?[44]

About a year later, by the time Ethel was 16, they were engaged. Her parents insisted
that she wait at least until her 20th birthday to get married, and sent her to the Gilman
School in Cambridge, Massachusetts, where her father's sister, Caroline Bottum Hall,
the wife of the head of the physics department at Harvard, could look after her.[45]
Ethel didn't like the boarding school because of its regimentation and rules. After
she graduated she attended Radcliff College for two years, this time living with Dean
Everett, a professor at Harvard Divinity School, and his daughter. She admired Mr.
Everett, and eventually gave her younger daughter (Caroline Everett Benton) his name.

Ethel's daughter Elizabeth recalled a photograph of her mother from those days,
showing "a lovely, tall, beautifully proportioned erect young girl in faultless Gibson
style dress, with bull dog (the Everett's) on leash, walking down Garden Street." Years
later she retained her beauty, as Elizabeth explained, "Her poise was always noticeable, for when I went shopping with her and she slipped on coat or dress, salesgirls
always stopped what they were doing to turn and admire her as [a] 'model.'"[46]

For the first chaotic months after the 1892 merger of type foundries, which created
the American Type Founders Company based in New York City (see Chapter 6), the
Benton family remained in Milwaukee. It soon became evident, however, that Linn
Boyd's genius and experience were required at the main offices. He and Jessie moved
to New York in 1893 and the foundry equipment was shipped there the following
year, while his partner Robert Van Valkenburgh Waldo remained in Milwaukee to
handle a sales office. Morris was in charge of renting out the house on Wells Street
and spent a few summer vacations away from Cornell looking after the family prop-
erty. Several years later Morris handled most of the arrangements for its sale.

Morris Benton (top) with Cornell classmates

Morris Benton (center) with friends from Cornell
University's Class of 1896

Morris's best grades at Cornell were in mechanical drawing. He designed a cannon, built
a five-inch model of it out of brass, and for years afterwards fired it every Fourth of July.
Morris told his daughter Caroline about his struggle with Cornell's language requirement:

> He kept going in to take the test in French … He only had to have a read-
> ing knowledge, I think … And finally, senior year, he had his thesis all writ-
> ten (and he had a little trouble on that—the professor lost the thesis and
> had to give him a grade off the top of his head)—but finally, the French pro-
> fessor said, 'I've seen too much of you. You [study] once more and come in
> and we'll see what we can do.' So he went in and took it once more and he
> gave him a passing grade.[47]

A copy of Morris Benton's "lost" thesis is actually still in the family—"A Test of the
Steam Power Plant of the Buffalo and Niagara Falls Electric Railway," by Benton and
classmate Philip Bevier Hasbrouck. It is a bound carbon copy of the original manuscript, complete with an embossed title on the cover, many photographs, meticulously
lettered tables and graphs, and detailed fold-out schematics of engines and the eleva-
tion of the boiler room.

Morris was about five feet four inches tall and liked sports. He was too light for football,
at about 135 pounds, and Cornell didn't have a basketball team at the time, so Morris
went out for rowing, even though he was too light to be an oarsman and too heavy to
be coxswain. He didn't make the team, but nevertheless went to all the practices and
watched all the races. He also enjoyed playing tennis[48] and had a keen sense of humor.
Photographs from his Cornell days reveal a rich social life; one of them depicts a "Regular Meeting of the S.P.L." and identifies each member of the group on the back:

Regular meeting of the S.P.L.

Morris Benton, right, displays his impish side, evidently in a student play at Cornell.

Cornell University, 1896

Beginning at the right,
No. 1 (Chairman of meeting) surprised
No. 2 Disgusted
No. 3 Makes a motion, namely: "To get up and do something"
No. 4 Indifferent
No. 5 Tired
No. 6 [Morris Benton] Don't know nothin 'bout it (never had a thought)

Morris graduated from Cornell in June 1896 with a degree in mechanical engineering, taking prizes in freehand drawing, mechanical drawing, and machine shop work.[49] Soon afterwards, he decided to start working with his father at the American Type Founders Company in New York. "I think it was because he and my mother wanted to get married, and that was an obvious salary and start for them," his daughter Caroline said. "And I have letters covering all that period. They were very much in love, and it was a long, hard wait."[50]

Chapter 2 Endnotes

1. "Benton, Morris Fuller," 15 January 1951, typewritten, for the *National Cyclopedia of American Biography* (New York: James T. White and Company).

2. Charles R. Benton to Linn Boyd Benton, 1 July 1907 (copy), 12; Benjamin F. Bryant, ed., *Memoirs of La Crosse County: From earliest historical times down to the present, with special chapters on various subjects, including each of the different towns, and a genealogical and biographical record of representative families in the county, prepared from data obtained from original sources of information* (Madison, Wis.: Western Historical Association, 1907), 248, http://murphylibrary.uwlax.edu/digital/lacrosse/Bryant-Memoirs/02480248.htm.

3. "Lamented Dead: Colonel Charles S. Benton Called from the Scene of Action," unnamed La Crosse, Wisconsin newspaper (5 May 1882), Cooney Room, Arphaxed Loomis Notebook, Book E, 99, Little Falls (N.Y.) Historical Society.

4. Charles R. Benton to Linn Boyd Benton, 14.

5. Bryant, ed., *Memoirs*, 248.

6. "Nathaniel Benton," typewritten notes, Little Falls (N.Y.) Historical Society.

7. "Benton, Nathaniel Seley," The Political Graveyard: Index to Politicians, http://politicalgraveyard.com/bio/benton.html#R9M0IPBTO.

8. "Told About Little Falls' Prominent Men," unnamed Little Falls (N.Y.) newspaper, April 17, 1948, Cooney Room, Book 6, Little Falls Historical Society.

9. Henry Lewis Bullen, "Linn Boyd Benton—The Man and His Work," *Inland Printer* 70, no. 1 (October 1922): 61.

10. "Lamented Dead."

11. Obituary, Hon. Charles L. [*sic*] Benton, *Little Falls Courier Journal*, n.d., Cooney Room, Arphaxed Loomis Notebook, Book E, 99, Little Falls Historical Society.

12. Bryant, ed., *Memoirs*, 248.

13. Handwritten eulogy of Charles S. Benton, 1882, Little Falls Historical Society.

14. Charles R. Benton to Linn Boyd Benton, 14.

15. Several anecdotes regarding Boyd's early boyhood after the death of his mother can be found in my original thesis, "The Contributions of Linn Boyd Benton and Morris Fuller Benton to the Technology of Typesetting and Typeface Design" (Rochester, N.Y.: Rochester Institute of Technology, May 1986).

16. Bullen, "Linn Boyd Benton," 60.

17. "Achievements of Linn Boyd Benton Vital to Industry's Progress," *Inland Printer* 89, no. 5 (Aug. 1932): 53–54.

18. William E. Loy, "Typefounders and Typefounding in America. No. XVII—Edward Miller," *Inland Printer* 28, no. 4 (January 1902): 584.

19. Maurice Annenberg, *Type Foundries of America and their Catalogs*, 2nd ed. (New Castle, Del.: Oak Knoll Press, 1994), 62.

20. "Benton, Charles Swan." Bigraphical Directory of the United States Congress. http://bioguide.congress.gov/scripts/biodisplay.pl?index=B000394.

21. Handwritten eulogy, 4.

22. Bryant, ed. *Memoirs*, 249.

23   Charles R. Benton to Linn Boyd Benton, 14.

24   Obituary, *Little Falls Courier Journal*.

25   Caroline Benton Gregg, in discussion with the author, Milwaukee, March 20, 1984.

26   Bullen, "Linn Boyd Benton," 60.

27   Gregg, discussion.

28   Ibid.

29   Bullen, "Linn Boyd Benton," 60; Annenberg, *Foundries*, 63.

30   Linn Boyd Benton, "Inventions of Linn Boyd Benton," to David Gustafson (Carnegie Institute of Technology), 30 June 1932, for inclusion in the United Typothetae of America's *Who's Who in Printing in the United States*.

31   RIT's Cary Graphic Arts Collection contains one of Morris Benton's original riddle booklets and copies of some other items he printed as a boy.

32   Ido Yavetz, "A Victorian Thunderstorm: Lightning Protection and Technological Pessimism in the Nineteenth Century," in *Technology, Pessimism and Post-Modernism*, ed. Yaron Ezrahi, Everett Mendelsohn and Howard Segal (Dordrecht, Boston and London: Kluwer Academic Publishers, 1994), 74n31.

33   Morris Benton's version of the poem contains several typos: "brght" for 'bright;" "travler" for "traveler," and an omission of the comma in the last line; the poem as rendered in the 1994 source cited above contains a different grammatical error, perhaps a typo, and several stylistic differences from Benton's.

34   Linn Boyd Benton to Gustafson.

35   "Printing products from MFB's boyhood press," copied from the collection of Caroline Benton Gregg, March 1984.

36   Elizabeth Benton Swain, telephone interview with the author, July 6, 1985.

37   Laurence Gregg, email message to the author, 26 March 2007.

38   Harry H. Seckler, "Short Pants or Long Trousers Gave Hint to Pioneer Parents," Leavenworth County Historical Society and Museum, Kansas State Library, Blue Skyways website. http://skyways.lib.ks.us/genweb/leavenwo/library/LONGPANT.htm. The article also states that most boys whose parents were better situated financially "wore the shorties because their parents insisted."

39   Morris's grandson Laurence Gregg agreed that the boy in the tree probably is Morris. A careful inspection of this photograph reveals a line or cord going across the base of the tree to the right of Linn Boyd, which appears to follow behind the group, toward the left. The boy in the tree has his left hand up in the air, holding on to the rope of the swing, but maybe also pressing a switch to trip the camera's shutter. But perhaps this scenario is too far-fetched and Morris could not have taken the picture from that far away.

40   Caroline Gregg, discussion.

41   Swain, "Mary Ethel Bottum," n.d., 1.

42   Ibid.

43   John Allen Murphy, "Morris Benton—Type Designer-Executive," *Inland Printer* 96, no. 6 (March 1936): 33.

44   Morris Fuller Benton to Ethel Bottum, Ithaca, 8 January 1893 (copy).

45   Elizabeth Benton Swain, "Mary Ethel Bottum," n. d. (copy), 1.

46   Ibid.

47   Caroline Gregg, discussion.

48   "Benton, Morris Fuller," 1951.

49 "Morris Fuller Benton," 3 October 1925, typewritten notes among the papers of Caroline Benton Gregg.

50 Caroline Gregg, discussion.

PART ONE

Type Founding in Milwaukee
1873 to 1892

The North-Western Type Foundry

Like his father, Linn Boyd Benton welcomed new opportunities. At 22, he was hired as a bookkeeper for the Milwaukee type and electrotype foundry owned by his father's friend Josiah Noonan. When Noonan went bankrupt seven years later in the Panic of 1873 (a nationwide economic depression that lasted until 1877), Benton saw it as an opening for himself, and with a partner named Edward Cramer he purchased Noonan's Northwestern Type Foundry in 1873.[1] Although he had no actual training in typefounding, Benton handled the manufacturing side of the business.[2] Years later he said that if he had known anything about typefounding at the time, he "would have thrown the entire plant into the lake as a measure of economy,"[3] because it was probably the worst equipped foundry in the country. Instead, he went on to master that difficult art and change it dramatically with a series of important inventions.

In the late 1870s, the American typefounding industry was congested with about 40 highly competitive foundries. Fifty years earlier, only 14 plants or so were in the business of casting type in the U.S., most of them on the East Coast.[4] According to Maurice Annenberg, author of the definitive reference *Type Foundries of America and Their Catalogs*, the following U.S. type foundries issued casebound type specimen books during Benton's typefounding years in Milwaukee (1873–1892):

Baltimore Type Foundry, 1799–1892
Barnhart Brothers & Spindler, 1868–1929 (New York, then Chicago)
Benton, Waldo & Co., 1873–1892 (Milwaukee)
Boston Type Foundry, 1817–1892
Bresnan Type Foundry, 1856–1896 (New York)
Bruce's New York Type Foundry, 1813–1901
Buffalo Type Foundry, 1835–1892

California Type Foundry, 1867–1898 (San Francisco)

Central Type Foundry, 1872–1892 (St. Louis)

Cincinnati Type Foundry, 1817–1892

Cleveland Type Foundry, 1875–1892

Collins & M'Leester, 1853–1892 (Philadelphia)

Conner Type Foundry, 1827–1892 (New York)

Cortelyou's Type Foundry, 1850–1875 (New York)

Curtis & Mitchell, 1864–1892 (Boston)

Dickinson Type Foundry, 1839–1892 (Boston)

Empire State Type Foundry, 1888–ca.1892

Farmer, Little & Co., 1862–1892 (New York)

Franklin Type & Stereotype Foundry, 1856–1892 (Cincinnati)

Hagar Type Foundry, 1826–1887 (New York)

H. C. Hansen Type Foundry, 1872–ca.1922 (Boston)

Ph. Heinrich, 1855–1892 (New York)

Curtis & Mitchell, 1864–1892 (Boston)

Illinois Type Founding Co., 1872–1892 (Chicago)

Kansas City Type Foundry, 1872–1892

Keystone Type Foundry, 1888–1919 (Philadelphia)

Lindsay Type Foundry, 1852–1903 (New York)

MacKellar, Smiths & Jordan, 1867–1892 (Philadelphia)

Manhattan Type Foundry, ca.1886–1890 (New York)

Marder, Luse & Co., 1855–1892 (Chicago)

Mechanics Type Foundry, 1872–1883 (Chicago)

John G. Mengel & Co., 1881–1892 (Baltimore)

Minnesota Type Foundry, ca.1870–ca.1900 (St. Paul)

New England Type Foundry, 1824–1886 (Boston)

Pacific States Type Foundry, ca.1888–1906 (San Francisco)

Palmer & Rey, 1882–1892 (San Francisco)

Philadelphia Type Foundry (Pelouze & Co.), 1841–1892

Richmond Type Foundry, 1858–1901 (Richmond, Va.)

John Ryan Type Foundry, 1854–1892 (Baltimore)

St. Louis Type Foundry, 1840–1892

Union Type Foundry, 1883–1892 (Chicago)

Washington Type Foundry, 1869–1892 (District of Columbia)

These were by no means the only type establishments in the country at that time. Others sold wood type instead of metal type, advertised with pamphlets or broadsides, or had outside help with their type specimen books. Also, the popularity of the electro-deposition process for making type matrices had enabled entrepreneurs only marginally familiar with the typefounding business to enter it. Roy Rice, a metal type enthusiast, wrote that by the mid-1800s, "anyone wishing to could duplicate a founder's matrices, and numerous foundries sprung up whose only stock in trade were other founders' designs."[5]

Benton, Gove & Co.

In 1874, just a year after going into business with Benton, Cramer sold his half-interest in Northwestern to Lieutenant-Commander Frank M. Gove, a Naval officer who knew nothing about the type business but who would prove to be a successful and popular salesman for the firm. Gove had been born in New Hampshire in 1843 and graduated from the Naval Academy in 1865. After marrying Emma Beck of Milwaukee, he resigned his commission in the Navy to move to her home town. An 1882 issue of the *Typographic Adviser* referred to him as "a genial, noble-hearted, generous companion, possessed of a highly cultured mind and fascinating social qualities, which endeared him to all with whom he came in contact."[6]

The new partners changed the name of the firm to Benton, Gove & Company, retaining the company's original name, now modified to "North-Western Type Foundry," on its letterhead. In November 1874, its address was 354 & 356 Broadway, Milwaukee,[7] and by 1877, the company had moved to Nos. 292 E. Water and 77–79 Detroit Streets.[8] While Gove handled the business end, Benton continued to learn everything he could about manufacturing type in a highly competitive market.

Many years later, Henry Lewis Bullen, historian and publicist for the American Type Founders Company (ATF), described this period of Boyd's life in an article for the *Inland Printer* magazine:

> Before Gove died, Benton had completed his self-instruction in typefounding and found himself on the most intimate terms with decimal fractions and measurements of ten thousandths of an inch. He had and still has a mania for accuracy to the vanishing point, not only knowing, as the books tell us, that a hot breath impinged on a small piece of steel changes its dimensions, but actually taking that solemn fact to heart, grieving that it cannot be overcome. The bane of Benton's career has been the limitations of error which are made necessary by the disposition of all metals to refuse to resist molecular action. What other mortals cheerfully accept as accuracy Benton regards as a calamity.[9]

Soon after they joined as partners, Benton and Gove began producing a house publication, *The North-Western*, for patrons, friends, and potential customers. It contained editorials, news of the printing business, whimsical essays, jokes, political commentary, type specimens, and advertisements for the presses and inks the company also sold. An early attempt at humor brought mixed results, as an article from July 1876 relates:

> In a recent number of this able and interesting publication, which should be in every family, regardless of expense, to us, we attempted to work off

Linn Boyd Benton, the editor/publisher of *The North-Western*, at his desk in Milwaukee, late 1880s

Front page of *The North-Western*, January 1885

an editorial in the style of some of the funny editors of the day. We went on to state, in all apparent seriousness, that we had invented a new type metal, the component parts of which were silver and bar soap, and, in imitation of some of the flatulent type-folding benefactors of the human race, we claimed that our new centennial type metal was bound to supercede all other kinds, inasmuch as it could be used not only for printing papers of a political nature—which of course contain more or less lye—but it could be demonetized and used as a circulating medium, and then soaked up and used as a lubricator for washing feet. Had this editorial appeared in our friend Geo. Peck's La Crosse *Sun*, or our friend Hauser's *Christian States-man*, it would have been taken as a joke with several grains of allowance, everybody knowing that those editors are given to exhibitions of elongated truth, that is painful to see, especially the La Crosse methodist [*sic*] fellow. But appearing in our staid, business *North-Western*, it was received in all candor. We have received several letters, inquiring into the *modus operandi* of its manufacture, from parties who evidently believe that we are going to turn the printing business bottom side up … Our experience in trying to be funny has been a lamentable failure, and hereafter our readers can look for the squarest kind of business talk in the *North-Western*. We will leave the field of humorous journalism to the other boys, and we will pay strict attention to editing our customary roller composition.[10]

Most of the articles in the *North-Western* were not signed, and some signed letters were written as spoofs. For example, a letter in the winter 1876–77 edition about introducing copper as an alloy for type metal is signed by C. Alloy.[11] Type historian

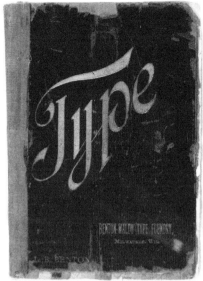

Benton, Waldo & Company, Milwaukee, Wisconsin · The *Portable Book of Specimens*, circa 1888

Dr. James Eckman implied that the humorous offerings in the publication were written by Benton himself, since he inserted Benton's name into an excerpt he reproduced from an 1877 issue of *The Printers Register*, the house organ of the Central
Type Foundry in St. Louis:

> The funny man of *The North-Western* [Linn Boyd Benton] is filling in his
> time between drinks writing correspondence to his paper, about the new
> type metal invented by the North-Western Type Foundry, composed of
> silver and soap. If the type sent us is a fair sample—to use the words of our
> friend A. Ward—"the cuss lies." Not a particle of silver or soap in it; noth-
> ing in fact but pure lead.[12]

Eckman sent this paragraph and other Benton references that he had retyped on
several sheets of paper to Linn Boyd Benton's granddaughter Caroline in 1964. Near
this particular reference he noted in handwriting: "They were hard on each other in
those days." The Central Type Foundry, according to Eckman, was "very tough competition" for the North-Western Type Foundry. The trade reached its height in the
1880s, and by then, "fewer than fifty foundries located in a dozen cities supplied the
nation's printing offices."[13]

Benton, Gove & Company issued type specimen books in 1876[14] and 1882, copies
of which are preserved today in the rare book collections at Columbia University
Library in New York. In his 2000 book about 19th century type specimen books,
Alastair Johnston wrote, "The rare books of Benton-Gove of Milwaukee are among
the earliest to display the waggings of loosetongued gabblespeak."[15] Perhaps the compositors at the foundry wrote their own text for the 1876 type specimens they set, but

it was no doubt Benton who permitted their whimsical entries. For example, the text of the specimen for Centennial Script reads,

Hallucinations of a Disordered Intellect

and a hillbilly proverb illustrates Antique Condensed No. 4,

LAFF AND GRO PHAT
Phun for Boys in Oshkosh 123

Johnston reserved the last word in his book for Benton-Gove's entry for Antique Condensed and Gothic:

OH DON'T YOU REMEMBER THE SPOT BEN BUT
Where You and I Used to Steal a Little While Away with the Spoons

BUT THE BULL-DOZER IS THERE NOW BEN BUT
And You and I More's the Pity Must Start Two Saloons

THE POET OF THE FUTURE
Hiding His Light Under the Bushel of a Specimen-Book[16]

A short notice in the winter 1876–77 *North-Western* announced the death of Gove's two-year old son Francis. Five years later Gove himself died, at age 38, while recovering from a slight case of paralysis at his brother's home in Waukesha, Wisconsin. His June 14, 1882, obituary in Milwaukee's *Daily Republican-Sentinel* stated that he had a large circle of friends and acquaintances in the "Cream City," and left behind a wife and "bright little 2-year-old daughter."[17]

Benton, Waldo & Co.

After Gove's death, Benton sold a one-third interest in the company to Robert Van Valkenburgh Waldo, a wholesale grocer who, like Gove, knew nothing about type but proved to be an ideal partner. Again the firm's name changed, this time to Benton, Waldo & Co. During the transition the *North-Western* took a brief hiatus, but resumed publication in the summer of 1883. The company moved again, to 89 Huron Street, and established a branch office at 311 Robert Street in Saint Paul, Minnesota, under the management of Mr. Waldo. Bullen wrote, "R. V. Waldo maintained [the company's] success and gave to the firm that enviable reputation for those qualities of stability and integrity which are preeminently characteristic of both its members."[18] Benton, Waldo & Co. also issued a series of type specimen books, again sporadically using light-hearted texts that were often in the form of surreal advertisements, bizarre news headlines, or fantastic stories.

BE IT KNOWN, That on and after the 29th day of March, 1985, passengers desiring transportation on the Rapid Transit Air Line, between the planets Jupiter and Mars, must procure their tickets three seconds before the advertised time of flying.

8-POINT (BREVIER) MOTHER HUBBARD.—P
18 A $1.90

TOBOGGANNING

HAIR RAISING ADVENTURES

DULL TRUD 5

12-POINT (PICA) LATIN CONDENSED.
30 A 50 a $2.70

MAIDENS BEWARE FOR THE
Impecunious Dude Stalketh Abroad in
Tight Fitting Raiment

12 A 12 A   12-POINT (PICA) GALLICAN. $2.15

CONSISTENCY THOU ART
A JEWEL BUT SELF SPACING TYPE IS
INFINITELY BETTER 24

7 A   24-POINT (DOUBLE PICA) EPITAPH.—B $3.25

WRITES ❖ EPITAPH
THEN DIES

14 A 20 a   18-POINT (GREAT PRIMER) MOSLEM.—B $3.25

MARSHVILLE RANGERS ANNUAL TARGET SHOOT
Visitors will Avoid all Risks by keeping as near the Target as Possible

12 A 20 a   22-POINT (DBL. SMALL PICA) GOTHIC CONDENSED, No. 5. $2.70

CHOICE FLAVORED GAME TIDBITS
Imported Boned He Fleas Stuffed with Gnats

Clips from the Benton-Waldo specimen book

Chapter 3 Endnotes

1   Henry Lewis Bullen, "Linn Boyd Benton—The Man and His Work," *Inland Printer* 70, no. 1 (October 1922): 60.

2   Linn Boyd Benton, "Inventions of Linn Boyd Benton," to David Gustafson (Carnegie Institute of Technology), 30 June 1932, for inclusion in the United Typothetae of America's *Who's Who in Printing in the United States*, 2.

3   Bullen, "Linn Boyd Benton," 60.

4   Maurice Annenberg, *Type Foundries of America and their Catalogs*, 2nd ed. (New Castle, Del.: Oak Knoll Press, 1994), 36.

5   Roy Rice, "Matrix Making at the Oxford University Press, Part I," Atlanta: Recalcitrant Press, 1982, http://bellsouthpwp.net/r/_/r_rice2/mmoup/Text1.htm

6   Obituary of Frank M. Gove, *Typographic Advertiser* 28 (Fall 1882): 774, quoted in material sent to Caroline Benton Gregg in 1964 by Dr. James Eckman.

7   Benton to Mrs. L.B. Benton, Milwaukee, 16 November 1874 (copy).

8   *North-Western* 3, nos. 12–13 (Summer and Autumn 1877): 1. Seven original editions of *The North-Western* are part of RIT's Cary Graphic Arts Collection, courtesy of Laurence Gregg.

9   Bullen, "Linn Boyd Benton," 61.

10 "The Peril of Attempting a Joke," *North-Western* 2, no. 8 (July 1876): 1.

11 "Correspondence," *North-Western* 3, nos. 9–10 (Winter Quarter 1876–77): 1.

12 "Sorts and Quoins," *Printers Register* 3 (February 1877), quoted in material sent to Caroline Benton Gregg in 1964 by Eckman.

13 William S. Pretzer, review of *Recasting a Craft: St. Louis Typefounders Respond to Industrialization* (Carbondale: Southern Illinois University Press, 2005), in *Technology and Culture* 47, no. 4 (2006): 844.

14 Alastair Johnston, *Alphabets to Order: The Literature of Nineteenth-Century Typefounders' Specimens* (London and New Castle, Del.: British Library and Oak Knoll Press, 2000), 103. Johnston writes, "many of the leaves have dates of 1876 but these may be in anticipation of the Centennial," and gives 1873 as the date of the first Benton-Gove specimen book, even though Gove joined Benton in 1874.

15 Ibid.

16 Ibid., 184.

17 "Death of Lieut. F. M. Gove, at Waukesha," *Daily Republican-Sentinel*, Milwaukee, June 14, 1882, quoted in material sent to Caroline Benton Gregg in 1964 by James Eckman.

18 Quadrat [Henry Lewis Bullen], "Discursions of a Retired Printer, No. VI," *Inland Printer* 38, no. 3 (December 1906): 353.

Challenges and Solutions

ONE OF THE MAIN PROBLEMS plaguing printing establishments until the late 1800s was the lack of dimensional standardization in the metal type they used. Each type foundry had its own peculiar system of type dimensions and its own formulas for the metal alloys used to cast its type,[1] so type sizes, widths, base alignment and durability varied tremendously. These differences actually benefited the foundries, since a printing shop's initial type purchase would most likely dictate where subsequent purchases would be made, simply to avoid the confusion and technical difficulty of introducing various type standards into the shop.

MEASURING TYPE SIZE

A brief history of type sizes and the point system might be helpful here. Type sizes were traditionally denoted not by measurement but by the names given to them at the foundries. At first the name of a typeface described both its style and size; later it referred to the size only. The fact that the sizes of early type bodies were entirely arbitrary was deplored by writers as early as Moxon.[2]

Pierre Simon Fournier, a French type designer, punch-cutter, type founder, printer, publisher, and historian, introduced a typographic sizing system in 1737 with the publication of a type measuring scale in a booklet entitled *Tables des Proportions qu'il faut observer entre les caractères*. The system was based on dividing the common French type size "cicero" (0.1648 inch in height) into 12 "typographical points."[3] When it became apparent that Fournier's scale for measuring type, printed on wet paper, shrank with the paper when it dried, he revised it to allow for shrinkage. Fournier described this new scale in his classic two-volume printing reference *Manuale Typographique*, published in Paris between 1764 and 1766. After Fournier

A type's body size is not simply the size of the character on it; type size also includes the non-printing space that surrounds the character above and below it.

died in 1768, François-Ambroise Didot reworked his system, basing it on an authorized linear measurement—the *pied du roi*—12 French or 12.7892 American inches.[4] This resulted in a larger typographical point, measuring 0.0148 inch compared to Fournier's point (0.0137 inch).[5] However in 1795 France adopted the metric system, making the Didot system, based as it was on the *pied du roi*, obsolete.

Other attempts at standardizing type sizes followed. The Bruce Type Foundry in New York initiated a geometric system for measuring type in 1822, in which every seventh successive size would measure twice as high as the original face; "although ingenious, the system resulted in a most cumbersome set of dimensions and was not adopted by other founders."[6] In 1824, James Fergusson of Scotland devised a simple plan for sizing type, *Plain and Accurate Rules for Obtaining Permanent Uniformity in the Sizes of the Bodies of Types, and in Their Height to Paper*, but it was never adopted.[7] In 1841, the Bower Brothers foundry of Sheffield, England, published *Proposals for Establishing a Graduated Scale of Sizes for the Bodies of Printing Types, and Fixing their Height to Paper Based upon Pica as the Common Standard and Referable to the English Inch*, suggesting that each pica, measuring one-sixth of an inch, contain 16 points. Their proposal was not accepted by the trade. And in 1857, the Shanks Patent Type Foundry in England introduced a proprietary system in which the pica would measure 20 points.[8]

After the Great Chicago Fire of 1871 destroyed the entire Marder, Luse & Co. type foundry in that city, John Marder calculated that it would be possible to rebuild and refurnish the foundry by selling his Chicago residence and collecting the money due him from the insurance company.[9] While he initially planned to adopt "a system of bodies based on six picas to the American inch," ultimately the decision was made to take for its standard the "pica" size of the MacKellar, Smiths & Jordan foundry of Philadelphia, since it was felt that this size "would be preferred by the greatest number of printers and founders."[10]

In 1874, Marder convinced a new partner in the firm, Nelson Crocker Hawks, to move from his home in Milwaukee to Alameda, California, to establish a branch printing supply house in San Francisco. Since the printers in California were already using type from various American foundries, as Richard L. Hopkins explained in *Origin of the American Point System for Printers' Type Measurement*,

> Hawks had to stock, in addition to type, separate fonts of spacing, quads, borders, leads and so on, all from different manufacturers and varying in size only enough to prevent mixing. Spacing items, especially, differed so little that they caused much confusion at the San Francisco agency, bringing Hawks to ponder seriously the need for more uniformity in type bodies.[11]

Hawks subsequently invented his own system for measuring type sizes, remarkably similar to the Fournier and Didot systems although he had apparently never heard of them. Hawks's point measured 0.0138 inch. A 2006 article in the *Alameda* (California) *Sun* newspaper explained how he came up with the system:

> Hawks … was forced to stock type and supplies from many foundries. While studying these typefaces, Hawks noticed that pica type was one-sixth inch high. He studied other type [sizes] and discovered that nonpareil was half the size of pica. But five other sizes stood between nonpareil and pica.
>
> Hawks asked himself, "What whole number has five whole numbers between it and its double?" He discovered the answer was the number six, which has five whole numbers—7, 8, 9, 10 and 11—before its double 12.
>
> So Hawks decided to assign nonpareil six points. From there, he could assign all other named sizes a point size very close to their actual size. In Hawks' scheme, 12 points make up one pica and six picas make up one inch; so there are 72 points in one inch.[12] [Actually, Hawks's decimal point equivalent of 0.0138 inch is not exactly 1/72 of an inch, a fact that was to plague the industry for years to come.]

Hawks tried to convince several foundries to adopt his point system, with no immediate success. Here the story breaks down into various versions, but at some point Hawks convinced Marder, Luse & Co. to adopt his point system. Type historian Dr. James Eckman implied that Hawks's invention preceded his move to California, and that Marder, Luse & Co.'s "work on the new system started in 1872."[13] Richard Hopkins, on the other hand, wrote that Hawks initially explained his system of point bodies to John Marder in California in 1877,[14] after which Marder, Luse & Co. adopted it, based on Marder's recommendation. When Hawks had a falling out with the firm and severed his ties with it,[15] magazine articles began to credit Marder with originating the system. (However, as Maurice Annenberg noted in *Type Foundries of America and Their Catalogs*, "personal correspondence written from Marder to Hawks, now preserved in the Kemble Collection of the California Historical Society,

NOTE.— Since the seventh discursion was written, the author has come across a table showing the actual variations in the old type-bodies, the measurements for which were taken by the author in 1885, just before the general adoption of the point system, from types furnished by the various typefoundries for the purpose. This table most effectively shows the younger printers under what evil conditions the former generation of printers did their work. Special attention is directed to the variations in height-to-paper, the consequences of which to the pressroom may better be imagined than described. Let us not forget that we owe the abolition of these evils to the initiative of the venerable John Marder, now in active business in Chicago.

FOUNDRY.	Height.	Diamond.	Pearl.	Agate.	Nonpareil.	Minion.	Brevier.
Boston Type Foundry	.9200		.0700	.0760	$.0833\frac{1}{3}$	.0955	.1100
Cincinnati Type Foundry	.9170	.0625	$.0694\frac{1}{4}$	.0764	$.0833\frac{1}{3}$	.0972	.1911
Marder, Luse & Co	.9180	$.0622\frac{1}{2}$	$.0691\frac{3}{4}$	$.0760\frac{2}{3}$	.0830	$.0968\frac{1}{3}$	$.1106\frac{3}{4}$
Johnson Type Foundry	.9180				.0830		
Farmer, Little & Co	.9180		.0667		.0830		
James Connor's Sons	.9180		.0665		.0840		.1062
Geo. Bruce's Son & Co	.9190	.0595	.0668	.0750	.0841	.0944	.1060
Benton, Waldo & Co	.9200		.0665	.0725	.0835	.1010	.1070
Barnhart Bros. & Spindler	.9200		.0664	.0706	.0838	.0949	.1065
Phelps, Dalton & Co	.9200		.0667		.0824		.1060

A comparison of 1885 type body sizes and height-to-paper measurements in various American type foundries

prove it was Hawks's idea."[16]) Thus, Marder's role in the standardization of type sizes was agreeing to use Hawks's system. The first type that the foundry produced using it was Parallel Shaded, patented in 1877.[17] Marder, Luse & Co. then announced that after July 1, 1880, all of its new types would be cast on what it called the "American System of Interchangeable Type Bodies."[18]

As late as the mid 1880s, however, the majority of American type founders still referred to the sizes of their type bodies using the "grand old names," such as diamond, brevier, pica, small pica, two-line small pica, bourgeois, double paragon, two-line Columbian, double great primer, and two-line mignonette.[19] To compound the problem, foundries did not agree as to what each name meant; for example, according to a 1907 *Inland Printer* article by Henry Lewis Bullen, a comparison of the heights of type bodies from ten 1885 type foundries showed that brevier could mean anything from 0.1060 inch to 0.1911 inch.[20]

Although printers who worked with type based on Hawks's point system appreciated it, most American type founders were initially unimpressed and unwilling to follow suit—especially since using the system would mean scrapping all the type they had in stock and starting over. But when the Central Type Foundry of St. Louis decided to adopt the system, the tide turned,[21] and on September 17, 1886, the "American System of Interchangeable Type Bodies" was formally adopted at a meeting of the United States Type Founders' Association in Niagara, New York.[22] This meeting also established the standard height-to-paper (the height from the foot of a piece of type to its face) to be 0.918 inch. Before this, variations of five one-thousandths of an inch were not uncommon.[23]

At the same meeting, a steel rule for measuring the newly adopted point system furnished by MacKellar, Smiths & Jordan, another leading type foundry, was accepted as the official standard. On this steel rule, 83 12-point bodies equaled 35 centimeters, and 15 heights-to-paper also equaled 35 centimeters. It was soon discovered that the standard was inaccurate (this can easily be shown mathematically[24]), and apparently it was Linn Boyd Benton who challenged it. "It [was] only approximately correct," Bullen stated in 1907, "and the term 'approximate' as applied to type standards of body, width or line does not exist in the dictionary of L. B. Benton, whose investigations, tested by other experts, have established the absolute standards."[25]

SELF-SPACING TYPE

Marder, Luse & Co.'s American System of Interchangeable Type Bodies related only to what its name suggested, the body size of type, not its alignment or set width. Type foundries may have been careful to base-align their own fonts (that is, to correctly place the face on each type body relative to the font's baseline), but printers could not mix types from different fonts or foundries because they wouldn't necessarily have a common baseline. (This problem was finally addressed by the American Type Founders Co. around the turn of the century; see Chapter 12.) Another problem was that type characters came in so many different widths that justifying lines of text was tedious.

As he struggled to make his type foundry in Milwaukee a successful business, Linn Boyd Benton recognized and tried to overcome the problems that had plagued the type industry for centuries. His first type-related patent was granted in 1882 for a machine that cast spacing material. Spurred on by this success and eager to find additional solutions for his business, he started working on another invention in 1882, an "automatic justifying machine." In the process, he instead invented a font of type that changed the way designers would approach type design.

Since Gutenberg's day, the hand mold and later the automatic casting machine could accommodate a type matrix of any width, and so type designers enjoyed the freedom of drawing or cutting each letter to whatever width seemed appropriate. This however complicated the compositor's job, since finding the right spacers to justify a line was often a hit-and-miss endeavor. In the early 1880s the number of different set widths in a font of type remained unnecessarily high—Henry Lewis Bullen maintained that there were "more than 100 widths normally found in an ordinary body-type font."[26]

Benton decided to limit the number of type character widths he would allow for his justifying machine, so he designed a special font of type for this purpose. Each character in his new "unit-width" system fit on one of eight different pre-determined type body widths for each size of a font. A ninth width was used for a long dash and two commonly used type ornaments. When the foundry produced the first font of body type for Benton's justifying machine, it became apparent immediately that the time

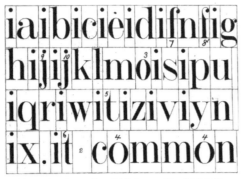

Self Spacing Type, from U.S. Patent No. 290,201

BENTON'S PATENT SELF SPACING TYPE.

The most important advance in printing type in four centuries. A type which increases the speed of the compositor 25 per cent., and completely revolutionizes the principle of type making.

From the Benton & Waldo specimen book

abcdefghijklmnopqrstuvwxyz

1 2 3 4 5 6 7 8 9 0   ⅛ ½ ¾ ¼ ⅜ ⅝ ⅞ ⅜   *1 2 3 4 5 6 7 8 9 0*

Benton's Self Spacing Type, from a Benton-Waldo specimen pamphlet

it took to hand-justify text with the type had been greatly reduced. Benton applied for a patent for this font of type that followed "the point system both ways"[27] on May 8, 1883, and received U.S. Patent no. 290,201 on December 18 of the same year for what he called "Self Spacing" type.[28]

Legros and Grant explained that all of the type characters in the Self Spacing font were "made on set widths each multiples of one-sixth of the body, so that any combination can be made up to a multiple of the em by the addition of some of the self-spacing spaces which are also equal multiples of the sixth of the body."[29] (The "em" is a unit of measure named after the capital M, which is as wide as the point size of the character.) For example, the lower case "i" was two units wide; the lower case "e" was three units wide; the em was six units wide; and the capital "W" was seven units wide.[30] An undated Benton, Waldo & Co. brochure advertising Self Spacing Type stated:

> In a complete font of the old kind of body type there are about 190 widths of bodies … [With this new typeface] there are but nine widths of bodies all told, and … the four-unit width predominates over any other, there being fifty-nine characters of this width.[31]

The term "self-spacing" was obviously an exaggeration. (The hyphen in "self-spacing" came and went in ads, promotional pieces and magazine articles.[32]) The term was first

```
1 unit  —Space.................................  1
2 units—Space, f i j l , : ; . - ' ! ſ ɪ ʃ ' |..  16
3 units—Quad, c e r s t z ? ) ] * † ‡ § ‖
        ¶ I J s z - °..........................  22
4 units—Quad, a b d g h k n o p q u
        v x y fi fl ff $ £ 1 2 3 4 5 6
        7 8 9 0 S Z A B C D E F G L
        N O P Q R T U V X Y & .. ~ ⟨
        ſ ⟩ ⟨ ⟩ |.............................  59
5 units—æ A B C D E F G L N O P Q
        R T U V Y H K M .....................  21
6 units—Quad, m ct w ffi ffl œ H K X
        & w æ œ lb ₧ @ — ... ¼ ½
        ¾ ⅓ ⅔ ⅛ ⅜ ⅝ ⅞ ...................  28
7 units—M W ....................................  2
8 units—Æ Œ ...................................  2
12 units—Quad, ......  —              ......  5
9 sizes.        Roman characters. .........233
                Italic characters............ 77
                                           233
```

The nine set-widths of Benton's self-spacing type

coined by Walter Stoddard, who later became one of the founders of the Curtis Publishing Company in Philadelphia. Benton had hired Stoddard, a compositor, to determine what gain, if any, the "unit width" types could afford over a non-unit font of the same size. Bullen recorded this version of the story in the *Inland Printer*:

> Three comparative trials showed that Stoddard set the unit-widths thirty-three and a third per cent faster than the non-unit types. Stoddard's average with unit widths, per one thousand ems, was forty-five and one-half minutes as against an average of sixty minutes. When asked what he thought of the justification, he pondered a while and said, "I never thought of that—why, the d—d thing spaces itself!" The types had not been named, and thus it came to be called "self-spacing." Benton was granted a strong pioneer patent for this system of making types.[33]

The Benton, Waldo & Co. brochure claimed that using self-spacing type increased the speed of a compositor by 25 percent, while the 1884 Spring issue of *The North-Western* stated, "Repeated experiments with the new type have shown that the average compositor can gain about 33 per cent in speed."[34] Soon the demand for self-spacing type grew at such a pace that Benton decided to suspend work on his justifying machine and instead concentrate on getting the new type to the market.

Benton by this time already had a reputation for being a perfectionist. Bullen told a story about a boy named William Ferdinand Lietke who grew up working in the Milwaukee foundry. Will's earliest task was to sharpen 15 pencils and have them ready on Benton's drawing table each morning so that when he arrived at the foundry, he could examine them under a magnifying glass. If five of the fifteen were accepted Will was lucky—most of them would be considered too flat, too round, or too sharp. "Benton knew what he wanted and trained his people to give it to him, without compromise."[35]

Self-spacing types were designed for use in the newspaper industry, where fast justification would be a great benefit. Newspaper offices generally used one series of body type in any one size, instead of a variety of types in the same size. Bullen explained

Variations of self-spacing type

that while the initial price of a self-spacing font was higher than other non-unit types, the compositor could work so much faster that the total cost of composing with the type was far less than for composing with other body types. If the Linotype machine had not entered the field of newspaper composition, Bullen later maintained, self-spacing types would have come into general use.

Even in the earliest advertising pamphlets for self-spacing types, two different fonts were available, old style and roman, both with italic versions. In the undated *Portable Book of Specimens from The Benton & Waldo Foundry Operated by the American Type Founders Company*, additional variations called Self Spacing Old Style Bold and Self Spacing German also appeared.[36] Each size of Self Spacing Roman, from 5½ to 12 point, came in a number of discreet versions, as Benton, Waldo & Co.'s advertising pamphlet explained:

> The following table gives the sizes of bodies, units of measure, and lengths of alphabets. In the first column will be found the various sizes of bodies; in the second, the number of units contained in one em Pica; and in the third the measurements of a lower case alphabet in the ems of each particular body.[37]

In other words, different versions of the same size of self-spacing type had different numbers of units to the em and thus different lengths for the complete alphabet! However, within any one font there were only eight different widths of type characters (nine counting the long dash).

Despite its novelty and initial success, a major drawback to using self-spacing type soon became apparent in commercial printing offices: its spaces and quads could

Body.	Number Units to Pica em.	Length of Alphabet.
5½ Point (Agate).........	13	15⅝
5½ Point (Agate).........	12	16⅞
6 Point (Nonpareil)...	13	14⅓
6 Point (Nonpareil)...	12	15½
6 Point (Nonpareil)...	11	16⅞
6 Point (Nonpareil)...	10	18⅝
7 Point (Minion).......	12	13¼
7 Point (Minion).......	11	14½
7 Point (Minion).......	10	16
8 Point (Brevier).......	10	14
8 Point (Brevier).......	9	15½
8 Point (Brevier)	8	17½
9 Point (Bourgeois)...	10	12⅜
9 Point (Bourgeois)...	9	13¾
9 Point (Bourgeois)...	8	15½
10 Point (L'g Primer).	9	12⅜
10 Point (L'g Primer).	8	14
11 Point (Small Pica)..	8	12⅔
11 Point (Small Pica)..	7	14½
12 Point (Pica)...........	8	11⅝
12 Point (Pica)...........	7	13¼
12 Point (Pica)...........	6	15½

Each point size of self-spacing type was available in different versions

not be mixed with the spaces and quads from other self-spacing fonts, even in the same size, because of the differences in width between them. "In Benton's system," Dr. Eckman explained, the "width of the quads and spaces depended on the width of the unit on which a given face was cast, so that an 8-point quad cast for use with one design would not be as wide as the 8-point quad of another design, even though both 8-point designs were said to be 'self-spacing.'"[38] Benton the perfectionist had perhaps gone a little too far trying to give options to printers.

Self-spacing spaces and quads could not be mixed with spaces and quads in the same point size from other foundries for the same reason. Commercial printing offices used a variety of fonts every day, and it was impossible in practice for them to keep the various spaces separate. With time, the justifying economy of self-spacing types would be lost as the spaces of a new font of self-spacing type mixed in with those of other fonts. Thus, the *concept* of self-spacing type was more important than the actual product.

There was a larger problem with self-spacing type. "The aesthetic result was not impressive," Dr. Eckman wrote.[39] In the early self-spacing fonts, Benton distorted certain characters to make them fit his system. "This is most noticeable," Bullen wrote, "in the round character 'e' which is three-unit, and the 'o' which is four-unit, thus giving the 'o' an unfortunate prominence."[40] Benton reworked and redesigned several self-spacing fonts and overcame many of these distortions, which Bullen praised in a 1922 *Inland Printer* article:

> In the Old Style series of roman and italic, based on the Ronaldson Old Style design, and in Self-Spacing Old Style Bold, the characters are adjusted to their prescribed widths so judiciously as to leave no room for criticism.[41]

An anonymous article in the December 1886 *Inland Printer* had made the same point: "Finally, the changes in the proportions of the letters have made the type more legible and less injurious to the eyes."[42] These changes did not, however, completely overcome the aesthetic problems with self-spacing type. Daniel Berkeley Updike, the founder of the Merrymount Press in Boston and author of the 1922 classic *Printing Types: Their History, Forms, and Use*, commented that

> self-spacing or point-set schemes which involve either lateral distortion of letters or too much space between them, may for the moment seem clever, convenient, lasting, and money-saving "improvements," but they are merely unintelligent, temporary, and inartistic expedients ... The fundamental trouble with these schemes is, that they make types hard to read.[43]

Benton received Design Patent No. D18,775 on December 4, 1888, for a lower-case italic self-spacing font, apparently an improved version of the lower case of an earlier font. (Two years later he was also granted a patent for a font of fancy letters, subsequently found in several Benton, Waldo & Co. promotional brochures.) Benton's italic self-spacing letters were cut on the same body widths as the corresponding roman characters. In order to accomplish this, he did not use a conventional italic but rather a sloped roman face.[44] This method of creating an italic letter design was later outlined by the British typographer Stanley Morison in the 1926 *Fleuron*:

> Indeed, if we make up our mind to reduce italic to identity of design with roman—and nothing less will content the consistent mind—we can only do so by going back on our definitions and for the future treating *inclination* and not informality as the essential property of italic. This however is so radical a change as perhaps to be the occasion of protest.[45]

Without knowing it, Morison was explaining how Linn Boyd Benton had produced his self-spacing italic fonts more than 40 years before. Bullen pointed this out in a 1927 personal letter to Beatrice Warde, who had been his assistant at ATF's Typographic Library and Museum:

> Speaking of Morison reminds me that his discovery that italic should be slanting roman was put into manufacture in 1883 by L. B. Benton, in his self-spacing types, in which all the italics are slanting romans. Good God, what an asset it appears to be to know a little about a subject and make much noise about that little![46]

Self-spacing type was the first step in the industry's move to more uniform type widths. William A. Schraubstadter of the Central Type Foundry and later the Inland Type Foundry, both in St. Louis, perfected Benton's system by casting type to a standard system of units. In Schraubstadter's system, the unit measured one-eighth of one point, and the number of widths used on body-type fonts varied from 13 to 20, allowing more subtle variations than Benton's limit of eight widths. Schraubstadter's system was widely praised and eventually adopted by American type foundries. Bullen wrote, "This system, by its compromise between the speed advantage of a lesser number of widths and the requirements of the designer, and its use of justifiers applicable to all fonts, overcomes all the drawbacks of Benton's system."[47] Updike, however, was unimpressed: "Something suffers when ninety different adjustments [the older fonts had about that many different widths] are reduced to from thirteen to twenty, and the 'something' that suffers *is the effect of the type*."[48]

In the meantime, another advantage of Benton's self-spacing types had become evident: since typecasting machines must be stopped and readjusted each time type of a different set width is cast, reducing the number of set widths in a font of type greatly reduced the amount of time that the machines were idle. Even so, it remained a formidable undertaking for the Benton-Waldo foundry to cut all of the steel punches that were required to cast self-spacing types. Solving this problem led to one of Linn Boyd Benton's most significant achievements.

Chapter 4 Endnotes

1   N. J. Werner, "Saint Louis' Place on the Type Founders' Map," *Inland Printer* 79, no. 5 (August 1927): 764.

2   Daniel Berkeley Updike, *Printing Types: Their History, Form and Use* (Cambridge: Harvard University Press, 1922), 1:25–26.

3   Nicholas Fabian, "The History of the American Point System" (School of Computer Science, McGill University, 1997), http://cg.scs.carleton.ca/~luc/fabian-point.html.

4   Updike, *Printing Types*, 1:31.

5   Fabian, "History."

6   Richard L. Hopkins, *Origin of the American Point System* (Terra Alta, Va.: Hill & Dale Private Press, 1976), 8.

7   Theodore Low De Vinne, *The Practice of Typography: A Treatise on the Processes of Type-Making, the Point System, the Names, Sizes, Styles and Prices of Plain Printing Types* (New York: The Century Co., 1900), 132–33.

8   Hopkins, *Point System*, 5–8.

9   Dr. James Eckman, "The Chicago Type Foundry of Marder, Luse & Company, 1863–1892," *Printing & Graphic Arts (PaGA)* 7, no. 3 (September 1959): 74.

10 De Vinne, *Plain Printing Types*, 149.

11 Hopkins, *Point System*, 27–28.

12 Peter Johnson, "How Alameda Changed the World (for Printers)," *Alameda Sun* 5, no. 22 (February 16, 2006): 9.

13 Eckman, "Chicago Type Foundry," 74.

14 Hopkins, *Point System*, 28–29.

15 Maurice Annenberg, *Type Foundries of America and Their Catalogs*, 2nd ed. (New Castle, Del.: Oak Knoll Press, 1994), 191 (in caption).

16 Ibid.

17 Eckman, "Chicago Type Foundry," 77.

18 G. Willem Ovink, "From Fournier to Metric, and from Lead to Film," *Quaerendo* 9, no. 4 (Autumn 1974): 291.

19 Werner, "Saint Louis' Place," 764.

20 Quadrat [Henry Lewis Bullen], "Discursions of a Retired Printer, No. VII," *Inland Printer* 38, no. 4 (January 1907): 520.

21 Werner, "St. Louis' Place," 764.

22 De Vinne, *Plain Printing Types*, 150.

23 Quadrat, "Discursions No. VII," 515.

24 One centimeter = 0.393700787 inches, so, by simple multiplication, 35 centimeters = 13.779527559055119 inches. While 15 heights-to-paper equals very close to 35 centimeters (15 x 0.918 inch = 13.77 inches), 83 12-point bodies equals slightly less than that (83 x 12 points = 996 points; 996 points x 0.0138 inches per point = 13.7448 inches).

25   Quadrat, "Discursions No. VII," 515n.

26 Ibid., 517.

27 Ibid.

28 The original specimen booklet for self-spacing type does not use a hyphen, but by the time Benton, Waldo & Co. was located at 89 Huron Street and produced a magazine ad for the type, a hyphen was being used. The hyphen appears as early as September 1886: "Of Interest to the Craft," *Inland Printer* 3, no. 12 (September 1886): 789.

29 Lucien A. Legros and John C. Grant, *Typographical Printing-Surfaces: The Technology and Mechanism of Their Production* (New York, London: Longmans, Green and Co., 1916), 77.

30 The "en" is the relative unit of measure equal to one-half the width of the em.

31 "Explanation of the Principle of Benton's Self Spacing Type," *Typographic Specimens: Benton's Self Spacing Type* (Milwaukee: Benton, Waldo & Co., n.d.), 1.

32 In this chapter the original spelling—no hyphen—introduces the type and is its proper "specimen book" spelling; later the hyphen is added for general discussion of the concept, as the subsequent Benton, Waldo & Co. spelling dictates.

33 Henry Lewis Bullen, "Linn Boyd Benton—The Man and His Work," *Inland Printer* 70, no. 1 (October 1922): 61.

34 "Self Spacing Type," *The North-Western* 9, nos. 37–38 (Springtime 1884): 2.

35 Bullen, "Linn Boyd Benton," 62.

36 *Portable Book of Specimens from the Benton & Waldo Foundry Operated by American Type Founders Company, Patentees and Manufacturers of Benton's Self-Spacing Type* (Milwaukee: American Type Founders Company, ca. 1893). An original copy, embossed with "L. B. BENTON" in gold on the cover, is part of RIT's Cary Graphic Arts Collection, courtesy of Laurence Gregg.

37 "Explanation," 1.

38 Eckman, "The Inland Type Foundry, 1894–1911," *Printing & Graphic Arts (PaGA)* 8, no. 2 (June 1960): 32.

39 Eckman, "The Immortal Century Type Face And the Bentons, Father and Son," *Printer's Digest* (November 1964): 4.

40 Quadrat, "Discursions No. VII," 519.

41 Bullen, "Linn Boyd Benton," 62.

42 "Self Spacing Type," *Inland Printer* 4, no. 3 (December 1886): 180.

43 Updike, *Printing Types*, 1:37.

44 "Self Spacing Old Style Italic," *Typographic Specimens: Benton's Self Spacing Type* (Milwaukee: Benton, Waldo & Co., n.d.), 14.

45 Stanley Morison, "Towards an Ideal Italic," *Fleuron* 5 (1926): 109–110.

46 Bullen to Beatrice Warde, 14 February 1927, 4, Typographic Library Manuscripts, Rare Book and Manuscript Library, Columbia University.

47 Quadrat, "Discursions No. VII," 519.

48 Updike, *Printing Types*, 1:35.

The Development of Benton's Punch-Cutting Machine, and How It Made the Linotype a Success

W HEN LINN BOYD BENTON decided to market his self-spacing type and abandon his work on the automatic justifying machine, he was immediately faced with the challenge of cutting punches for every character of each size of each self-spacing font and making matrices from them as quickly as possible. According to Henry Lewis Bullen

> There were more than three thousand punches to be cut and not one punch-cutter was available either in America or in Europe. The dilemma was the turning point of Benton's career—it eventually disclosed to himself that he had mechanical genius of the highest order.[1]

Did Benton hand-cut the originals for his self-spacing type trials? There is no evidence that he did, and we know that his youthful tombstone letter-engraving experience was less than successful. At some point he decided that the best answer to the problem was to invent a machine that would cut the letters for him. He explained much later, "Unable to engage the services of expert type-punch cutters, I was compelled to invent my type-punch engraving machine, the success of which became much more important to our art than I ever dreamed of …"[2]

The first version of the punch-cutting machine worked perfectly, Bullen wrote in 1922, "showing that the principle was correct. The second machine did no better work but was easier to manipulate."[3] Benton applied for a patent for the third version of his machine on February 29, 1884. After repeated rejections, amendments and clerical and legal problems (see Chapter 8), U.S. Patent No. 332,990 was granted on December 22, 1885, for Benton's "Punch Cutting Machine."[4] As De Vinne later wrote,

> The inventor claims, and the claim is not disputed, that punches completed

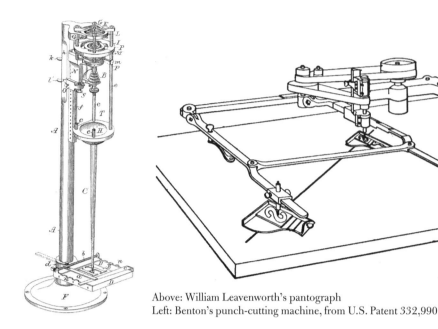

Above: William Leavenworth's pantograph
Left: Benton's punch-cutting machine, from U.S. Patent 332,990

by this machine produce matrices that are more readily fitted up and justified than those cut by hand. Models for accents, fractions and borders can be made in sections, and accurately conjoined in proper position before the cutting of the punch. The punches for accents are always truly flat on the face, and all kinds of kerns can be provided with proper supports … As the counters are deeper and the bevels truer, the types do not show distortion when they have been flattened by wear.[5]

EARLIER PANTOGRAPHIC DEVICES USED FOR MAKING TYPE

Many sources give Benton credit for having invented the first pantographic punch-cutting machine, not mentioning any of the other similar machines invented and used prior to 1885. One obscure 1960 source states that "the pantograph proper was invented by Christoph Schreiner, rector of a Jesuit college at Neisse in Silesia, who developed the principle in the years following 1603."[6] Schreiner published his discovery in 1631, in a treatise entitled *Pantographice, seu are delineandi resquiaslibet per parallelogrammum linare mobile.* Within a hundred years the pantograph, or parallelogram as it was called, was being used to copy and enlarge maps and fortification plans.

William Leavenworth of Allentown, New Jersey, adapted the pantographic principle to the manufacture of wood type in 1834,[7] eliminating the need for drawing letters by hand on wood. De Vinne explained: "From one set of models attached to the pantograph an unskilled workman could cut on untraced wood various sizes from two-line pica upward, and every size would be a faithful reproduction of the model."[8]

According to type designer N. J. Werner, writing in 1930, an early pantographic machine for cutting steel punches was imported from Germany for the Cincinnati Type Foundry in 1880, but when no one in the foundry was able to operate it, it was sold to the Central Type Foundry of St. Louis in 1882.[9] Later, William Schraubstadter, one of the sons of the owner of the Central Type Foundry, engraved characters directly into matrices by machine. Bullen wrote, "metal-engraving machines had been made and used before 1885 in Germany, and William Schraubstadter made and used one in this country in 1881, but these all lacked precision and required to be supplanted by hand work."[10] Apparently the Central Type Foundry's matrix engraving machine was not adequate for the job, since William's brother Carl Jr. wrote a few years later in the *Inland Printer* about the prevalence of the electrotype process for making matrices (see Chapter 1). Werner also noted that the machines used in St. Louis were "flat pantographs," as opposed to Benton's patented upright machine.[11]

Another early machine for engraving type matrices was shipped to Chicago from Germany in 1881 by Herman Wiebking, a type engraver, when he moved his family to America. Herman's son Adolph wrote this about his father's German matrix engraving machine:

> My father's original engraving machine was made by somebody in Berlin, possibly during 1870 or even before, for it was in his house as far back as I can remember. We children were never permitted to touch it, and it was carefully covered up when not in use. I made wax seals on this very same machine when only fourteen years old.[12]

Herman Wiebking is said to have engraved a matrix in 1882 from which type was cast by Marder, Luse & Co. of Chicago. Another son of his, Robert, who had been born in 1870 in Schwelm, Westphalia, engraved his first successful matrices in 1894. Robert later worked in Chicago for many years as a type designer and engraver at several foundries, including Barnhart Brothers & Spindler, until his death in 1927.[13] Robert Wiebking engraved some of Frederic W. Goudy's typefaces and the Centaur face designed by Bruce Rogers (see Chapter 14). R. H. Middleton, the director of typeface design at the Ludlow Typograph Co. in Chicago from 1933 to 1971,[14] claimed that Robert Wiebking and William A. Reade, the founder and first president of the Ludlow Company, made an arrangement whereby Ludlow purchased one of Wiebking's machines, and Wiebking provided Ludlow employees a brief period of training in engraving methods. Middleton gave no dates for the transaction, but merely stated that "this arrangement … launched the Ludlow Company on an independent engraving program."[15]

Did Benton know about these machines? We don't know. The Wiebking machine was a matrix engraver, and Benton's first patented machine was for cutting letters in relief, although he did modify it to skip the punch-cutting step entirely and engrave matrices instead. Despite Milwaukee's proximity to Chicago, where Wiebking lived and worked, no evidence has been found that the two men met before 1885.

The First Version of Benton's Machine

While Benton was struggling to find a way to produce self-spacing types, his foundry was making type matrices by electro-deposition, and therefore Benton's invention was first used to cut type metal, not steel. "The machine which brought Benton fame was his punch-cutting machine," type historian Dr. James Eckman wrote, "patented in 1885, which, oddly enough, Benton did not use for the cutting of punches. He used it to cut type metal, for the Benton & Waldo foundry at this time was making matrices by the electrotype process."[16]

Some sources erroneously claim that the first version of Benton's invention was used to engrave matrices, not relief letters. For example, Richard E. Huss wrote in 1985 in *The Printer's Composition Matrix* that Benton "originally used 'sorts' *patterns* for cutting soft-metal 'dummy' matrices from which electrotype matrices were made, in order to replace worn or damaged matrices in his foundry, thereby avoiding the necessity for hand-cutting punches."[17] Huss was apparently confusing the 19th-century electrotype method of making matrices with the 20th-century electrotyping process commonly used to duplicate a relief form for mass production. In the same book, Huss also mistakenly identified the drawing from the first page of Benton's 1885 "Punch-Cutting Machine" patent as a "pantographic matrix-engraving machine."[18]

In an earlier book about mechanical typesetting methods, Huss also confused Benton's punch-cutting machine with his later matrix-engraving machine. "An obscure printer-typefounder named Linn Boyd Benton suddenly had the answer in 1885 when he patented a matrix-engraving machine, which produced matrices quickly, accurately, and economically,"[19] Huss wrote. In fact, Benton's invention was not patented as a matrix engraver until more than 20 years later.

Benton's 1885 patent was strictly for a punch-cutting machine; no mention is made about engraving matrices. Benton's colleague at ATF, Henry Lewis Bullen, heard the details about the history of the machine from Benton himself, and wrote that the first version was "A machine to cut letter punches! … The Benton punch-cutter … was cutting in type metal, for Benton was using electrotyped matrices."[20]

William Charles Gregan, the last master engraver at the American Type Founders Company in Elizabeth, New Jersey, spoke with Morris Benton on several occasions in the 1940s about Benton's late father's "engraving odyssey." As a result of these conversations, Gregan also deduced that Linn Boyd Benton originally used his pantograph invention to engrave the original models to be used for making electrotype matrices.[21] But by July 1884, less than a year after Benton's self-spacing type had been patented, the *Inland Printer* was already reporting that Benton had changed his process, from working in type metal to steel:

> Benton, Waldo & Co., of Milwaukee, claim to have invented a machine for cutting punches for original characters for type foundries in steel—an invention which will much cheapen the ordinary process of cutting by hand. It will cut from the largest to the smallest punch—even to half diamond; while as a time-saver, we may state that a piece of work now requiring four hours to perfect by the hand process can, under its operation, be turned out in *half an hour.* [22]

Why, if this statement was true, was Benton's machine cutting punches in steel instead of cutting originals in type metal for electrotyping? To understand what had happened, we need to look elsewhere in the country.

MERGENTHALER'S LINOTYPE MACHINE

The story of Benton's punch-cutting machine is intertwined with another type story. Ironically, Benton's invention to aid type founding was to become what Bullen called "the greatest ally of a machine which at the time was expected to destroy the type-founding industry." [23] While Benton was busy in Milwaukee making self-spacing type, Ottmar Mergenthaler in Baltimore was working on his own revolutionary justifying typesetting machine.

It all started in the 1860s when James Olivie Clephane, a court stenographer and later a practicing lawyer, felt oppressed by the tediousness of producing manuscript copies of his notes and the notes of his employees for the law courts. He became interested in devising a system of mechanical writing in about 1866. Even though he bought and used the first seven Remington typewriters (invented by Christopher Sholes), Clephane wanted more. His objective was "to produce a machine that would mechanically produce copy that would eliminate the cost of type composition." [24]

Charles T. Moore, an inventor whose 1872 patent for a "double-cylinder typesetter" proved impractical, persuaded Clephane to help finance another of his inventions that used a keyboard to create characters on lithographic paper, which would then be transferred to lithographic stone. Moore called it a "transfer typewriter," and in 1876 he asked A. Hahl & Co. in Baltimore to build a prototype. August Hahl, the owner of the shop, also succumbed to Moore's charismatic persuasion and accepted the job.

At that time, 20-year-old Ottmar Mergenthaler was the foreman of Hahl's machine shop. Mergenthaler, the son of a schoolteacher, had been born in 1854 in a small town in southern Germany. At the age of 14 he became an apprentice for Louis Hahl, his stepmother's brother and a watchmaker. In 1872, young Mergenthaler moved to Washington, D.C. to work for August Hahl, Louis's son, who had already established himself as a watchmaker and model builder there. A few years later they moved the machine shop to Baltimore. "At this time," explained Elizabeth Harris, former curator of the Division of Graphic Arts at the Smithsonian's National Museum of American History, "the Patent Office required that every patentee provide a scale model in support of an application for a patent. Clearly there was business for clever modelmakers."[25]

When Mergenthaler first received the assignment to build a model of Moore's newest invention, he criticized its basic design but worked on it anyway because his cousin August had already agreed to make a prototype. To Mergenthaler's doubts about the feasibility of the design, Clephane replied, "I am a man possessed by an idea. I intend to overcome all obstacles to see it carried through. If you tell me that it cannot be done, I will answer in the words of Napoleon who, when he wanted to cross the Alps and was told of the difficulties, cried, 'There are no Alps.' I tell you now: the machine has got to be built."[26]

Mergenthaler modified and simplified Moore's design and even patented a Rotary Impression Machine in 1879, but he became disenchanted with the work and severed his ties with the new company that had been formed to manufacture it, the National Machine Printing Company. Mergenthaler sold his three shares of company stock in 1881 for $60. August Hahl held onto his three shares for about a year longer, after which he sold them for $900. By 1924, those shares would be worth tens of thousands of dollars.

Mergenthaler started his own machinist business in 1883, reconsidered Clephane's objective, and evolved his first "band machine." It employed small bands or bars of metal with letters and other characters used in type composition engraved in relief on their edges. Bullen explained how it worked in an *Inland Printer* article:

> At the touch of the corresponding key on the keyboard, the bar dropped until the required letter came into alignment with other letters which formed words and lines. The line of punches was then pressed into a long strip of papier-maché, which in turn was assembled on paper and justified … after which each page was stereotyped in a hand mold.[27]

Mergenthaler soon improved his original band machine: first, by assembling and justifying a line of matrices instead of punches, and second, by then casting type directly from those assembled matrices. In 1884 the first "line of type" was cast in Mergenthaler's shop in Baltimore on the revised band machine. To justify the lines, Mergenthaler used a wedge system that had been patented in 1872 by Merritt Gally, an inventor who had constructed a printing press for artistic work called "the Universal Press." (Some reports call Gally's spacing device "the most effective detail on the Linotype."[28]) The National Typographic Company bought two of Mergenthaler's machines and helped him set up a factory.

But Mergenthaler soon realized the impracticality of his improved band machine: it

The Mergenthaler Linotype Machine of 1886   Ottmar Mergenthaler

was much too expensive to build and he could not satisfactorily align the matrices. Clephane and another backer encouraged him to conduct more experiments, but leading newspaper publishers were interested in the band machine and formed a syndicate that bought 7,000 of the 40,000 shares of stock in what had come to be called the Mergenthaler Printing Company. Mergenthaler, however, persisted in his experimentation, and his first single-matrix or "blower" machine came out in 1885. "The matrices were held in perpendicular channels," Bullen wrote, "and, dropping down onto a wire rod in the horizontal assembling channel, were brought to the justifying point by means of blasts of air provided by a blower—a most unmechanical makeshift, which did not work satisfactorily."[29] But the directors of the company thought the 1885 blower was good enough, and ordered 100 to be manufactured. Mergenthaler persuaded them to reduce this number to 12, and by July 1886, the first one was installed at the *New York Tribune*.

Mergenthaler's revised 1886 model was an improvement over the 1885 blower machine, but again, although he wanted to perfect it before beginning mass production, he was ordered to make 200 more machines. By February 1888, about 60 machines were in use in the composing rooms of members of the newspaper syndicate, but their performance remained problematic. "As a consequence of various disagreements," Bullen wrote, "Mergenthaler severed his ties with the company in April 1888, leaving with it an unsatisfactory machine, which he had been prohibited from improving."[30]

Mergenthaler sold his stock in the company that bore his name and again set up his own small workshop. By the end of 1888, he had completed drawings for an improved machine, which eventually became what is now called the 1890 model, the Linotype in its final form. He asked Clephane again for financial assistance, and after much negotiation, the manufacture of the new machine began.

The Benton Moment

But a new problem with the Linotype system had become apparent, which Bullen explained in the *Inland Printer:*

> Here was a machine; but no adequate means of supplying it with matrices had been devised. The rapid production of matrices required the rapid production of steel punches. The typefounder may use a steel punch only once; he seldom would use it half a dozen times. But each linotype matrix requires the use of a punch, and punches are fragile things. A steel punch may break the first time it is used. Where steel punches are used thousands of times a day the percentage of breakages is serious. Steel punches also wear out and must be replaced immediately they show signs of wear. Steel punches cut by hand are very expensive. It is said that the hand-cut punches of the Mergenthaler Printing Company cost $5 each. This cost, however, was a small matter compared with the slowness of production when cut by hand. In 1890 the Linotype company had six or seven punch cutters in its employ, and these could do no more than keep up the supply of matrices for about two hundred machines. Not in all the world could enough steel punch cutters be found to furnish an adequate supply of matrices, without which the machines were as useless and unsalable as a gun where powder is unprocurable.[31]

An earlier account of the same problem, also by Bullen in the *Inland Printer*, had brought out the additional problem of matrix alignment:

> Every one of my readers has seen a Linotype matrix; on one edge of a thin piece of brass the matrix is made by driving into the brass a steel punch on which the character is engraved. For every character used on a Linotype machine a steel punch was required to be made with greater exactness as to the position of the character on the punch than a typefounder demanded … Punches soon wore out; they might last one hour or a year, as breakages were frequent. The Linotype company was paying as high as $8 per letter-punch.[32]

According to his autobiography, written in the third person and dictated to his associate Otto Schoenrich during the winter of 1897–98, Mergenthaler had realized from early on that obtaining enough matrices for his machines to work would be a challenge. "Probably the most difficult problem connected with the first manufacturing attempts," Schoenrich wrote, "was the production of the matrices at a price not prohibitive. Attempts to have them made outside under contract failed entirely."[33] Mergenthaler had decided to solve this problem himself, and devised a system of producing matrices from steel punches that "required some thirty special machines and machine attachments."[34] It took months for him to perfect his method of producing matrices at an acceptable cost, but the problem of obtaining the original steel punches remained. Mergenthaler, writing through Schoenrich, revealed that he was acutely aware that he needed a breakthrough like Benton's punch-cutting machine. The third-person account of his trials, *The Biography of Ottmar Mergenthaler*, explained:

> One great difficulty in the matrix department was found to be the expense and trouble of maintaining the original steel stamps which produced the matrix proper. There was no machine existing at that time by means of which these stamps could be engraved at a small cost with an absolute certainty of maintaining the same size and shape, but they had to be engraved by hand at a cost of $5 per piece, and their accuracy as a matter of course was far inferior to those later produced by the Benton & Waldo type engraver. Without the help of this machine it may well be said that good matrices as we now have them would be an impossibility. Mr. Mergenthaler soon discovered the need for such a machine, and failing to find anything in the market, he at once went to work designing an engraving machine. The work on this machine had already well advanced when the above named parties brought out theirs, thus causing work on his design to be discontinued.[35]

Mergenthaler was an excellent mechanic and had the integrity to pursue his goals against great odds. Elizabeth Harris characterized him as a "brilliant and impulsive inventor" whose misunderstandings with businessmen "grew to become overwhelming."[36] Bullen, on the other hand, was not so complimentary: "[Mergenthaler's] path as an inventor was that of a plodder, and is marked by an unusual number of machines that failed. Had he possessed the genius of a great inventor he would have confined his failures to paper."[37]

Linn Boyd Benton was not aware of Mergenthaler and his machine, preoccupied as he was with getting self-spacing types manufactured for the newspapers that had ordered them and marketing the idea to newspapers that hadn't. Once he had invented the punch-cutting machine as a means of cutting the originals from which electrotype matrices could be made to cast his self-spacing types, he concentrated on production. In the meantime, his partner, R. V. Waldo, made a trip to New York City to try to sell self-spacing type to some of the larger newspapers, and landed in the composing room of the *New York Tribune*, the only paper at the time that was using the Linotype for daily production.

Waldo had never heard of the Linotype machine, and so did not realize its limitations, namely, that every time a steel letter-punch used to make matrices for the Linotype broke, a new one had to be cut by hand. This meant that there were minute differences in some of the letters in the paper, which no one but perhaps a type founder would notice, under a microscope. Bullen, recounting the story in 1922, maintained

The second version of Benton's punch-cutting machine, which cut the first sample steel punch for Mergenthaler's Linotype machine

that the *Tribune's* type left much to be desired:

> We remember, as some of our readers may, the peculiar appearance of the *New York Tribune* when it was first set by linotypes. Each line had wrong font characters in it. There would be two or three kinds of letters e or c or t in each line, each change of character indicating the breakage of a punch.[38]

Oblivious to these concerns, Waldo handled his marketing endeavors with gusto and integrity, undaunted by the *Tribune's* Linotype machine and persisting in his sales pitch of the self-spacing types. The superintendent of the *Tribune's* composing room, Mr. Milholland, wasn't interested in what he was saying until Waldo made the claim that better stereotypes could be made from 'self-spacing' types "because the punches from which the matrices were made were cut by a machine which finished the bevels below the face of the letters as smoothly as the faces of the letters."[39] Milholland was familiar with the troubles of the Mergenthaler Company, and asked Waldo to repeat his story to Whitelaw Reid, who represented the majority of the *Tribune's* stockholders. When Reid replied to Waldo's sales pitch by simply saying that he wasn't interested in the self-spacing types, Waldo considered his trip a failure and returned to Milwaukee.

Soon after Waldo arrived home, Philip T. Dodge, the Mergenthaler Company's patent attorney, appeared in Milwaukee at Benton, Waldo & Co. He asked to see the punch-cutting machine, and realized that it was cutting in type metal, not steel, because Benton was using electrotyped matrices to cast the self-spacing types. Dodge asked whether the machine could cut in steel, and Benton replied that he didn't know whether it could. He didn't want to stop production to experiment, but Dodge offered to pay him $50 if the trial did not succeed, as compensation for lost time.

That evening, Benton slightly changed the cutting tools and successfully cut a steel punch for Dodge. Soon he received an order to cut 90 steel punches, and when this also proved successful, Benton and the Mergenthaler Printing Company entered into an agreement for leasing Benton's machines.

Perhaps some other device would eventually have been invented had Benton's machine not been brought to the attention of the Mergenthaler Company. Yet in his characteristically enthusiastic way, Bullen claimed, "Thus Benton saved the Linotype machine, with an invention much more marvelous than the Linotype machine."[40]

Leasing Benton's Machine

Benton had refined his invention and patented it in 1885, and Benton and Waldo continued to promote and peddle self-spacing types to the newspaper industry. By late 1885 these were selling beyond the capacity of the foundry to produce them, even with Benton's invention in full use.[41] Bullen wrote in 1922 about this frantic period:

> Mr. Benton, working night and day, looked much older than he does now, and his face was then much more furrowed than it is now, forty years after. He was a hero of the same character as Palissy, the renowned potter. At that time, like Palissy, he was ready to "burn his furniture," and to let his inventive ardor "know no brother," if need be, to accomplish his self-imposed task.[42]

During these hectic years Benton began to acquire a reputation outside Milwaukee. The September 1886 *Inland Printer* reported that he was

> an intelligent, entertaining, unostentatious gentleman, a mechanical genius of whom [Milwaukee] has every reason to feel proud; and, it is needless to add, a thorough, enthusiastic believer in the success and merits of his "system." One such man is of more value to the community than all of the brainless dudes to be found throughout the length and breadth of the country.[43]

The first Benton punch-cutting machine to be leased was shipped to the Mergenthaler Printing Co. on February 13, 1889. Less than one month later, John Dunbar of the Mergenthaler manufacturing plant in Brooklyn wrote to Benton:

> I was a little in doubt as to the practical working of your Punch Cutter. Mr. Mills has this week dispelled that doubt, as I find that he has cut 19 splendid punches that are a credit to any machine, and much better I think than hand work.[44]

After a few months Dunbar reported to Benton, Waldo & Co. that Mr. Mills was already training others on the machine.

> There is one important fact that I forgot to mention in relation to the logograms that were gotten out by your machine. The young man that we put to help Mr. Mills got out 7 in one day of 3 letter[s] on each punch. Wages $12.00 per week. Our hand cutter charges us $2.00 a letter or $6.00 a punch.[45]

Brochure for leasing the punch-cutting machine   Linn Boyd Benton, circa 1889

Dunbar continued writing about his experience with the machine. "I thought that you would like to know," he wrote that same year, "that on August 1st the young man that works on your machine, cut 11 Roman Long Primer punches in seven hours—accented letters to go to Paris with our machine."[46]

To summarize, the first version of Benton's pantograph machine was engraving type metal originals at Benton, Waldo & Co. in Milwaukee by 1884. The second version of the machine cut the sample steel punch for Dodge. Benton received a patent for the third version in 1885, and this was the version of the machine that the Mergenthaler Printing Company leased. The arrangement with Mergenthaler became so successful that Benton, Waldo & Co. began planning to lease more machines.

An undated pamphlet from the Benton-Waldo Type Foundry, probably produced in 1891, describes "Benton's Punch Engraving Machine" and includes dated testimonials regarding the machine's effectiveness from several companies that had already leased it: the Mergenthaler Printing Co. of Brooklyn, N.Y.; the Rogers Typograph Co. of Cleveland; the Electro Matrix Co. of Minneapolis and another Electro Matrix Co. of New York; the Linotype Company, Limited, of London; and the Lanston-Type-Machine Co. of Washington, D.C. For example, L. C. Bright of London wrote on September 18, 1890:

> It gives me much pleasure to say that the two Punch Cutting Machines which you made for us and which are running at the present time in our factory in Manchester, give us the most complete satisfaction. They work smoothly and well. They delight all who see them, and are constantly pronounced to be the perfection of ingenuity, accuracy and delicacy in machinery.[47]

During the late summer or early fall of 1890, Linn Boyd Benton and his 18-year-old son Morris traveled to Washington, D.C. to assist Tolbert Lanston who was working on another type-composing machine. Lanston's Monotype automatically cast individual pieces of type, as opposed to the Linotype's slug ("line-of-type") system, but it also required large quantities of matrices. Lanston had leased several punch-cutting machines from the Milwaukee foundry, and the Bentons instructed his employees in their use. A few months later Benton received this letter:

> The Lanston-Type-Machine Co.
> Washington, D.C. November 3, 1890.
> Messrs. Benton, Waldo & Co.,
> Milwaukee, Wis.
>
> Gentlemen:
>
> During last August you delivered to us one of your punch cutting machines. Since then we have cut an entire set of punches in Brevier, several logotypes being included. From our experience I am able to deduce the following conclusions:
>
> That the punches are exact reproductions of the patterns, size only excepted.
> That in finish, taper, counters, in all the elements of good punch cutting, they are superior to the hand made.
> Our inexperienced cutter gave us double the output of the average hand worker.
> The alignment of the characters upon the faces of the punch pieces, is to us important in simplifying the work of driving. The punch-cutter secures that alignment.
>
> Your machine is a remarkable example of the perfection of mechanical construction. To us it is invaluable, and others in a like situation cannot afford to forgo it.
>
> > Very sincerely your friend,
> > Tolbert Lanston, Superintendent.[48]

Benton's Paradox

The March 1896 *Inland Printer* magazine reported that Benton's punch-cutting machine was judged to be the most perfect mechanical exhibit in the World's Columbian Exposition held in Chicago. Accompanying the medal given to Benton was an award—"in the highest degree commendatory," the *Inland Printer* noted—which read, in part: "This machine is the embodiment of the highest order of mechanical construction; cuts a line in steel to one ten-thousandths of an inch, and produces perfect punches."[49] Despite this award, Linn Boyd Benton himself was surprised at the eventual fame of his invention, writing much later that it

> became much more important to our art than I ever dreamed of, the machines being now employed in America, England, Europe and Japan, in which countries almost all type punches now in use are cut on machine[s] made by myself, or copies of my machine. This invention proved as fundamental to the success of the Linotype, Monotype and Intertype and other composing machines as Edison's improvements on Bell's invention were to the success of the present Bell-Edison telephone. My steel type-punch engraving machine was the first to cut a perfect type punch in metal; it was probably the first attempt in that direction. Its importance to the Linotype machine, then in its infancy, was acknowledged in the first annual report of the Mergenthaler Linotype Company issued following the date on which my punch engraving machines were first put to work in their Brooklyn factory, in the sentence, "By the acquisition of the Benton punch-cutting machine a seemingly insurmountable obstacle to our success has been overcome."[50]

De Vinne reiterated the Linotype Company's statement in *Plain Printing Types*: "The success of the Linotype … machine is largely due to the accuracy of the matrices made from Benton machine punches."[51] Bullen, however, took the compliment one step further: "Thus an invention to aid the typefounder became the greatest ally of a machine which at that time was expected to destroy the typefounding industry."[52] Benton, for his part, did not regret this outcome of his invention. "Though a typefounder I am fully appreciative of the importance of the composing machines to the printing industry," he wrote. "It is a great satisfaction to me to have aided in their efficiency."[53]

In fact, the composing machine manufacturers came relatively close to being deprived of Benton's machine altogether. Before Benton knew of Mergenthaler's efforts, he had offered to sell the patents and exclusive control of his invention to the wealthy MacKellar, Smiths & Jordan type foundry in Philadelphia. A price was agreed on, but the prospective purchaser balked when Benton stipulated that one machine remain in his own type foundry, and the sale did not go through.[54]

If Benton had known of the Linotype's problem when he first met Philip Dodge, and if he had sold his punch-cutting machine outright, he might have made a fortune on the spot. Then the Mergenthaler Printing Company would have had sole access to the machine, a great disadvantage to later composing machine manufacturers. Instead, Benton's machine in effect replaced manual punch-cutting and ushered in the era of the composing machine. In 1925, an anonymous author in the *Inland Printer* (Bullen?) claimed that "all the matrices used in composing machines throughout the world are made by machines and appliances invented by Linn Boyd Benton."[55] This

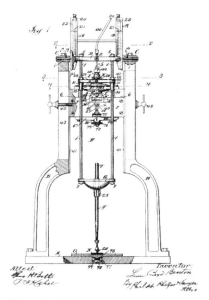

The revised Benton engraver

author must not have known that Robert Wiebking once sold the Ludlow Company one of his engraving machines.

Later Developments

It is clear that the original patent for Benton's punch-cutting machine came after a period of experimentation. As he continued tinkering with his invention, the foundry produced additional machines to lease. At some point Benton adapted his invention to engrave matrices ("mats") directly, skipping altogether the traditional intermediate steps of cutting the punch and driving it into brass to form the unjustified matrix. Former ATF employee Stevens L. Watts wrote in 1957 that the first mats to be cut on Benton's machine at ATF were for Cheltenham in March 1899,[56] although Bullen had previously claimed that the first type to be produced directly from matrices engraved on a Benton machine was 24-point Roycroft, on October 4, 1900.[57] In February 1899, Benton applied for a patent for the modifications that enabled the machine to engrave matrices directly in metal. U.S. Patent No. 809,548 was finally granted almost seven years later! In the meantime, the patent for the previous version of Benton's invention expired in 1901.[58]

Once the original punch-cutting machine patent had expired, type foundries around the world copied its design. Those companies that had returned their leased Benton machines to the American Type Founders Company in 1892 (see Chapter 6) had a head start—a Linotype punch-cutter was operational in about 1900,[59] and Monotype soon followed with its own version. Years later the Stempel type foundry in Frankfurt, Germany, was still using a machine based on Benton's invention.[60] Another copy was installed at the Lanston Monotype Corp. of London, established in 1897, when an American, Frank Hinman Pierpont, equipped the plant "to the highest standards,

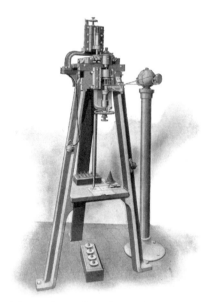

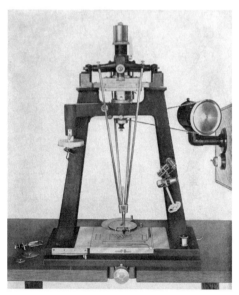

Linotype's punch-cutting machine   Monotype's version

redesigning the Benton-Waldo punchcutting machines on which the accuracy and quality of the product ultimately depended."[61]

While the original machine could now be legally copied, Benton's modifications to it were not even patented until 1906. In the meantime type designers began complaining that the letters produced by the punch-cutting machine were too "mechanized." They apparently did not realize that Benton had devised a system of altering the stem widths of different letter sizes to either condense or expand them. This elaborate and no doubt proprietary system of "optical scaling" is explained in Chapter 10.

Theo Rehak, proprietor of the Dale Guild type foundry in Howell, New Jersey, owns and operates two original Benton pantographic engravers, one dating from the Milwaukee foundry. He wrote at some length about Benton's methods:

> It is hard to imagine that such logistics as are found in the final versions of the Benton engraver did not come by way of some previous stages of development. Linn Boyd Benton (LBB) had always been fascinated with the "art and science" of mathematics, especially as applied in the classical nineteenth century approach, which was his metiér. He could not have avoided Pythagoras in such contexts, and he was known to be fond of mathematical puzzles, games and "conundrums," as they were referred to in his day. The formulae and working constants of the pantograph and its engineering principles must have surely caught his attention early on. Carefully filed away in his prodigious mind, he found pragmatic use for these things in type founding. That he freely improvised and actually improved upon such devices is a credit to his peculiar sort of genius.

The question is: what was the sequence of applications of this knowledge? Gregan [a contemporary of Morris Benton and fellow ATF employee] maintained that the first use of the early pantograph prototypes that LBB "played" with were used to cut letter-punch models for electroplating (using the copper electro bath) type matrices. This was a technique first patented by Edwin Starr around the year 1840. The electrotyping process was originally used to pirate competitors' type designs directly from their cast specimens and also to ease the workload of the human punch-cutter who produced models for replacement electro matrices. Benton conceived of creating even more accurately-cut, newly-designed models by engraving them in relief on the end of a blank piece of type.

My photos show some matrices, types and proofs for a fancy Benton, Waldo & Co. ornamented alphabet from the late 1880s. These were supposed to have been shown at the World's Columbian Exhibition in Chicago, although the actual event may have well have been earlier.

What is true is that a piece of type is merely "a punch in leaden form," which "reads wrong" and the business end of which carries a thin coating or "ribbon" of ink to sink into the fibers of a leaf of paper. There is also, of course, the reality of exactly how LBB changed his engraving protocols from lead to steel, thus producing the punches which saved Merganthaler and his machine. So Gregan thought that Morris Benton indicated that the type models for electrotyping came first. It seems logical, with LBB's ever restless engineering-oriented mind constantly going over and refining these processes. It also explains why he finally did away with electros and punches altogether, changed his device to produce a character "reading right," and to cut (or "sink") that character directly into a blank nickel brass "planchet," making it a finished engraved matrix.

When the time came to patent the processes involved, they were already part of a proven system (unlike many nineteenth century inventions, all Benton's device patents were first proved with real-world, operational models: without any speculation or conjecture), but the dating of his patent documents are neither absolutely reliable nor entirely chronological for compiling any exact time-line history for our purposes. These changes in engraving protocols likely occurred in rapid succession, thereby preventing any "paper trail" with enough time to be documented.[62]

Chapter 5 Endnotes

1   Henry Lewis Bullen, "Linn Boyd Benton—The Man and His Work," *Inland Printer* 70, no. 1 (October 1922): 61.

2   Linn Boyd Benton, "Inventions of Linn Boyd Benton," to David Gustafson (Carnegie Institute of Technology), June 30, 1932, for inclusion in the United Typothetae of America's *Who's Who in Printing in the United States*.

3   Bullen, "Linn Boyd Benton," 61.

4   Benton, "Punch Cutting Machine," U.S. Patent No. 332,990, December 22, 1895.

5   Theodore Low De Vinne, *The Practice of Typography: A Treatise on the Processes of Type-Making, the Point System, the Names, Sizes, Styles and Practices of Plain Printing Types* (New York: The Century Co., 1900), 353.

6   "From the Stork's Beak to Benton's Punchcutter," *Linotype Matrix* 33 (May 1960): 2.

7   De Vinne, *Plain Printing Types*, 348. However, N. J. Werner wrote that Leavenworth invented his wood-type cutting pantograph in 1843, not 1834 (most likely this is a typo), in N. J. Werner, "Wiebking Created Popular Faces in Chicago, Friend Discloses," *Inland Printer* 90, no. 2 (November 1932), 72.

8   DeVinne, *Plain Printing Types*, 348.

9   Werner, "Wiebking Created," 72.

10 Quadrat [Henry Lewis Bullen], "Discursions of a Retired Printer, No. VII," *Inland Printer* 38, no. 4 (January 1907): 517.

11 Werner, "St. Louis in Type-Founding History," *Share Your Knowledge Review* 22, no. 3 (January 1941): 21.

12 Werner, "Wiebking Created," 73.

13 Ibid., 71.

14 Stephen Glenn Crook, "The Contributions of R. Hunter Middleton to Typeface Design and Printing in America" (M.S. diss, University of Chicago, 1980), 25.

15 R. Hunter Middleton, *Chicago Letter Founding* (Chicago: The Black Cat Press, 1937), 13.

16 Dr. James Eckman, *The Heritage of the Printer*, vol. 1 (Philadelphia: North American Publishing Company, 1965), 111.

17 Richard E. Huss, *The Printer's Composition Matrix* (New Castle, Del.: Oak Knoll Books, 1985), 9.

18 Ibid., 8.

19 Huss, *The Development of Printers' Mechanical Typesetting Methods, 1822–1925* (Charlottesville: University Press of Virginia, 1973), 9.

20 Bullen, "Linn Boyd Benton," 62.

21 Theo Rehak, email to the author, 2 December 2006.

22 "Items of Interest," *Inland Printer* 1, no. 10 (July 1884): 21.

23 Quadrat, "Discursions, No. VII," 518.

24 Bullen, "Origin and Development of the Linotype Machine, Part I," *Inland Printer* 72, no. 5 (February 1924): 770.

25 Elizabeth Harris, introduction to *The Biography of Ottmar Mergenthaler*, ed. Carl Schlesinger (New Castle, Del.: Oak Knoll Press, 1989), ix.

26 Frank J. Romano, *Machine Writing and Typesetting* (Salem, N.H.: Graphic Arts Marketing Association, 1986), 26.

27   Bullen, "Origin and Development, Part I," 771.

28   Quadrat, "Discursions, No. VII," 518.

29   Bullen, "Origin and Development of the Linotype Machine, Part II," *Inland Printer* 72, no. 6 (March 1924): 936.

30   Ibid.

31   Bullen, "Origin and Development, Part II," 937.

32   Quadrat, "Discursions No. VII," 518.

33   Carl Schlesinger, ed., *The Biography of Ottmar Mergenthaler* (New Castle, Del.: Oak Knoll Press, 1989), 29.

34   Ibid.

35   Ibid., 29–30.

36   Harris, introduction to *Biography*, xii.

37   Bullen, "Origin and Development, Part II," 938.

38   Bullen, "Linn Boyd Benton," 62.

39   Ibid.

40   Bullen, "Origin and Development, Part II," 937.

41   John Allen Murphy, "Morris Benton: Type Designer-Executive," *Inland Printer* 96, no. 6 (March 1936): 34.

42   Bullen, "Linn Boyd Benton," 61–62.

43   "Of Interest to the Craft," *Inland Printer* 3, no. 12 (September 1886): 789.

44   "Benton's Punch Engraving Machine," pamphlet (Milwaukee: Benton-Waldo Type Foundry, ca. 1891).

45   Ibid.

46   Ibid.

47   Ibid.

48   Ibid.

49   "Foundation of Good Type," *Inland Printer* 16, no. 6 (March 1896): 676.

50   Benton to Gustafson.

51   De Vinne, *Plain Printing Types*, 353.

52   Quadrat, "Discursions, No. VII," 518.

53   Benton to Gustafson.

54   Bullen, "The Creators of the New Era in Typefounding," *Inland Printer* 73, no. 5 (August 1924): 764.

55   "Two Men Whose Work Greatly Benefits All Typographers," *Inland Printer* 76, no. 3 (December 1925): 453.

56   Stevens L. Watts, "'Chelt' Really Got Around," *Printing* 81, no. 5 (May 1957): 78.

57   Bullen, "Linn Boyd Benton," 63.

58   Bullen, "Creators," 764.

59   Lucien A. Legros and John C. Grant, *Typographical Printing-Surfaces: The Technology and Mechanism of Their Production* (New York, London: Longmans, Green and Co., 1916), 204.

60   Hermann Zapf, in discussion with the author, Rochester, N.Y., 9 August 1985.

61   James Mosley, "On Type: Eric Gill's Perpetua Type," *Fine Print* 8, no. 3 (July 1982): 90.

62   Rehak, email.

PART TWO

The Bentons and the
American Type Founders Company
1892 to 1948

The Formation of the American Type Founders Company

Aमेरican foundries such as Benton's in Milwaukee were not faring especially well in the late 1870s because there were too many of them. "[A]s manufacturing processes improved, and more foundries entered into business, a serious problem of overproduction confronted the industry."[1] Because of the overabundance of available type, foundries granted too much credit to unstable printers, outfitted whole printing plants for entrepreneurs with insufficient capital, and engaged in savage price wars with each other.[2]

In 1878, Benton's foundry joined five Chicago type foundries and one from St. Paul, Minnesota, in sending a letter to the United States Type Founders' Association about "the existing demoralization and abuses in the trade"[3] that were lowering the price of type. A proposed price list was included with the letter, which also observed that the members of the association had previously agreed to a uniform schedule of prices. But eight years later, the Chicago Type Foundry (Marder, Luse & Company) offered a discount of 25 percent on type manufactured on its American System of Interchangeable Type Bodies (see Chapter 4) for cash payments made between the first and tenth of the month. The company justified its action by arguing that older types of irregular sizes were being dumped on the market at ridiculously low prices by founders who were finally being forced to adopt the new point system. The *Inland Printer* magazine summarized the situation:

> It has been known for some months past that a rather spirited and lively competition for business has been going on between our various type-founding establishments, a competition which time only seemed to increase in intensity and volume. It was hoped, however, that wiser counsels would ultimately prevail and put an end to a strife which could only

result in loss to all concerned. But such has not proven to be the case. The chasm widened, active competition grew into open antipathy, and the rivalry became keener day by day. Prices were cut to the rocks, and the methods resorted to by some houses to secure business were alike injurious and indefensible.[4]

The *Inland Printer* editors were confident that a meeting in late September 1886 of the Type Founders' Association at Niagara Falls would resolve the problem: "the insurmountable difficulties about which we hear so much will disappear like snow before the summer's sun."[5] An agreement was in fact reached by the twenty foundries present to stabilize prices, allowing a maximum discount of 10 percent for accounts paid monthly or within 30 days of purchase.

However the Type Founders' Association disbanded in 1888,[6] and the following year, "in the face of an extremely lethargic business atmosphere,"[7] the Chicago Type Foundry repeated its earlier offer of a 25 percent discount on its types. Barnhart Brothers & Spindler, also of Chicago, matched this offer and then announced another discount of 40 percent on certain older types. When the Central Type Foundry of St. Louis and the eastern foundries decided to uphold the 1886 agreement and not lower their own prices, "the practical result was nation-wide confusion and endless recriminations and reprisals in the typefounding industry."[8]

Another problem was of course the invention of the Linotype machine. Before the Linotype came into general use, the main business of type foundries had been with the managers of daily newspapers, who wanted local foundries to provide them with type supplies on short notice. But the Linotype took most of the newspaper business away from the foundries. According to Dr. James Eckman, "Each machine could wipe out an entire type foundry."[9]

The Merger

Type foundry owners began to realize that there was no choice but to consolidate. After many meetings and much argument, a plan was drawn up, promoted by John Marder of the Chicago Type Foundry; Arthur T. H. Brower of the Union Type Foundry, also in Chicago; and two New York bankers.[10] When the oldest and most respected foundry, MacKellar, Smiths & Jordan of Philadelphia, joined the group advocating for a merger, its success was virtually guaranteed. A short, anonymous article in the November 1892 *Inland Printer* magazine announced the merger of 23 type foundries and their incorporation as the American Type Founders Company.

> The company is formed to acquire and carry on the business of the following firms and corporations: MacKellar, Smiths & Jordan, Philadelphia; Collins & McLeester, Philadelphia; Pelouse & Co., Philadelphia; James Conner's Sons, New York; P. H. Heinrich, New York; A. W. Lindsay, New

York; Charles J. Cary & Co., Baltimore; John Ryan & Co., Baltimore; J. G. Mengel & Co., Baltimore; Hooper, Wilson & Co., Baltimore; Boston Typefoundry, Boston; Phelps, Dalton & Co., Boston [renamed the Dickinson Type Foundry][11]; Lyman & Son, Buffalo; Allison & Smith, Cincinnati [renamed the Franklin Type & Stereotype Foundry][12]; Cincinnati Typefoundry, Cincinnati; Cleveland Typefoundry, Cleveland; Marder, Luse & Co., Chicago; Union Typefoundry, Chicago; Benton, Waldo & Co., Milwaukee; Central Typefoundry, St. Louis; St. Louis Typefoundry, St. Louis; Kansas City Type Foundry, Kansas City; Palmer & Rey, San Francisco.[13]

In 1907, Bullen described the same scenario in slightly different terms:

On February 8, 1892, the American Type Founders Company was incorporated, with a capital of $4,000,000 preferred and $5,000,000 common stock, and purchased a majority of the typefoundries in the United States, thus becoming the successor of the eminent houses of MacKellar, Smiths & Jordan (established 1796), Cincinnati Type Foundry (1817), Boston Type Foundry (1817), James Conner's Sons (1827), Dickinson Type Foundry (1839), Marder, Luse & Co. (1855), Benton, Waldo & Co. (about 1860), Central Type Foundry (1870), Palmer & Rey (1875), Cleveland Type Foundry (1881), and, at a later period, George Bruce's Son & Co. (1813). In addition it became the owner of eleven minor typefoundries. With the exception of the Boston, Central and Bruce foundries, which were purchased for all cash, the various owners disposed of all their interests in their individual foundries for part cash and part common stock in the new company.[14]

Only five major American type foundries did not join ATF when it incorporated in 1892: Barnhard Brothers & Spindler and its four subsidiaries; Farmer, Little & Co. of New York, which reorganized and became A. D. Farmer & Son; George Bruce's New York Foundry; the Keystone Type Foundry of Philadelphia; and the H. C. Hansen Type Foundry of Boston. By 1919, however, all of these had joined the group.[15]

The first order of business for the new company was to close the weakest foundries and concentrate on the remaining 12, in New York, Boston (two), Philadelphia, Chicago, St. Louis, Cincinnati (two), Milwaukee (Benton's foundry), Baltimore, Cleveland, and San Francisco. Robert Allison of the Franklin Type Foundry in Cincinnati became ATF's first president and a general office was established in New York, but Allison, continuing as manager of the Cincinnati branch, seldom traveled there. Thus there was no central control or policy; each foundry operated more or less as it had before the merger. Allison neglected two of the new company's most important assets, the Benton punch-cutting machine and the Barth typecasting machine. As part of Benton, Waldo & Co.'s agreement with ATF, Benton had to reacquire the punch-cutters that he had leased out.

Barth, Marder and Benton

Joseph Warren Phinney, the manager of the Dickinson Type Foundry in Boston, became an outstanding early leader in the new company. In fact, Phinney, Benton, and Henry Barth had talked about combining into a single type foundry in 1891, when the larger merger seemed uncertain.

Early Problems at ATF

For the first few months after the merger, a few of ATF's directors—Allison, Marder, Benton, Barth, and Phinney—had to use their personal credit to float the new company. Soon even larger issues began to take their toll, according to Bullen: "Never did a company need good management more and never was a company less ably managed than the American Type Founders Company during its first two years."[16] There was little company spirit among the 12 foundries—they continued under the management of their former owners, who in each case kept the original foundry name. There was no unified vision, and since the merger had generated little liquid capital, the financial situations of individual foundry offices did not improve. "The plants and stocks of most of the type foundries had been paid for with stock of the new company," Bullen explained. "As the valuations of most of the type foundries were on a liberal basis, the company was overcapitalized."[17]

In 1893 Linn Boyd Benton moved to New York as ATF's chief technical advisor. His stationery that summer, however, listed him as manager of the Conner Type Foundry. By 1894 ATF's general offices were located at the Conner Foundry in the Rhinelander Building on the corner of Rose and Duane Streets in Manhattan; that foundry's equipment was old and run down, and so very little of it was used.[18]

Two years into the merger, there still had been no improvement in ATF's situation. There was no consolidated type specimen book, there were no new typefaces, and no dividends had been paid. The new company was regarded as a trust, it was badly managed, and the stockholders were divided into two factions, each vying for control. Some directors sold out, and others held on in the hopes that if the merger were dissolved they might resume ownership of their former type foundries. Bullen explained the situation in the *Inland Printer*:

> The controlling interest … was composed of as honest, unplotting, and simple-minded a group of directors as ever undertook to manage a big company. This group had individual efficiency and collective inefficiency. They were helpless against a sea of troubles aggravated by the totally unmerited unpopularity of the company, which came to be known as the "Type Trust." They actually deserved the sympathy of the printers. There was not the slightest semblance to a trust in the American Type Founders Company. Its property, which before the formation had been owned by about a hundred persons, was now owned by thousands. It never had the power to control prices. Its first act was to reduce the prices of body types, probably as a measure of defense against the composing machines, completely (as it was afterwards discovered) depriving itself of any profits on body types. Propaganda instigated against the company at the time was decidedly dangerous, and added greatly to the embarrassments of a management not strong enough to overcome the adverse conditions with which it was confronted.[19]

ROBERT NELSON AND THE THORNE TYPESETTING MACHINE

At this time a man named Robert W. Nelson frequently bought large orders of type from ATF for his Thorne typesetting machines. Joseph Thorne had developed this first American typesetting machine around 1886,[20] and soon afterwards Nelson, having amassed a "moderate fortune" as a founder and sales manager of the American Press Association, became interested in Thorne's machine, purchased it, and became the principal owner of the Thorne Typesetting Machine Company.[21] Bullen noted that "as developed and marketed by Nelson, more Thorne machines were being sold than any other typesetting machine, and the demand for [them] continued from 1886 until 1910, over 2,000 being sold."[22]

Unlike the Linotype or Monotype machines, the Thorne actually set and distributed real foundry type.[23] As the Thorne typesetter operator typed on the machine's keyboard, individual types contained in vertical channels of a cylindrical magazine were released, awaiting justification by hand. Although it was advertised as a "one-man typesetter," it was more efficient when two workers collaborated on the task, one at the keyboard and the other justifying the output.

Thorne typesetting machines were sold in England, Australia, New Zealand, and the U.S. "By 1889 Publishers' Printing Company in New York (one of many owners) used six Thornes to set type, and others had been ordered from the Thorne factory in Hartford, Connecticut."[24] Since each machine needed to be equipped with foundry type, Nelson became ATF's best customer. In December 1893 ATF took over the Thorne Company, but about five years later, according to Bullen, "the Cox Typeset-

The Thorne typesetting machine   Robert W. Nelson

ting Machine Company, in which Barnhart Brothers & Spindler held a controlling interest, was merged with the Thorne company in a new company, under the title of The Unitype Company.”[25] The Thorne machine was again modified and renamed the Simplex, and apparently in 1904, two men operating a Simplex at the *Paducah Sun* in Kentucky set 315,700 ems of 8-point type in one 48-hour week[26] (over 6,500 ems per hour). Nevertheless, competition from the Linotype put the Unitype Company out of business some time afterwards.

As Nelson became familiar with ATF's history and some of its founders, Phinney talked him into making a study of possible solutions to the company's problems. In 1894, Nelson bought out one of ATF's directors who had lost faith in the merger, and, though unsalaried, immediately gave most of his time to ATF. Through his connections Nelson was able to bring new business to the company. Bullen wrote that although

> the New York house, being in close contact with the demoralized general offices of the company, had acquired an outlook probably more gloomy than elsewhere prevailed … Nelson quickly revived our hopes. His Cheerfulness and Optimism were infectious: these were his constant characteristics under all circumstances.[27]

Nelson united the two factions of stockholders, as far as each would permit, and when the old management was thrown out at a stockholders' meeting on October 24, 1894, a board of directors representing both viewpoints was elected. At the new board's first meeting, Nelson was elected general manager of the company, and John E. Searles, a prominent lawyer, was elected president. With Searles's approval, Nelson actually assumed all but the legal duties of the president, and when Searles resigned in 1901 Nelson was elected president.[28]

Nelson was determined to unite the foundries that had merged, and his first important directive was ordering them to remove their old signboards and stop using their letterheads, replacing both with the corporate name. He convinced the individual plants to stop issuing their own type catalogues and led them to understand that "The purpose of the consolidation was to sell under one name and to combine resources."[29] The first company specimen book, a small (4.5 by 7-inch), 727-page "Blue Book," published in 1895, was planned and partially printed before Nelson became general manager. A larger (9 by 12-inch) book came out the same year, followed by the *Collective Specimen Book* in 1896, which was issued in various editions with different title pages for each branch's geographic location.

Within a month of becoming ATF's general manager, Nelson requested 100 Barth type casters to be manufactured for distribution to ATF's foundries, and decided to prohibit the manufacture of ATF type from electrotyped matrices. Bullen explained:

> When the company was organized in 1892 many of the then standard typefaces of precisely the same design were made in several of the type foundries. As an instance, there was the series of Antique, originated by the Dickinson Type Foundry in Boston, cut in steel and cast from matrices driven from the original steel punches. This desirable series had been copied by the electro-matrix process by half a dozen other foundries. Nelson stopped such waste of effort and consequent unnecessary accumulation of stocks by concentrating the manufacture in the originating foundry, affording to the users better type and to the company important economies.[30]

Nelson organized an ATF design and matrix department in Manhattan, equipped it with several Benton punch-cutting machines, and put Benton in charge of it. Finally the Benton machine was being recognized as one of ATF's key assets. Phinney was given the task of procuring new type designs. Although it may have been too early at this time to tell, Nelson had managed to turn the company around.

Chapter 6 Endnotes

1   David Pankow, "The Rise and Fall of ATF," *Printing History* 43/44, vol. 22, nos. 1 & 2 (2002): 4.

2   James Eckman, *The Heritage of the Printer*, vol. 1 (Philadelphia: North American Publishing Company, 1965): 165.

3   Eckman, "The Chicago Type Foundry of Marder, Luse & Co., 1863–1892," *Printing & Graphic Arts (PaGA)* 7, no. 3 (September 1959): 80.

4   "Meeting of the Type Founders of the United States," *Inland Printer* 4, no. 1 (October 1886): 22.

5   "The Type Founder's Convention," *Inland Printer* 4, no. 1 (October 1886): 21.

6   Quadrat [Henry Lewis Bullen], "Discursions of a Retired Printer, No. XII," *Inland Printer* 39, no. 4 (July 1907): 514.

7   Eckman, "Chicago," 81.

8   Ibid.

9   Eckman, *Heritage*, 166.

10   Henry Lewis Bullen, "The Effect of the Composing Machines Upon the Typefounding Industry," *Inland Printer* 73, no. 4 (July 1924): 596.

11   Maurice Annenberg, *Type Foundries of America and Their Catalogues*, 2nd ed. (New Castle, Del.: Oak Knoll Press, 1994), 128.

12   Ibid., 140.

13   "American Typefounders' Company," *Inland Printer* 10, no. 2 (November 1892): 150.

14   Quadrat, "Discursions No. XII," 513.

15   Annenberg, *Type Foundries*, 41.

16   Quadrat, "Discursions No. XII," 515.

17   Bullen, "Robert Wickham Nelson: An Intimate History," *Inland Printer* 77, no. 6 (September 1926): 905.

18   Eckman to the author, 29 September 1986.

19   Bullen, "Effect of Composing," 596–97.

20   Edward Porritt, "Trade Unionism and the Evolution of the Typesetting Machine," *Journal of Political Economy* 2, no. 2 (March 1894): 293.

21   Fred Williams, "American Type Founders in Bankruptcy!" *Type & Press* 77 (Summer 1993): 2.

22   Bullen, "Creators of the New Era in Typefounding," *Inland Printer* 73, no. 5 (August 1924): 762.

23   International Printing Museum, "The Collection: Unitype Typesetting Machine, Circa 1900," http://www.printmuseum.org/museum/collection/

24   Richard Huss, *The Development of Printers' Mechanical Typesetting Methods, 1822–1925* (Charlottesville: University Press of Virginia, 1973), 99.

25   Bullen, "Creators," 762.

26   International Printing Museum, "Collection."

27   Bullen, "Nelson," 905.

28   "New President of the American Type Founders Company," *Inland Printer* 27, no. 1 (April 1901): 99.

29   Annenberg, *Type Foundries*, 41.

30   Bullen, "Nelson," 906.

Linn Boyd Benton and the Century Type

WHEN ROBERT W. NELSON became ATF's general manager he gave Linn Boyd Benton the authority to establish a letter-designing department, which soon became an important asset of the company. ATF branched out into several product lines, but Nelson retained his interest in type and championed the letter-designing department throughout the next 20 years.

Benton's first work in New York was to cut a series of punches in collaboration with Theodore Low De Vinne, the famous typographic scholar, printing craftsman, and publisher of the *Century Magazine*. De Vinne was not satisfied with the Caslon-derivative types his press was using for the magazine at the time, since they were thin and weak, both hard to read and "gray-printing." The types had been appropriate for earlier printing methods, but by the 1890s they were entirely outdated. De Vinne explained the situation:

> In the bewildering variety of faces devised during this century, one peculiarity, the sharp hair-line (a fashion introduced by Bodoni and Didot, in imitation of the delicate lines of the copper-plate printer), has never been changed. When printing was done upon wet paper, against an elastic blanket, the hair-line was necessarily thickened by its impress against the yielding paper, which overlapped the sides of every line. Under this treatment the hair-line appeared thicker in print than in type, and was unobjectionable to printer or reader; but when the new method began (as it did in 1872) of printing on dry and smooth paper against an inelastic surface, the hair-lines and light faces of types were not thickened at all. From an engraver's point of view, new types so printed were exquisitely sharp and clean; but from a reader's point of view, the general effect of the print was rela-

tively mean and wiry, gray and feeble … The readable presswork produced by all good printers during the first half of this century was supplanted by feeble impressions that compelled continual strain of eyesight.[1]

De Vinne had kept pace with new printing developments, experimented with wood engravings, and commissioned the Warren Paper Company to make a coated paper for his press,[2] so it was logical that he would also want to experiment with a new typeface.

LEGIBILITY STUDIES

Professor Louis Emile Javal of the University of Paris had performed a series of tests on typographic legibility and published his results in 1879.[3] Javal had found that, while reading, "the eyes move along a line of print in a series of quick jerks, which he called saccadic movements, and not in a smooth uninterrupted sweep as had previously been believed."[4] According to readability expert Edmund Burke Huey,

> [Javal] concluded that there was a pause about every ten letters, and thought that this was about the amount that could be seen clearly at one fixation. He found that after reading he had after-images of straight gray lines corresponding to the parallel lines of print, and concluded that the eye's fixation point did not leave the line as it moved forward in reading. Finding that the upper half of the line was most important for reading, as can be seen at once by dividing a line in halves horizontally and comparing the legibility of the upper and lower halves, he concluded, from this and other observations, that the fixation point moves along between the middle and top of the small letters.[5]

Javal's work suggested that x-height is an important component of legibility. De Vinne was aware of Javal's research,[6] and explained to his magazine audience that "increased expansion did not always secure increased legibility."[7] De Vinne returned to this theme in his book *The Practice of Typography*:

> Types are not always made more readable by giving them larger and blacker faces. The attractiveness of a very black-faced type when used in one line or in a few lines becomes repelling when it is used in a mass … What a reader needs for pleasurable reading is the instant visibility of every stroke in every letter; but this visibility is dimmed when the types have too much black.[8]

CENTURY ROMAN

In an attempt to design a more readable typeface, De Vinne decided to expand his letters only slightly, and also to increase their x-height and thicken their hairlines. He and Benton started with "some Scotch roman of the middle 1800s, possibly from the Miller & Richards foundry of Edinburgh."[9] Benton made enlarged drawings of each letter and adjusted them, adding a fixed percentage of weight to produce a heavier overall color, and redrawing the curves with a compass and the straight lines with a ruler. Century Roman, as the new typeface was later called, appeared in the *Century* magazine's November 1895 issue.[10] Former ATF employee Stevens L. Watts, who was also a type historian, wrote that Century Roman, "in sizes 8, 9, and 10 point (with italics), was cut in steel punches under the direction of Linn Boyd Benton, at the New York City casting foundry of ATF in 1895 or 1896."[11] These three sizes are shown on page 140 of the Philadelphia (MacKellar Smiths & Jordan) branch edition of ATF's 1898 *Specimens of Printing Types*; on page 34 of the Pacific Coast's edition of ATF's 1900 *Desk Book of Type Specimens*;[12] and according to Watts, on page 108 of the 1898 ATF *Desk Book*.[13]

Century Roman was slightly taller (by just 6.5 thousandths of an inch!)[14] than the type the magazine had been using since 1870. It had a condensed look, suited for the magazine's pages of two or three columns. Century Roman was praised by some and criticized by others who "protested that it was over-refined—with every trace of the original character squeezed out of it."[15] De Vinne explained in 1900 that

> to secure a proper relief of white space within each character the round letters were made a little taller. To proportion the type for a large page in two columns and with narrow margins, and to give the usual amount of text in the *Century* page, the characters were compressed a trifle.[16]

Type historian Alexander Lawson wrote that De Vinne called the Century face a

> practical protest of experienced printers against the growing effeminacy of modern types. Readers of failing eyesight ask for types that are plain and unequivocal, that reveal the entire character at a glance, and are not discerned with difficulty by body-marks joined to hairlines and serifs that are but half seen or not seen at all.[17]

In his March 1896 *Century* magazine article about the typeface, De Vinne explained how it was created:

> The story of the designing of this face is too full of technical detail to interest the casual reader. Perhaps it is enough to say that each character (first drawn on the enlarged scale of ten inches high) was scrutinized by editor and publisher, printer and engraver, and often repeatedly altered before it was put in the form of a working model. Only a maker of instruments of precision can appreciate the subservient tools, gauges, and machines that show aberrations of a ten-thousandth part of an inch; only an expert punch-cutter can understand why minute geometrical accuracy was a work of necessity upon some letters, and why it was discarded in others, for the humoring of optical illusions in the reader. Type-making does not tell its story; like other arts, it hides its methods.[18]

His body was embalmed, and in due season the funeral procession followed. The mummied king was placed aboard the royal barge, and, attended by the priests and the images of the gods Horus and Isis and Hathor, was floated up the Nile to the Theban city of the Dead — to Bîbân el-Mulouk, the St. Denis, the Westminster Abbey of the kings, and a great lamentation went up to the skies from stricken Egypt.

Original type used in De Vinne's *Century* magazine

abcdefghijklmnopqrstuvwxyzABCDEFGHIJS

THE NEW FACE.

abcdefghijklmnopqrstuvwxyzABCDEFGHL

THE OLD FACE.

Century Roman, from the *Century* for March 1896

CENTURY ROMAN

8 POINT CENTURY ROMAN

WHEN, in the course of human events, it becomes necessary for one people to dissolve the political bands which have connected them with another, and to assume, among the powers of the earth, the separate and equal station to which the laws of nature and of nature's God entitle them, a decent respect to the opinions of mankind requires that they should declare the causes which impel them to the separation. We hold these truths to be self-evident, that all men are created equal ; that they are endowed by their Creator with certain unalienable rights ; that among these, are life, liberty, and the pursuit of happiness. That, to secure these rights, governments are instituted among men, deriving their just powers from the consent of the governed ; that, whenever any form of government becomes destructive of these ends, it is the right of the people *to alter or to abolish it, and to institute a new government, laying its foundation on such principles, and organizing its powers in such form, as to them*

Lower case a to z, 12 ems

ABCDEFGHIJKLMNOPQRSTUVWXYZ
1234567890

Century Roman from ATF's 1900 *Desk Book of Specimens*

Details such as the ten-inch drawings, working models, and "tools, gauges and machines that show aberrations of a ten-thousandth part of an inch," indicate that Benton used his punch-cutting machine to cut Century Roman.[19] Shortly after the type made its debut in the *Century* magazine, De Vinne collaborated again with Benton to design a wider version for the De Vinne Press. This new type, Century Broad-Face, was meant for the longer line lengths used in book printing.[20] It was cut on the punch-cutting machine in 10-point roman and italic circa 1899, and became the inspiration for ATF's Century Expanded, which was released the following year (see Chapter 14).[21]

De Vinne's concern with legibility would later influence many other type designers, Century Roman becoming the fore-runner of the so-called legibility faces. After the De Vinne Century faces were produced, Linn Boyd Benton turned his attention back to the punch-cutting machine itself: refining it, making it safer, and designing the accessories and tools it required. He became the head of ATF's general manufacturing department in 1903, a post he held until he retired in 1932, and also remained a member of ATF's board of directors.

Chapter 7 Endnotes

1   Theodore Low De Vinne, "The Century's Printer on the Century's Type," *Century Magazine* 51, no. 5 (March 1896): 795.

2   Eugene M. Ettenberg, *Type for Books and Advertising* (New York: D. Van Nostrand Co., Inc., 1947), 109.

3   Alexander Lawson, "Anatomy of a Type: Century, Part 2," *Printing Impressions* 24, no. 7 (December 1981): 41.

4   Herbert Spencer, *The Visible Word* (London: Royal College of Art, 1968), 13.

5   Edmund Burke Huey, *The Psychology and Pedagogy of Reading* (New York: Macmillan, 1908; Cambridge, Massachusetts: The M.I.T. Press, 1968), 18. Citations are to the M.I.T. edition.

6   Lawson, "Century, Part 2," 41.

7   De Vinne, "Century's Printer," 795.

8   De Vinne, *Practice of Typography: A Treatise on the Processes of Type-Making, the Point System, the Names, Sizes, Styles and Practices of Plain Printing Types* (New York: The Century Co., 1900), 377.

9   Fred C. Williams, "Theodore De Vinne's Type of the Century," *Type & Press* 49 (Summer 1986): 1.

10 Apparently this was 9-point Century Roman, cut circa 1895, according to a 28 September 1962 memo that Stevens L. Watts wrote to Dr. James Eckman. Watts continued, "10 point size, 124 characters of the roman, was finished 8 August 1898; 8 point, 118 characters, on 11 February 1899." Only these three sizes of Century Roman were cut. The information in this 1962 memo is more detailed than what he wrote to Eckman the following year (footnote #11).

11 Watts to Eckman, 14 October 1963.

12 Copies of these two specimen books are part of RIT's Cary Graphic Arts Collection.

13 Watts to Eckman, 14 October 1963.

14 De Vinne, "Century's Printer," 795.

15 Williams, "De Vinne's Type," 1.

16 De Vinne, *Plain Printing Types*, 376.

17 Lawson, "After 70 Years Century Typefaces Hold Their Own," *Inland Printer/American Lithographer* 154, no. 4 (January 1965): 46.

18 De Vinne, "Century's Printer," 796.

19 Watts corrobotated this assumption in his 1962 Eckman memo.

20 Lawson, "After 70 Years," 46.

21 Watts to Eckman, 28 September 1962.

CHAPTER 8

An Overview of Linn Boyd Benton's Patented Inventions

LINN BOYD BENTON's famous punch engraving machine was by no means his only invention. On June 30, 1932, the day before he retired from ATF, he reported that he had received 20 patents in his life, 18 of which related to "the art of type making." The other two were from 1875 and 1876.[1] How did a man with a very informal and disjointed education produce so many patents? Theo Rehak suggested it was because Linn Boyd Benton was a mechanical genius: "He was one of those people who could see with his hands."[2]

Benton's first patent may have been for a float for a steam boiler "feed regulator." While researching the Bentons in 1984 at Columbia University Libraries, I found a hand-written note on stationery from the North-Western Type Foundry, Office of Benton, Gove & Co., Milwaukee, dated November 7, 1877, that read:

> Messrs. Benton, Gove & Co.
>
> Gents—
>
> We have for over two years been using one of Benton's Patent Floats in our Steam Boiler Feed Regulator. It has never given us a moment's trouble. It does not seem to be affected by heat or cold and is apparently as good today as when purchased. Don't see why it should not last a man's life time. Very Truly, (indecipherable)[3]

Photographic evidence exists for another Benton patent outside the type field, for a device that knit tubular socks from wool (see Chapter 11).[4]

Benton's first type-related patent, U.S. Patent No. 254,792 of March 14, 1882, described a multiple mold for casting printers' leads and slugs (spacing material).[5]

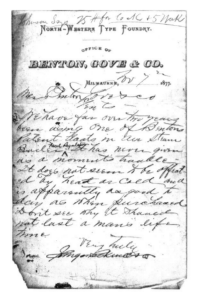

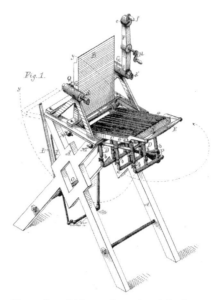

The original 1877 note   Benton's mold for casting printer's leads

Type historian Dr. James Eckman wrote in 1964 that Benton "claimed that his machine, with one man operating it, could cast more spacing material in a ten-hour day than ten men working the same period could turn out with other methods."[6]

Benton's second type-related patent, as we have seen, was granted on December 18, 1883, for self-spacing types set on pre-determined unit widths; his third was the 1883 British patent for the same types. His fourth type-related patent was for an attachment for the molds used in typecasting machines, to prevent, as he explained, "what are technically called by the type founders 'swell bodies'"[7] — variations too minute to be detected by the naked eye but troublesome to the type founder. The application for this patent was filed on May 18, 1884, and U.S. Patent No. 326,009 was granted to Benton and Isaac Baas Jr. more than a year later, on September 8, 1885.

Benton's next three patents were for the third version of his punch-cutting machine, invented to facilitate the production of his self-spacing types in Milwaukee. The original application was dated February 29, 1884, but the first U.S. and British patents were not issued until more than a year and a half later. A five-page hand-written document among the Benton family papers (apparently in patent attorney Elias H. Bottum's handwriting) explained the reason for the delay:

> After repeated rejection and amendments, the above application was
> allowed with 24 claims on May 16, 1885. Applications for the same inven-
> tion were filed in England, Germany, France and Canada on October 6,
> 1885, and it was carefully arranged beforehand to have the U.S. Patent
> issued on the same date in order to prevent the publication of the U.S.
> Patent from invalidating the foreign patents or the foreign patents from

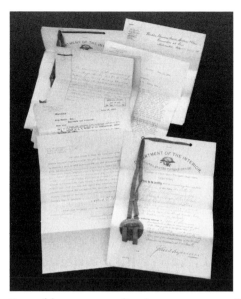

Some of the papers regarding the controversy over Benton's U.S. patent for his punch-cutting machine

limiting the term of the U.S. Patent in accordance with the usual practice in obtaining U.S. and foreign patents for the same invention.[8]

U.S. Patent No. 327,855 was issued on October 6, 1885. A few days later a clerical error in the documents was discovered, which in effect left out one of the agreed-upon amendments to the patent. The usual method of handling this type of error was then followed: Patent No. 327,855 was cancelled, the error was corrected, and a new patent was issued, U.S. Patent No. 332,990, on December 22, 1885. But British Patent No. 11,894 had also been issued on October 6, 1885, and had not been challenged. A flurry of correspondence in the early 1890s took place between Benton's patent attorneys and the U.S. Patent Office, finally concluding that, although the British patent actually pre-dated the re-issued U.S. patent because of the clerical error, the British patent did not limit or affect the term of the U.S. patent.[9] Many original papers surrounding this controversy are part of RIT's Cary Graphic Arts Collection.

Some time after the first two ATF Century faces had been produced, the decision was made to abandon the use of punches at ATF and instead to engrave matrices directly by machine. The patent for this new process came several years later. Benton wrote,

In 1906 (patent of Jan. 9, 809,548) I extended the usefulness of my punch engraving machine, adding accessories by the use of which the machines engrave the matrices directly in the metal without the necessity of using a letter punch. I was not the originator of this idea.[10]

A Listing of Linn Boyd Benton's Patents

The following summary of Linn Boyd Benton's printing-related patents is based on a number of sources: his own writing;[11] a list of ATF patents compiled by ATF employee Stevens L. Watts;[12] correspondence between the Milwaukee law office of Winkler, Flanders, Smith, Bottum & Vilas and the U.S. Patent Office;[13] a 1930 article about Linn Boyd Benton in the Plainfield, N. J., newspaper (patent listing #26); and the list of U.S. and British patents in Legros and Grant's *Typographical Printing-Surfaces*.[14] U.S. patents are searchable by patent number at http://www.uspto.gov/patft/, and so all of the U.S. patents listed here with numbers (except for #6, which was withdrawn) can be accessed online.

The tool grinder (#9 at right, and further explained in Chapter 10) was used to sharpen and refine the cutting tools used in the original punch-cutting machine. Patents for this tool grinder and other accessories to Benton's system reveal that he was involved with all of the processes related to type founding. In 1925, an anonymous writer admired Benton's mechanical versatility in the *Inland Printer*:

> In the type making division of the American Type Founders Company there is scarcely a tool, apparatus, machine or process the efficiency of which has not been advanced by Mr. Benton's inventive genius. Unlike many inventors, he is a thorough mechanic and himself translates his inventive ideas into practical mechanical movements.[16]

Benton's delineating machine (#15) was a refined pantograph with a microscope attachment that could reduce or enlarge a drawing, either proportionally or to make condensed, extended, italic, or back-sloped variations. "The delineator was actually the working gimbel mechanism of the Benton engraver, but instead of a cutter making an engraving," Rehak explained, "it was (merely!) an infinitely adjustable pantograph drawing device with a microscope attachment, which would render with precision, as well as distortion, anything traced from a drawing of a character."[17] When Benton first applied for a patent for the delineator, it was rejected by the patent commissioner on the grounds that the machine was a mechanical impossibility! Benton was much amused by this response. He explained,

> Our company had been using the "mechanical impossibility," and my answer to the Patent Office in Washington was to send drawings, all made from a single print of characters of 14-pt. Caslon Oldstyle roman, in italic, backslope, condensed and extended forms, whereupon the patent (No. 790,172, May 16, 1905) was issued. The machine has been in almost daily use since that time.[18]

"One Benton Delineating Apparatus is sufficient for the purposes of the American Type Founders Company," Bullen wrote in 1922, "and thus a second has never been built. It is a miracle of accuracy and flexibility."[19] Unfortunately, when ATF was forced

Linn Boyd Benton's Patents

Date	Patent No.	Title or Description
1. March 14, 1882	254,792	multiple mold for casting printer's leads
2. Dec. 18, 1883	290,201	"Self Spacing Type"
3. 1883	5,778	(British patent) type of multiples of standard units (i.e., self-spacing type)
4. Sept. 8, 1885	326,009	type mold, pivotal (with I. Baas Jr.)
5. Oct. 6, 1885	11,894	(British patent) single-column punch-cutting machine
6. Oct. 6, 1885	327,855	single-column punch-cutting machine [withdrawn]
7. Dec. 22, 1885	332,990	single-column punch-cutting machine (to replace Patent No. 327,855)
8. Dec. 4, 1888	D018,775	Italic type: a slanted roman to accompany the self-spacing type
9. March 14, 1890	422,874	tool grinder
10. Aug. 26, 1890	D20,120	font of printing type
11. Sept. 3, 1895	545,568	type: combination-fractions; superiors and inferiors each with part diagonal stroke (a method of making piece fractions)
12. Feb. 20, 1900	644,039	flexible pipe
13. Aug. 20, 1901	680,685	type dressing machine
14. 1904	unknown	grinding machine (This may be #9.)
15. May 16, 1905	790,172	delineating machine (tracing apparatus)
16. Jan. 9, 1906	809,548	accessories to enable the punch-cutter to engrave matrices directly
17. May 8, 1906	819,842	matrix trimming (fitting) machine
18. April 30, 1907	851,855	automatic typecasting machine, for casting types on angular bodies, with all kerns supported
19. 1913	unknown	depth gauge
20. July 8, 1913	1,066,576	parallel liner, a device for engraving matrices of shaded letters
21. July 29, 1913	1,068,478	apparatus for cutting matrices (parallel-lining device for making formers)
22. 1913	unknown	improvements in automatic typecasting machines (This may be #24.)
23. 1912–1916 (?)	unknown	machine for putting faces on brass rules of various thicknesses
24. Nov. 3, 1914	1,115,773	typecasting machine
25. 1922	unknown	fonting apparatus for use with multigraph types, jointly with Morris F. Benton
26. 1930	unknown	"an important improvement in the larger printing types used in newspaper headlines"[15]

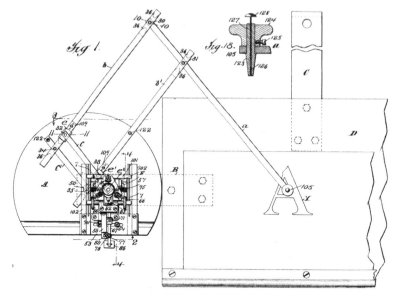

Benton's delineating machine

to move all its operations to one location in the 1930s, any supporting documentation that may have existed about the delineator was lost. No physical trace remains today of the machine. Its role in Benton's system is further explained in Chapter 10.

Another important invention (#23) was a machine for putting faces on brass rules. ATF's 1923 *Specimen Book and Catalogue* referred to it as "Benton's Automatic Brass Rule Facing Machine," and claimed that "the strips delivered by the machine [were] exact height-to-paper from one end to the other with perfect uniformity of face, an exactitude never attainable in brass rule made on brass rule benches."[20] The catalogue also mentioned a "Benton Brass Rule Cutter" machine. Brass rules were used for printing ruled lines of varying thicknesses. They were usually manufactured in lengths of 16 or 24 inches and then cut down to size.[21] For more than a century before this invention, brass rules could be faced only with hand planers. A paragraph in a 1930 newspaper article about Benton explained the machine:

> In typography brass rules have an important, absolutely essential place. For four centuries many expensive inventions were made with the object of facing the rules by machinery, but not until 1912 was such a machine perfected. Until that year brass rules were laboriously planed and faced by hand. Mr. Benton in 1912 overcame the mechanical difficulties which had baffled generations of inventors whose efforts had involved the expenditure and loss of hundreds of thousands of dollars, while the results on the machine are superior to that of hand planing.[22]

While Bullen and the *Plainfield Courier-News* give 1912 as the date for the invention of the brass rule facing machine, Benton himself wrote that he invented it between

1913 and 1916.[23] Unfortunately the patent number is not given in either source. Two weeks before he died, 88-year-old Linn Boyd Benton wrote, "There is still room for improvement in the machinery and appliances of our art, contemplation of which keeps my mind active, notwithstanding my advanced age."[24]

1   Linn Boyd Benton, "Inventions of Linn Boyd Benton," to David Gustafson (Carnegie Institute of Technology), 30 June 1932, for inclusion in the United Typothetae of America's *Who's Who in Printing in the United States*, 1.

2   Theo Rehak, in discussion with Elizabeth Benton Swain, Hingham, Massachusetts, 13 October 1987.

3   Hand-written message on stationery from the North-Western Type Foundry, Office of Benton, Gove & Co., Milwaukee, 7 November 1877, Typographic Library Manuscripts, Section I.C., Misc. Incomplete Mss., Rare Book and Manuscript Library, Columbia University.

4   Rehak to the author, 23 February 2006.

5   Benton to Gustafson; L. B. Benton, "Mold for Casting Printers' Leads," U.S. Patent No. 254,792, March 14, 1882.

6   Dr. James Eckman, "The Immortal Century Type Face and the Bentons, Father and Son," *Printer's Digest* (November 1964): 4.

7   I. Baas Jr. and L. B. Benton, "Type Mold," U.S. Patent No. 326,009, September 8, 1885.

8   Hand-written document attached to a letter from E. H. Bottum to Commissioner of Patents, 14 October 1885.

9   Winkler, Flanders, Smith, Bottum & Vilas, Counselors at Law, to U.S. Patent Office, 19 January 1894.

10   Benton to Gutafson, 2.

11   Benton to Gustafson.

12   Stevens L. Watts, "A Record of Patents Issued to Type Founders and Others," June 1952, in "Notebook of Stevens Lewis Watts, 1895–1966," Typographic Library Manuscripts, Rare Book and Manuscript Library, Columbia University.

13   Original correspondence and copies of originals regarding the patent mix-up, 1885–94, between the U.S. Patent Office; Benton-Waldo Type Foundry; E. H. Bottum, patent attorney, and later his firm, Winkler, Flanders, Smith, Bottum & Vilas; James A. Skilton, patent attorney, and Benjamin Kimball, Esq., general counsel for the American Type Founders Co., courtesy of Laurence Gregg.

14   Lucien A. Legros and John C. Grant, *Typographical Printing-Surfaces: The Technology and Mechanism of their Production* (New York, London: Longmans, Green, 1916), 577–607.

15   "Hails Linn Boyd Benton's Type Invention As One Of Greatest Of Present Era," *Plainfield, N.J. Courier-News*, October 9, 1930.

16   "Two Men Whose Work Greatly Benefits All Typographers," *Inland Printer* 76, no. 3 (December 1925), 453.

17   Rehak, email message to the author, 6 July 2006.

18   Benton to Gustafson, 2–3.

19   Bullen, "Linn Boyd Benton," 63.

20   American Type Founders Company, *Specimen Book and Catalogue, 1923* (Jersey City, N.J.: ATF Co., 1923), 811.

21   Leighton Linslade Virtual Museum, "Brass Rule – Jackson Printer" (2002), http://leighton-museum.org.uk/gallery1/printing/06.htm.

22 "Hails," *Plainfield, N.J. Courier-News*; "Linn Boyd Benton, 'Edison of Typographic Industry,' Is Dead at His Home Here," *Plainfield, N.J. Courier-News* (July 16, 1932): 1, 6.

23 Benton to Gustafson, 3.

24 Ibid.

Morris Benton at ATF

Morris Benton arrived at ATF on September 1, 1896, with a bachelor's degree in mechanical engineering from Cornell University. He had been hired as the assistant manager of the general manufacturing department under his father, and worked as an engineer and draftsman for ATF until 1900 when he became the company's chief type designer, retaining that position until his retirement in 1937.[1]

Much of Morris Benton's early work at ATF was in mechanical designing, i.e., helping his father with his inventions. Then he was assigned the task of standardizing the various type lines that ATF had acquired from the type foundries in the merger. This was a meticulous and no doubt exasperating undertaking. J. W. Phinney had begun the job before it was assigned to Benton. "While notable work had been done in the four years since the merger in unifying the 23 divergent lines into one well-rounded American Type Founders line," John Allen Murphy wrote in the *Inland Printer*, "the completion of this immense task became for Morris Benton an intriguing and immediate responsibility."[2]

The point system had been adopted by some foundries only a short time before the merger, so most of the types and matrices ATF inherited had been manufactured according to old, conflicting standards that were often imprecise.[3] In particular, base alignment had to be standardized in order to render them usable.[4] While at least some of the matrices from the various foundries in the merger were made from hand-cut punches, many of them were probably electrotyped. As discussed in Chapter 1, electro-deposition made it possible for a foundry to duplicate the typefaces of its competitors simply by purchasing complete fonts of type and electroplating copper onto them to make matrices. As a result, ATF's collection of matrices from the merger must have contained many of the same designs from different foundries. There were also undoubtedly several different original versions of popular faces. For example, four foundries may have contributed an original "Egyptian" font, no two being exactly identical in weight. The job of amalgamating and organizing ATF's eclectic collection of type matrices provided Morris Benton with a comprehensive introduction to type.

Even though the advent of the Linotype and other composing machines began to erode the demand for foundry type in the early 1900s, Robert Nelson decided to maintain type as ATF's chief product. While Nelson may have realized that the sales of body type to newspapers would at some point cease altogether because of the composing machines, and that the foundry type industry would have to find another market, he nevertheless believed that a market would be found. Henry Lewis Bullen explained Nelson's vision for ATF in a 1926 *Inland Printer* article:

> He foresaw that the future of the type industry depended on a never-ceasing succession of new typefaces of a new order of type design, now known as publicity type—type which is adapted as well for text pages as for display pages.[5]

In the years to come, Morris Benton would carry out Nelson's plan, creating more typefaces than any other American type designer. The flexibility and extreme accuracy of his father's inventions would help him along the way.

Working closely with his father, he began to design types and rework the drawings submitted to ATF by other designers. In 1903, ATF's central plant and general offices moved from Manhattan to a new building at 300 Communipaw Avenue in Jersey City, New Jersey, and Morris Benton was put in charge of the type-designing department there. "Since that time," the 1925 *Inland Printer* claimed, "almost every type face shown in the type-specimen book of the American Type Founders Company has derived its design quality from the head and hands of the younger Benton."[6] Many typefaces designed or revised by Morris Benton are discussed in Chapter 14.

MORRIS BENTON'S TYPE REVIVALS AND BULLEN'S TYPOGRAPHIC LIBRARY

Near the end of the 19th century, William Morris in England embraced the arts and crafts movement's goal of infusing everyday objects with beauty. After attending a lecture on printing at the Arts and Crafts Society in London in November 1888, he was inspired to revive the beautiful typefaces of earlier centuries, abandoning the sterile types being used at the time to print books. His subsequent "Golden" type was based on the 15th-century types of Nicholas Jenson. But according to G. W. Ovink in the 1956 *Penrose Annual*, designers like William Morris, who revived classic types, treated

> every little detail of a letter as the organic result of one governing principle of form, with respect—at least so they thought—for the valuable parts of tradition, but otherwise entirely from their own sense of beauty … The actual result, however, was often an unbridled individualism, in which tradition was lost entirely, including the basic shape as an "agreed sign"—in short, legibility.[7]

HERE BEGYNNETH THYNTERPRETACION OF THE NAME OF SAYNT VYNCENT.

VYNCENT is as moche to saye as brennyng vyces or ouercomyng brennynges & kepyng victorye, for he brente and destroyed vyces by mortificacion of hys flessh, he vaynquys- shid the brennyngis of tormentis by stedfast suffraunce, he helde the victorye of the world by despysyng of the same. He vaynquys- shyd thre thynges in the world, that is to wete false errours, foule loues, and worldly dredes, whyche thynges he ouercam by wysedom, by clennesse, and by constaunce. Of whom saynt Austyn saith that the martirdoms of sayntes haue enseygned that the world is ouercome wyth all errours, loues, and dredes. And somme afferme that saynt Austyn wrote and compyled hys passyon, whyche prudencien sette right clerly in versis.

The Golden type of William Morris, from *The Golden Legend*

Ovink realized that the logical outcome of the arts and crafts view of typography would be a reaction against it. Sure enough, the Boston printer, typographer, and type historian Daniel Berkeley Updike and his companions began to revive more read- able faces like Caslon and Bell, but Ovink felt that these did not "have an appreciable influence on ordinary commercial printing until much later." Instead, Ovink wrote, "the real movement towards a revival of 'true' historic types [began] with M. F. Ben- ton's Bodoni in 1907, followed by his and Cleland's Garamont in 1917." These reviv- als were finally "legible, universally acceptable and beautiful."[8]

Indeed, many of Morris Benton's typefaces were restorations of classic European types that had originally been developed for printing on wet paper and had been cut in only a few sizes. Because of the efforts of one of his colleagues, Henry Lewis Bullen, Benton had access to many examples of these types right in the ATF plant. Bullen had begun working at ATF right after the merger in 1892, first as manager of the New York office and later as advertising manager. He started ATF's free Typographic Library and Museum in 1908 with the collections of specimen books and other early printed matter that the original foundries had gathered, supplemented by his own collection of incunabula (that is, books produced before the year 1501) and early printed ephemera. Bullen regularly added to the collection, and in time it contained type specimens from around the world, histories of printing and publishing, biogra- phies of famous printers, books from early presses, and many other historical items. By 1915, for example, the library possessed the only known copy of William Caslon's first type specimen broadside of 1734, the Oxford University type foundry's speci- men book of 1693, Erhard Ratdolt's 1486 specimen broadside, and a 1628 type spec- imen from the Vatican.[9] At one time the library housed more than 80,000 volumes.[10]

Henry Lewis Bullen in ATF's   Morris Benton at ATF in   Morris Benton at ATF, 1935
Typographic Library and Museum   Jersey City, 1922

Richard C. Marder, whose grandfather John Marder of Chicago's Marder, Luse & Co. was one of the original founders of ATF, remembered seeing Morris Benton in the company's typographic library on Saturdays, which were then half-workdays for employees. "I used to spend a lot of my time on Saturdays in the library," he said. "[Benton's] inspiration came from that library. That's one of the reasons it was created."[11] The extent to which Bullen himself influenced Morris Benton's type revivals is hard to assess since the two colleagues did not document how they worked. Printing historian James Moran, writing in 1971, did not want to underestimate Bullen's effect on Benton:

> How much certain typefaces owe to [Bullen] and how much to … Morris Fuller Benton will perhaps never be known. But since Bullen was responsible for accumulating the great ATF library, from which he gained a formidable amount of knowledge, it is reasonable to assume that he supplied the inspiration, and Benton the mechanical skill, or, as is often the case, there may have been an interplay of ideas between the two men, which produced the final result in the shape of type-faces for ATF.[12]

Benton's historic type revivals became popular for advertising typography. For example the *Inland Printer*'s "Typographic Scoreboard," a regular feature of the magazine from 1929 to 1945, consistently ranked Benton's Bodoni and Garamond as the most popular faces for advertisements in *The Saturday Evening Post*. And yet at the time, Morris Benton was not regarded as one of America's important type designers. That distinction usually went to Frederic W. Goudy, the famous type designer who worked out of his own small studio, "Deepdene," in Marlboro-on-Hudson, New York. In 1961, Alexander Lawson wrote, "It is safe to say that there are more Benton types in use at the present than Goudy faces, and it is unfortunate that Benton's name has been obscured in spite of the importance of his contribution."[13]

In the Jersey City plant, Morris Benton was responsible for managing several assistant designers and a type committee that worked as a group to determine what types the market would support. In this capacity, Benton learned to decipher the significance of trends in advertising types, deciding which ones were fads and which would meet a real need. Painstakingly researching each new typeface idea, he studied the market to determine what sort of face it wanted, since his policy was not to flood the market with new type designs. "He does not bring out a new face until there is every reason to believe that it satisfies an actual typographic need," Murphy wrote, "and that the demand for it is much more than a mere whimsy of the day."[14]

THE TYPE FAMILY

Some sources give Morris Benton credit for inventing the "type family"—a group of types closely related to a "parent" design but expanded, condensed, or otherwise varied from the original face—but actually, the concept pre-dates Benton. Perhaps the earliest example of a type family is from Pierre-Simon Fournier in France, who showed various sizes and weights of the same basic face in his *Manuel Typographique* (1764–66). Among the many chapters Fournier wrote to accompany his specimens was one entitled "The Poetry Face." He explained that this type was

> a roman, but more condensed and elongated than the normal. I have cut it for works to which it is desired to give an air of lightness by somewhat shortening the lines, especially for setting poetry, which, to gain elegance, needs a greater interval between the lines than usual.[15]

Fournier grouped his type specimens according to size, and then into "various nuances of size," literally translated from French as *small eye, ordinary eye, average eye, large eye, Dutch eye, tight eye,* and *poetic eye.* "These denominations announce letters a little more or a little less nourished and extended, though on the same body," Fournier explained.[16] For example, in the specimens for St. Augustine (what would later be known as a 14-point body), we find these variations of the same basic typeface:

St. Augustin Poétique (condensed roman)
St. Augustin Poétique (condensed italic)
St. Augustin Ordinaire (roman)
St. Augustin Ordinaire (italic)
St. Augustin, Oeil Moyen (literally, "average eye;" a slightly expanded and larger version)
St. Augustin, Oeil Moyen ("average eye" italic)
Saint-Augustin dans le goût Hollandois (extra condensed)
St. Augustin, Gros Oeil (expanded, or "large eye")[17]

St. AUGUSTIN POÉTIQUE.

Guénevil conſerve avec
les Grands le caractère qu'ils
ont avec leurs inférieurs ; il
ſonge à les faire ſervir à ſes in-

St. AUGUSTIN ORDINAIRE.

A un homme vain, altier,
qui eſt un mauvais plaiſant
& un grand parleur , qui

St. AUGUSTIN, ŒIL MOYEN.

A quoi aboutiſſent tous
les ſoins & toutes les veil-
les des Savans ? Le valet

St. AUGUSTIN , GROS ŒIL.

Cromwel alloit ra-
vager toute la Chrétien-
té : la famille Royale étoit

From Fournier's *Manuel Typographique*

More than 100 years later in Italy, Giambattista Bodoni followed Fournier's example
and also cut types in various weights. The 1818 specimen book of Bodoni's types,
published by his widow after he died, shows many series of types in different sizes,
weights, and set widths.[18]

For many years the ideas of Bodoni and Fournier regarding the practicality of a variety
of sizes and weights of one basic typeface lay dormant. Theodore Low De Vinne and
other typographers and commercial printers would have welcomed such variety in
the late 1800s, but at that time, according to type historian Dr. James Eckman, "Most
text faces could only be had in text sizes, and without variants, so that a printer who
wanted a 24 or 36-point heading for a text was forced to use some other display face,
often one which did not harmonize with the text."[19]

As if responding to De Vinne's complaints about the types he had to work with,
Gustav Schroeder of the Central Type Foundry in St. Louis cut the famous De Vinne
face,[20] without any "promptings or suggestions."[21] By the time the type was patented
in 1893,[22] Schroeder's colleague Nicholas J. Werner had already drawn De Vinne
Italic and De Vinne Condensed, which Central produced in 1892 to make what many
came to regard as the first American type family.[23] ATF came out with De Vinne
Extended in 1896, and Chicago's Barnhart Brothers & Spindler foundry offered De
Vinne Compressed, Extra Compressed and Bold by 1898.

Alexander Lawson cited Philadelphia Lining Gothic, a late 19th-century face made by
the McKellar, Smiths and Jordan foundry in Philadelphia, as another example of an
early type family. It was cut in several widths and weights, and its popularity "proved

the success of the so-called family idea in printing types."[24] Bullen maintained in a 1924 *Inland Printer* article that it was J. W. Phinney of Boston who came up with the "type family" concept, later introducing it to ATF.[25] Eckman wrote that Phinney designed the Jenson type family for the Dickinson Type Foundry[26]; its parent face was cut by John F. Cumming in 1893.[27] But two years after Bullen had given Phinney credit for the concept, he switched gears and wrote that Robert Nelson had invented it:

> Nelson conceived the idea of the type family, an idea which, while of inestimable value to printers both from the esthetic and the economic point of view, has had a marvelous effect upon type sales. This was the master idea in modern typemaking. It was wholly Nelson's.[28]

According to James Moran, Beatrice Warde (Bullen's assistant in ATF's famous library) said that Bullen himself invented the concept of the type family. "It may well be," Moran wrote, "that once again Bullen thought the matter out and that Benton put it into practice."[29]

No matter where the concept actually originated, it is generally agreed that with Morris Benton's handling of the Cheltenham type, the value of a type family began to take hold. Benton designed Cheltenham Bold in 1904 and at least ten other variations by 1913.[30] According to Bullen, by 1924 Cheltenham had become, in all its various permutations designed by Morris Benton, "the best seller in the history of typography."[31]

Robert Nelson purchased the original drawings for Cheltenham Oldstyle, a book type designed by Bertrand Grosvenor Goodhue, against the advice of the majority of his associates. They felt it was too expensive, but Nelson's decision proved to be a good one, as the story of the type in Chapter 14 reveals. Morris Benton took the original drawings for Cheltenham Oldstyle and steered them through "the mechanical maze through which all drawings must pass before they materialize into actual type."[32] Then Benton designed 21 Cheltenham variations; eventually "the type became practically a household word far beyond the confines of the nation's composing rooms."[33]

In John Murphy's 1936 *Inland Printer* article, he gave Morris Benton credit for both the idea and actualization of the Cheltenham family.

> In Cheltenham ... he saw an opportunity to give a type face a range of possibilities and an extent of usefulness by giving it different variations in weight and proportion that no type had yet had in all the long and fascinating history of printing. Thus was born the invaluable "type family."[34]

Murphy then claimed that Morris Benton denied having originated the concept of type families: "When I asked him how he got this revolutionary concept in type designing, his typically laconic reply was, 'I didn't. I merely accepted an assignment.'[35] Murphy's contradictory statements reveal Morris Benton's lack of concern

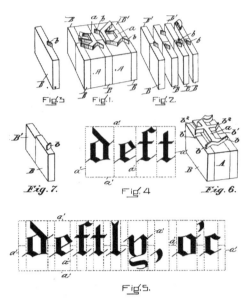

Morris Benton's Patent No. 720,314

for attention, since if Benton had cared, he would have corrected them. But instead, as Murphy wrote:

> Morris Benton seems one of the most difficult men to interview I have ever talked to—and I have interviewed thousands in my time. Try to pin some honor on him, or give him credit for some achievement, and he will modestly sidestep with the remark that "Lady Luck helped me a lot there."[36]

While Morris Benton may not have conceived of the idea of the type family, it is certain that he carried it out with great success. In addition to Cheltenham, Morris collaborated with his father on a variant of Century Roman No. 2, and by 1924 had expanded that family to include at least 16 offerings. These and other Benton type families are discussed in Chapter 14, including Bank Gothic, Bodoni, Clearface, Cloister Oldstyle, Franklin Gothic, Globe Gothic, Louvaine, and Typo Roman and Script.

An Ingenious Method for Kerning

Like his father, Morris Benton was interested in solving problems in the industry. In 1903, Morris received U.S. Patent No. 720,314, entitled "Type," for a method of imitating hand engraving by using "extension characters" in addition to the main metal "face" bodies. Elaborate, embellished letters on full metal type bodies would create irregular spacing within words, but by using Benton's system this problem could be easily eliminated. Figure 4 (see above) from the original patent is the "before" illustration with too much space between the d and the e. Benton's system shown in Figure 5 tightens the spacing by overlapping the serifs of the letters with extension characters. The patent documentation explained:

> These extension characters may be made on bodies the same as that of the

letter, as shown in Figure 1, or divided in halves, as shown in Figure 2, this latter arrangement being preferable in that with a fewer number of extension characters a larger number of designs may be made up. It is also possible to divide them into other fractions, if thought best.[37]

While this clever method of kerning embellished metal type solved the problem of too much spacing between letters, it would have been a nightmare for compositors to set because of all the tiny extension characters.

Morris Benton's Other Work

Throughout the years Morris Benton continued to collaborate with his father on the concerns of ATF's General Manufacturing Division. For example, Linn Boyd Benton's 1932 list of inventions states that his 1922 "fonting apparatus for use with multigraph types" was invented "jointly with my son, Morris F. Benton."[38] Theo Rehak's *Practical Typecasting* explained that Morris Benton "devised the final engineering refinements for the shading device used on the Benton Engraving Machine."[39] And Morris's daughter Caroline wrote that,

> Sometimes my grandfather and father would talk for a few minutes about some good happening of the day, as we all sat at the dinner table, and if some problem had developed about which they needed to talk, they would arrange for a quiet conference after dinner. My grandfather might be bringing up some detail about which his draftsman, Mr. Bower, had enquired.
>
> Some years later, on a visit home, I asked my father, "Did you, with your engineering training, ever help Grandpa with some of the machines he invented or improved?"
>
> My father answered, "I worked on almost all of them."[40]

Apparently Morris Benton was also involved with the formulations of metal alloys used at ATF. In 1906 he outlined two algebraic formulas of type metal composition in a letter to A.T.H. Brower.[41] And in 1912 he received a letter from Elwood Haynes discussing the best way to obtain an exceptionally hard steel alloy:

> From your description I would advise you to use a high class 3½% nickel steel, carrying about 25/100% to 3/10% of carbon. You can get this from the Midvale Steel Company of Philadelphia at about 10 cts per pound or possibly a little less.
>
> After making the desired pieces, they should be placed in pulverized "bone dust" and case hardened for about 10 hours at a temperature approximating 750 C. They should then be heated to a full orange say about 900 C and then quenched in oil. You will find that the parts will then have a glass

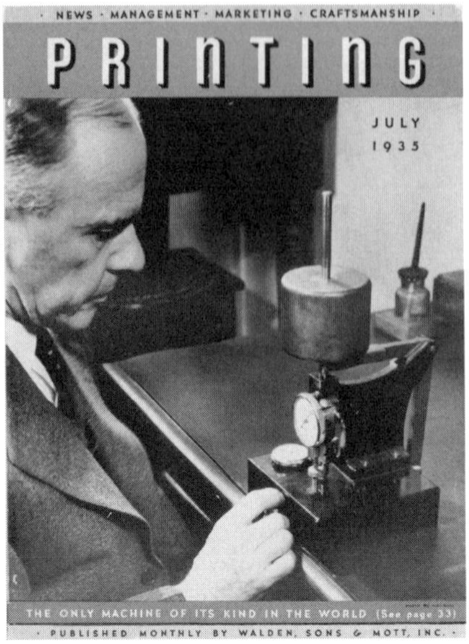
NEWS · MANAGEMENT · MARKETING · CRAFTSMANSHIP
PRINTING
JULY
1935
THE ONLY MACHINE OF ITS KIND IN THE WORLD (See page 33)
PUBLISHED MONTHLY BY WALDEN, SONS & MOTT, INC.
The cover of *Printing* for July 1935, showing Morris Benton and the Benton Hardness Tester

> hard surface and that the hardness will extend inward about 1/16 inch, which should afford ample stock for grinding.
>
> Not only will this steel be very hard on the surface, but very elastic throughout and at the same time remarkably tough and strong.[42]

Later correspondence includes a letter from Morris Benton to William Kelly in the 1940s, outlining a process of nickel-facing a matrix. "A mat. punched in copper and then nickel faced should wear a little longer than an electrotype of copper," Benton wrote, "as the copper is compressed in the punching."[43]

Morris was also a member of ATF's safety committee, and his short biography for the *National Cyclopedia of American Biography* indicated that his later work for ATF included inventing a number of type founding devices, processes, and machines.[44] Theo Rehak wrote that Morris Benton's last projects at ATF "were tests involving type hardness and the effect of age on this factor. He was particularly adept in performing accurate Brinell testing."[45] A photograph of Morris using the "Benton Hardness Tester" appeared on the cover of the July 1935 issue of *Printing* magazine. No other evidence of a Benton Hardness Tester turned up in the research for this book, and it is not on Linn Boyd Benton's list of inventions. If Morris Benton himself invented it, he didn't leave much evidence to establish that fact.

Morris Benton spent his entire professional life at ATF. His lack of pretension apparently won him considerable respect within the company, even if accounts of his work did not reach far beyond Jersey City. Rehak, who worked at ATF from 1980 until it closed in 1993 and heard stories about Morris Benton from others who had known him, called Benton "a reticent man whose outward manner seemed stern. He was in fact shy and modest when among peers."[46] In 1925, an anonymous author in the *Inland Printer* wrote

> What shall be said of the younger Benton, whose designs cover every requirement of typography; who has produced the greatest type successes of this century; yet has considered these achievements as "all in a day's work," and has never sought or received any notoriety through advertising's artful aid? No other type designer has done such good work with less pretension; no other type designer has produced so many designs that are in daily use by the printers everywhere.[47]

Chapter 9 Endnotes

1 "Benton, Morris Fuller," 15 January 1951, for the *National Cyclopedia of American Biography* (New York: James T. White and Company).

2 John Allen Murphy, "Morris Benton—Type Designer-Executive, Part 1," *Inland Printer* 96, no. 6 (March 1936): 34.

3 M. F. McGrew, "The Bentons, Father & Son," *Typographic i*, March 1978, reprinted by Mac McGrew, 2.

4 David Pankow, "The Rise and Fall of ATF," *Printing History* 43/44, vol. 22, nos. 1 & 2 (2002): 7.

5 Henry Lewis Bullen, "Robert Wickham Nelson: An Intimate History," *Inland Printer* 77, no. 6 (September 1926): 906.

6 "Two Men Whose Work Greatly Benefits All Typographers," *Inland Printer* 76, no. 3 (December 1925): 453.

7 G. W. Ovink, "Back to Humanism in Type Design," *Penrose Annual* 50 (1956): 70.

8 Ibid.

9 "The Printers' Library and Museum," *American Bulletin*, April 1915.

10 *American Type Founders Company: Photographic Views of Central Plant*, facsimile edition, 2002.

11 Richard C. Marder, in discussion with the author, Plainfield and Elizabeth, N.J., November 1984.

12 James Moran, *Stanley Morison: His Typographic Achievement* (New York: Visual Communication Books, 1971), 26.

13 Alexander Lawson, "Morris Fuller Benton Deserves More than Obscurity," *Inland Printer/American Lithographer* 148, no. 1 (October 1961): 80.

14 Murphy, "Benton, Part 1," 36.

15 Harry Carter, ed., *Fournier on Typefounding. The Text of the Manuel Typographique* (New York: Burt Franklin, 1973), 170.

16 Fournier, le jeune [Pierre Simon], trans. Google.com, "Advertissement Préliminaire" in *Manuel Typographique, Utile Aux Gens de Lettres* ..., Tome II (Paris: Chez l'Auteur, 1766), viii. http://books.google.fr/books?id=FP4BAAAAQAAJ&pg=PR32&source=gbs_toc_r&cad=0_0#PPR7,M1 (accessed March 18, 2009).

17 Fournier, le jeune, *Manuel Typographique*, Tome II (Paris: Chez l'Auteur, 1767), 42–49.

18 Giambattista Bodoni, *Manuale Tipografico*, vol.1 (Parma: Presso La Vedova, 1818).

19 James Eckman, "The Story of an Historic Typeface—Century and the Bentons," *Industrial Arts Methods* 3, no. 12 (December 1964): 24.

20 Eckman, "On the True Ancestry of Old Type Faces," in *Heritage of the Printer*, vol. 1 (Philadelphia: North American Publishing Company, 1965), 189.

21 William E. Loy, "Designers and Engravers of Type, No. XI: Gustav F. Schroeder," *Inland Printer* 22, no. 3 (December 1898): 338.

22 McGrew, *American Metal Typefaces of the Twentieth Century* (New Castle, Del.: Oak Knoll Books, 1994), 119.

23 N. J. Werner, "St. Louis in Type-Founding History," *Share Your Knowledge Review* 22 (January 1941): 21.

24 Lawson, "Anatomy of a Type: Cheltenham," *Printing Impressions*, March 1971: 55.

25 Bullen, "The Effect of the Composing Machines Upon the Typefounding Industry," *Inland Printer* 73, no. 4 (July 1924): 595.

26 Eckman to David L. Ritter, 24 March 1965.

27 McGrew, *American Metal*, 189.

28 Bullen, "Nelson," 906.

29 Moran, *Stanley Morison*, 26.

30 McGrew, *American Metal*, 85.

31 Bullen, "Effect of Composing Machines," 595.

32 Murphy, "Morris Benton, Part 2," *Inland Printer* 97, no. 1 (April 1936): 42.

33 Lawson, "Cheltenham," 55.

34 Murphy, "Benton, Part 2," 42.

35 Ibid.

36 Ibid.

37 M. F. Benton, "Type," U.S. Patent No. 720,314, February 10, 1903, 1–2.

38 Linn Boyd Benton, "Inventions of Linn Boyd Benton," to David Gustafson (Carnegie Institute of Technology), 30 June 1932, for inclusion in the United Typothetae of America's *Who's Who in Printing in the United States*.

39 Theo Rehak, *Practical Typecasting* (New Castle, Del.: Oak Knoll Press, 1993), 116.

40 Caroline Benton Gregg, "Personal Remembrances of My Father, Morris Fuller Benton," Milwaukee, n.d., 9.

41 Morris Benton to A.T.H. Brower, 13 January 1906.

42 Elwood Haynes to M. F. Benton, 25 January 1912.

43 Morris Benton to William H. Kelly, 13 March 1942.

44 "Benton, Morris Fuller," 1951, 2.

45 Rehak, *Practical Typecasting*, 116.

46 Ibid., 115.

47 "Two Men," 453.

How Type Was Made at ATF

I N DECEMBER 1909, the *American Machinist* magazine published an article by W. J. Kaup about the American Type Founders Company, noting that type making "is an art where the little things, measured in fractions of a thousandth of an inch are the big things as exemplified by [ATF], whose system makes each small step a refinement link in the whole chain of microscopic accuracy."[1] This accuracy was what both Linn Boyd and Morris Fuller Benton demanded of themselves and others. Father and son were perfectly suited to the work, and the results they achieved were phenomenal.

One of ATF's advertising devices, used as early as 1922, was a piece of type on which was cast the entire Lord's Prayer—66 words, made up of 271 right-reading characters, including punctuation. (The matrix was cut wrong-reading so that the type would be right-reading). On the eight-point version of the Lord's Prayer, the lowercase letters were .0044 inch in height; the matrix was cut by a tool measuring .0005 inch in diameter; and the image area was constrained to a six-point square, that is, a square measuring 1/144th of a square inch.[2] Amazingly, the words are entirely legible under a microscope. ATF also cut another matrix using the same pattern for a four-point type body and cast the type,[3] but Linn Boyd Benton was not satisfied with it. He maintained that the eight-point example was the smallest successful cutting done directly into a matrix.[4]

The microscopic detail of this advertising piece was made possible by Linn Boyd Benton's greatest invention: the matrix-engraving machine. But an accurate matrix engraver would be of little use if each image to be engraved was not also absolutely precise. Luckily it was Morris Benton who oversaw the type design department at ATF, with a zeal and passion for quality that equaled his father's. As independent type designer Frederic W. Goudy wrote, "The machine itself may be hard and uncompro-

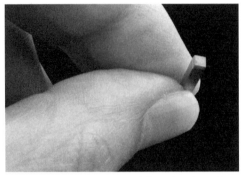

The Lord's Prayer cast on an eight-point piece of type

mising, but its product is entirely within the control of the pattern—if the pattern is right, then the more accurate and precise the machine, the more perfect the reproduction of the designer's art."[5]

INITIAL DRAWINGS

As the first step in the creation of a new typeface, Morris Benton studied the historic exemplars in ATF's extensive typographical library. Even for a completely modern face, Benton first conducted extensive research. He believed that gathering thorough background information was an essential part of the designer's job. Benton studied original type founders' specimen sheets and books printed in a wide variety of typefaces. Many of these resources were located in ATF's splendid library and museum.

Morris Benton and his colleagues began with pencil drawings, which would then be inked in for evaluation. These would be used to get a sense of what the letters would look like. An original drawing could be of any size, but preferably was 96 point or larger. Some faces began life as just one word: ATF's Balloon Light and Extrabold, for example, started with Max R. Kaufman's drawings of the letters in the word CHAMPION.[6]

Every year ATF received hundreds of proposed typefaces from enthusiastic letterers. The drawings they provided could seldom be used as working drawings because independent designers rarely realized the complexities of the type manufacturing process. A 1947 *Inland Printer* article by A. Raymond Hopper explained:

> Even among printers the belief is widespread that a type face originates by some designer submitting the drawing of an alphabet to the founder who buys it for a Hollywood figure and then proceeds to photograph it to the various sizes to make up a series. Nothing, even the imaginary Hollywood figure, could be further from the facts than this over-simplified conception of the birth of a type face.[7]

Designs submitted from the outside had to be redrawn to conform to technical limitations and peculiar word combinations. For example, Bertram Goodhue's drawings for

Cheltenham were not directly translated into patterns for cutting matrices upon their reception by ATF's design department. Morris Benton first had to adapt them to the appropriate specifications for typecasting. In the process of preparing such drawings for production, the original work went through "what Goudy referred to as Benton's 'army of smoothers and effacers.'"[8] Standard type body measurements for each size and standard character height ratios between drawings, patterns, and matrices were all part of the Benton system.[9] ATF also standardized such parameters as the available area allotted for a typeface on a given size body, and the proportions of character height according to size and type of baseline (common line, title line, script line, or ultra line).[10] The original drawings, then, were simply the starting point for the design department.

Other type foundries used somewhat similar systems. In 1927, Oswald Cooper, a Chicago type designer who worked for Barnhart Brothers & Spindler, was asked to make pattern drawings for a new type from the original drawings of August Dietz Sr. of Richmond, Virginia. It was an arduous task, and Cooper became "fed up." He wrote:

> I put in two months of drudgery on Dietz. The Wiebkings refused to touch
> it and Zim pleaded inability, naturally, seeing that I was there. So I drew it,
> and re-drew it, from the stump up. Anybody who wants to sell a type face
> to Barnhart's should be required to furnish pattern size drawings. Why
> should the foundry take on all the real WORK? Hell, anybody can make a
> scratchy type design an inch high.[11]

The Delineating Apparatus

To help the designer evaluate and adjust the preliminary drawings, Linn Boyd Benton invented a special machine to make an enlarged outline of each letter—so large, in fact, that all errors could easily be seen and corrected. The machine could enlarge up to a factor of 25:1,[12] and after adjustments were made, the letter was again reduced to a usable size. The delineator was a refined pantograph with a microscope attachment, enabling the operator to enlarge or reduce a single character very accurately. The focal length of the delineator's magnifier was changed for its various tasks.

To enlarge a preliminary drawing, the original letter (usually not larger than 96 point) was clamped in place on a small bed or plate directly under the microscope attachment. The face of the microscope held two single filaments of spider silk, crossed in the center of the focal point. The larger bed of the machine held a sheet of paper under the pantograph's tracing point, which for enlarging purposes held a small pencil. The operator focused the cross-hairs of the microscope on the outline of the character and then, "grasping the pencil holder and keeping his eyes entirely on the focal point of the microscope,"[13] followed the outline of the design by moving the pencil holder and, in so doing, traced an enlarged outline of the character.

The bed of the holder on which the original character was clamped could be swiveled to any angle, "thereby changing the style of the letter to wide, narrow, back slope or italic, both the italic and back slope being produced though the combination of angles,"[14] the *American Machinist* explained. In the patent's description of the machine, Benton used the terms "pattern-table" for the bed of the delineator, and "letter-pattern" for the original drawing:

> By rocking the pattern-table … so as to incline the pattern more or less to the horizontal … the component of the tracing movement that determines the enlargement of the letter vertically is more or less decreased relatively to the other component of the tracing movement which determines the enlargement of the letter horizontally or sidewise, and thus different varieties of type-patterns may be produced from the same letter-pattern, all having the same proportional enlargement sidewise, but varying in enlargement vertically. If it be desired to vary the enlargement of the letter horizontally or sidewise, retaining the same enlargement vertically, it is obvious that this result may be secured by turning the pattern-letter on the pattern-table at right angles to [its original] position.[15]

Thus Benton's delineator enabled the design department to create variants of standard faces by modifying the approved original drawings. Benton further explained the process in a 1906 essay:

> With the aid of the delineating machine, the operator, besides being able to produce an accurately enlarged outline pencil tracing of a design, is also enabled, by various adjustments, to change the form of the pencil tracing in such a manner that it becomes proportionately more condensed or extended, and even italicized or back-sloped. That is, from a single design, say Gothic, pencil tracings can be made condensed, extended, italicized, and back-sloped, as well as an enlarged facsimile.[16]

The resulting enlarged outline drawings were normally made about ten inches high, and then were evaluated by the designer. Judging enlarged letters and visualizing them in a text size required considerable skill. ("Believe me, it isn't easy," said Richard Marder.[17]) Inevitably the drawings of an independent letter designer not thoroughly trained and experienced in type making had to be adjusted by a trained specialist. After the enlarged outline drawings were modified to meet the requirements of ATF's standard lining and point systems, they went back to the delineating machine. This time, however, the microscope attachment was removed, and in its place a tracing pen was attached to trace a small-scale outline of the letter. The operator clamped the enlarged letter onto the machine and guided a pointer over its outline as the tracing pen reduced it to a practical size, say, 36 point or less. Then he inked in the reduced outline, giving it the appearance of a sharp impression from a piece of type. A solid letter so made lent itself more readily to further evaluation. If the reduced image was

The Benton delineating machine, as seen in *American Machinist*

not satisfactory, its enlarged outline drawing was again altered, and the process was repeated until the letter was approved. If the original drawings came in very large, the process was simply reversed, first reducing the image and inking it in for evaluation, and then making the appropriate ten-inch outline drawings for modifications.

After Morris Benton died, the delineating machine was no longer used.[18] However evaluating letters by enlarging them remained a common practice among type designers. For example, type designer William A. Dwiggins drew his originals at 120 point. He explained in 1940, "I can *modify* [characters] in the large outline drawings, but so far I can't *originate* in that medium."[19]

Working Drawings

Before final drawings were released by the design department, they were worked and reworked many times. Because the delineating machine enabled a designer to reduce the original outline drawings to various sizes and study them without the expense of actually casting the type, adjustments could easily be determined at the drawing stage for different type sizes.

The approved traced outline of a character was used to make a ten-inch "working drawing" on special paper. If the designer wanted a vertical line to be perfectly straight, he would use a straight-edge on the working drawing. Measurements and other information that would be helpful during later processes were noted on the margins of the paper. Today, a complete set of Morris Benton's working drawings for Bodoni is part of RIT's Cary Graphic Arts Collection. In 1970, ATF gave the Smithsonian "almost 500 sets of pantograph drawings for matrix engraving, dating between 1900 to 1940 and including the work of such as M. F. Benton, Goudy, Warren Chappell, and Lucian Bernhard."[20] Even before they were completely catalogued, these working drawings were available for researchers, and about ten years later Paul Shaw wrote in *Fine Print*:

> The characters are pattern drawings, not rough sketches, representing the
> final stage before the design is transferred, via the Benton matrix-engraving

Benton's wax plate machine

Wax plate machine at far right

machine, to metal. Although virtually finished, they still bear measurements, notations, doodles, and other comments regarding the design of each character, and offer insights into the creation of ATF typefaces. The Smithsonian's ATF drawings constitute an invaluable, yet practically unknown and untouched, resource for the study of type designs.[21]

In the 1990s, type designers studied these drawings before designing digital versions of Benton faces (see Chapter 14). "In transferring a type design to a new technology, the selection of the best model is of critical importance," explained Charles Bigelow, contemporary type historian, designer, and RIT professor, "and original drawings by the designer are obviously the best choice."[22]

The Pattern

Once the ten-inch working drawings were approved, the next step was to create a pattern plate for each character. These were made either in wax and then electrotyped, or directly in metal, depending on whether a punch or a matrix was required. Another Linn Boyd Benton pantograph machine was used to make the patterns. Henry Lewis Bullen called one early version "Benton's Wax Plate Machine."

The patterns for cutting punches or type characters on blank type bodies had raised (relief) images. When a raised-image pattern was required, the wax plate machine was fitted with a glass or brass plate coated with wax. Theo Rehak identified the following hand-written formula for the wax used on the wax plate machine as being in Linn Boyd Benton's handwriting:

Formulae for wax used on patterns

64–oz White wax

20– " Yellow wax

12– " Zinc white

Heat in water-bath and stir for 3 hours, add 4 oz. Spirmacetti [*sic*], 6 oz. Burgundy-pitch, 8/10 oz. Venice turpentine, stir for ½ hour. Before adding pitch crush the same into small pieces.[23]

Linn Boyd Benton's handwriting

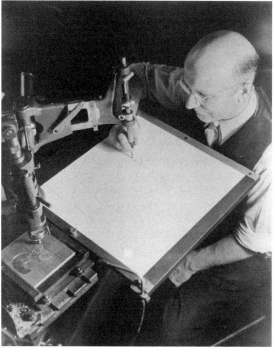

An ATF pattern with a raised outline image: Benton's Cloister Italic, initial cap A

The operator of the Gorton engraving machine followed the pattern drawing to produce a brass pattern plate.

The operator used a "follower" on the wax plate machine to trace the ten-inch outline drawing, while the cutting tool engraved a smaller outline of this character entirely through the wax on the pattern plate. The character was reduced in the process to about a third of the working drawing's size, or about three and a half inches high. A thin layer of copper was electrically deposited on the wax plate, which was then backed up with metal, trimmed, and finished. The result, turned upside down, was the pattern. It had a raised outline image and was ready to be used on Benton's punch-cutting machine.

Pattern plates to be used for engraving matrices were made of lead or zinc, into which right-reading characters were incised. Later, copper electro-wax shells (backed with lead) were produced by outside contract. During the war materials shortage years of 1941 to 1946, Gorton-engraved brass plates were used. After 1948, photoengraved zinc plates were used. When what remained of ATF in Elizabeth, New Jersey, was auctioned in 1993, many hundreds of brass and copper pattern plates were scattered helter-skelter over table tops and cabinets.[24]

In general, matrices of all the regular type sizes could be cut from these pattern plates. Exceptions included certain descenders and (rarely) ascenders that required special truncated patterns enabling them to fit within the available vertical confines of certain body sizes.[25] As Linn Boyd Benton explained, the pattern determined the shape of

An ATF pattern plate on the bed of the Benton engraving machine in Elizabeth, New Jersey, 1984

the letter, but its size and any design variations from the pattern were determined by means of adjustments on the engraving machine.[26]

Engraving a Matrix

In Milwaukee, Benton's pantographic machine cut "models" or letter-punches from which matrices were made to cast Benton's self-spacing types. The matrix-engraving machine was an adaptation of this punch-cutting machine and was developed in the early 1900s when ATF decided that engraving directly into a matrix blank was more practical than either cutting a punch or cutting a model from which new matrices could be grown electrolytically.

Rehak defines Benton's engraving machine as "a reduction-reproducing, skewed gimbal engraving device, capable of infinite horizontal proportional adjustment."[27] He owns and operates two Benton engravers at his Dale Type Foundry in Howell, New Jersey. His vertical No. 55, circa 1885, was rebuilt in 1903 and can cut matrices up to 72-point type. It appears to be the only existing engraving machine with the Benton & Waldo builder's plate still attached. Rehak's other engraver is Benton's only known surviving horizontal machine, the No. 5 or "adcut" engraving machine for larger matrices, which can cut up to 144 points and beyond.[28]

The No. 55 engraver, as described in the *American Machinist*, consists of "two housings between which swings a long pendulum or arm … delicately suspended in a compound yoke [at the top of the machine] by means of gimbal screws which gives it a toggle-joint effect."[29] (In the *American Machinist*'s image of the Benton engraver, the pendulum is labeled F; the yoke, G; the quill, H; the flexible shaft drive, I; the matrix, J; the micrometer adjustment, K; and the follower, L.) The free end of the pendulum, with a "follower" tip inserted, can be moved all around the pattern secured on the bed of the machine, directly in front of the operator. Matrices can be cut for different point sizes of a given type design by adjusting the distance between the pattern and the cutting tool.

Benton engravers at ATF, 1984

ATF's matrix cutting department

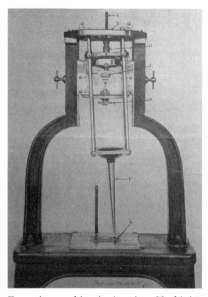

Engraving machine, in *American Machinist*

A man operating the Benton matrix engraving machine

To engrave a matrix at ATF, a nickel brass blank was fixed in a jig and inserted into the cutting platform of the engraver; there it was held fast by a thumbscrew above the operator's head. This blank or "planchet" became the matrix after the cutting protocol was completed. Minute cutters like fine dentist drills, spinning in ball-bearing races within the "quill" assembly, cut the character step by step. The quill, or the head that housed the cutting tool, was perhaps the most highly developed part of the engraving machine. "The steel is specially selected and machined, and then laid away for three or four months for seasoning or adjustment of the various strains inherent in

The cutting-tool end of a quill assembly

A case for six quill assemblies

all steels," the *American Machinist* explained.[30] Only after such time was it fitted into its guides. At ATF, the allowable tolerance for all dimensions in the construction of this head was within .0002 inch.

The Benton machine was originally furnished with five cutting tools, each used in turn to engrave the matrix.[31] The first, second, and third were roughing cutters, also used to cut the counter areas of a character. The fourth was the first finishing tool, and the fifth was the final finishing tool. When Theodore Low De Vinne described Benton's punch-cutting machine, he was especially impressed with the precision of its cutting tools: "The cutting tools are exceedingly minute, but they are made with the nicest accuracy, and are rotated at high speed by steam power."[32] When these cutting steels (or "wires") were improved by way of tougher alloys, the battery of tools was reduced to three—rough, medium, and finishing cutting tools. The final Benton system used carbide rods ground on diamond wheels as cutting tools, and this reduced the number of tools to just two: a rougher and a finisher.

Once in place, the cutting tool was driven by a flexible shaft spinning at a speed of 8,000 to 10,000 revolutions per minute. The dimension of the facet of the cutting edge of each tool varied from .001 inch to .080 inch in width (depending on the amount of metal to be removed). The largest was used to rough out the major portion of the design, while the smallest was used for finishing.

The "follower," inserted in the taper-end collet of the pendulum, was carefully held by the operator to trace around the pattern. There were large followers, which fit into a ball-end shank, and smaller, finisher followers with tapered shanks to fit the collet. The *American Machinist* described the precision required to cut an accurate matrix:

> A light spring in tension against the end of the pin holds the follower always in position. The size of the follower is in direct ratio with the size of the tool, as for example, the pendulum arm with a ratio of 10 to 1, using a tool with a 0.008-inch face, would require a follower ten times as large, or 0.080-inch diameter.[33]

Tracing the pattern

A blank matrix slides into the matrix holder…

… and then is inserted into the cutting platform of the Benton engraving machine. Notice the point of the cutting tool.

The cut but unfitted matrix, still in its holder

The operator guided the follower along the inside edges of the pattern, while the cutting tool above simultaneously cut the character into the matrix. The matrix moved in unison (but at a proportionately reduced scale) with the follower and was pushed against the fixed tool in the cutting-head assembly. The work moved, not the cutting tool, which rotated at high speed in place, perpendicular to the matrix blank. A rough character was made first, and the surplus metal removed. After an adjustment, another circuit of the pattern was made, refining the incision and removing more metal. The operator also guided the follower/cutting tool over the inner area of the pattern between the character's outlines. Different cutting tools were used for many successive cuts, and finally a finishing tool made the last precision cuts. In Rehak's foundry today, a correctly calibrated engraving machine can engrave a matrix for a large, ornate capital letter in about two hours. The same font's period can be engraved in ten minutes.[34]

The Measuring Microscope and Benton's Tool Grinder Device

The engraving machine operator periodically examined the cutting tools through a special "measuring microscope," since the accuracy of the matrix depended to a large extent on the accuracy of the cutting tools. The microscope was made of cast iron,

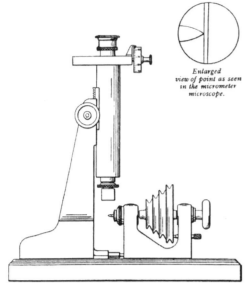

Enlarged
view of point as seen
in the micrometer
microscope.

Benton's measuring microscope

Benton's tool grinder as seen in *American Machinist*

modeled after a similar microscope used by Louis Pasteur. The engraving procedure was so perfectly ordered that only if a tool was damaged was the resulting matrix faulty. In those cases where a tool edge was broken or damaged, necessitating its removal in the middle of the operation, it was essential that some means of grinding or renewing the edge be available to the operator to ensure that the tool remained within proper tolerances.

Not surprisingly, Linn Boyd Benton invented a special device to grind the cutting tools automatically and with extraordinary accuracy when a gauge on the machine was properly set. Any desired width of tool face could thus be obtained. Benton's tool grinder was patented in 1890, and it remains a vital part of the Benton system today at the Dale Guild Type Foundry. Benton once gave an extemporaneous explanation of the device at ATF, which was later typed up and revised by his son Morris and the Engraving Department foreman, John Bauer. The resulting six-page, undated document is reprinted in Rehak's *Practical Typecasting*.[35]

The cutting tools, after being reground, were again inspected under the microscope. "Across the center of the face or lens of the microscope, is arranged a fine scale reading in 0.0005 of an inch," the *American Machinist* explained.[36] This is about half the thickness of a cigarette paper. A cutting tool looks like a heavy nail under this microscope, and so the accuracy of its point could easily be gauged by eye—the .080-inch tool covered 160 lines on the scale, and the .001-inch tool covered two lines.

Cutting Punches v. Engraving Matrices

Some confusion remains about ATF's methodologies. Bullen explained in a 1922

A pattern for Morris Benton's Wedding Text

Inland Printer article that Benton's machine could adapt to either punch-cutting or matrix-engraving, depending on whether a raised character (punch) or a sunken one (matrix) was needed: "When the Benton punch-cutting machine is required to cut a punch, the outside of the pattern is used; when it is required to engrave a matrix, the inside of the pattern is used."[37] This statement of Bullen's seemed to me to be a gross oversimplification, so I asked Theo Rehak whether it was true. Rehak replied that Bullen was correct, but that he had left out one important detail: different types of patterns were used for cutting punches and matrices.

> The punch is cut by following the pattern's extreme perimeter, *i.e., in relief*. The matrix is cut from the interior of an *incised* pattern … and so is made "within" the planchet of brass. (Only with a character cut within it does a raw planchet of brass become a rough—first stage—matrix.) These are two different-looking patterns: the ones I use for matrices are "sunk" into a flat sheet of metal. As for the punch ones, I saw some at Hartzell's [Hartzell Machine Works, Philadelphia] and they were somewhat smaller but still on plates, only "built up" from the surface, so the follower could trace around the outside perimeter of the character.[38]

According to Bullen, after ATF's letter-designing department was established and Morris Benton was appointed chief designer in 1900, "it was determined to abandon the use of punches."[39] However, Linn Boyd Benton wrote in 1906 that two different engraving machines were still being used in the foundry:

> At present there are two styles of engraving machines employed, one cutting the letter in relief,—called a "punch" if cut in steel, and an "original" if cut in type metal,—and the other cutting a letter in intaglio,—called a "matrix."[40]

The patterns for Morris Benton's Wedding Text, dated June 21, 1907, show wear mainly on the inside edges of the characters, suggesting that the operator traced around these inside edges. Wedding Text is a special case, however. As explained in Chapter 14, over a period of years, it was produced with both type punch originals and matrices.

Name *Freehand*
S. Lineparallel Crossing   *top* %   Body . . . *8* . . . Points
Height ~~Cap H~~ *.0806* . . . . *C* Line. Head bearing *.215*. Side bearing *8/pts* Depth *0.235*.

Machine No. *55*. Leverage *31*. Picas & *.0165 / .089*. ~~Normal.~~ Expansion *4/7 pts* ~~Condensation~~ . . . . . .

Machine No. . . . . . . Leverage . . . . . Picas & . . . . . .

Size of Finishing Follower *.038*. Medium Follower *.166*. Large Follower *.300*. Extra Follower . . . .

Size of Finishing Tool *.0.015*. Medium Tool . . . . *.004*. Large Tool . . . . *.007*. Extra Tool . . . .

Figures $ £ cut with *38* . . . . . . Points under screw. Bevel Stop . . . . *1/4 Pt* Follower *.038* . . . . . .

Stop for cap and fig. counters with largest tool . . . *.017* . . . . Stop for l.c. and pts. counters with largest tool *.017* . . . . .

A cutting slip for casting Morris Benton's 8-point Freehand

6 point 12 point 24 point 80 point

Kingsley/ATF Corporation generated these examples of its optical scaling capability in 1989.

Cutting Slips and Optical Scaling

At ATF, engraving instructions or "cutting slips" were written out for each size of each typeface. These slips guided the engraving machine operator in choosing the proper followers, cutting tools, engraving depth, and other variables. Apparently Benton used an early version of these cutting slips from the very beginning. An 1888 advertisement for his punch-cutting machine reads,

> The operator is provided with a card on which is printed a series of numbers, corresponding with numbers stamped on the followers, opposite which are a series of figures identical with figures on the micrometer. This card indicates to the operator the order in which the different followers should be used, and the number to which the micrometer is to be set for each succeeding change of follower.[41]

Cutting slips also directed the operator to use precision steel adjustment standards for the proportional changes needed to produce different letter sizes. Briefly put, to accommodate the inherent limitations of the human visual system, as the size of a letterform gets smaller it needs to be expanded, and as it gets larger, it needs to be condensed. "Traditional punchcutters and scribes made such proportional changes in order to optimize legibility," Charles Bigelow wrote. "Recent research in visual perception suggests that such proportional changes are necessary because the human visual system has non-linear sensitivity to visual features of different spatial frequencies."[42]

Benton understood that slightly distorting the characters as they went up or down in size enabled a basic typeface design to retain its integrity, and so he built this capabil-

Scaling type

TRUE 6 POINT TYPE

Scaling type

6 POINT TYPE MAGNIFIED TO 24 POINT

Scaling type

TRUE 24 POINT TYPE

The micrometer wheel adjusts the depth of engraving.

ity into his engraving machine. For example, according to the Day Book, a hand-written ATF reference book, each size of Morris Benton's Wedding Text was expanded or condensed relative to the pattern for the typeface; not even one size of the type was strictly proportional to the pattern. Many years later, ATF's successor, the Kingsley/ATF Type Corporation, coined the term "optical scaling" to describe this phenomenon of distorting letters.

> Typographers have always known to change the relative weights of strokes, serifs and even the character's width from one size of character to the next, to compensate for the way we see. They also know to change the relative amount of white space surrounding the character to preserve its legibility. These changes are known as Optical Scaling.

> Contrast this with linear scaling, where all parts of the character change size at the same rate, making large characters look wide and heavy (strokes too thick, serifs too big) while small characters look thin and weak.[43]

Kingsley/ATF Corporation was a pioneer in utilizing optical scaling in its early digitized fonts. To advertise this feature of its digital type, various sizes of a letter were magnified to a uniform height to show how they had been expanded or condensed.

Aside from such optical considerations, the three-dimensional nature of type also dictated that different sizes be slightly distorted. For example, hairlines and serifs on metal type had to be well supported to prevent breakage, and counters needed to be deep enough and large enough, especially in the smaller sizes, to avoid filling up with ink and paper dust during printing. Although the adjustments made for different sizes of metal type were minute, they were nevertheless critical. Benton's engraving machine was routinely adjusted to vary the characters cut for different sizes so that each size could reflect its ideal proportions. The slight distortions that the Benton matrix engraver was capable of making rendered it a more valuable tool than a straight pantograph could ever be. Henry Lewis Bullen explained in 1907 that Benton's engraver was capable of "infinitesimal gradations in all directions."[44]

Some typographers, however, either did not understand this capability of the machine or were not impressed with Benton's optical scaling. For example, in 1922 Daniel Berkeley Updike wrote in *Printing Types: Their History, Forms and Use*,

> Benton of Milwaukee invented … a punch-cutting machine, thereby at once enormously simplifying the cutting of punches, as well as cheapening their production. At first sight it would appear that this was a wholly admirable invention; and it would be, if it did not tend to mechanize the design of types. But a design for a type alphabet that may be entirely successful *for the size for which it is drawn*, cannot be successfully applied to all other sizes of the same series. Each size is a law unto itself, and is often bettered by modifications in the original design made by the feeling and taste of the designer. To a trained eye, looking over impressions of a series of modern machine cut types, it is often possible to tell which was the size originally designed because it stands out as the most harmonious and successful. In this particular size the designer's eye had most modified his rules, and in all others the necessary modifications proper to the varying sizes had not been so carefully made.[45]

The first great American book designer, Bruce Rogers, agreed:

> It is a truism that almost every face of type has its ideal size, and lessens in merit as this size is either increased or decreased. The modern practice of cutting all sizes (at least down to 8-point) from one pattern on a pantograph machine, is accountable for much of the mechanical appearance of our books. But before the pantograph was invented, each size, although based on one model, was really a separate design. For the punch-cutter was then in effect the ultimate designer of each size he cut, in proportion to the fidelity with which he followed his model.[46]

Was Benton's optical scaling system really that deficient? Type designers had strong opinions about the subject, which still occupies the minds of digital type designers today. "Despite Benton's ingenuity, [his optical scaling system] may not have been as effective as true hand-cut punches by a master punch cutter," Bigelow admitted. "However, in Benton's favor is the fact that there were very few master punch-cutters in the twentieth century."[47]

Linn Boyd Benton devised ratios for the horizontal expansion and condensation that were the basis of his optical scaling system. In 1901, according to Rehak, "Benton embarked upon the formulation of his Engraving Factor Tables, a work of great skill and a most notable achievement."[48] The original Benton Engraving Factor Tables no longer exist since many of his original notes and papers were lost when ATF moved from Jersey City to the Kelly Press factory in Elizabeth, New Jersey in 1935 (see Chapter 12). By then he had already been dead for about three years, and apparently no one carefully evaluated his papers during the move. Rehak explained in *Practical Typecasting*:

> The contents of Benton's "room" (curiously never referred to as an office proper, perhaps because, like Edison, Benton would sometimes sleep overnight in it) were not intelligently cared for. What remains is, however, impressive for its usefulness and accuracy. Just how such marvelous devices could spring so effortlessly from, and be developed by, a man without formal engineering training is intriguing. Benton kept most of his discoveries and information secret; and he trained no successors, although there were several apprentices and his son was certainly well versed in his theories.[49]

Rehak studied what remained of Benton's notes—from what was left at the ATF factory in Elizabeth, New Jersey; from the ATF collection at Columbia University; and from the holdings of the Smithsonian Institution in Washington, D.C. and Suitland, Maryland—and marveled at Benton's "formidable amount of experimentation and calculation, especially in an era without computers."[50]

Benton's ratios linked the height and width of pattern images, desired characters, and blank matrices. For example, to determine the width of a character using the "common line" baseline (see Chapter 12), the width of the pattern's image was divided by a common line constant that Benton had determined for each size. The width of both side bearings and a "fitting allowance" (see below) was then added to this character width to arrive at the blank matrix width. Benton standardized all possible variables in his factoring tables.

Perhaps it was this standardization that so offended other typographers. While the survival of the type industry demanded that it move in the direction of standardization, the ingenious capacity of the Benton engraver to make adjustments for cutting different sizes of the same letter remained unappreciated, not necessarily by the users of metal type, but by typographers. D. B. Updike, as we have seen, was apprehensive of accomplishing optical scaling by adjusting a machine. He wrote in *Printing Types*:

> I have sometimes questioned whether a machine can be so managed that it will ever produce those fine and almost imperceptible qualities of design given to it by the hand of a clever type-cutter—which mean so much to the appearance of type in the mass, and which vary in nature and degree in dif-

ferent sizes of the same series of characters. In point of fact, the first types produced by punch-cutting machines did seem to show a certain rigidity from the point of view of design. That there has been an improvement of late in type cut by machine is undeniable, and yet there has been practically no change in its mechanism. This improvement, I learn, has come to pass through a more sympathetic and subtle manipulation of the machine itself, and by modifications of rules by the eye of the workman who operates it.[51]

Updike concluded that the trained eye must remain the primary judge of good design, no doubt unaware that the "improvement" he referred to came by following cutting slips that encoded Benton's optical scaling ratios. Benton machine operators did not make design decisions.

Updike's fellow critic Bruce Rogers must have also been under the impression that engraver operators altered the patterns according to their own aesthetic sensibilities, since some time before 1922 he wrote to him:

> Even with strict instructions and with best intentions, it is difficult for the habitual user of a very accurate machine *not* to insensibly smooth out what he has always been taught to consider "imperfections" and to make as mechanically perfect a letter as is possible … I have come to believe that perhaps only hand-cut punches, *cut by the designer of the type*, can preserve the real feelings of the design.[52]

These objections were made despite the general availability of ATF specimen books, showing various typefaces in various sizes, all optically scaled according to Benton's system. Frederic W. Goudy's personal experience with an engraving machine enabled him to appreciate its precision and its ability to retain the feeling of an original drawing, and as a result he disagreed with Rogers:

> Since my pattern letter is made by hand from drawings by the same hand, the contention that type cast from a machine-engraved matrix must necessarily be too "mechanical," seems to me to fall on the ground. We do not design by machinery—design is the artist's creation, and, when necessary, it may be exactly *reproduced* by a machine.[53]

Beatrice Warde mentioned the optical scaling capability of the Benton matrix engraver in a footnote to a 1935 article about machine-cut types, but apparently she also mistrusted it. At the time, she was working for the British Monotype company, which certainly did not have access to Benton's Engraving Factor Tables. "There exists an ingenious mechanism by which a certain amount of reproportioning can be done by adjusting the machine," she wrote. "Opinions differ as to the wisdom (from the designer's point of view) of *using* the adjustment."[54] [Italics mine.]

EXHIBIT GREAT SUCCESS Sight
LAVISH business arrangement
in western city amazed visitor
from the slumbering lakeside

Clockwise from top: 72 point Bodoni at actual size,
72 point Bodoni reduced to 8 point; 8 point Bodoni at actual size.

Carl Purlington Rollins of the Yale University Press berated Benton's system for being too "mechanical." As late as 1947, he did not grasp the matrix engraver's capability for optical scaling.

> It was the two basic machines invented and developed by Linn Boyd Benton which made it possible for those unskilled in the intricacies of type making to provide the basic designs for type. The machines were very ingenious, and the designs partook of the "faultily faultless, icily regular" perfection of the mechanical device. This method of making type faces involved the drawing of the design and the making of two or three patterns in thin brass of the outline of the letter—each pattern good for several sizes of type, and slightly modified for another group of sizes. This is the way in which type is designed.[55]

As late as 1956, the Dutch type historian G. W. Ovink remained unaware of Benton's complex system.

> With enlarging camera, drawing pantograph and curves, large-scale patterns could be made of absolute technical perfection, and from these the punch-cutting machine could produce punches and matrices in any size in absolute identity of form—*and it did so, even when subtle variations were necessary.*[56] [Italics mine.]

Updike, Rogers, Warde, Rollins, and Ovink must not have understood that Benton engraving machine operators exactly followed both the patterns and their cutting slip instructions, precisely and consistently adjusting the machine for every point size. Operators were not permitted to deviate from these specifications, thereby ensuring continuity and uniformity. This enabled properly trained day workers to produce as fine and accurate a matrix as Benton himself,[57] meeting the reproduction tolerance for replacement work at ATF of ±.0002 inch.

The opposition to Benton's system, clearly essential to the metal type industry, may have reflected a simple unwillingness to move forward. "Each typographic technology has its own limitations and advantages to which the forms of the letters become adapted through time," explained Charles Bigelow. "A new technology must imitate the forms of the previous technology because of reader conservatism, but at the same time such imitation leads to problems of inferior quality which ultimately can only be solved through innovation."[58] To a large extent, Benton's own innovation of optical scaling, built right into the matrix engraving machine, enabled ATF's type to bypass the expected "inferior quality" stage.

The point size of a character on the Benton engraving machine is determined by the "leverage" adjustment.[59] The distance between the pattern and matrix on the machine can be changed (the entire middle section containing the matrix jig and cutting assembly moves up and down) by adding or subtracting equivalent precision steel standards to the inside of both legs of the machine. These act as a stop to the vertical movement of the middle section of the machine. Leverage is always set first.[60] The precision steel standards come in two sizes: pica standards and smaller shims measured in decimal inches. For example, for 6-point Freehand, each leg of the machine was fitted with steel standards adding up to 32 picas, and an additional steel shim, or combination of them, measuring .025 inch. To increase the height of a letter, the leverage dimension is reduced, and to reduce the height, the leverage dimension is increased. Once the correct steel standards are in place for the size of matrix desired, they are locked in.

The small shims were measured in decimals of an inch to compensate for the inherent problem in the American System of Interchangeable Type Bodies, adopted in 1886, which, as discussed in Chapter 4, was based on a point that measured 0.0138 inch (or, according to Linn Boyd Benton, 0.013837 inch).[61] This meant that 72 points, and therefore 6 picas, was equal to 0.9936 inch (or, according to Benton, 0.996264 inch). An ATF standard measurement table reproduced in Rehak's *Practical Typecasting* goes so far as to list inch equivalents in eighth-of-a-point intervals from 1/8 to 84 points, and in point intervals up to 144 points.[62]

The other set of precision steel standards, independent of the leverage setting and used to adjust for narrower than normal or wider than normal characters, was operational at least by 1906. These standards are added or subtracted from a "normal" height of 40 points of steel inserted under two screws on either side of the top of the machine. The screws attach to a circular plate (yoke) above the gimbal arms. Linn Boyd Benton wrote:

> The adjustments are such that the operator is enabled to engrave the letter proportionately more extended or condensed, and lighter or heavier in face, than the pattern. All these variations are necessary for the production of a properly graded modern series containing the usual sizes. In fact, on account of the laws of optics, which cannot be gone into here, only one size of a series is cut in absolutely exact proportion to the patterns.[63]

THE BENTONS

84 Bodoni

	Pur.	Exp-Cond.	Fd	Tool
6	.0550	+5½ Pt	.046	.0015
8	.0776	+4½ "	.038	.0015
10	.0962	+3¾ "	.035	.0015
12	.1100	+3 "	.033	.0015
14	.1239	+2½ "	.032	.0015
18	.1654	NORMAL	.034	.002
24	.2200	-3¼ Pt	.034	.002
30	.2745	-6½ "	.032	.002
36	.3295	-10 "	.029	.002
42	.3745	-13 "	.028	.002
48	.4396	-16½ "	.027	.002
60	.5500	-23.5M	.027	.0025
72	.6604	-29½5M / -33¼M	.027	.0025
78	.812	-93 LM	.028	.003
84	.963	-51 LM	.027	.0035
96	1.159	-71 LM	.026	.004

128 Bulmer

	Schine	Exp-Cond.	Fol	Tool	
6	.0665	+2½ Pt	.051	.0015	+.0004
8	.0806	+2½ "	.048	.0015	+.00028
10	.0947	+2¼ "	.045	.0015	+.00016
12	.1015	+2 "	.043	.0015	NORMAL
14	.1224	+1¾ "	.042	.0015	-.0001
18	.1629	NORMAL	.049	.002	-.00015
24	.2168	-3¼ Pt	.052	.0025	-.001
30	.2706	-6½ "	.047	.0025	-.0015
36	.3245	-10 "	.049	.003	-.002
42	.3713	-13 "	.051	.0035	-.0025
48	.4322	-16½ "	.052	.004	-.003

Bulmer Italic

		Exp-Cond.		
6	.0665	+2½ Pt	.051	.0015
8	.0806	+2½ "	.048	.0015
10	.0947	+2¼ "	.045	.0015

Two pages from the ATF "Day Book," a quick reference guide for setting up the Benton engraving machine

Like the leverage setting, this system is counter-intuitive: adding steel shims to the "normal" setting of 40 points under the screw condenses the type engraved into the matrix, and subtracting points (by substituting the 40-point block for shims in smaller increments) expands the type.[64] For example, only the 18-point size of Bodoni was cut exactly proportional to the pattern. Going down in size, the letters were made wider (expanded). Above 18-point, they were narrowed in width (condensed) relative to the pattern's image. For both adjustments, leverage and expansion/condensation, the total measurement of steel standards must be exactly the same on both sides of the machine: for leverage, on the inside of its two legs, and for expansion/condensation, under both screws on the top.

After Benton's Engraving Factor Tables were lost, the company apparently tried to reconstruct them. Dr. James Eckman, an avid historian of American type foundries, wrote in 1985: "In the matrix-engraving department of the American Type Founders Company, I have seen, on the walls, great charts of trigonometric projections of curves for use in correcting aberrations produced by magnification of letter forms from a beginning prototype of one size of letter."[65]

In the 1940s, the great contemporary type designer Hermann Zapf was designing for the German Stempel type foundry while it still used a pantographic matrix engraver. He explained that the normal practice at Stempel was to produce three sets of patterns for every typeface.[66] Adjustments on the machine were made only to widen characters in the very smallest point sizes.

While type designers in Benton's day may have objected to his methods of optical

Checking the depth of each point on an ATF matrix

An ATF fitter rubs the matrix on a fine stone to bring its face absolutely parallel to its engraved surfaces.

scaling by machine, some digital typographers today, such as Raph Levien, a software engineer at Google, Inc., who has also designed digital type, admire his ingenuity. (For an extended discussion on the relevance of Benton's optical scaling system to digital type design, see Appendix A.)

FITTING OR JUSTIFICATION

After a matrix came off the Benton machine, any burrs that had formed on its edges were removed. When a number of clean matrices were ready, they were placed face up on a piece of iron, their cavities were filled with mineral oil, and they were exposed to heat. "When the oil boils," Linn Boyd Benton wrote, "remove matrices and blow the oil out."[67] He also explained two other methods for getting matrices ready for the "matrix fitter" in a 1917 document on how to set up the No. 59 matrix engraving machine.

Then the matrices were fitted. "Fitting is one of those seemingly insignificant details in the production of a type face which are of paramount importance in the appearance of the printed page," the American fine printer Joseph Blumenthal wrote in 1935. "Poor fitting can nullify fine letter design and render almost valueless the most careful type composition."[68] He stressed the importance of the "extra metal (side-bearing, it is called) [that] remains to the right and left of the face of the letter." Linn Boyd Benton also explained why fitting was so important:

> The adjusting of the matrix to the mould is technically called "fitting," and requires great skill. If type is cast from unfitted matrices, be the letters ever so cleverly designed and perfectly cut, when assembled in the printed page they will present a very ragged appearance. Some letters will appear slanting backward, others forward, some be above the line, others below; some will perforate the paper, while others will not print at all; the distances between the letters will everywhere be unequal, and some will print on but one edge. Indeed, a single letter may have half of these faults, but when the matrices are properly fitted, the printed page presents a smooth and even appearance.[69]

THE BENTONS

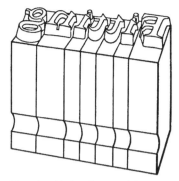
Note the side bearings on this type.

The matrix is trimmed with microscopic precision.

Fitting assured a uniform depth on the engraved surface of the matrix (making the face precisely parallel to the foot), adjusted the character's baseline, adjusted the side bearings (the non-printing surfaces around each letter), and adjusted the matrix to perfect squareness to prevent "squirts" (molten lead leakages) in the typecasting machine. Perfectly fitted and square matrices insured a uniformly printed image, with no alignment variations.

Simply put, "the matrix as delivered from the Benton engraving machine required very precise trimming in order to place the engraved letter cavity exactly central to the to-be-cast body and absolutely straight and on the proper baseline."[70] So it was clamped onto yet another Benton invention, the matrix-trimming machine. As its patent stated, this machine trimmed the "matrix-blocks to secure the proper relation of the sides and head of the matrix block to the matrix formed in it, which is usually called 'fitting' the matrix."[71]

The position where each character should sit in relation to the baseline of the type was of course not necessarily apparent, as noted in Chapter 1. If all letters were placed exactly on the "true" baseline, they would appear to be bouncing up and down on it, because letter combinations and shapes give rise to optical illusions. "A large proportion of characters contain some lines that are departures from the rules which must be observed in their mated characters," A. Raymond Hopper explained in a 1947 *Inland Printer* article.[72] Deviations have to be made to trick the eye into believing that all the letters in a font of type sit on a common baseline. These irregularities cannot be systematized, but vary with each new alphabet design, and, to an extent, with every size of a given design. Richard Marder explained that Morris Benton was a master at determining these irregularities. "The spacing of a letter on its body is a very critical thing, creating a pleasing amount of white space [around it]. All these things Morris Benton did with complete confidence and tremendous skill."[73]

The left and right edges of the matrix determined the "set" of a letter, or, how much white space would appear next to that letter when it was placed beside another character in the font. As new designs were readied for production, proofs were made for each letter in combination with every other letter, and the results would be studied for legibility and beauty. The letters H, O, o, and m, because of their shapes and proportions, were used as standards and printed beside each character in the font to judge the set. Approved proofs were kept in cabinets in the ATF fitting area for consultation.

"When I was first confronted with the need of fitting a type face," Blumenthal wrote, "I endeavored to fit as closely as possible. I was puzzled by the curious, uneven, and crowded result of the trial proofs and soon discovered where the errors lay."[74] After studying "the masterpieces of the past," Blumenthal decided that he needed to give his letters more room. "Ample fitting clarifies the individual letters and 'opens up' the readability of the page," he wrote. For example, Blumenthal found that in the *Ecclesiastical Histories* by Eusebius, printed in 1470 by Jenson, "the optical distance between all letters, whether straight or round, is always generous."[75]

The importance of the fitting department cannot be overstated, since the final appearance of a printed page depended on the adjustments it made. "Fitters are lonely, usually tiresome, and for the most part irascible people—perhaps their work makes them so," Rehak wrote. "[Fitting] is demanding, taxing of the nerves, and never fully appreciated … Perfection being taken for granted, the fitter never hears about the work, unless it is wrong … Even praise is seldom considered without suspicion."[76] But fitters commanded a great deal of respect at ATF. According to Rehak, "In earlier days, the most important workers in the foundry were the *fitters* and the *liners*."[77]

> Liners insured that every casting job "lined" with the samples (kept of every design) in their specimen cabinets. Each job had to be signed off by the liner, as being inspected and approved before commencing the casting. Liners usually used a cap H or lower case m to check the alignment. There were also "alignment steels" or standards for setting special jobs, including Title Line, Art Line, etc., all specified by the production department or the needs of the type customer's specs. This was the basis for ATF's legendary consistency of cast quality.[78]

Larger than any other of its kind, Linn Boyd Benton's personal type alignment gauge was even more exacting than most:

> It takes 8 revolutions of the micrometer-type adjustment to equal the travel of just one revolution of … a typical point-set micrometer. Even to the most

Linn Boyd Benton's personal type alignment gauge

adept machinist, this piece is awe inspiring. Its see-thru window is unique, and allows the user several options in viewing the baseline. This is, by far, the finest alignment gauge ever made. It can align types from the smallest to 96 pt. baseline, and does it much faster than an optical comparitor.[79]

CASTING

ATF's type was cast from a mixture of tin, antimony, lead, and a small amount of copper. There were also traces of arsenic in the alloy. "As antimony expands in solidifying," Linn Boyd Benton wrote in 1906, "advantage is taken of this quality, and the mixture is so proportioned that the expansion of the antimony will practically counteract the shrinkage of the other ingredients."[80] Actually, antimony does not expand but rather acts as a retardant in the shrinking process of the alloy.

The proportions of ingredients of type metal varied according to the size and style of the type and the purposes for which it would be used. The alloy used for large type was generally softer, especially if there were ornate or delicate details in the design. Scripts and italics were also somewhat softer, with added tin and lead to ease the type through the finishing operations on the Barth typecaster. Rehak recalled from his ATF days:

> Italic [type], when cast in high-antimonial alloy (ATF's famous "No. 4" alloy contained 28% antimony) was often quietly "adjusted down" with an ingot of Linotype metal, by an experienced production caster, "softening" it somewhat. This enabled the cast type to more easily pass through the trimming knives without ragged cuts or breakage of the kerns.[81]

The casting machine was a marvel of engineering. Invented in 1888 by Henry Barth, president of the Cincinnati Type Foundry, the Barth automatic type caster not only cast the type, but broke off the jets, ploughed grooves to form the feet, cut four trimmed edges on each type character at the mold/mixture interface, and delivered the type in lines ready for inspection. Soon after the formation of ATF, Barth was made a director, with his son Henry O. Barth as his assistant. After the senior Barth's

The Barth casting machine   An ATF employee casting type with the Barth machine

death in 1905, Linn Boyd Benton made several improvements to the machine and received patents for them (see Chapter 8).

Each Barth machine at ATF was set up to cast a single body size. The matrices for a font of, say, 12-point Cheltenham, were held firmly and accurately in turn against the Barth machine's adjustable mold, which allowed each character's set width to be properly fixed. After every cast, the matrix was pulled away from the mold and the piece of type was sent on its way to a series of finishing operations. Benton further described the casting sequence:

> The mould for this purpose is made of hardened steel, and in it is formed the body of the type. The printing end is formed in the matrix. The mould is provided at one end with guides and devices for holding the matrix snugly against it while the type is being cast, and for withdrawing the matrix and opening the mould when the type is discharged. At the opposite end from the matrix is an opening through which the melted metal enters. The moulds are made adjustable so that each character is cast the proper width, the opening of course being wider for a "W" than for an "i." Only one mould is necessary for one size of type, and with it all the matrices for that size may be used. Commercially, however, it is often necessary to make several moulds of the same size in order to produce the requisite amount of type.

> After the adjustments are made, the casting of the type follows. Type are now cast in a machine which is automatic, after it is once adjusted to cast a given letter. The melted type metal is forced by a pump into the mould and the matrix, and when solidified, the type is ejected from the mould and moved between knives which trim all four sides. The type are delivered side by side on a specially grooved piece of wood, three feet long, called a "stick," on which they are removed from the machine for inspection. Type are cast at the rate of from ten to two hundred per minute, according to the size, the speed

ATF's main font dividing room, circa 1910

Ready for fonting, the type is checked once again for smooth face, accurate body, and proper alignment.

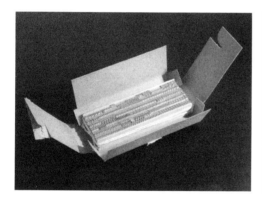

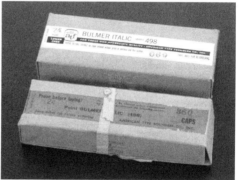

An ATF font of 24-point Bulmer Italic requires one box for the capitals and another for the lower case.

being limited only by the time it takes the metal to solidify. To accelerate this, a stream of cold water is forced through passages surrounding the mould, and a jet of cold air is blown against the outside.[82]

Casting is explained in much greater detail in Rehak's *Practical Typecasting*.

FONTING

An inspector examined each cast type character under a magnifying glass and discarded any flawed pieces. The perfect type was then sent to the "fonting" room, where it was weighed, counted, and packaged for sale. The exact number and placement of every character was dictated by the standard "font scheme" for each face; display types, body types, scripts and title faces were each fonted differently according to how they were most commonly used.

Chapter 10 Endnotes

1   W. J. Kaup, "Modern Automatic Type Making," *American Machinist* 32 (December 16, 1909): 1042, Typographic Library Books FF-5-8, Rare Book and Manuscript Library, Columbia University.

2   "A Demonstration of ATF Craftsmanship: The Entire Lord's Prayer on a Piece of 8-point Type" (envelope), Elizabeth, N.J.: American Type Founders, n.d.

3   "The Entire Lord's Prayer on a Single Type" (four-page booklet to accompany 4-point example), Elizabeth, N.J.: American Type Founders, n.d.

4   Theo Rehak, *Practical Typecasting* (New Castle, Del.: Oak Knoll Books, 1993), 106–07.

5   Frederic W. Goudy, "Type Design: A Homily," *Ars Typographica* 1, no. 4 (Autumn 1934): 21.

6   A. Raymond Hopper, "Fitting: A Vital Step in the Perfection of a Type Face," *Inland Printer* 119, no. 1 (April 1947): 52.

7   Hopper, "Fitting," 50; Mac McGrew, *American Metal Typefaces of the Twentieth Century* (New Castle, Del.: Oak Knoll Books, 1993), 21.

8   Rehak, email message to the author, 6 July 2006.

9   Rehak, *Practical Typecasting*, 181, 202, 204.

10   ATF/Kingsley Archives, Cary Graphic Arts Collection, Rochester Institute of Technology.

11   Richard N. McArthur, "On Cooper Type Faces … With Some Digressions," in *The Book of Oz Cooper: An Appreciation of Oswald Bruce Cooper* (Chicago: Society of Typographic Arts, 1949), 97–98.

12   Rehak, *Practical Typecasting*, 108.

13   Henry Lewis Bullen, "Linn Boyd Benton—The Man and His Work," *Inland Printer* 70, no. 1 (October 1922): 64.

14   Kaup, "Modern Automatic," 1043.

15   L. B. Benton, "Tracing Apparatus," U.S. Patent No. 790,172, May 16, 1905, 5.

16   Benton, "The Making of Type," in *The Building of a Book*, ed. Frederick H. Hitchcock (New York: Grafton Press, 1906), 32–33.

17   Richard C. Marder, in discussion with the author, November 1984.

18   Rehak, in discussion with the author, February 16, 2008.

19   William Addison Dwiggins, *WAD to RR: A Letter about Designing Type* (Cambridge, Mass.: Harvard College Library, 1940), 2.

20   Elizabeth Harris, "ATF & the Smithsonian Institution," *Type & Press* 78 (Fall 1993): 1.

21   Paul Shaw, "On Type: The Century Family," *Fine Print* 7, no. 4 (October 1981): 141.

22   Charles Bigelow, ed., introductory remark to "Century Family," by Paul Shaw, 141.

23   Benton, "Formulae for wax used on patterns," handwritten, n.d. Courtesy of Theo Rehak.

24   David Pankow, "The Rise and Fall of ATF," *Printing History* 43/44, vol. 22, nos. 1 & 2 (2002): 7. See also Gregory Jackson Walters, *ATF: The Auction of the Century, August 24, 1993* (privately printed, n.d.), Cary Graphic Arts Collection, Rochester Institute of Technology.

25   Rehak, *Practical Typecasting*, 111.

26   Benton, "Making of Type," 33.

27   Rehak, *Practical Typecasting*, 110.

28   Rehak, email message to the author, 30 June 2006.

29   Kaup, "Modern Automatic," 1043.

30   Ibid.

31   Rehak, email message to the author, 25 January 2007.

32   Theodore Low De Vinne, *The Practice of Typography: A Treatise on the Processes of Type-Making, the Point System, the Names, Sizes, Styles and Practices of Plain Printing Types* (New York: The Century Co., 1900), 352.

33   Kaup, "Modern Automatic," 1044.

34   Rehak, email message to the author, 10 July 2006.

35   Rehak, *Practical Typecasting*, 116–23.

36   Kaup, "Modern Automatic," 1045.

37   Bullen, "Linn Boyd Benton," 63.

38   Rehak, email message to the author, 17 June 2006.

39   Bullen, "Linn Boyd Benton," 63.

40   Benton, "Making of Type," 34–35.

41   American Type Founders Co., "Benton's Punch Engraving Machine." (advertising brochure, n.d.), 2.

42   Bigelow, "On Type: Form, Pattern, & Texture in the Typographic Image," *Fine Print* 15, no. 2 (April 1989): 77.

43   Kingsley/ATF Type Corp., "ATF-Type-Club" (ad brochure), ca. 1990, ATF/Kingsley Archives, Cary Graphic Arts Collection, Rochester Institute of Technology.

44   Quadrat [Bullen], "Discursions of a Retired Printer, No. VII," *Inland Printer* 38, no. 4 (January 1907): 520.

45   Daniel Berkeley Updike, *Printing Types: Their History, Forms, and Use* (Cambridge, Mass.: Harvard University Press, 1922), 1:11.

46   Bruce Rogers, with James Hendrickson, *Paragraphs on Printing* (New York: William E. Rudge's Sons, 1943), 107.

47   Bigelow, in discussion with the author, June 2007.

48   Rehak, *Practical Typecasting*, 108.

49   Ibid., 115.

50   Ibid., 114.

51   Updike, *Printing Types*, 1:12–13.

52   Ibid., 1:11–12.

53   Goudy, "On Designing a Type-Face," *Dolphin* 1 (1933): 21.

54   Beatrice Warde, "Cutting Types for the Machines: A Layman's Account." *Dolphin* 2 (1935): 67.

55   Carl Purlington Rollins, introduction to "American Type Designers and Their Work" (Chicago: R.R. Donnelley & Sons, 1947), 3.

56   G. W. Ovink, "Back to Humanism in Type Design," *Penrose Annual* 50 (1956): 69.

57   Rehak, *Practical Typecasting*, 108.

58   Bigelow and Jonathan Seybold, "Technology and the Aesthetics of Type," *Seybold Report* 10, no. 24 (August 24, 1981): 5.

59   The explanation given here came from conversations I had with Theo Rehak at his Dale Type foundry in February 2008.

60   Rehak, *Practical Typecasting*, 112.

61 Benton, "Making of Type," 39.

62 Rehak, *Practical Typecasting*, 186–87.

63 Benton, "Making of Type," 35.

64 Benton appears to have been intentionally secretive about how this adjustment worked. He included all the information that an operator would need to know in a document he wrote to accompany a matrix engraving machine sold to the Japanese government (see note 67 below), but not enough to facilitate reverse-engineering the mechanism.

65 Dr. James Eckman to the author, 8 July 1985.

66 Hermann Zapf, in discussion with the author, Rochester, N.Y., August 9, 1985.

67 Benton, "Instructions for Setting-Up the Benton Matrix Engraving Machine, No. 59, Written and Signed by Linn Boyd Benton in March, 1917" (Jersey City, N.J.: American Type Founders Co., 1922), 18, Typographic Library Books FF-5-9, Rare Book and Manuscript Library, Columbia University.

68 Joseph Blumenthal, "The Fitting of Type," *Dolphin* 2 (1935): 71.

69 Benton, "Making of Type," 33.

70 Marder to the author, 21 May 1993.

71 L. B. Benton, "Matrix-Trimming and Similar Machine," U. S. Patent No. 819,842, May 8, 1906, Specification 1.

72 Hopper, "Fitting," 51.

73 Marder, discussion.

74 Blumenthal, "Fitting," 78, 80.

75 Ibid., 80.

76 Rehak, *Practical Typecasting*, 165.

77 Ibid., 5.

78 Rehak, email message to the author, 25 January 2007.

79 Rehak, "Typefounding Artifacts: Type Alignment Gauge 3," http://www.daleguild.com/Artifacts.html.

80 Benton, "Making of Type," 31.

81 Rehak, email message to the author, 25 January 2007.

82 Benton, "Making of Type," 37–38.

The Benton Family's Early Years in Plainfield, New Jersey

ON SEPTEMBER 1, 1897, after a three-year engagement, Morris Benton married Mary Ethel Bottum, the daughter of his father's patent attorney, at Grace Avenue Congregational Church in Milwaukee. Ethel had just turned 20, and although her college education was unfinished, she had her parents' permission to marry. She was an iconoclast, her daughter Caroline said,[1] because she didn't want to wear what she called "white mosquito netting" on her head. But her mother insisted, and she complied, although she had wanted to get married as simply as possible. Even before Morris and Ethel were married, one of Ethel's classmates at the Gilman School had said that she had never known a more devoted couple.

The young couple took up residence in a small, somewhat dingy apartment on Staten Island, ten blocks away from the senior Bentons. Each morning, Morris and his father would meet and take the ferry to New York City. The American Type Founders Co. was located at that time on the southernmost tip of Manhattan. Ethel was alone all day, and when her first daughter, Elizabeth Boyd, was born the following year, she became terribly lonesome. Caroline explained, "She didn't know anybody, not a soul, on Staten Island." Shortly after the baby's birth, the young family moved in with Boyd and Jessie, who had bought a large house at 19 Central Avenue in Tompkinsville. Another daughter, Caroline Everett, was born in 1902. The two families lived together on Staten Island for nine years.

Some time after ATF moved to 300 Communipaw Avenue in Jersey City, New Jersey, in 1903, Boyd and Morris decided to leave Staten Island and move closer to the company. They chose Plainfield, New Jersey, for its schools and because it was famous for its clean artesian well water. In 1906, Boyd rented a home for the whole family at

Morris and Ethel's apartment, Staten Island, 1897

The extended Benton family's first home, 19 Central Avenue, Tompkinsville, Staten Island

Elizabeth Boyd Benton and her grandmother, Jessie Elizabeth Benton, 1899

The Benton homestead at 107 Crescent Avenue, Plainfield, N.J.

131 Crescent Avenue. About two years later, he bought a large Victorian house down the street at 107 Crescent Avenue, with three and a half acres of lawn and gardens. Boyd had always wanted a large family, and both he and Jessie were pleased with the three-generation arrangement. The two men took the 7:20 a.m. Jersey Central train to Jersey City every morning and returned at about 6:30 p.m.[2]

The first floor of the Plainfield house had twin living rooms and a dining room, and Jessie was queen of the kitchen, although she didn't cook—the family always had help. The third floor's three large rooms and several smaller ones were set aside exclusively for Morris and his family. There, Morris and Ethel read aloud current novels such as *The Virginian* by Owen Wister, *The Riverman* by Stewart Edward White, and *The Crisis* by Winston Churchill. They also enjoyed the serials in the *Saturday Evening Post*, and reread from time to time all of Mark Twain.[3]

The Benton family's domestic life was rich and varied. Boyd kept copies of humor magazines such as the British weekly *Punch*, and had them bound. Morris appreciated humor as well. He "would tell an anecdote with a grave face, eyes twinkling, and then after the punch line, break into a sudden, warm grin," Caroline remembered. "He liked American folk wisdom, such as in Mark Twain, and often quoted from him, from Ben Franklin, George Ade or Will Rogers."[4] One of his favorite sayings was, "Them that ain't up on things is usually down on them."

Morris's interest in hobbies was as keen as ever. He took photographs and developed them in his darkroom on the third floor of the Benton home. Morris also amused himself with target shooting, though he did not care for hunting. He had inherited a collection of fourteen guns from his father-in-law and belonged to a local gun club. He kept the guns, oiled and cleaned, locked in the darkroom, along with target records and ammunition. When they were old enough, Morris taught his daughters how to shoot at tin cans.

Music was an important feature of family life in the Benton household, and both of Morris's daughters were encouraged to study the piano. Very much like his father, who expected perfection from mechanical parts, Morris often retuned the piano after the regular piano tuner had left the house. Caroline recalled: "He had the theory that every individual piano had certain tonal areas which needed to be balanced with extra care in the tuning."[5] He owned an Edison phonograph and, later, a Victrola, and loved to listen to Enrico Caruso and most classical music, except Brahms, whom he felt was "insincere." He also owned an Aeolian Orchestrelle, a pump organ with stops that Morris would manipulate to get the tone he wanted, while the paper roll took care of the notes. His daughter Elizabeth remembered, "He used to play *Tannhäuser*, and my little bed upstairs would rock!"[6]

Morris belonged to the American Society of Mechanical Engineers, the National Rifle Association, the Cornell Club of New York City, and the Plainfield Country Club. He attended the Presbyterian Church and was a Republican.[7] Morris and Ethel also belonged to a card club in Plainfield. One Halloween, the club's members invited additional guests to a costume party. Ethel made Morris a jack-o-lantern costume—a big, full ball that covered his head and body. Because he was a fairly small man he also had small feet, which fit into women's shoes for the party. Morris didn't say a word at the party, and no one was able to guess his identity. "They kept looking at his feet," Caroline said, "trying to decide if they were big enough to be a man's … They never guessed who he was."[8]

Morris was a patient man who explained things carefully to his daughters. He drew diagrams for them or, after dinner, would move the salt and pepper shakers around on the table to explain in simple terms some complex piece of machinery. The children had toy pantographs and Morris once electrified a mechanical train for them, before electric trains were readily available. He and his father designed toy blocks and had a carpenter make them out of maple, with edges that were absolutely true. Once

Morris Fuller Benton

Ethel Benton with her daughters, Elizabeth
(left) and Caroline, circa 1910

when Caroline asked her father about his work, he picked up a current magazine and
"pointed out page after page of advertisements and articles using his designs. I was so
proud and excited," she wrote, "and he seemed very pleased at my enthusiasm."[9]
Letters that Morris kept from Clay Belsley, a mechanical engineer from Peoria, Illinois, reveal a lively and playful relationship between the two young men. A letter that
Morris kept from Clarence C. Marder, John Marder's son, asked him for help with an
article he was writing about magic squares for the *Atlantic Monthly* magazine. At the
bottom of the page Clarence wrote: "I am coming over for some gossip one of these
days if you can sandwich in an idle hour among your busy ones."[10]

Ethel made dresses for herself, the children, and their dolls with her two sewing
machines, a lock stitch and a chain stitch. Elizabeth remembered that the dresses
her mother designed and finished were styles ahead of the times. "I can distinctly
remember one of my small friends asking in wonder to see my bloomers that
matched my dress!"[11] Ethel taught her daughters handcrafts, sketching and painting, coached them in tennis and ice skating, and learned to swim with them. When
the girls were in high school she organized a group of Campfire Girls and continued
friendly relations with the group for six years. "She was not only a good executive and kept her part of the house immaculately," Elizabeth remembered, "but she
found time to mother her 'lame ducks' as we called them—to help and counsel other
women less able than herself."[12]

Looking back on her youth, Elizabeth was also impressed with her mother's intelligent attitude toward physical care. Ethel was a student of the early childhood psychologists Friedrich Froebel and Madame Maria Montessori. "When we were sick there

The extended Benton family, circa 1909. From left, Ethel, Elizabeth, Morris, Ethel's mother Caroline ("Kit"), Ethel's father Elias Bottum, young Caroline, and Linn Boyd behind his wife, Jessie.

Ethel Benton, 1915

were always special delicious and nourishing dishes she prepared herself," Elizabeth wrote. "We almost enjoyed our misery."[13] Ethel also taught Elizabeth how to relax when she was going through adolescent difficulties.

Both Morris and Ethel loved the outdoors. He was an avid figure skater and bicyclist, and took the family camping in the Adirondacks for vacations, where they would hike with map and compass. Caroline described one of her father's foolproof methods of finding their way back: "He would take red tags and hang them on the trees, and then coming back, he'd collect the tags again." Later he gave slide shows of the family vacations.

The younger Bentons frequently took Sunday outings in the family car. Caroline felt that her father's interest in automobiles was more than an interest in transportation.

Morris and Ethel with two of their first cars

> The series of cars the family owned, beginning before my birth in 1902, consisted of mechanical problems which my father was "expected" to solve. Each car was expected to run perfectly; my father did all the work on them himself for many years, and careful records were kept on all repairs and adjustments made, in addition to records on fuel consumption, oiling, greasing, tires, etc. Hours might be spent (and much conversation with my mother on the road) tracking down an elusive body squeak, or a strange ping or "birdie" in the engine.[14]

Caroline's story reinforces the notion that Morris's meticulous attention to detail was an essential aspect of his character.

The family's first car, circa 1898, was a Stanley Steamer, and Morris needed a locomotive operator's license to take it on the road. This was followed by a Haynes-Apperson (gasoline) touring car that the family kept until about 1907; a 1902 one-cylinder Oldsmobile two-seater runabout with a top speed of about 20 miles per hour that was licensed until 1914; a four-cylinder Haynes touring car; several Reo touring cars, with a permanent-top Reo coming in about 1925; and then a variety of Buicks and Chevrolets. Boyd, 28 years older than his son, left the driving and repairs to Morris, who would roll himself underneath a car to work on it.

Ethel kept a journal from April 1904 to November 1906 of outings and car repairs, entitled "The Book of the Oldsmobile with the Bentons In It." The journal records both Morris Benton's desire for perfection—"It had been thoroughly cleaned, even to polishing the muffler with stove polish"—and Ethel's whimsy:

> The little black devil who made his home with us inside the machine during our first weeks of ownership and who had seen fit to leave us alone for some time had put his finger on some screw or other and we were missing explosions to beat the band … Thump, thump, thump—"I don't want to go," miss, thump, thump— "I won't go, so there," miss, miss, thump, thump, thump. "Now do go and be a good auto." "But I don't want to," thump, miss, thump, miss, miss, & co.[15]

The dog-shaped letter reads (starting from the tip of the ear on the left): MY DEAR CAROL. DOES THIS LOOK LIKE YOUR NEW DOG. I RECEIVED YOUR DEAR LITTLE LETTER A FEW DAYS AGO AND SOMETHING INSISTED THAT IT MUST BE ANSWERED TODAY. AM SITTING ON THE PORCH AND JUST A MOMENT AGO A RED SQUIRREL RAN UP ONE OF THE TREES. YOUR PAPA IS NOW VISITING UNCLE HARRY. AND DINNIE IS TRYING TO FLY IT. IT WAS NUT AFRAID OF HER A BIT YESTERDAY AND LET IT GO AGAIN. IT WAS A YOUNG ONE JUST LITTLE. COUSIN JEANNIE CAUGHT A RED ONE IN HER HAND. AND LOTS OF LOVE FROM—YOUR GRANDPA. A KISS FOR YOU.

Boyd Benton's letter of July 26, 1908

In 1914 Morris gave the Oldsmobile to the gardener.

Boyd Benton was more sociable than his son. His grandchildren described him as a "big, powerful character." He could recite whole pages of Dickens and would often orate at the dinner table, especially about politics. He was a "single taxer," who did not support the 1913 income tax law, saying, "That's terrible! It's socialism." He would often slap the table to make a point, startling everyone in the process. But Boyd loved the children. When they were young they often sat in his lap before going to bed while he told them stories about his own childhood. He would buy tremendously large Valentines for the girls, placing each in a big box. On at least one occasion, he pretended to go off to catch the train to work as usual on Valentine's Day, but then sneaked back, set the two large boxes up against the house, rang the doorbell, and hid behind a tree to see his granddaughters' faces when they found the surprise. Boyd Benton wrote a letter to Caroline in the shape of a dog on July 26, 1908, when she was about six years old. Even the dog's toenails are apparent! The letter reads starting from the tip of the dog's ear on the left:

> My dear Carol, Does this look like your new dog? I received your dear
> little letter a few days ago and something insisted that it must be answered
> today. Am sitting on the porch and just a moment ago a red squirrel ran up

Boyd Benton using his sock-knitting machine

one of the trees. Our papa is now visiting Uncle Harry Pond. Cousin Jeannie cought a robbin [*sic*] in her hand yesterday, and let it go again. It was a
young one just learning to fly. It was not afraid of her a bit. I would like to
see you now. This is his nose. A kiss for you.

For exercise Boyd Benton bought a croquet set and had the lawn rolled often. Morris
and his father were very good at the game and taught the girls how to play. "Grandpa
was very scientific about it," Elizabeth remembered.

He taught us how to make split shots, like in billiards, so that one ball
would go one way and the other ball would go the other way. And when he
couldn't see very well, he used to have us tie a handkerchief on the wicket.[16]

Using this method, Boyd could still make shots from 30 or 40 feet away.

During World War I, Boyd knit socks in the evenings for the soldiers. He had invented
a sock-knitting machine which he could easily operate, although by that time he was
already nearly blind, according to a handwritten notation on the back of a photograph
of him using the machine.[17] His wife Jessie cast off the socks and finished them. "He'd
crank away and the socks would come out," Caroline said. "He'd get the yarn free from
the Red Cross."[18] Boyd donated several hundred pairs of socks through Caroline's
school to help the war effort. At one time Theo Rehak owned the original patent for
Benton's sock-knitting machine in his collection of ATF memorabilia.[19]

Chapter 11 Endnotes

1   Caroline Benton Gregg, in discussion with the author, Milwaukee, March 20, 1984.

2   Caroline Benton Gregg, "Personal Remembrances of My Father, Morris Fuller Benton," typewritten manuscript, n.d., 9.

3   Ibid., 6–7.

4   Ibid., 9.

5   Ibid., 8.

6   Elizabeth Swain, telephone interview with the author July 6, 1985.

7   "Benton, Morris Fuller," 15 January 1951, typewritten, for the *National Cyclopedia of American Biography* (New York: James T. White and Company).

8   Gregg, discussion.

9   Gregg, "Remembrances," 10.

10   Clarence C. Marder to Morris Benton, New York City, n.d.

11   Elizabeth Swain, "Mary Ethel Bottum," typewritten manuscript, n.d.

12   Ibid.

13   Ibid.

14   Gregg, "Remembrances," 4.

15   Mary Ethel Bottum Benton, "The Book of the Oldsmobile with the Bentons In It," handwritten diary, Apr. 1904–Nov. 1906, copy.

16   Swain, interview.

17   "Nearly blind" is written in pencil on one of the original prints of a photograph of Linn Boyd Benton operating the machine.

18   Gregg, discussion.

19   Theo Rehak to the author, 23 February 2006.

Prosperity and Hard Times

W HEN ROBERT W. NELSON was elected general manager of ATF in 1894, 12 of
the original foundries were still producing type.[1] By 1900, six foundries were
manufacturing type, in St. Louis, Philadelphia, Chicago, Cincinnati, Boston, and
New York.[2] Consolidating these into one location became a priority of Nelson's when
he was elected president of ATF in March 1901, and by 1903 he had installed both
ATF's general offices and a new physical plant in a new building at 300 Communipaw
Avenue in Jersey City, New Jersey.

Realizing that the advent of the composing machines in the early 1900s would eventually cause foundry type sales to plummet, Nelson was convinced that ATF should
diversify its product line into other markets besides type. Since he was especially fond
of the type department he continued to encourage the production of new designs, but
at the same time he increased the scope of ATF, introducing products such as presses,
composing room furniture and equipment, inks, paper cutters, and stitchers made by
other manufacturers.

ATF collective specimen books had replaced the type books of the individual foundries, and now the company also had to provide information about the machinery,
equipment, and supplies it offered. For example, as early as 1896, an illustrated
catalogue was printed in Spanish of machinery, equipment, and supplies, to supplement a special ATF specimen book of types with appropriate accents that had been
produced for Spanish-speaking customers in Latin and South America. "Nelson had

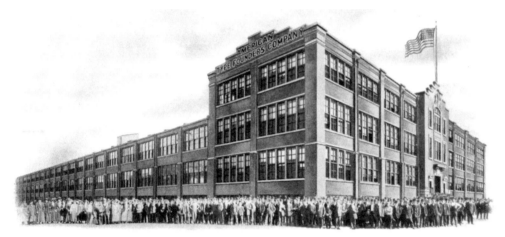

ATF's Jersey City manufacturing plant

An artist's rendering of ATF's Jersey City building

5,000 of each book distributed in person by a trusted Spanish-speaking salesman," Bullen wrote in 1926, "whose work, during a most profitable year abroad, laid the foundation for the present immense business in those countries."[3]

A number of ATF specimen books of various sizes and page counts were produced almost every year between 1895 and 1913. Then smaller, supplementary catalogues were issued until 1923, when ATF's most famous specimen book was printed.

The company's hefty, green, 1,186-page 1900 *Desk Book* boasted that ATF carried "Everything for the Printer." It measured 5.63 by 8.5 inches and featured 165 pages of printing machinery and supplies in addition to 682 pages of type, 33 of which were for foreign languages: German, Hebrew, Greek, Rabbinic, Armenian, and Russian. The book also included music type, signs of all kinds, borders, ornaments, cast and electrotyped cuts and initial letters, brass rule, wood type, and 43 pages of "useful information for printers."

ATF specimen books

The slimmer (292-page), black 1903 specimen book explained and illustrated ATF's new "American Lining System," which insured that types from different fonts would base align (at the bottom of the x-height) when composed together on a single line.

It's something that's *assumed* by most folks dealing with type today, but prior to "lining" systems, virtually no two 12-point faces could be composed together on a single line without some vertical adjustment (us[ing] strips of paper or leads) to get their so-called base lines to appear visually aligned in the printed piece. American Type Founders settled on three basic alignments: one for "common" types (the majority of the faces they manufactured), one for "title" faces (all-cap fonts which required little space for ascenders and descenders), and last, the "script" line for scripts and other faces with very long descenders.[4]

Another ample (1,181-page), red *American Line Type Book* was published in 1906. The various editions of ATF's red 1912 *American Specimen Book of Type Styles* were even fatter, containing between 1,301 and 1,323 pages. The tag line "Originator of Type Fashions" appeared on the title page, and this one claimed to showcase only up-to-date styles:

Another Specimen Book as big as this one might be compiled of type faces which were in regular demand a few years ago, but which cannot now be used profitably. Not the least service the American Type Founders Company has rendered to the printers is that of discarding hundreds of series of type faces which do not conform to the present higher standard of typographic taste which has been created and fostered by the "Originator of Type Fashions."[5]

The 1912 book included 15 pages of foreign language and music fonts. Its 148-page printing equipment section was divided into three categories: machinery and supplies, modernized furniture for the composing room and press room, and steel and iron equipments.

In 1923, ATF issued a blue 1,148-page *Specimen Book and Catalogue*. Sixty thousand copies were printed entirely from type and brass rules (no electrotypes of the original forms were used) in ATF's Specimen Printing Department, at a cost of about $300,000. The Preface insisted that all of ATF's type designs, borders and decorative pieces were either original or were purchased, and that the copied designs prevalent in the offerings of composing machine manufacturers were for the most part copies of ATF's original type designs.

> Whether these copied designs are sold in matrices or in fonts of type the American Type Founders Company receives not the slightest compensation; but it asks printers who use composing machines to realize that whatever merit any machine composition may have in the matter of typographic design, such merit is, with few exceptions, derived from designs original with the American Type Founders Company; and printers are asked to give the credit to the originator and not to manufacturers of typesetting machines and other copiers.[6]

The 1923 *Specimen Book and Catalogue* contained more than 250 pages of presses, inks, binding equipment, and composing room equipment and furniture in addition to its vast selection of type. In contrast, of the few remaining specimen books that ATF produced after 1923, the most elaborate was its 1934 *Book of American Types: ATF Standard Faces*, at a slim 207 pages. Supplemental price lists were produced periodically.

For awhile the Benton engraving machine itself was successfully sold to select customers. In 1899, ATF's Rose and Duane Street office in Manhattan printed a Japanese-language notice regarding the Benton punch-cutting machine.[7] In anticipation of the expiration of the machine's patent, the foundry apparently was advertising an earlier (and outdated) version of it to customers who wouldn't become competitors. ATF records showed that nearly three dozen Benton engraving machines were produced and eventually sold and/or leased.[8]

By 1912, according to the Japan Association of Graphic Arts Technology (JAGAT), the Japanese Ministry of Finance Printing Bureau had obtained a Benton machine for government work.[9] An incomplete journal written by Benton's foreman, John Bauer, confirmed that ATF supplied the Japanese government with two machines in the early 1920s.[10] Soon three commercial enterprises in Japan obtained original Benton machines: Tokyo Tsukiji Printing and Sanseido Co., Ltd., in 1922; and Toppan

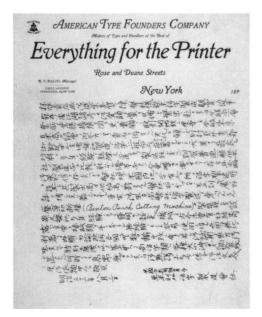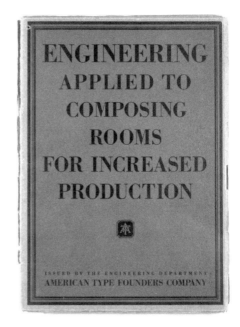

Printing Co., Ltd., shortly afterwards. The Benton machine was a boon to the Japanese printing industry, not only improving the quality of its printing type, but also enabling "big reform to a printing type style of handwriting design,"[11] according to an online translation of JAGAT's history of printing in Japan. In 1948 Sanseido and Dai Nippon Printing Co. began manufacturing replicas of the original Benton engravers for the domestic printing industry. Today the Engineering Department at Chiba University still has a Japanese version of the Benton engraver in its collection of 77 early media-related artifacts.[12]

In 1913, ATF established an Efficiency Department[13] to help customers increase production, especially in the composing room. "Its aim was high, its purpose determined, and the results achieved beyond the fondest hopes and dreams of those whom the Department was intended to benefit,"[14] reads a 64-page promotional booklet (circa 1926), no doubt written by Henry Lewis Bullen. The booklet's logo, "Concentration and Efficiency are Inseparable" also suggests Bullen's hand. Stevens L. Watts, who worked at ATF for many years, gave Bullen credit for creating and managing the department, calling it his principal accomplishment.[15] "Bullen's genius as an inventor was called into play," Watts wrote, "resulting in the revolutionary line of Cost Cut Equipment. Patents for a number of items in the line were assigned to American Type Founders Company by the inventor, Henry L. Bullen of 18 Shepard Avenue, Newark, N.J."[16]

The distance between ATF's Communipaw Avenue plant and the nearest shipping docks on the Hudson River was just a little over a mile, and the Lehigh Valley Railroad ran alongside the building, so ATF was an obvious choice for war work. Normal ATF activities were interrupted by the country's entrance into World War I in 1917

Ideal Alleys formed with American Cut-Cost Type
Cabinets. They discount the Payroll in a com-
mon-sense way and turn Loss into Profit

From ATF's Engineering Department booklet

and, according to Watts, "the company's facilities and those of its suppliers were largely converted to the war effort."[17]

In the meantime, William M. Kelly, a printer and mechanic from Kansas who had also been an overseas equipment salesman for ATF,[18] invented a small, two-revolution automatic cylinder press in 1911 that he believed would meet the requirements of most commercial printers. After convincing Nelson that the press would be profitable, Kelly developed it into a three-roller, two-revolution flat-bed cylinder press with an automatic feeder and jogger.[19] ATF introduced the first model of the press, called the Style B, in 1914. It had a 19½ by 22⅜-inch bed and could handle a variety of sizes and papers from onion-skin to four-ply poster board. Its top speed was 3,600 impressions per hour. Fred Williams, editor of *Type & Press*, explained in 1985 how the press worked:

> The Kelly press employs a small cylinder revolving in stationary bearings over a horizontal bed that supports the type form. The bed moves back and forth under the inking rollers with a reciprocal movement beneath the rotating cylinder. Grippers, closing on a sheet of paper, hold it against the turning cylinder, which applies sufficient pressure to print as it passes over the inked form. Shooflies then lift the printed sheet off the cylinder after being released by the grippers and pass it on to the delivery.[20]

Printers were so enthusiastic about the new press that more than 2,000 were sold before it was advertised. Sheet detectors automatically stopped the press if a sheet was torn or crooked, and corrections or changes could be made right on the press bed without having to remove the form. By 1922 more than 2,500 Kelly B presses had been sold, and ATF was producing 50 presses per month at the Jersey City factory. This success

Manufacturing plant of the Kelly Press Division

The Style B Kelly Press

led to the Kelly #2 in 1921, which could print a 22 by 34-inch sheet and had a top speed of 3,000 impressions per hour. In order to meet the demand for Kelly presses, ATF built a new three-story plant in Elizabeth, New Jersey, in 1923–24, the Kelly Press Division, which provided 280,000 square feet of floor space.[21] Two years later an additional 20,000 square feet of manufacturing space was added in another building.[22]

The Style A or "Baby" Kelly was introduced in 1925. It could print from the size of a postcard to a 13½ by 20-inch sheet, at speeds up to 4,500 impressions per hour. The Kelly Automatic jobber was introduced in 1925, followed four years later by the Kelly #1. The Kelly Clipper was developed in 1938, one of the first presses to come with a chain delivery. By the time of Kelly's death in 1949, about 11,000 Kelly presses had been sold.

During the mid-1920s the sales of Kellys soared, and ATF's annual report for 1926 showed the largest profit in the company's history. But Robert Nelson died in July of that same year, and soon afterwards the company's fortunes began to change. Frank Belknap Berry, one of the founders of the Cleveland Type Foundry ("a radical among radicals as far as type designing was concerned" because it dared to bring out a number of extreme typefaces soon after it was formed in 1879[23]), replaced Nelson as

Robert W. Nelson.

Joseph F. Gillick

president in August, and by September, opposing factions on the board of directors had already begun to disagree about the company's future.

Joseph F. Gillick was elected the president of ATF in 1927.[24] One of his first decisions was to buy out Barnhart Brothers & Spindler of Chicago, which had been an ATF subsidiary since 1911. The BB&S type foundry was closed and its equipment shipped to ATF in Jersey City and Elizabeth.[25] By 1929 ATF's sales again showed a profit, but the comeback was short-lived. The Depression began to seriously affect ATF in 1931: working hours were cut, inventories reduced, and financial reserves depleted. By 1932 sales were down by 25 percent, and salaries had to be reduced. When major accounting errors turned up in the company's books showing that assets had been exaggerated and the company had serious liabilities,[26] Gillick resigned.

Thomas Roy Jones, a businessman with no experience in type founding, was put into the position of company president. Soon afterwards, Bullen submitted a report to Jones that stated, "Since Nelson's death there has been no leadership."[27] The report went on to outline the problems of the Type Design Committee, and ended with a pledge of support for Jones as president. But by October 1933, Jones had filed a voluntary petition for bankruptcy. ATF was placed under the control of the association of banks to which it owed money, and was forced to focus on decreasing its debt instead of honoring its contracts.[28] "To understand the desperation of its situation," David Pankow wrote in a brief history of ATF, "it may be useful to consider that year-end figures for 1933 showed that type sales were 29.2 percent of its 1926 sales and Kelly press sales were just 6.8 percent of what they had been in 1926."[29]

In 1935, ATF's manufacturing division and general offices moved to the Kelly Press factory in Elizabeth, New Jersey, and the following year the Jersey City plant was sold for only $250,000.[30] As of the summer of 1936, Bullen's Typographic Museum and Library was still located in Jersey City,[31] but soon afterwards it was moved to Columbia University, where it remains today. These extreme measures paid off for the company, because, according to Pankow, "by means of drastic cost-cutting, centralization of resources, and the implementation of commission-based compensation for the sales force, ATF clawed its way back from the brink, or out of the melting pot, whichever metaphor you prefer."[32] In 1936 the court approved plans for its reorganization. Type founding was no longer to be the mainstay of ATF's business; in 1938 the company bought the Webendorfer-Wills Company, manufacturer of lithographic presses.[33] However the intervention of World War II forced a complete change of emphasis for ATF. "Eventually the main plant was entirely converted to war work, and it is reliably reported that even some of the faithful Barth casters were drummed into service to produce firing pins."[34]

Morris Benton's daughter Caroline attributed some of ATF's problems to a lack of planning. "Everybody was getting old, and I think that was the trouble … It was very short-sighted not to take in younger men and train them, and they didn't. They were satisfied with getting their profits."[35] ATF stock had been selling at more than $100 a share but plunged into the $30s during the Depression. All ATF directors owned stock in the company and didn't take large salaries because of the dividends. When the value of the stock fell, Boyd Benton held onto his shares. After he died in 1932, Morris "sold out pretty fast. He couldn't afford to hold it and see it go down, he said."[36]

Chapter 12 Endnotes

1   Henry Lewis Bullen, "Robert Wickham Nelson: An Intimate History," *Inland Printer* 77, no. 6 (September 1926): 905–06.

2   American Type Founders Company, *Desk Book of Type and Printing Materials* (San Francisco: ATF Co., 1900), preliminary page.

3   Bullen, "Nelson," 906.

4   Fred C. Williams, ed., "The Issue of Several Sizes of Type on One Body!" *Type & Press* 68 (Spring 1991): 1.

5   ATF Co., *American Specimen Book of Type Styles, Complete Catalogue of Printing Machinery and Printing Supplies* (Jersey City, N.J.: ATF Co., 1912), v.

6   ATF Co., *Specimen Book and Catalogue, 1923* (Jersey City, N.J.: ATF Co., 1923), 8–9.

7   An original copy of this document is part of RIT's Cary Graphic Arts Collection, courtesy of Caroline Benton Gregg.

8   Theo Rehak, *Practical Typecasting* (New Castle, Del.: Oak Knoll Books, 1993), 107.

9   Yoshihiko Sawada, tr. Yahoo! Japan, "It Is Photocomposition Style of Handwriting and Digital Style of Handwriting (11)," Japan Association of Graphic Arts Technology, n.d., http://www.jagat.or.jp/story_memo_view.asp?StoryID=7745 (accessed April 10, 2008).

10   Rehak, *Practical Typecasting*, 107.

11   Sawada, "It Is."

12   Takashi Ono, tr. Yahoo! Japan, "The Industrial History That a Thing Recites," Engineering Department, Chiba University, n.d., http://www.chiba-u.ac.jp/message/prs/koho118/tokushu07.htm (accessed February 5, 2009).

13   ATF Co., *Specimen Book,* 1923, 12.

14   ATF Co., Engineering Department, *American Cut-Cost System of Printing Plant Equipment* (Elizabeth, N.J.: ATF Co., ca. 1926), 7.

15   On the title page of the booklet itself, however, C.W. Kellogg is listed as manager.

16   Stevens Lewis Watts, "A Tribute to the Memory of Henry Lewis Bullen and His Work," a lecture in the series *Heritage of the Graphic Arts*, New York, March 30, 1966 (Warren County, Va.: The Privateer Press, n.d.): 13.

17   Watts, "Tribute," 13.

18   ATF Co., *The Kelly Press* (Elizabeth, N.J.: ATF Co., Kelly Press Division, 1927), 14.

19   James Eckman, *The Heritage of the Printer*, vol. 1 (Philadelphia: North American Publishing Co., 1965), 71.

20   Williams, ed., "The Rise and Fall of the Kelly Press," *Type & Press* 44 (Spring 1985): 1.

21   Eckman, *Heritage*, 72.

22   ATF, *Cut-Cost*, 5.

23   "A New Leader in Our Industry," *Inland Printer* 78, no. 1 (October 1926): 111. According to this article, the Cleveland Type Foundry brought out "a number of sensational typefaces in the extreme of the fashions of that twisted-rule period."

24   "American Type Company's New President," *American Printer* 85, no. 6 (December 1927), 88.

25   David Walker Mallison, "Henry Lewis Bullen and the Typographic Library and Museum of the American Type Founders Company" (Ph.D. diss., Columbia University, 1976): 206.

26 Thomas Roy Jones, "Printing in America—and ATF" (New York: Newcomen Society of England, 1948), 23.

27 Mallison, 210.

28 Mallison, 212.

29 David Pankow, "The Rise and Fall of ATF," *Printing History* 43/44, vol. 22, nos. 1 & 2 (2002): 9.

30 Eckman, *Heritage*, 72.

31 Morris Fuller Benton to N. J. Werner, 9 June 1936.

32 Pankow, "Rise and Fall," 15.

33 Jones, "Printing," 23–24.

34 Pankow, "Rise and Fall," 10; Milton Anderson to Pankow, 4 November 1994.

35 Caroline Benton Gregg, in discussion with the author, Milwaukee, March 20, 1984.

36 Ibid.

The Typographic Climate
in the Early Twentieth Century

T HE TYPOGRAPHIC INDUSTRY went through profound changes during the careers of the two Bentons, who in turn played pivotal roles in bringing about those changes. Linn Boyd Benton's invention and perfection of the mechanical matrix-engraving system paved the way for the composing machine industry, which ultimately replaced the type founding industry itself. Morris Benton affected the course of type history at least as much as his father with his historic type revivals, type families, and innovative advertising type designs, which were rapidly copied for use on the composing machines.

Before the Linotype machine came into general use, most type designers were affiliated with printing establishments or type foundries, and their types were usually designed for a specific purpose. As Morris Benton came into his own at ATF in the early 1900s, the typographic climate was radically changing: the type founders' main business, supplying newspapers with composition type, was being taken over by the composing machines. Even so, since the best type designers were working for established type foundries, the composing machine manufacturers looked to the foundries for new ideas. This was to be expected. "Two stages in the evolution of type design can be recognized following the introduction of each new technology," Charles Bigelow wrote in 1983.

> First, there is a period of imitation, in which the outstanding letterforms of the previous typographic generation serve as models for the new designs. Second, as designers grow more confident and familiar with the new medium, innovative designs emerge that are not merely imitative but exploit the strengths and explore the limitations of the medium.[1]

It wasn't until the 1920s that composing machine manufacturers began to produce their own original type designs,[2] and their really first-class original designs didn't come until the late 1920s and 1930s.[3] Richard N. McArthur, the sales manager of Barnhart Brothers & Spindler, explained: "The oldtime type founders had been guilty of taking freely from each other, and the typesetting machine makers all got their starts by taking over bodily the best-selling foundry faces."[4] For example, even though in 1900 the English Monotype Corporation's production team already included letter draftsman Fritz Max Steltzer and punch-cutter Theodor Bisser, for the next 22 years they concentrated on simply imitating foundry types.[5] Chicago type designer Oz Cooper said of the "slug machine folks" in the U.S.: "They remind me of an old vaudeville joke: 'We write all our own songs. Whenever we hear a good one, we write it.'"[6]

ADVERTISING TYPOGRAPHY

An important development in the 1920s was the introduction of advertising typographers and advertising agencies. Previously, advertisements were typically placed directly with the newspapers or magazines that would design and print them. A publication's compositors would set up ads as they saw fit, using the typefaces that were readily available in the composing room. Newspapers did not stock a wide variety of types because the average printer would rather use the type he had than buy new type for every job, so type choices were limited. It was natural for a new business model to evolve out of this situation—advertising agencies gave businesses much greater freedom in ad design.

With the ad agency came advertising photographers and artists, as well as the demand for new, "exciting" typefaces. The Linotype machine couldn't set display sizes, so type shops had to buy foundry type for the display faces they needed. The growing demand for appropriate advertising faces prompted the type founders and eventually the typesetting machine companies to develop new type styles. New typefaces were expected to help sell products, appealing not only to ad agencies but to businesses, printers, and especially the general public. "Advertising demands more of type—in variety, in novelty, in eye appeal—than any other use to which it is put," John Murphy wrote in his 1936 *Inland Printer* article about Morris Benton.

> It puts type in the position of *having* to produce results—that is, of having to win the attention of the reader to the message that it clothes. Presumably all type is intended to be read, wherever it is used. A book is printed to be read, but if the book does not sell, rarely is the type blamed for the apathy.[7]

However, if a printed advertisement didn't sell a product, very often the type was blamed for the failure. This put pressure on the ad agencies to obtain new types, on designers to design them, and ultimately on type foundries to produce them. Thus the foundries had a new market. Robert Nelson at ATF quickly picked up on the new trend, and encouraged the type design department to follow through. As Henry Lewis Bullen claimed,

> Undeniably, the greater effectiveness of printing in advertising, the greater is the demand for printing. This is the basic idea in Nelson's policy: to increase the demand for types by increasing the demand for printing. Nelson moves his type families as generals move their divisions, not haphazardly, but with deliberation.[8]

To ensure harmonious layouts, ad agencies at first bought type families instead of single fonts. But Cheltenham Bold and Goudy Bold outsold Cheltenham Old Style and Goudy Old Style, their parent designs, because they became popular for headlines in advertising. This led to the development of a category of type dedicated strictly to advertising purposes, called "publicity types." While their use may have been limited to headlines and eye-catching call-outs, they had to be as well designed as any type.

TYPE DESIGNERS

So during Morris Benton's career, the type designing field expanded. Searching for new types, the composing machine manufacturers called on independent type designers in addition to the type foundries. Frederic W. Goudy was perhaps the most well-known of the independent American designers, but he was by no means the only one. In his 1947 book *Type for Books and Advertising*, Eugene M. Ettenberg credited 22 type designers with what he considered the major 20th-century typefaces up to that time.[9] Two of them—De Vinne and Updike—were not actually type designers, but made "so important a contribution to the literature of world typography that they could not fairly be excluded."[10] He gave short biographies and briefly outlined the contributions of the type designers in the following order:

Will Bradley
Theodore Low De Vinne
Bertram G. Goodhue
Daniel Berkeley Updike
Frederic W. Goudy
Bruce Rogers
Morris Fuller Benton
Thomas Maitland Cleland
Lucian Bernhard
Rudolph Ruzickca
Eric Gill
Rudolf Koch
Stanley Morison
George William Jones
Frederic Warde

Emil Rudolf Weiss
Robert Hunter Middleton
William Addison Dwiggins
Jan van Krimpen
Warren Chappell
Joseph Blumenthal
Victor Hammer

Another listing of Benton's contemporaries comes from a 1947 R. R. Donnelley exhibition entitled American Type Designers and Their Work, which recorded more than 500 type designs by 46 men and one woman. All of the American type designers chosen for Ettenberg's book were represented in the exhibition, as well as Linn Boyd Benton, Wadsworth A. Parker, Robert E. Smith, Willard T. Sniffin, and Gerry Powell from the American Type Founders Company; Sidney Gaunt, Carl Steven Junge, Richard N. McArthur, Ralph Fletcher Seymour, Robert Wiebking, and John Zimmerman of Barnhart Brothers & Spindler; Ernst Frederick Detterer and William E. Fink of the Ludlow Typograph Co.; C. H. Griffith at Mergenthaler Linotype; Sol Hess of the Monotype Company; and Elizabeth Colwell, Tommy Thompson, and Oswald Cooper, among others.

How did Morris Benton compare with other designers? Although most of his typefaces were not attributed to him in ATF publications, Benton was generally regarded as a prolific type designer. In his introduction to the 1947 R. R. Donnelley exhibition catalogue, Carl Purlington Rollins wrote, "It is unfortunate that the names of the designers of the types put out by the American Type Founders Company have not been preserved except in rare instances."[11] Yet the catalogue goes on to list 178 of Morris Benton's type designs!

Ettenberg wrote about the Donnelley exhibition in the May 1948 *American Printer* magazine, crediting Morris Benton with "the greatest number of type faces designed by any one American."[12] But 23 years later, Alexander Lawson maintained that "this was the period when such figures as Frederic W. Goudy, Bruce Rogers, Daniel B. Updike, and Carl Rollins were building reputable careers. Goudy attained recognition as the foremost American type designer of his time, while Benton remained relatively obscure to most of his contemporaries."[13]

Why this incongruity? Most likely it is because Morris Benton worked for ATF his entire professional life, which had a profound impact on what he produced. He needed to design types that would sell, or, as Murphy put it, would "satisfy thousands of printers and tens of thousands of discriminating buyers of printing."[14] Freelance type designers such as Frederic W. Goudy did not have the same imperative since they worked for commissions. In the process they became experts at promoting themselves.

Bullen revealed his feelings on the subject in a February 14, 1927, letter to Beatrice Warde, his assistant at ATF's Typographic Library and Museum from 1922 to 1925:[15]

> You mention "Publicity." Things related to the vital interests of printing receive little of that, outside of the allied industry. On the other hand scarce a dozen initiates—the playboys of typography—whose yearly product might be carried in a wheelbarrow, know how to get columns of the very best kind of publicity for their perfectly innocent, if innocuous purpose— the glorification of themselves. Little, sweet and perfectly proper playthings become "masterpieces," provided you print few enough of them on hand-made paper, while works of pith and moment, essential to the world's work and used tremendously, are "unhonored," though their production is quite beyond the capacity of the much lauded playboys. The truth is that the critics in our literary supplements, etc., don't know much about print-ing, but have learned the names of the playboys, and it's a case of "If it has _____'s colophon it is _____!" (Here add adjectives ad lib.)[16]

Another reason that ATF did not generally promote the work of its employees was explained by Theo Rehak in his 2004 book *The Fall of ATF*. The company's managers (including, most likely, the Bentons) were Masons, keeping apart from the mostly Catho-lic workers.[17] While Freemasonry today has become less of a secret society and more of a "society with secrets,"[18] during the early to mid 20th century, one of its chief charac-teristics, at least to outsiders, was its tendency towards privacy. Apparently ATF's man-agement ran the company with a policy of keeping quiet about processes and people.

Morris Benton and Frederic W. Goudy

Goudy has been called "the greatest type designer in the world,"[19] and "America's widely known and respected type designer."[20] Even Laurance B. Siegfried, the editor of the *American Printer* magazine from December 1929 to December 1940, in his remarks for the ninth annual Frederic W. Goudy Distinguished Lecture in Typogra-phy in 1977 at the Rochester Institute of Technology, commented that, "with the pos-sible exception of Bodoni—I never was able to check this or run it down—he [Goudy] did design more type faces than anybody in the history of the Graphic Arts."[21]

Goudy was warm, outgoing, and ready to lend a hand. Aspiring typographers were welcome to visit Deepdene, his private studio in the Catskill Mountains in New York, where he was never too busy to talk. He made friends easily. Morris Benton, on the other hand, was reserved. William Gregan, who worked at ATF with Morris Benton, remembered that Benton "wouldn't say two words, when none would do."[22] It is no wonder that Goudy became famous while Benton remained obscure.

Benton and Goudy also differed in the way they approached their work. Trained as a letterer, Goudy at first felt that type designers should be inspired by early hand-written letter forms, and complained in 1918 that types "as produced by the founders are not based on a study of classic models of the times before printing …"[23] However, by 1934 he had changed his mind:

> One writer speaking of modern type design says, "It is doubtful whether the type designer benefits from a close study of hand lettering," meaning of course a study of the MS. hands of the past. For myself, in the main I am inclined to agree with him. I do find manuscript letters intensely interesting, but at the same time only occasionally do they suggest new type expressions to me. As a general thing I prefer to get my suggestions from a study of the earlier types that appeal to me.[24]

A few years later Goudy admitted that his familiarity with early printed specimens was severely limited, but that in fact, he drew his letters freehand.[25]

> I find it so difficult to concentrate my thoughts when faced with a wealth of information contained in a large library that I have practically limited my research to the materials in my own modest collection, picking freely from sources within easy reach and making the most of things close at hand instead of searching for less accessible matter.[26]

Morris Benton took a completely different approach, since a wide range of early type specimens were easily accessible to him in ATF's extensive Typographic Library and Museum. Benton studied the original works of the masters and based his type revivals on them. While Benton studied, Goudy wrote. "For more than thirty years he was the most listened to and widely read public spokesman about esthetics in type design and lettering,"[27] wrote one of his biographers. Goudy's Village Press (1903–39) won several awards for its fine books by various authors, including himself. He even apologized in 1934, as editor of the periodical *Ars Typographica*, for being so verbose:

> The Editor realizes the over-large amount of his own matter introduced both in text and types, the reason being that they were ready to hand, and he hopes that the articles not by his hand which are presented will be found sufficiently interesting to mitigate the effect of "too much Goudy."[28]

Despite, or perhaps because of his verbosity, Goudy was much loved in the industry. "It is because he is the truest embodiment of that familiar yet vague thing we call friendship," Paul Standard wrote in 1936. "Seeing him for the first time, any stranger must feel that Goudy is the friend he's been seeking all his life. For here is a man who doesn't take himself or his work too seriously."[29]

Goudy and Benton must have met at some point because, as he recorded in *A Half Century of Type Design & Typography*, Goudy made "frequent visits to the Company, then located in Jersey City."[30]

According to the R. R. Donnelley exhibition catalogue, Goudy's first typeface was Camelot, produced in 1896 by the Dickinson Type Foundry, ATF's Boston branch foundry.[31] Correspondence regarding the patent for Camelot Old Style suggests that it was designed by Goudy (living in Chicago at the time) and modified by J. W. Phinney (manager of the Dickinson foundry) to make it useable in type.[32] It may be that Goudy drew the upper case and Phinney added the lower case.[33] Camelot Old Style was patented on February 27, 1900 (U.S. Patent D32,298); F. W. Goudy and J. W. Phinney are listed as the patent holders.[34]

Some time after Camelot came out, Robert Nelson asked Goudy to design another face for ATF to produce, not an uncommon request at the time. When his preliminary drawings were submitted to the Type Designing Department, Benton or someone under him redrew some of the letters. Even though this was a common and necessary practice (see Chapter 10), Goudy became furious. "The first proofs of my design from the foundry showed differences from my drawings," he wrote. "I immediately took the matter up with Nelson and reminded him of his promise that my design would be followed exactly."[35] Nelson sided with Goudy, but Benton did manage to retain a few changes in the letters, and the type, Goudy Old Style, was produced in 1915. "I am almost satisfied that the design is a good one," Goudy wrote, "marred only by the short descenders which I allowed the American Type Founders to inveigle me into giving p, q, g, j, and y—though only under protest."[36]

The 1947 R. R. Donnelley exhibition catalogue listed three other ATF faces in the Goudy family that Goudy designed: Goudy Old Style Italic (1915), Goudy Cursive (1916),[37] and Goudytype (1916).[38] But it was Benton who developed Goudy Old Style into an extensive family of type, with nine additional variations by 1927:

Goudy Bold (1916)
Goudy Bold Italic (1919)
Goudy Catalogue (1919)
Goudy Catalogue Italic (1921)
Goudy Extrabold (1927)
Goudy Extrabold Italic (1927)
Goudy Handtooled, with Wadsworth A. Parker (1922)
Goudy Handtooled Italic, with Wadsworth A. Parker (1922)
Goudy Title (1918)[39]

Goudy did not receive any commission for these variations because he had sold his original drawings outright to ATF. Benton's first variation, Goudy Bold, became one of ATF's most popular faces. Frederic Goudy acknowledged that Goudy Bold was "a face which seems to be more successful than [he] could have anticipated," and while he admitted that it was not his design, he didn't feel that Benton should have received credit for it. He explained in 1922:

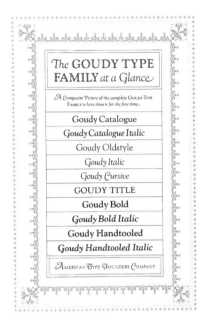

> It is the writer's contention that simply thickening or thinning an existing
> type, or making it wider or narrower, is not real design. A letter should
> be thought of at the outset as possessing a particular character in which
> weight and widths are mere details in its presentation.[40]

J. L. Frazier, editor of *The Inland Printer* from April 1928 to May 1951 and author
of its monthly "Specimen Review," would have disagreed. "A bold face variation," he
wrote, "requires an entirely different treatment than that necessary in the basic design,
and almost as much originality."[41]

Goudy captured what he called the "particular character" of the letters in his typeface revivals by drawing them freehand, without rulers, compasses, or photographic
enlargements. He "not only insisted that he was right to take such freedoms in designing types; he thought all designers should."[42] Goudy explained his freehand designing
methods in a 1933 article he wrote for the *Dolphin*, "On Designing a Type-Face,"[43]
and a two-page photo spread in the May 1938 *American Printer* magazine showed
how he produced his types.[44] Morris Benton, on the other hand, did not document
his method of designing typefaces at ATF. Nevertheless, one of Goudy's biographers,
D. J. R. Bruckner, implied that Benton's methods were not as good as Goudy's:

> At the time, the foundries had many people who were adroit in changing
> older faces in small ways so the foundries could justify selling them as new
> faces. If one accepted such small adjustments as invention, we would have
> to say that Morris Benton of American Type Founders created at least two
> hundred faces. (In fact he made some changes to a few famous old types
> that, to adapt Dr. Johnson's praise of an editor of Shakespeare, raise the

corrector to the level of the inventor.) Goudy was not always gentle with such people; he said with annoyance that they would tinker with an edge or add a curlicue and call the result a new type. That was unacceptable. For Goudy, the designer—unlike a typographer, who might make minor adjustments in an existing type to achieve certain results in a single project—had to start every new face from the beginning.[45]

Bruckner has completely missed the point of Morris Benton's work. Before he redrew them, typefaces such as Bodoni, Garamond, Bulmer, and Civilité existed in America only as printed samples in old books. Printers had no way of using most of these faces until Benton redrew them and ATF produced and sold them. For each revival, Benton had to decide which characteristics of the original letters to retain and which to alter, and also make all of the fitting decisions. "The integrity of an alphabet results from the structured way in which each letter relates to all the others," Chuck Bigelow wrote. "When a type face is copied, this coherence is one of the first items of information lost, and it is extremely difficult to restore it to its original form without real understanding of the design."[46] And yes, many of Benton's types were members of families and therefore closely related to each other, but again, he had to make the design decisions, and he was a master at making them. The fact that Morris Benton's Goudy Bold sold much better than Goudy's original Goudy Old Style, for example, is not without significance.

Milton McKaye told the story of Goudy Old Style in a 1933 *New Yorker* magazine article.

> Some of his friends … thought it was a happy circumstance when the American Type Founders Company purchased Goudy Old Style, today one of the most widely distributed fonts. The company bought the type outright for fifteen hundred dollars, and has never regretted its bargain. In addition to the profitable return from Goudy Old Style, the company succeeded in making three types sprout where one had grown before. The designer at its plant redrew the original letters (this still annoys Goudy) to produce two additional alphabets. Goudy nowadays never sells a design outright to a foundry.[47]

Goudy designed a few other typefaces for ATF, but most likely worked out the details more to his advantage.

Morris Benton has often been called an engineer and Goudy an artist, and it is true that Benton had a mechanical engineering degree and Goudy had an artistic temperament. But Benton's mechanical ability and affinity for engineering did not therefore make him aesthetically insensitive. He simply saw type as a means of communication rather than as an art form.

Goudy cutting a master pattern by hand with a knife

Making a metal working pattern from the master pattern

Cutting a brass matrix using the working pattern

Inspecting type and mats

Goudy did not believe that engineers could also be good type designers: "Types of distinction," he wrote in 1940, "are created by artists only, and not by engineers or artisans."[48] He felt that engineers were too concerned with precision and accuracy. Perhaps he was still smarting from the misunderstanding he had had with ATF regarding Goudy Old Style. Three years after Goudy Old Style was issued, when his ego was still recovering, he claimed in *Ars Typographica* that "Every bit of finish and refinement not necessary to the expression of the design is useless and is wasted effort … The demand for perfection is an evidence of a misunderstanding of the true ends of art."[49]

Goudy's assumption that the incompatible categories of "artist" and "engineer" could never be bridged is narrow-minded. Hermann Zapf, the leading German type designer of the late 20th century, regarded Benton as a designer and Goudy as an artist. "There's a lot of creative work that goes into type designing," Zapf said, "and Morris Benton is one of the great designers we should not forget." Zapf attributed Benton's relative obscurity to his personality. "In this country [the U.S.], you have to make noise to get recognized." He likened the Benton situation to Seward's purchase of Alaska in the 1800s—a very important move on Seward's part, but one that is not recognized by most Americans.[50]

But Goudy's "noise" was not necessarily that of boasting—he had to be vocal because he did not have a steady salary like Morris Benton. Paul Standard wrote, "Despite his now reverberant acclaim, Goudy has never presumed to be a pontifical. He has always remained humble, with a humility directly proportional to his output."[51] Some ATF employees however, particularly Henry Lewis Bullen, did not regard Goudy as highly as the general public did. The personal notebook of Stevens L. Watts, who was in charge of ATF type sales and the production of new typefaces from 1948 to 1955, contains the following hand-written entry:

> Henry Lewis Bullen had this to say about Morris F. Benton: "In the experienced opinion of the writer, he is the most experienced and best letterer of type designs in the world and has perfected more designs than any other man, *including the boastful man* who claims to have designed 100 type faces, few of which are used in the printing industry, while there would scarcely be any printing industry if at this time all the types lettered by M.F.B. were excluded. He is not as great a man as his father, but he is a 'chip off the old block.'"[52]

The bottom line in this discussion must be that while Benton's job at ATF gave him a regular paycheck, Goudy as a freelance type designer had to struggle to obtain work. Self-promotion was therefore a necessary part of Goudy's profession.

On July 28, 1932, Goudy wrote a letter to Morris Benton upon hearing of the death of his father. "I trust you will accept my sincere sympathy & condolences," he said. "I had the highest regard for Mr. Benton, and the American [Type Founders Company] as well as his friends have suffered a very great loss."[53] A notation on the bottom of the letter in Morris Benton's handwriting states, "Answered Aug. 1, 1932, M.B."

In her famous 1932 address to the British Typographers' Guild, "The Crystal Goblet, or, Printing Should Be Invisible," Beatrice Warde said:

> I once was talking to a man who designed a very pleasing advertising type which undoubtedly all of you have used. I said something about what artists think about a certain problem, and he replied with a beautiful gesture:

'Ah, madam, we artists do not think—we *feel*!' That same day I quoted that remark to another designer of my acquaintance, and he, being less poetically inclined, murmured: 'I'm not *feeling* very well today, I *think*!' He was right, he did think; he was the thinking sort; and that is why he is not so good a painter, and to my mind ten times better as a typographer and type designer than the man who instinctively avoided anything as coherent as a reason.[54]

It would appear that the two type designers to whom Warde was referring were Goudy and Morris Benton, respectively. This was confirmed by Richard Marder in 1986.[55]

Judging Morris Benton's contribution to the development of typography will ultimately depend on the criteria used for assessing his work. Even if creativity is considered the main ingredient for a great type designer, Morris Benton will score highly since he designed several original faces that are still widely used, such as Franklin Gothic and the Century variations. But the bulk of Benton's work was practical, as opposed to "creative." He was the first to revive many European typefaces that otherwise may not have become available commercially, all the while insisting on their legibility and practicality. He fashioned many of these into type families to extend their usefulness to printers. After consulting several legibility studies and conducting his own research, he designed a typeface specifically for youngsters learning to read. He also satisfied the advertising agencies with novelty faces that made their layouts attract attention. Many of these types became good sellers for ATF, enabling the company to prosper.

In 1957 Steve Watts explained what appears to have been Morris Benton's motive in designing type:

> It should be borne in mind that the makers of type and composing machines are in business to produce profits for the shareholders of their companies, and not, as Tommy Thompson [the designer of ATF's Quillscript] expresses it, "to make arrowheads for museums." As a matter of business, they must be concerned about only two kinds of type: the kind that sells readily and the kind that never pays for making the matrices and the expenses of introductory sales promotion. A rough estimate shows that perhaps two out of three new faces brought out in the last 50 years were financial failures.
>
> Even with signal successes like Cheltenham to take up the slack, the employee who recommends the cutting of new faces is vulnerable if he goes longhair on the job and cultivates esthetic ideals that will not "stand the strain of weaving into human stuff on the loom of the real." He must learn to pray with Henry Van Dyke: "Keep me from caring more for books than for folks, for art than for life." Working as a typemaker can be an enchanting

experience, but to continue at it one must take the folklore out of type lore, and give the customer what he wants and needs. Too many "bloomers" in a row will send him down the road talking to himself.[56]

Chapter 13 Endnotes

1   Charles Bigelow and Donald Day, "Digital Typography," *Scientific American* 249, no. 2 (August 1983): 110.

2   M. F. McGrew, in discussion with the author, Pittsburgh, September 3, 1984.

3   Bigelow, in discussion with the author, June 2007.

4   Richard N. McArthur, "On Cooper Type Faces … With Some Digressions," in *The Book of Oz Cooper: An Appreciation of Oswald Bruce Cooper* (Chicago: The Society of Typographic Arts, 1949), 110.

5   Bigelow and Jonathan Seybold, "Technology and the Aesthetics of Type," *Seybold Report* 10, no. 24 (August 24, 1981): 5–6.

6   McArthur, "Cooper," 90.

7   John Allen Murphy, "Morris Benton, Part 3," *Inland Printer* 97, no. 2 (May 1936): 69.

8   Henry Lewis Bullen, "The Effect of the Composing Machines Upon the Typefounding Industry," *Inland Printer* 73, no. 4 (July 1924): 595.

9   Eugene M. Ettenberg, *Type for Books and Advertising* (New York: D. Van Nostrand Company, Inc., 1947), 109–116.

10 Ibid., 109.

11 Carl Purlington Rollins, introduction to "American Type Designers and Their Work" (Chicago: R. R. Donnelley, 1947), 4.

12 Ettenberg, "American Type Designers and Their Work: An R. R. Donnelley Exhibition," *American Printer* 126, no. 5 (May 1948): 18.

13 Alexander Lawson, "The Prolific Career of Morris Benton," *Printing Impressions* 13, no. 11 (April 1971): 76.

14 Murphy, "Morris Benton, Part 3," 69.

15 David Walker Mallison, "Henry Lewis Bullen and the Typographic Library and Museum of the American Type Founders Co." (Ph.D. diss., Columbia University, 1976): 140.

16 Henry Lewis Bullen to Beatrice Warde, 14 February 1927, 1–2, Typographic Library Manuscripts, Rare Book and Manuscript Library, Columbia University.

17 Theo Rehak, *The Fall of ATF* (privately printed, 2004), 7.

18 Wikipedia, Freemasonry, http://en.wikipedia.org/wiki/Freemasonry.

19 Milton McKaye, "Profiles: Glorifier of the Alphabet," *New Yorker*, January 14, 1933, 20.

20 Lawson, "Introduction" to *Typographer's Digest* 27 (Spring 1969): 3.

21 Laurance B. Siegfried, "Ninth Annual Frederic W. Goudy Distinguished Lecture in Typography" (Rochester, N.Y.: The Press of the Good Mountain, 1977), 7.

22 Theo Rehak, email message to the author, 2 December 2006.

23 Frederic W. Goudy, "Type Designs: Old and New," *Ars Typographica* 1, no. 1 (Spring 1918): 39–40.

24 Goudy, "Type Design: A Homily," *Ars Typographica* 1, no. 4 (Autumn 1934): 13.

25 Goudy, in *A Bibliography of The Village Press*, by Melbert B. Cary Jr. (New York: Press of the Woolly Whale, 1938), 21.

26 Goudy, *Typologia: Studies in Type Design & Type Making* (Berkeley: University of California Press, 1940), ix.

27 D. J. R. Bruckner, *Frederic Goudy* (New York: Harry N. Abrams, Inc., 1990), 27.

28   Goudy, "The Editor's Workshop: By Way of Apology," *Ars Typographica* 1, no. 4 (Autumn 1934): 47.

29   Paul Standard, "Goudy at Seventy," *Penrose Annual* 38 (1936): 58.

30   Goudy, *A Half-Century of Type Design & Typography, 1895–1945* (New York: The Typophiles, 1946), 1:92.

31   The original matrices for Camelot are part of the Cary Graphic Arts Collection at RIT.

32   J. W. Phinney to Benjamin Kimball, Esq., Boston, 18 January 1900, Typographic Library Manuscripts, Rare Book and Manuscript Library, Columbia University.

33   McGrew, *American Metal Typefaces of the Twentieth Century*, 2nd ed. (New Castle, Del.: Oak Knoll Press, 1993), 57.

34   F. W. Goudy & J. W. Phinney, "Font of Type," U.S. Patent No. 32,398, February 27, 1900.

35   Goudy, *Half-Century*, 93.

36   Ibid.

37   Stevens L. Watts listed this as a 1922 font in "Some Type Series Originated or Restyled by Morris Fuller Benton," June 1965.

38   "American Type Designers and Their Work" (Chicago: R. R. Donnelley, 1947): 7.

39   Maureen D. Hitchcock, "Benton Types" (Rochester, New York: The Press of the Good Mountain, 1978). The dates of production given by Watts in "Some Type Series Originated or Restyled by Morris Fuller Benton" conflict in some cases with the dates in the hand-annotated copy of the American Type Founders' 1923 *Specimen Book and Catalogue*, Book Arts Collection, Rare Book and Manuscript Library, Columbia University. Here ATF dates are given, except in the cases of Goudy Extrabold, Goudy Extrabold Italic, Goudy Handtooled, and Goudy Title, which are listed as Benton faces only by Watts.

40   Goudy, *Elements of Lettering* (New York: Mitchell Kennerley, 1922), 42.

41   J. L. Frazier, *Type Lore: Popular Types of Today, Their Origin and Use* (Chicago: Frazier, 1925), 105.

42   Bruckner, *Goudy*, 30.

43   Goudy, "On Designing a Type-Face," *Dolphin* 1 (1933): 3–23.

44   "How Frederic W. Goudy Cuts a Type Face," *American Printer* 106, no. 5 (May 1938), 20–21.

45   Bruckner, *Goudy*, 30.

46   Bigelow and Seybold, "Technology," 7.

47   McKaye, "Profiles," 23.

48   Goudy, *Typologia*, 28.

49   Goudy, "Old and New," 40.

50   Hermann Zapf, in discussion with the author, Rochester, N.Y., August 9, 1985.

51   Standard, "Goudy at Seventy," 59.

52   Watts, "Notebook of Stevens Lewis Watts, 1895–1966," n.d., Typographic Library Manuscripts, Rare Book and Manuscript Library, Columbia University.

53   Goudy to Morris Benton, 28 July 1932.

54   Beatrice Warde, *The Crystal Goblet: Sixteen Essays on Typography* (Cleveland and New York: World Publishing Company, 1956), 14–15.

55   Richard Marder, handwritten note on a copy of the original Benton thesis, 1986.

56   Watts, "'Chelt' Really Got Around," *Printing* 81, no. 5 (May 1957): 79, 114.

Morris Benton's Type Designs

HERMAN ZAPF IDENTIFIED THREE PARAMETERS within which a type designer must work: "The designing of a typeface demands knowledge of historical trends of the evolution of type design, artistic perception and a thorough understanding of typefounding techniques."[1] These three requirements were indeed the foundation of Morris Benton's types. He continually added to his knowledge of historical trends in type design by studying the examples of classic European types in ATF's typographic library. Zapf felt that artistic perception should embrace practical considerations ("the art of type design must be harmonious with type's primary task—instant recognition"); Benton, too, insisted on legibility. And who could possibly have better understood the techniques of typefounding at the turn of the 20th century than the son of Linn Boyd Benton?

"Despite his relative obscurity (the result of his great modesty), Benton was arguably America's most influential type designer," wrote calligrapher and typographer Paul Shaw in 1981. "With over 200 faces to his credit, he was certainly the most prolific."[2] The quibbler may ask: "But exactly how many typefaces did Benton design?" It is a valid question, not easily answered. During the years that Benton oversaw ATF's Type Designing Department he had many employees working under him, and so there is some question as to whether he designed all of the types that have been attributed to him.

In 1978, RIT student Maureen Delaney Hitchcock published a small booklet listing 251 different Morris Benton typefaces and 38 accessories and decorative materials (fractions, ornaments, and borders).[3] It was compiled from two sources: a copy of the 1923 ATF *Specimen Book and Catalogue* in one of Columbia University's rare book collections,[4] anonymously annotated by handwriting in pencil (possibly by Henry Lewis Bullen);[5] and a list that Stevens L. Watts compiled in June 1965 for RIT student David L. Ritter, entitled "Some Type Series Originated or Restyled by Morris Fuller Benton."[6] Hitchcock included 25 typefaces that Watts indicated were later abandoned; if these are discounted, Hitchcock's total becomes 226. The list compiled by Watts gives 199 typefaces and an additional 31 that were either abandoned or renamed.

Type expert Mac McGrew of Pittsburgh listed 201 "Typefaces from the hand of Morris Fuller Benton" in "The Bentons, Father & Son," an article he wrote for the March 1978 issue of *Typographic i*, published by the International Composition Association, Inc. McGrew qualified his findings by adding, "This list is derived from several sources which we believe to be reliable, but because Morris Benton's work was seldom published during his lifetime, there may be errors or omissions. If so, we are sorry."[7] Although McGrew had uncovered 201 Benton typefaces, the list compiled by Steve Watts included 15 faces that were not on McGrew's original list. After more research, McGrew concluded, in his 1993 book *American Metal Typefaces of the Twentieth Century*, that Morris Benton designed 221 typefaces, making him by far the most prolific on his list of type designers.[8]

Another source was found among the papers of the Benton family. On April 23, 1936, Morris Benton wrote a letter to Harold Kathman, an ATF colleague in the sales department,[9] containing what he specifically called a "partial list" of his designs: 101 typefaces, of which 52 were starred. Benton indicated that the starred items should be selected if the whole list was too long for the article that Kathman was writing. The value of this document is limited because at the outset Benton did not intend to include all of his type designs, but it does identify the typefaces that Benton considered his best or most significant. Benton's own list includes one typeface that is not attributed to him in any other source: Gallia.

Not all of the types credited to Morris Benton were solely his creation. In some cases, ATF employees in the Type Designing Department collaborated on new typefaces. Watts explained:

> Mr. Benton had full charge of the type design program at ATF for many years. It is hard for anyone to say just what designs brought out during his tenure were his own work as a designer. Many faces accredited to him as designer were undoubtedly based on ideas conceived by workmen in his department. One such face was Novel Gothic, a "modernist" attempt, originated by Charles Herman Becker, a hand engraver in the Matrix Cutting Department whose regular job was putting the finishing requirements on matrix patterns.[10]

ATF's hand-annotated 1923 *Specimen Book*, the list compiled by Watts, and McGrew's *American Metal Typefaces of the Twentieth Century* all indicate some types that were only partly designed by Morris Benton; however, these three sources do not entirely agree. The following 18 examples of collaborations do not include Benton's historic revivals. In cases of conflicting data, the sources are indicated as ATF (the annotated *Specimen Book*), SLW (Watts), or McG (McGrew).

	Typeface	Notation
1.	Bulfinch Oldstyle	"partly" (ATF); designed by William Martin Johnson, adjustments by MFB (McG)
2.	Century Expanded	with Linn Boyd Benton
3.	Clearface	Linn Boyd Benton, advisor
4.	Clearface Italic	Linn Boyd Benton, advisor
5.	Clearface Bold	Linn Boyd Benton, advisor
6.	Clearface Bold Italic	Linn Boyd Benton, advisor
7.	Cloister Black	with Joseph W. Phinney
8.	Cloister Cursive Handtooled	with Charles H. Becker
9.	Della Robbia Light	after design by T. M. Cleland (SLW)
10.	Engravers Old English	"Cowan" and MFB before 1903 (ATF) / has also been ascribed to J.W. Phinney (McG)
11.	Goudy Handtooled	with Wadsworth A. Parker (SLW) / with Charles H. Becker (ATF)
12.	Goudy Handtooled Italic	with Wadsworth A. Parker (SLW) / with Charles H. Becker (ATF)
13.	Lithograph Shaded	MFB and W. F. Capitan (ATF)
14.	Norwood Roman	design suggested by J. S. Cushing (SLW)
15.	Novel Gothic	with Charles H. Becker
16.	Packard Bold	after an Oswald Cooper design (SLW, McG)
17.	Piranesi Bold	after basic design by W. T. Sniffin (SLW)
18.	Roycroft	"partly" (ATF) has been credited to Lewis Buddy (McG)

One supposedly reliable source for information about Morris Benton's type designs would appear to be the U.S. patent for each design. However, ATF's purpose in pursuing patents was strictly to prohibit other companies from copying its type, and the company stopped patenting type designs around 1920. "Before that time," Watts explained,

> Mr. Benton's name appeared on patent applications for some designs
> that were the united efforts of several people under his supervision. In
> the old days, it seems to me, patents were obtained under the name of

an individual who assigned his patent rights to the Company. Due to this practice, many type designs have been accredited to people such as John K. Rogers of Boston Type Foundry, for faces that were designed by other persons.[11]

While a definitive numerical accounting of Morris Benton's type output is not possible at this late date, even a casual study of his designs reveals that his body of work is amazing for more than just its volume. First, Benton typefaces encompass a wide range of styles, from ultra-modern to purely classical. Professor Alexander Lawson, who taught typography at RIT from 1947 to 1977, wrote, "diversity should of course be the hallmark of a good designer."[12] Watts greatly admired Benton for this quality. "Sentimentalists among type lovers regard Mr. Benton's work in reviving old faces and making them available in type suited for modern printing as being his greatest achievement," Watts wrote in 1965.

> It is true that he brought back Bodoni, Baskerville, Garamond, Bulmer, and other faces that became popular and were copied or approximated by the machine composition people, but those "esthetic" faces were not Benton's best money-makers for American Type Founders Company… [Morris Benton] excelled not as a creator of new type designs but as a perfectionist who translated the basic ideas of others into metal type that was most useful to printers. His rendering of a type design had "architectural" merit. He was capable of making numerous variants of a typeface without having them lose identity. Plain faces cut under his supervision were the ones that paid off commercially and many of them are still in use.[13]

Their long life span is another hallmark of Benton types. Advertising typographers and other designers introduced many new faces after Morris Benton retired from ATF, yet some of his types remained popular. The *Inland Printer's* "Typographic Scoreboard" judged the popularity of typefaces on how frequently they appeared in ads for the *Saturday Evening Post*; from 1929 to 1945, Garamond and Bodoni, both Benton types, were the consistent winners.[14] Although the composing machine manufacturers copied these revivals, type historian Mac McGrew wrote, "in both these cases, his versions have won out over competing adaptations to become the American standards."[15] McGrew maintained that Morris Benton "designed more good typefaces than anyone else I know of. Not only good, but many of them so practical that they are among the most extensively used faces in the world."[16] Many digital versions of Benton's typefaces are available today—even a basic Internet search turns up digital versions for more than half of the 226 faces attributed to him in Appendix B, a compilation of information about the types he is thought to have designed.[17]

Morris Benton was one of the first to give typographers new design options. Although he may not have originated the "family" concept in type design, he was the first to develop the idea. Richard Marder went so far as to call Benton the father of the type family, because he did more than anyone else to exploit it.[18] Morris Benton should also be remembered for his legibility studies, resulting in Clearface, the Century Schoolbook family, and News Gothic, the typeface judged to be "the most legible face" by Barbara Roethlein's famous 1912 type legibility study.[19]

The stories of some of Morris Benton's noteworthy designs follow, grouped chronologically within seven basic categories.

1. Blackletter

Blackletter types are based on the letterforms of the first movable types, which in turn were based on the handwriting of the 14th and 15th centuries. (The term "blackletter" is an American one; in Europe, typefaces reminiscent of the earliest types are known as "gothic.") To modern eyes these early types are difficult to read, as Alexander Lawson explained in his book *Anatomy of a Typeface*:

> The illegibility stems primarily from unfamiliarity—the types are infrequently used today—but in addition the form has certain peculiarities, particularly in the construction of the capitals … Because capitals were frequently used for decorative initials, the scribes chose to embellish them; they also added lines and flourishes to fill in the counters (enclosed white spaces) of the capitals that appeared to be excessively open in relation to the narrower and heavier lowercase characters. This practice, although creating an art form, reduced the cohesiveness of the letters as units of an alphabet and made them difficult to distinguish.[20]

Wedding Text, about 1901
Benton's Wedding Text is a comparatively light blackletter face. McGrew explained that the 12-point size of Wedding Text was cut in type metal in 1901, and electrotype matrices were made from these originals. Apparently the electrotyped matrices caused problems in casting, and new matrices were cut on the Benton engraving machine, since the type was hailed as "new" in 1907, and again in 1909.[21] Benton designed one variant, Wedding Text Shaded, in 1913 or 1916, but only the parent design is included on his 1936 typeface list.

Although Wedding Text became popular for its intended purpose, for printing wedding invitations, some type historians felt that it was overrated. Lawson and fellow RIT Professor Archie Provan wrote in 1983, "Admittedly more appropriate for funeral notices, Wedding Text was nevertheless the prime type for many years."[22] Today Linotype's digital version of Wedding Text is called "Mariage Regular."

Engravers Old English, before 1903
According to the annotated 1923 ATF *Specimen Book*, Morris Benton collaborated

𝔚𝔞𝔰𝔥𝔦𝔫𝔤𝔱𝔬𝔫 𝔖𝔪𝔦𝔱𝔥𝔰𝔬𝔫𝔦𝔞𝔫 𝔍𝔫𝔰𝔱𝔦𝔱𝔲𝔱𝔦𝔬𝔫 𝔒𝔭𝔢𝔫𝔰
𝔓𝔯𝔦𝔫𝔱𝔢𝔯 ℭ𝔬𝔫𝔱𝔯𝔦𝔟𝔲𝔱𝔢𝔰 𝔅𝔢𝔞𝔲𝔱𝔦𝔣𝔲𝔩 𝔄𝔫𝔫𝔬𝔲𝔫𝔠𝔢𝔪𝔢𝔫𝔱

𝔑𝔲𝔪𝔢𝔯𝔬𝔲𝔰 𝔚𝔬𝔫𝔡𝔢𝔯𝔣𝔲𝔩 𝔍𝔫𝔟𝔢𝔫𝔱𝔦𝔬𝔫𝔰 𝔇𝔦𝔰𝔠𝔬𝔟𝔢𝔯𝔢𝔡 𝔕𝔢𝔠𝔢𝔫𝔱𝔩𝔶
𝔏𝔞𝔱𝔢𝔰𝔱 𝔕𝔢𝔪𝔬𝔡𝔢𝔩𝔢𝔡 𝔐𝔞𝔠𝔥𝔦𝔫𝔢𝔯𝔶 𝔍𝔫𝔟𝔞𝔯𝔦𝔞𝔟𝔩𝔶 𝔄𝔭𝔭𝔯𝔢𝔠𝔦𝔞𝔱𝔢𝔡

Benton's Wedding Text

10 Point   5 A 11 a

𝔐𝔢𝔱𝔯𝔬𝔭𝔬𝔩𝔦𝔱𝔞𝔫 𝔥𝔦𝔰𝔱𝔬𝔯𝔦𝔠 𝔓𝔞𝔤𝔢𝔞𝔫𝔱
𝔅𝔲𝔦𝔩𝔡𝔦𝔫𝔤𝔰 𝔇𝔢𝔠𝔬𝔯𝔞𝔱𝔢𝔡

ATF's Engravers Old English

with a Mr. Cowan on Engravers Old English, a plain rendition of the blackletter style. In 1910 Benton designed a heavier weight, Engravers Old English Bold. The unfamiliar characters of this face, according to McGrew, were often misused. Two variations of "H" and "I" were included in the font, but when Monotype copied it, the two forms of the "I" became "J" and "I," with no alternates.[23] Morris Benton did not include Engravers Old English or its bold variation in his 1936 list.

Cloister Black, 1904
ATF's most famous blackletter typeface, Cloister Black, must not be confused with Benton's Cloister Oldstyle. Some historians credit Joseph W. Phinney of ATF's Boston foundry with Cloister Black, and others give some or all of the credit to Morris Benton,[24] who himself indicated on his 1936 list that he had designed it. Cloister Black is similar to the type that Gutenberg used for his 42-line Bible.

Apparently the idea for Cloister Black was conceived by Phinney, but Benton may have done most of the work on the type because its November 15, 1904, patent (U.S. Patent No. D37,235) lists Morris Benton as the type's inventor.[25] Flemish Black was patented the same day with Morris Benton again listed as inventor (U.S. Patent No. D37,234). Flemish Black may actually have been Phinney's design.

Lawson calls Cloister Black a true English blackletter;[26] today it is used in the U.S. for diplomas and certificates. According to Lawson and Provan, Cloister Black remained one of the most popular versions of blackletter type in America.[27]

A fragment of an early 15th-century manuscript

Detail from Gutenberg's 42-line Bible

18 Point   8 A $1 60   22 a $1 70 $3 30

𝕾ixth 𝕬nniversary of 𝕮onnecticut 𝕷eague

Cloister Black

𝕮ontinuation of the 𝕾ixth 𝕮hapter	
22 Blessed are ye, when men shall hate you, and when they shall separate you from their company, and shall reproach you,	30 Give to every man that asketh of thee; and of him that taketh away thy goods ask them not again.

Flemish Black

The Trajan Column

2. Roman

Harry Carter defined roman type "as one whose capital letters reproduce classical inscriptional models and whose miniscules are made to conform with the capitals in their style or construction."[28] The inscription on the base of the Trajan Column (A.D. 113) in Rome is perhaps the most famous example of ancient roman capital letters. Roman type also has "serifs at the terminals of the straight strokes," Carter continued. "Serifs are added strokes, not continuations of terminal thickenings. The mysterious and modern word comes, I suppose, from the Dutch 'schreef' for a scratch or flick of the pen."[29]

Roycroft, circa 1898

While this typeface departs significantly from the inscriptional models to which Carter referred, it is nevertheless loosely based on them and does have serifs, and so is included here as a Roman type. In 1898 Morris Benton apparently worked on Roycroft at ATF; the catalogue of the R. R. Donnelley exhibition American Type Designers and Their Work, held in 1947 in Chicago, listed Roycroft as Benton's first type.[30] But perhaps the most authoritative compilation of Morris Benton's type designs, that prepared by Stevens L. Watts, did not list Roycroft at all. Alexander Lawson, who disliked the Roycroft face, wrote, "Some doubts may be cast on whether Benton could have survived the reputation of having fathered such a letter."[31]

Aa Bb Cc Dd Ee Ff	Characters in Complete Font
Gg Hh Ii Jj Kk Ll	A B C D E F G H I J
Mm Nn Oo Pp Qq	K L M M N O P Q R R
Rr Ss Tt Uu Vv	S T U V W X Y Z &
Ww Xx Yy Zz	$ 1 2 3 4 5 6 7 8 9 0
ſ R Æ Œ œ œ &	a a b c d e f g h h i
$ 1 2 3 4 5 6 7 8 9 0	j k l m m n n o p q
. , ; : ! ? a æ	r s t t u u v w x y z
	fi fl The ct f ſh fi fl ft
	. , - ' : ; ! ?

Buddy's drawings and ATF's Roycroft, from the June 1937 *Inland Printer*

Explaining the intended or proper uses of extra letters in the Roycroft Series.

From an ATF stand-alone specimen booklet for Roycroft

The type was first drawn by Lewis Buddy III, a former artist on the staff of *The Saturday Evening Post* who hand-lettered his own headings. Shortly after he left the *Post* in the 1890s to become art editor of *The Chatauquan Magazine* in Cleveland, Buddy received a telegram from J. W. Phinney of ATF's Boston office, asking him to design a complete font of type based on the letters he had drawn for the *Post*. Buddy rushed through a set of drawings and mailed them the same day. He wanted to call the type "Carbudy," after his grandfather Edward Will Carr and himself, but Phinney had other ideas. At the time, Elbert Hubbard and a group of craftsmen called the Roycrofters in East Aurora, New York, published a periodical called *The Philistine*, similar to the *Reader's Digest* in size and popularity, with untrimmed pages, printed on antique paper, and butcher paper for the cover. "The vigorous, 'homespun' style of typography the Roycrofters affected was widely favored," A. Raymond Hopper explained in a 1937 *Inland Printer* article,

> and Mr. Phinney very likely thought it good salesmanship, as surely it was, to attach the luster of the Roycroft name to this new offering in rugged types. So permission was sought, and granted, to call this type Roycroft— though the Roycrofters had nothing to do with its design, even by way of inspiration, and, so far as I know, never used the face.[32]

Buddy's original drawings had to be reworked to be made into type at ATF, and years later, Hopper was displeased with ATF's revisions. His *Inland Printer* article included a photograph that Buddy had made of his drawings before sending them to ATF, alongside a reproduction of the font as it was cut. "A comparison shows how much the face was narrowed in the rendering," Hopper wrote. "This, in this writer's opinion, is a lamentable deficiency in a design so suited to its time, however much its great and long popularity might seem to contradict the criticism here made."

The anonymously annotated copy of ATF's 1923 *Specimen Book and Catalogue* at Columbia University gave Benton partial credit for Roycroft, with 1898 as the date of its design.[33] Morris was working for his father in ATF's letter-designing department at the time and would have been the logical employee to be assigned to this project; it was the type of work that would engage him in subsequent years. Roycroft in 24 point was the first font of type to be cast from matrices that were directly engraved on Linn Boyd Benton's machine, on October 4, 1900,[34] and Morris Benton was almost certainly involved in the project.

Whether or not it was Morris Benton who redrew the Roycroft letters, he began designing other types and reworking drawings submitted to ATF by other designers. When ATF's central plant moved to Jersey City, New Jersey, in 1903, Morris was put in charge of the Type Designing Department. "Since that time," the 1925 *Inland Printer* claimed, "almost every typeface shown in the type-specimen book of the American Type Founders Company has derived its design quality from the head and hands of the younger Benton."[35]

Roycroft achieved wide popularity as a reaction against the weak book types of the late 19th century: Lawson wrote that the type "was an immediate success. ATF stated in an advertisement one year after the introduction of the type that on one day the foundry had shipped 10,000 pounds of Roycroft"[36]; Hopper noted that "at one time it was in the case of almost every printer in this country"[37]; and Lawson wrote in 1965 that Roycroft became perhaps the best-known of the so-called "rugged" letters.[38] But Roycroft is not one of the typefaces that Morris Benton included in the partial list of type designs he compiled in 1936. While it seems likely that he was at least tangentially involved in its production, he didn't regard it as his own. Or perhaps, like Lawson, he was not particularly fond of the face.

Century

Several ATF type families bear the Century name. All of them were based on Morris Benton's ongoing study of the two typefaces that his father and Theodore Low De Vinne designed before Morris began working at ATF. These Century faces have been grouped together here because of their shared derivation.

Century Expanded, 1900

The original steel punches for Century Roman type were cut in 1895 by Linn Boyd

In the mean time a great change has taken place in the taste of readers, who have wearied of light types and gray impressions. There is an unmistakable demand for bold and stronger print. William Morris has printed books in many styles of letters; all of them are black and rugged, yet they find readers and buyers. American type-founders have recently introduced other styles of bold and black letter—for publishers and advertisers, as well as for bibliophiles. The «Jenson,» the «Monotone,» and the «De Vinne» are in high favor with all, not for their novelty of form, but for their greater legibility. With these evidences before them of a general preference for bolder types, the publishers of THE CENTURY decided that they would swim with the tide, and have new types of larger face and thicker hair-lines.

Century Roman, from De Vinne's *Century Magazine*

11 POINT
POINTS WORTH NOTING
CLEAR-CUT and legible face, with strong-wearing qualities

12 POINT
CENTURY EXPANDED
A SERVICEABLE letter for magazines and text books

14 POINT
OUR TYPE STYLES
Are decidedly original

18 POINT
PLAIN LETTER
Delighted readers

Century Expanded

Benton in collaboration with De Vinne for the *Century Magazine*. Century Roman was used by the magazine for several years, but it did not come into general use because, according to J. L. Frazier's *Type Lore*, the measure was a little too narrow[39] (condensed) for book work. Therefore, Linn Boyd Benton and De Vinne collaborated again on a slightly wider version for the De Vinne press, Century Broad-Face. Morris Benton became interested in and began experimenting with the two typefaces after he started working at ATF. His father was involved in the work as well, and in 1900, ATF produced a revised Century, based on Century Broad-Face.[40] The matrices were cut on Benton's matrix-engraving machine, and the new type was first shown as Century No. 2 in the 1901 ATF *Desk Book*, on page 61.[41] Two years later it was shown as Century Expanded, in sizes 6, 8, 10, 11, 12, 14, 18, 24, 30, and 36 point, in ATF's 1903 *Specimen Book of American Line Type Faces*.[42]

Century Expanded was easy to read and had good wearing qualities. According to a 1927 article in the *Inland Printer*, the type proved to be "a great success, especially in newspaper offices in the smaller towns; it also found much favor in commercial printing offices …"[43] Type historian Mac McGrew called it "a basic, much used American typeface,"[44] and it was found in newspapers up into the 1980s.

One of the sets of ATF drawings in the Smithsonian is labeled "Century Extended," although no type by that name appears in ATF specimen books or matrix records. Two of these drawings are dated 1899, suggesting that Century Extended may have been an early name for Century Expanded.[45] The name Century Expanded may cause some confusion because the type does not resemble a typical expanded face.[46] McGrew explained in 1978 that it was "'expanded' upward in relation to some of the weak faces of the 19th century, and outward in relation to the original Century Roman, which has long been obsolete now, but not in relation to most contemporary faces."[47]

Some printers were not happy with Century Expanded. Frazier wrote:
> Its chief drawback is a commonplace, mechanical, rather severe appearance; esthetic considerations appear to have had little influence in its design. Century Expanded, in effect, is a busy, efficient workman dressed in denims. It is a typeface for common "ads" and booklets on common subjects. Lacking in style and grace, it is wholly unsuited for job work.[48]

Watts also admitted in 1962 that he had never liked Century Expanded, "it being too pedestrian for my taste. The italics are graceful but kerned characters in the larger sizes break off and cause trouble in use."[49] Even so, in 1925 the *Saturday Evening Post* was set in the Monotype version of Century Expanded. It was also copied by other composing machine manufacturers, and as late as 1965 was still available on most typesetting machines. Alexander Lawson called Century Expanded "the most popular of all the Century types"; and as of 1982, he felt that it had "survived as a type for the text composition of advertisements."[50] It was also used in newspapers into the 1980s, as previously noted.[51]

In 1997, type designer Tobias Frere-Jones worked on improving the *Boston Globe*'s text type. Later he decided to widen that face for the *Detroit Free Press* and in so doing, returned to the proportions of Morris Benton's Century Expanded. The result was "Benton Modern," drawn for The Font Bureau, Inc. Its companion, Benton Modern Italic, drawn by Richard Lipton and Christian Schwartz for the Font Bureau, is a modified version of Century Schoolbook Italic.[52]

Morris Benton included Century Expanded in his 1936 list of typeface designs.

Variants of Century Expanded
Morris Benton designed an italic version of Century Expanded, and the two were produced in an unusually large number of sizes. In 1904 he started designing two more Century faces that ATF released in 1905: Century Bold, which would become a major display face, and Century Bold Italic. "Although the name doesn't include 'Expanded,' they are obviously the companion boldfaces," McGrew noted.[53] Benton designed Century Bold Condensed in 1906, and it was introduced in 1909, rapidly becoming, according to the Font Bureau, "one of the most popular headline typefaces for American newspapers and magazines of our time."[54] In 1938 Sol Hess designed Century Bold Condensed Italic for Monotype, and Linotype came out with Century Bold Extra Condensed for newspaper headlines. More recently, the Font Bureau's Greg Thompson digitized Century Bold Condensed for the headline sizes in *Road & Track* magazine. In 1992 the Font Bureau adapted this face as "Century FB" for general use.[55]

Century Expanded
Century Expanded Italic
Century Bold
Century Bold Italic
Century Bold Condensed
Century Bold Extended
Century Oldstyle
Century Oldstyle Italic
Century Oldstyle Bold
Century Oldstyle Bold Italic

Century Catalogue

Augmenting a Popular Family

An extremely legible face designed for fine catalogue and booklet printing. Its uniform tone and fine contour make it a useful letter for various other jobs

AMERICAN TYPE FOUNDERS COMPANY

Benton's Century Family, as of 1912

Century Catalogue

Benton also designed Century Bold Extended in 1906; it was released in 1910. Benton's Century Bold Condensed Title of 1924 was abandoned. Four of the Century variations—Century Expanded Italic, Century Bold, Century Bold Italic, and Century Bold Condensed—are included on Benton's 1936 list.

Century Oldstyle, 1908–09

In 1906 Morris Benton began to depart from the Century Expanded series with a lighter face, Century Oldstyle, without the curled tail on the capital R and the long, straight vertical serifs of the capital T. The upper serifs of the ascending lower case letters (b, d, i, k, and l, for example) were slanted instead of straight—"old-style" serifs. After Century Oldstyle was released, Benton grew it into its own sub-family, with bold, italic, bold italic, and bold condensed variations. The Font Bureau claims that Benton's Century Oldstyle was based on a typeface from the Scottish foundry of Miller & Richard, designed and cut by Alexander Phemister in 1860.[56] "Although closely related," McGrew wrote, "the *Century Oldstyle* family is not really a part of the *Century Expanded* family."[57]

Frazier called Century Oldstyle "a desirable body or text letter, especially where a large face in relation to the body is desirable, as when six point must be used or when a pocket size booklet is in prospect."[58] Frazier regarded the foundry version of Century Oldstyle Bold as more attractive than Cheltenham and the bold Caslons. Century Oldstyle was popular with printing school teachers,[59] but it never achieved the success of the other members of the Century family. Today the Adobe website states: "Century Old Style [*sic*] is still renowned for its readability, and is a good typeface for magazines and other publications."[60] Century Oldstyle is also available from the Font Bureau

---

as "Bureau Roman," designed in 1997 for the *Washington Post* by David Berlow and Cyrus Highsmith. The Font Bureau expanded Bureau Roman into its "second Readability Series, offering choices between the five closely spaced grades [weights]."[61]

Morris Benton included Century Oldstyle, Century Oldstyle Italic, and Century Oldstyle Bold on his 1936 list of typefaces.

Century Catalogue, 1914
According to the annotated 1923 ATF *Specimen Book*, Benton designed Century Catalogue, a medium-weight letter, in 1914. McGrew's *American Metal Typefaces of the Twentieth Century* states that Century Catalogue "was brought out by Benton in 1917, with longer ascenders but essentially the same design [as Century Oldstyle]."[62] Watts gave the date for Century Catalogue as 1922, and wrote that it was "One of the very finest straight-matter letters ever made ... [but] it never caught on salewise, probably because it was not made available on the slug machines."[63] Century Catalogue Italic, according to McGrew, was cut from the patterns for Baskerville Italic, with minor changes in a few characters. In smaller sizes, however, Century Catalogue Italic was cut wider than the pattern by adjusting the Benton engraving machine.

Morris Benton's 1936 list of typefaces includes both Century Catalogue and Century Catalogue Italic.

Century Schoolbook, 1920
In his book *Typologia*, first published in 1940, Frederic Goudy maintained that, although many legibility experiments and studies had been completed up to that time, no designer had used them in devising a new typeface. "It is a pity," he wrote,

> that the experiments have dealt only with existing forms (not always well chosen), and so far as the writer is aware, no suggestions for incorporating any results making for increased legibility by devising new forms based on the experiments have been made. Why haven't there been enlisted in these experiments the services of a designer who has given thought to the question of legibility of letters as well as to physical representation and their esthetic expression?[64]

Goudy must not have realized that Morris Benton had long since consulted type legibility studies and experiments, and had designed more than one typeface based on this research.

In 1915, the schoolbook publisher Ginn and Company asked Morris Benton to design a legible typeface for its young readers. The company felt that a type "that would be better for the eyesight of students logically should be designed by an expert."[65] Benton was a good choice since he had been involved in both the preliminary stages and the final evaluations of a legibility study published in 1912 by Barbara Elizabeth Roethlein of Clark University in Worcester, Massachusetts.[66] Roethlein had found that "legibility depended on form, size and heaviness of the letters and on the margin, position in group and on the shape and size of adjacent letters."[67]

Morris Benton had already collaborated with his father in 1907 on a typeface designed to be especially legible (see the entry for Clearface), and he and his wife, both avid readers, were raising two young readers (they were 13 and 17 years old in 1915), so the subject of legibility was close to him. When his father had collaborated with Theodore Low De Vinne on Century Roman for the *Century Magazine*, they had discussed Emile Javal's legibility studies from 1879 (see Chapter 7). Javal's work must have come up again in 1900 when Morris experimented with Century Roman and worked on Century Expanded with his father. It is not surprising, then, that Morris Benton turned to the Century types as a basis for his Ginn and Company face.

He had also found a 1913 investigation by the British Association for the Advancement of Science entitled "Report on the Influence of School-Books Upon Eyesight."[68] The British report discussed the visual apparatus of the child, the psychology of the reading process, the care of one's eyesight, and lighting, paper, bookbinding, illustrations, type, line length, printing, and other topics. "Speaking generally," it said, "no definite principles or rules as to printing and other conditions of legibility have been adopted in the selection of school books, atlases, diagrams, & c."[69] The report lamented that, although "the existence of a very serious amount of visual defect [*sic*] among children of school age is established as a result of official inspection,"[70] no specific attention was being given to the legibility of school textbooks.

The report's supposition was that the immature optical apparatus of the growing child required books specially printed for children; it then gave recommendations for an ideal textbook. It argued, "The best type for isolated letters is not necessarily the best for word-wholes, and attention must be given to the comparative legibility of letters as seen in context."[71] The report recommended that compressed or condensed type should not be used in books for children, and that the contrast between fine and heavy strokes should not be too great. It went on,

> In an ideal type the whites and blacks are well balanced in each letter, and it is easy to discriminate between *e*, *c*, and *o*, between *i* and *l*, and between *h* and *k*; and to recognize *m, nn, nu, nv, w, in*.[72]

The report concluded by urging the "responsible authorities" to establish textbook production standards to protect the eyesight of children.

Benton responded by making tests of his own to determine what would constitute the best possible typeface for school textbooks. His studies of eyesight and reading led to the design of Century Schoolbook, which "subsequently turned up on nearly every list of legible types."[73] Century Schoolbook is bolder than Century Oldstyle or Century Expanded, although it is a normal-width type. Its wide open counters, large x-height, and squared-off serifs bring to fulfillment the original legibility ideals of De Vinne. Benton explained in a letter to N. J. Werner in 1936 that "the height of the 'm' is 65% of the height of the 'H' and the ascenders do not come above the 'H'."[74]

Morris Benton also designed Century Schoolbook Italic and Century Schoolbook Bold. Century Schoolbook Italic, according to Paul Shaw, is "basically a sturdier version of Century Expanded Italic, but the top serifs on the lowercase letters are flat … Thus, there is a strong x-height line for the eye to follow."[75]

Century Schoolbook was first advertised in the 1920 *Supplement No. 2* to the 1912 ATF type catalog. On Saturday, June 13, 1925, Morris Benton addressed the Industrial Educators of New Jersey at a luncheon given for them at the Jersey City ATF plant.[76] His talk, one of three at the event, was entitled "A Special Type for Educational Purposes," no doubt his own Century Schoolbook. Frazier wrote in 1925 that Century Schoolbook "reflect[ed] the composite opinion of those seeking to determine the most legible type."[77] But at first, the type was "a flop as a foundry face," as Watts explained in 1962:

> Very few printing teachers in junior and senior high schools specified Century Schoolbook. It is too black. Under a densitometer it shows up as bold as Bookman Oldstyle. Sales of foundry Schoolbook faces amounted to very little until advertising specifiers went for it around twenty years ago.[78]

Even though Century Schoolbook was initially overlooked, legibility remained an important value among those who used type. "Legibility is all that matters in 6- to 10-point types; so that their successful design is a technical, and not in the ordinary sense an artistic, achievement," Harry Carter wrote in 1937.

> None of the classical old-face types is good value in the small sizes. The punchcutters of the 16th–18th centuries when they cut diminutive types were thinking of footnotes and marginal notes to texts set in larger fonts, and they had not to think seriously of the problem of making long texts readable in small type. When newspapers came in fashion this problem became an urgent one.[79]

Century Schoolbook would eventually go "far beyond the schoolbook field to become one of the most popular designs for advertising and other printing,"[80] according to McGrew; but only when it was finally copied by other foundries and the composing machine manufacturers did it become popular. Century Modern by R. Hunter Middleton became the Ludlow Typograph Co.'s 1964 version of Century Schoolbook. The design was also acquired by the Mergenthaler Linotype Co. in the

A RIDE IN THE CARS

Evelyn cars ride one these ticket
two aboard New York all Donald

Characters. May, Grace, Evelyn, George, Donald,
Jack, Will, Frank, Ticket Man

(Arrange chairs for a train of cars, and have one chair with
a table or a desk for a ticket office. Let the children make
tickets for busy work)

Donald. Do you wish to ride in my
cars?

Evelyn. Yes, thank you. I wish to
ride in your cars.

Century Schoolbook

16 pt. 9A 20a 10-1   Lower case alphabet 220 pts.   Characters per pica 1.5

THE EARLY PRINTERS CAST THEIR
THEY INSTRUCTED some local blacksmith
to make the iron frame or chases in which
Century Schoolbook

16 pt. 9A 21a 9-1   Lower case alphabet 214 pts.   Characters per pica 1.6

THE EARLY PRINTERS CAST TYPE
They instructed some local blacksmith to
make the iron frame or chases in which
Century Schoolbook Italic

16 pt. 9A 17a 9-1   Lower case alphabet 245 pts.   Characters per pica 1.4

PRINTERS CAST THEIR TYPE IN
They instructed the local blacksmith
to make the iron frame or chases in
Century Schoolbook Bold

1960s.[81] Other names for adaptations of the face were Century Medium and Century Text, and the International Typeface Corporation (ITC)'s version was called Century Book. According to Alexander Lawson, in 1965 Century Schoolbook was "the most widely used member of the [Century] family … available on all composing machines as well as foundry type from ATF."[82] J. I. Biegeleisen wrote in 1976, "No respectable American printer is ever without a good supply of Century Schoolbook."[83] Today Century Schoolbook is a standard Microsoft typeface, and many digitized versions are available.

Benton included all three variations of the type in his 1936 list.

In her September 2006 thesis entitled *Searching for Morris Fuller Benton: Discovering the Designer through his Typefaces*, Juliet Shen argued that for her, Century Catalogue was the most readable of the Century typefaces. "However," she added, "Century Schoolbook is quite readable if typeset with open leading and extra word spacing as it would be in a child's book."[84]

Cheltenham, 1904–14

Although Morris Benton's name is associated with the great Cheltenham family of type, he did not design the original face. Cheltenham Oldstyle was drawn by Bertram Grosvenor Goodhue, an architect who designed St. Thomas Church in New York, the Nebraska State Capitol, and some buildings at the U.S. Military Academy at West Point, New York. He was also interested in the graphic arts, and designed the Merrymount typeface for Daniel Berkeley Updike's Merrymount Press.

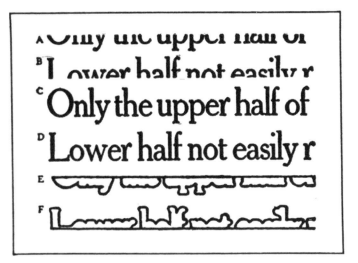

Illustrating greater importance to legibility of the upper half of lower-case letters and the individual outline of words in lower-case due to ascenders and descenders

From *Type Lore* by J. L. Frazier

Goodhue met a man named Ingalls Kimball when they both worked on the production of Stone and Kimball's *Chap Book*, first published in Boston in 1894. Years later Kimball, then owner of the Cheltenham Press in New York, commissioned Goodhue to design a type for the exclusive use of his press. Realizing, as Louis Emile Javal had in the late 1800s, that the upper half of a letter is more important than the lower half for recognition, Goodhue drew an alphabet with lengthened ascenders and shortened descenders. Goodhue and Javal's theory was corroborated in 1923 when a legibility study at Ohio State University found that Cheltenham was more legible than Baskerville and Bodoni types.[85] J. L. Frazier explained that "reading is a matter of recognizing word forms rather than of spelling out the letters that go to make up the words. In Cheltenham the long ascenders accent the word forms, which accounts for its very good legibility."[86] In *Type Lore*, Frazier used an illustration from *The Linotype Bulletin* to make this point; notice that line B can easily be read, but line A cannot.

There is some confusion as to the next steps in the evolution of the type. According to Frazier, the *Linotype Record* for October 1923 claimed that "the creation of the Cheltenham type (Old Style) is entirely owing to the Mergenthaler Linotype Company."[87] According to Watts, Kimball decided not to hold Goodhue's drawings exclusively for the use of his press, and instead sold the design to Mergenthaler Linotype, which brought out its Cheltenham type in 1906. In the meantime, however, Kimball, who had retained the rights to the foundry version of the type, sold these rights to ATF, whose Cheltenham preceded Mergenthaler's, since it came out in 1902.[88] Dr. James Eckman told a slightly different story:

There is an interesting tale of a feud in relation to the Cheltenham design.

It was told to me by Paul A. Bennett. It appears that when Bertram Gros-venor Goodhue brought out the design (and his version is not the one ultimately cut) for Cheltenham, the agreement was that the Mergenthaler Linotype Company was to cut the sizes which could be composed on the Linotype machine, and the American Type Founders Company was to manufacture and sell those sizes which could not be composed on the Linotype machine. But it is said that the American Type Founders Company proceeded to cut all sizes of the Cheltenham design, from 6 points upward, and I believe the Mergenthaler organization regarded this occurrence as an act of piracy. Morris Fuller Benton, as designer of the series, of course must have been in the very midst of this controversy.[89]

Watts wrote in the May 1957 issue of *Printing* magazine:

Hardly a man is now alive who knows that Cheltenham was first named "Boston Oldstyle" and that the mats for the 11-point size were the first complete font, for production purposes, to be cut on Linn Boyd Benton's matrix engraving machine. The cutting was done by Cuthbert W. ("Cubby") Lütke, in March, 1899. Subsequently, Morris Fuller Benton, only son of "the Edison of typemaking," masterminded the production of over a score of variations on Goodhue's basic design, Cheltenham Oldstyle.[90]

John Murphy indicated in the *Inland Printer* that the work of steering Goodhue's original drawings through production was Morris Benton's first type designing assignment.[91] This seems logical, since, as we have seen, someone would have had to modify Goodhue's original drawings considerably before they were ready to use. However the type's original name, Boston Oldstyle, suggested to some type historians that the modifications for the original typeface may have been done by J. W. Phinney at the Boston branch of ATF.[92] ATF produced its first version of Cheltenham (Cheltenham Oldstyle) in 1902, and Benton's first variant, Cheltenham Bold, was introduced in 1904. By 1912, 85 pages of the current ATF specimen book were used to show Cheltenham variations.

Cheltenham is a compact type with a condensed lower case and small x-height. The combination of short descenders and long ascenders enables Cheltenham to be set solid (that is, without extra "leading"—space between the lines). "This feature allowed for economic composition," Lawson wrote, "since leading could be dispensed with, even in longer than average lines."[93] The *Linotype Bulletin* reported that compositors could increase the number of words per thousand ems by almost one-fifth by using Cheltenham.[94]

Cheltenham's legibility made it a natural for advertising work, and when Benton expanded it into a family, its sales increased dramatically. Cheltenham never became

NEWEST FASHION FOR PRINT SHOPS

Cheltenham
Oldstyle
Type

Showing the
14 and 12 point
sizes, set solid
¶Compact and
legible

No. 5606A. Mortised. $1.00

MUCH can be said of Cheltenham, England, but its origin, like the origin of almost every town, is involved in doubt and obscurity. The revolutions to which this kingdom, in its earlier history, has been subject, and the consequent fluctuations of local customs and manners prescribe but limited bounds to the spirit of inquiry. Whether, as the affirmation goes, the word Cheltenham owes its rise to a river, a mountain, or the nature of its soil, is a subject more

as popular for straight-matter composition as Goodhue had hoped, but it did become one of the first great advertising types. "Up to the time that Cheltenham was created there was really no advertising type," John Murphy wrote in 1936. "It is true that a number of types were used effectively in advertising composition, but these types lacked the variety [of sizes and weights] needed in advertising work."[95] While earlier types such as De Vinne and Philadelphia Lining Gothic had already been made into type families (see Chapter 9), with Cheltenham the concept of a type family "really blossomed."[96] Benton's Cheltenham variations had "much greater popularity and sales than the parent design,"[97] and the family was becoming, according to Lawson, "a veritable goldmine for the foundry." He continued, "There was not a printing office in the land which didn't proudly accommodate one or more fonts of 'Chelt,' as it was more fondly described by the comps who were vaguely uncomfortable with the true British connotation of the full name."[98] (Cheltenham is simply the name of a town in Gloucestershire county in central England.)

Morris Benton did not take credit for the original design in his 1936 list of type-faces,[99] but he did include these Cheltenham variations:
    bold
    bold italic
    bold condensed
    bold extended
    bold extra condensed
    medium
    medium italic
    wide

Several other Cheltenham variations were also attributed to Benton:
    bold condensed italic

Cheltenham Oldstyle	
Cheltenham Wide	
Cheltenham Medium	*Cheltenham Medium Italic*
Cheltenham Bold	***Cheltenham Bold Italic***
Cheltenham Bold Condensed	***Cheltenham Bold Condensed Italic***
Cheltenham Bold Extra Condensed	CHELTENHAM BOLD EXTRA CONDENSED TITLE
Cheltenham Bold Outline	**Cheltenham Bold Extended**
Cheltenham Oldstyle Condensed	**Cheltenham Extrabold**
Cheltenham Italic	Cheltenham Inline

Cheltenham Inline Extended

Cheltenham Inline Extra Condensed

From ATF's 1912 specimen book.

bold extra condensed title
bold outline
bold shaded
bold italic shaded
extrabold
extrabold shaded
inline
inline extended
inline extra condensed
medium condensed
medium expanded
oldstyle condensed

In addition to these, at least five Benton Cheltenhams were abandoned at some stage in their production: bold black outline, bold condensed shaded, bold initials, monotone (all letter strokes being equal in width), and rimmed. Alexander Lawson gave Benton credit for all 21 usable variations of the original Cheltenham Oldstyle produced by 1915.[100]

Printers everywhere wanted Cheltenham. "Something new and decidedly different, Cheltenham took hold with a grip," Frazier wrote. "Its selection amounted to a rage; the universal order, seemingly, was 'When in doubt, use Cheltenham.'"[101] The Mergenthaler Linotype Co. brought out ten variants, Monotype followed with 15, Ludlow produced 13 Cheltenhams, and Intertype cut a dozen variations under the name Cheltonian. American type foundries outside the ATF merger also copied the face, the Inland Foundry calling it Kenilworth, and the Western Foundry, Chester-field. Cheltenham even became internationally popular: in England it was Gloucester at Monotype; Stephenson, Blake & Company named it Winchester; and a Dresden foundry called it Pfeil Antiqua. Steve Watts loved to tell of a version he found from the Morikawa Ryobundo Type Foundry in Osaka, Japan, called Chentury Bold.[102]

As early as 1915, Benjamin Duffield wrote the following about Cheltenham in the *American Bulletin*, ATF's advertising periodical:

> One cannot have too much or too great an assortment of this ideal letter. A font or so will prove but to create a desire for more, more, until its beauty and utility are convincingly recognized, then will come the wonder why one held aloof so long, and a general "stocking up" ensues.[103]

Cheltenham was overused, though, and began to lose popularity in the 1920s. Certain individual characters were criticized, especially the capitals A and G, the lower case a, and the final trilled r. Goudy Bold, introduced in 1917, greatly slowed up the sales of Cheltenham for a few years,[104] and, according to Lawson, from about 1928 to 1941, "Chelt was a black sheep."[105] Type designer and printing historian Douglas McMurtrie went so far as to say, "The appearance of most magazine and commercial printing will be improved by the simple expedient of denying any variants of the Cheltenham design to compositors."[106] Stanley Hlasta wrote that the type was tricky to work with, and that an advertisement set in Cheltenham and laid out improperly would appear lifeless. But in his 1950 book *Printing Types & How to Use Them*, he called Cheltenham the most widely known pure American typeface, very popular for newspaper advertising.[107]

Cheltenham had become a basic American design, going through frequent revivals but never actually dying. In 1983 Lawson and Provan called it "the best known type to be designed in the United States."[108] Although some typographers still regard it as old-fashioned, Lawson and Provan felt that "Cheltenham continues its long and happy existence as a valuable marketplace type." RIT Professor Charles Bigelow called Cheltenham "the Helvetica of its era—a ubiquitous face."[109]

ATF's 1934 *Book of American Types* offered Cheltenham Bold Italic in sizes 24 to 72 point both on a regular type body and on its new "angle body." Traditional italic type fonts included several kerned characters, and kerns had a tendency to break off with use; angling an entire font eliminated this problem. The specimen book explained:

> By this greatly improved method sizes 24 point and larger are cast on a sloping body practically eliminating the overhangs that break frequently when the form is being stereotyped or while it is on the press. Angle Body is as easy to set as type cast in regular molds. It is the modern way of making italic type.[110]

5-point Clearface

An angle body italic from ATF's 1934 specimen book   A 30-point Clearface d, enlarged

ITC brought out a version of Cheltenham in 1975, redrawn by Tony Starr. This Cheltenham became "one of the most popular typeface families that International Typeface Corporation offers."[111]

Clearface, 1907

The Clearface design came as a result of more than seven years of study by both Bentons. It was an earlier attempt at a legibility type than Century Schoolbook, as the July 1910 *American Bulletin* explained:

> The intention of the designer is to adapt the characters, singly and when assembled in words and lines, to the necessities of normal eyesight in a design agreeable to the senses of form and color. A glance at the smaller sizes (where the test is most severe) shows Clearface to be extremely optical ... favorable to vision, legible without strain to the optic nerves ... These characteristics of the Clearface ... are not, then, the results of a straining for oddity or "something different" upon which to hang a patent, but constitute the first deliberate, practical attempt in the history of type founding to make a type design conform to optical laws. We see that conformity to those laws has produced a design not only helpful to the eyesight, but agreeable and refreshing to every artistic sense, and therefore better adapted to fulfill the sole mission of types, which is to convey information or ideas to our intelligence without fatigue or shock.[112]

Most likely written by Henry Lewis Bullen, this article compares certain Clearface lowercase letters with those of other fonts. The top curves of many of Clearface's lowercase letters are varied to distinguish them, and the openings or white spaces at the junctions of curved and perpendicular lines are magnified by deflections of the lines. The lower end of the perpendicular line in the lowercase "d" is an example of this deflection.

Juliet Shen calls Clearface "eclectic."

> It combines oldstyle features—a pronounced oblique axis on the curved strokes, a Jensonian e, teardrop terminals and oblique ascender terminals—

CLEARFACE BOLD BECOMES MORE POPULAR EACH DAY TO USERS OF DISTINCT PRINTING This beautiful type design commands the attention of the reader's eye wherever displayed. As is signified by the name it possesses the exquisite feature of clearness together with the desirable character of boldness. The combination makes it a series which advertisers desire

Clearface Bold

Hotel Elizabeth
BROADWAY AND HURON STREET
CHICAGO

This is the newest and one of the greatest hotels in America. Hotel Elizabeth is a two million dollar structure, at the apex of the busiest section of Broadway, embodying in every feature the important idea of doing everything perfectly. It is the only hotel in this great city that caters exclusively to the women folks, thus enabling them to secure accommodations which are pleasant and entirely free from the annoying and very objectionable scrutiny of a curious throng in the lobbies and corridors. There is the rare quality of perfect taste, as well as of richness, permeating the whole house. The restaurant is the finest in this city, or in all America. The dignified, quiet comfort, the restful repose, the tasteful furnishings of the sleeping rooms, the reception and the reading rooms are similarly characteristic

Clearface Gothic

with nineteenth century features like slab serifs. The teardrop terminals grow abruptly out of the hairlines like the ball terminals of modern style romans instead of swelling naturally out of the stroke as in traditional old-style faces.[113]

According to Columbia University's 1923 annotated *Specimen Book*, Morris and his father designed Clearface Bold first, in 1905. They collaborated on Clearface Bold Italic in 1906, and Clearface and Clearface Italic in 1907. Morris Benton designed Clearface Gothic, a sans-serif type (see this chapter's explanation of gothic types, below), in 1908, and then Clearface Heavy and Clearface Heavy Italic, a non-kerning font.

Clearface Gothic seems to have been an experiment, since only one weight was designed. While McGrew felt that "it can hardly be considered part of that family,"[114] the characteristics of Clearface Gothic are remarkably similar to its roman cousin. Juliet Shen calls Clearface Gothic "likely the first instance of a fully harmonized san serif design based on a serif typeface, an idea several decades ahead of its time."[115] (Designing a "serial family," i.e., a type family encompassing both serif and sans-serif fonts, was attempted by Jan van Krimpen in 1932 with Romulus, although the sans-serif variants were never issued. In 1976–77, Gerard Unger designed his Demos and Praxis typefaces as a serial family; and in the early 1980s, Charles Bigelow and Kris Holmes began designing the Lucida family of fonts, which grew to encompass an extensive range of type styles.)

While Clearface Gothic most likely was the first sans serif designed to harmonize with a serif typeface, Shen concludes that the concept was "too far ahead of its time to make any inroads on the public taste. Perhaps Benton did not push the idea far enough by not making a bolder variant of the gothic."[116] Leave it to Morris Benton to have been the first to produce a serial type family, but to have had that accomplishment go unrecognized, even by his colleagues. ATF's 1912 *American Book of Type Styles* placed the printed samples of Clearface Gothic immediately after other members of the Clearface family, but 12 years later, in the 1923 *Specimen Book*, Clearface Gothic had been moved almost 300 pages away from the rest of the family, between Roycroft and Bold Antique.

Clearface became an advertising letter, but with the advent of sans-serif display types, advertisers lost interest in it.[117] None of the Clearface types are included in Morris Benton's 1936 list, but many digital versions are available today.

Bodoni, 1909

Giambattista Bodoni was born in Italy in 1740, and he became, according to Joseph Blumenthal in *The Art of the Printed Book*, "a master of the art of printing and a great and prolific type designer."[118] By 1788 he had cut a large number of fonts. In general, his roman types had exceptionally long ascenders and descenders, with very thin fine lines, thick heavier strokes, and apparently horizontal serifs, although upon close inspection the serifs had a very slight curve.

Bodoni's types were copied extensively in the early 19th century while he was still alive,[119] but these copies did not generally retain the beauty of the originals. "With a very few exceptions," Blumenthal wrote, "most of the so-called 'Bodonis' are libelous versions which perpetuate the name but not the designer's skills."[120] According to Charles Bigelow, in order to successfully revive a typeface, the designer must make it his own.

> This is the crucial paradox of type design imitation, and the force which drives type design evolution. A designer skilled and knowledgeable enough to perceive and render all the subtle nuances of another master craftsman is really too good to do a slavish copy. A master designer will inevitably transform an imitation into a creative act, which will give the new design true individuality.[121]

Benton did just this in his revival of Bodoni's types. They had "suffered much of an eclipse because of rank abortions and abuses," wrote A. Raymond Hopper in 1944, "until the American Type Founders brought it to public notice again in 1911 with Morris Benton's brilliant series, at present much adored and popular with most printers."[122] (Other sources give 1909 as the date of ATF's initial Bodoni offering.) Alexander Lawson called ATF's Bodoni "the first successful revival of the Italian master's type to be manufactured in this country."[123] McGrew agreed: "There have been numerous interpretations of Bodoni's typefaces, but the most popular in America are

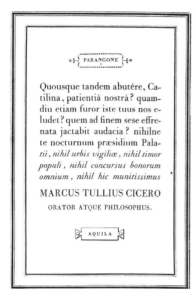

Bodoni's original type

UNIQUE BODONI SPECIMEN
Exquisite Series Nicely Designed
Display Remarkably Handsome

Benton's 36-point Bodoni

those drawn by Morris F. Benton for ATF or adopted from his work by other manufacturers."[124]

Henry Lewis Bullen said that Morris Benton spent three years studying the Bodoni
type models in ATF's Typographic Library before ATF issued a specimen of the
face.[125] In a 1927 letter to Kent D. Currie, Bullen explained that Benton's
preliminary studies disclosed the fact that Bodoni had made as many as
eighteen variations of his roman type design, the group forming an entirely
new division of type design which we now call "modern" to distinguish the
new divisions from the earlier romans which we now call "Old Style." These
variations compelled Mr. Benton to either select one of Bodoni's renderings of his idea or to effect a compromise. A compromise was made, which
resulted in the completion in February, 1910, of our Bodoni series, roman
and italic. This is a free interpretation of Bodoni's basic idea, but in no sense
a copy. For the purpose of present day printers it is, in the opinion of the
writer, an improvement on Bodoni's own cutting, especially in the italics."[126]

In 1911, the manager of the Nebiolo Type Foundry of Turin, Italy, Mr. Lobetti-
Bodoni (a descendent of Giambattista Bodoni), asked ATF for permission to use
Benton's Bodoni for a national commemoration of the death of Bodoni the following
year (1912).[127] ATF agreed, and Benton's interpretation of Bodoni's roman letters
became popular in Italy and Germany as a result. Lobetti-Bodoni in turn sent ATF's
Typographic Library and Museum copies of the materials that were printed for the
commemoration event: circulars, cards, menus, programs, and a biography of Bodoni.

ATF's Bodoni revival was also admired in the U.S., and after several years, copies began to appear. In 1923 Bullen verified in the *Inland Printer* that Morris Benton and the ATF Company were the "originators of the Bodoni type family," and accused the American composing machine manufacturers of copying it:

> The advertisers, now beginning to create their own designs, will understand how unpleasant it is to find one's design property, developed at a cost of thousands of dollars, copied so closely that the types fit into the originator's matrices with absolute precision.[128]

The Bodoni types by then had been copied extensively, and so Bullen's displeasure is understandable. A letter that Watts wrote in 1965 to RIT student David Ritter may explain why ATF's Bodoni was initially copied so often:

> Benton's rendering of Bodoni was introduced in 1910 but printers regarded it as too "precious" for everyday use, and ATF did not obtain a patent for the design until 1915. Its sharp serifs and hairlines made it a fragile face for everyday use, but when it was made available on non-distribution use and the demand for contrasty faces that developed around 1927 made Bodoni a "natural" for newspaper headings and advertising display lines, Bodoni came into its rightful popularity.[129]

In the meantime, Morris Benton developed his Bodoni revival into a type family. At first he concentrated on the typical variations: italic, bold, and bold italic. But over the years, Benton came back to Bodoni again and again. By 1933 the extended Bodoni family included 15 viable variants; three additional faces were abandoned.

Bodoni Italic
Bodoni Bold
Bodoni Bold Italic
Card Bodoni and Card Bodoni Bold (all-cap)
Bodoni Book, Bodoni Book Italic, and Bodoni Book Expanded (the latter abandoned)
Engraver's Bodoni and Engraver's Bodoni Open (the latter abandoned)
Bodoni Open (discontinued and then reintroduced in 1930)
Bodoni Bold Shaded
Bodoni Shaded Initials
Bodoni Bold Condensed (abandoned)
Ultra Bodoni, Ultra Bodoni Italic, Ultra Bodoni Condensed, and Ultra Bodoni Extra Condensed

The first Bodoni that Benton drew appears somewhat mechanical, but is very legible. The long ascenders and descenders, marked contrast between thicks and thins, and flat serifs give the face a distinction that is easily recognized. Hlasta called it "an aggressive face and unusually brilliant when printed on smooth, hard-finish stock."[130]

SOME KNIGHTS OF
After an apprentice as
Bodoni

KNIGHTS of the middle
Bodoni Book

KNIGHTS of the middle
Bodoni Book Italic

KNIGHTS ARE THE
After an apprentice has
Bodoni Italic

ALL KNIGHTS OF THE
After he serves as an
Ultra Bodoni Extra Condensed

ALL Knights of the
Bodoni Bold

ALL KNIGHTS
Ultra Bodoni

SOME KNIGHTS OF
After an apprentice is
Bodoni Bold Italic

THE KNIGHT
An apprentice
Ultra Bodoni Italic

Benton's family treatment of the original Bodoni roman made it ideal for newspaper headlines and magazine ads, and in the mid to late 1920s it became a very popular face. Bodoni consistently headed the list of most-used faces in the *Inland Printer*'s "Typographic Scoreboard," and the magazine even published a five-page article in 1939 quoting contemporary typographers on their reasons for Bodoni's success.[131] Type designer William A. Dwiggins, for example, rated Bodoni a 75 percent as compared with his ideal type, ATF Caslon No. 471. And J. L. Frazier wrote, "Bodoni suggests cleanliness—yes, even the 'hard' aspect found in hospital wards … On the whole it appears to be wearing a stiff collar and looks best in precise surroundings."[132]

As of 1934, Ultra Bodoni Italic in sizes 24 to 72 point was offered only in angle body fonts. Morris Benton included seven Bodoni typefaces in his 1936 list.

Cloister Oldstyle, 1913
The *American Bulletin* of April 1914 gave this background about Nicolas Jenson for an article about Cloister Oldstyle:

> Nicolas Jenson was born in France in 1420. He served as apprentice in the mint in Paris as an engraver of dies, and in 1458, while master of the mint in Tours, he was sent by the king to learn the secret of printing in Mainz, with a view to introducing the new art in France. He returned to France in 1461, but meanwhile another king was reigning, who apparently was not interested in printing, and the next we learn of Jenson is that he commenced printing

iube. Quod poſteaq̄ lictor ille q apparebat:cito intellexit : Maximum
‚pcoſule deſcedere iuſſit. Fabius imperio paret.& filiu collaudauit:quu
imperiu:quod populi eſſet:retinetet.
 Qua ratioe uerbis quibuſdā uocabuliſq; ueteres imiſerūt .h.litteræ
ſpiritū. Caput.iii.
  .Littera:ſiue illam ſpiritū magis q̄ litterā dici oportet:inſerebant
 eam ueteres noſtri pleriſq; uocibus uerboᷓ firmādis roborādiſq;:
ut ſonus earum eſſet uiridior:uegetiorq; .Atq; id uidétur feciſſe ſtudio
& exemplo linguæ atticæ.ſatis notum é atticos ιχθῡν ίροɴ: id eſt piſcé
pauperem.multa itidem alia : citra morem gentium græciæ cæterarum

Jenson's original type

ɴDREWE is expowned and is as
moche to saye as fair, or answeryng
vnto strengthe, & it is said of andor,
that is as moche to saye as strengthe.
Or andrewe is said thus, as antipos of
ana, which is to saye hye, & of tropos
which is conuersion, so that andrewe
is to saye a man hyely conuerted, and
in heuen adressyd vnto hys maker.
He was fayr in his lyf, answeryng in
wysedom and in doctryne, stronge in payne, and conuerted
hie in glorye. The prestes and diacones of achaye wrote his
passyon lyke as they had seen it with theyr eyen. ·

The Golden type of William Morris

in Venice in 1470, the second printer there. In his first year he produced
four important editions and more than one hundred and fifty-five during the
remaining ten years of his life. He used Roman types of one design and one
size until 1475, when he added two sizes of beautiful types.[133]

Jenson designed a roman typeface in 1470 to print his famous book *De Evangelica
Praeparatione* by Eusebius. He was influenced by humanist handwriting and by
previous attempts to capture that handwriting in type. He cut and cast the type in
only one size, about 16 point. Frazier explained in *Type Lore*, "In the preparation of
this type Jenson is said to have cut but one set of punches, the cutting being so well
accomplished that he concluded no changes were necessary."[134] Jenson's type has
been acclaimed by many type designers as one of the most beautiful ever cut. Hlasta
called him "the world's first great type designer, perhaps the greatest in all typographical history."[135]

Nicolas Jenson's 1476 edition of *Historia naturalis* by Pliny and another book
printed in Venice in the same year, the Jacobius Rubeus edition of *Historia Florentia*
by Aretino, inspired William Morris in England more than four centuries later to do
something about the cheap, ugly printing brought about by the Industrial Revolution
in England.[136] In 1888 Morris attended a lecture in London given by Emery Walker, a
master printer, typographic designer, and engraver, entitled "Letterpress Printing and

Illustration." Walker projected images of beautiful typefaces from early printed books and manuscripts onto a screen, and compared them to the weak, condensed Victorian typefaces that were common at the time. After the lecture William Morris asked Walker to help him design a new font of type. They enlarged photographs of Jenson's type, and Emery Walker drew the face, adjusting the fine details to his liking. The punches were then cut by Edward Prince.

This new typeface, called the "Golden" type, was much heavier than Jenson's letters and lacked the subtlety of the Roman stone inscriptions, but nevertheless it was a significant departure from the weak book types of the late 19th century, and it started a typographic trend. The Golden type was copied so frequently that "printers were soon awash in a sea of awkward imitations of the Morris type: Jenson Old Style (1893),[137] Mazarin (1895), Kelmscott (1897) and others."[138] Frazier noted that "the use of the style became so widespread that, despite its superiority over the thin modern styles that started William Morris on his reformation, the public soon tired of it."[139] And according to Bullen, although William Morris's characters were "full of faults, stiff, ungraceful and not easy to read—defects excusable in a beginner in type design—the Golden types had a tremendous influence in bringing typefounders and printers to a knowledge of how far they had departed" from Jenson's type.[140]

When Morris Benton began his research for an ATF version of William Morris's type, he did not turn to the Golden types but went back to Jenson's original. Benton was a long-time admirer of Jenson, and found the work a labor of love. Linn Boyd Benton acknowledged that it was Bullen who suggested to Morris Benton in 1913 that he revive the Jenson type.[141] "Through my initiative," Bullen later wrote, "the printers are enjoying the use of the Cloister Old Style series."[142]

Benton's preparatory work was exhaustive. He read extensively in the literature of the period, "saturated himself with the Venice of 1470, the year Jenson established his press,"[143] and tried to put himself in Jenson's place by visualizing the conditions under which he worked. Then, according to John Murphy, he asked himself, "What would Jenson do if he had the facilities of a type foundry like ATF?" In the process of designing ATF's version of Jenson's type, Morris Benton "gave full and untrammeled expression to the artistic side of his nature."[144] The result was Benton's favorite type,[145] Cloister Oldstyle, a face that captured the beauty and grace of the original Jenson letter. Alexander Lawson characterized it as "having many of the recognizable features of the Jenson letter but none of the oddities of the Golden type."[146]

ATF announced Cloister Oldstyle in 1913. It retained many of the details of Jenson's type, including the diagonal stroke of the e, the oblique stress (leftward inclination) of the lower case o and capital O, and the further extension of some serifs to the right. For example, in the capital A, the longer extension of the serif moves to the inside of the letter. The ascenders and descenders are unusually long, but because the letters are rounded, they are still very legible. The ascenders of the lowercase letters rise above the capitals, which are rather wide, and the lower case itself is somewhat close-fitting. There is only a slight variation between thin and thick strokes.

The family grew to include 11 members—by 1924 Benton had designed the following Cloister Oldstyle variations:

> italic
> bold
> bold italic
> bold condensed
> bold title
> cursive
> cursive handtooled
> lightface
> lightface italic
> title

Since Jenson cut his type before italic types were developed, Benton had to invent an italic for Cloister Oldstyle. He drew 12-degree inclined capitals based on the roman and added 14 alternate capitals, and used the type cast by Aldus Manutius in 1501 as a starting point for the lower case. Philip B. Meggs, "who developed the first academic curriculum for the study of graphic and advertising design,"[147] called Cloister Italic "far more compatible with the roman face than are most italics based on Renaissance models."[148]

The parent design was praised by typographers all over the country. "Of the productions of the American Type Founders Company in later years none can compare with the Cloister Oldstyle," wrote Harry Hillman, editor of the *Inland Printer*, in 1927.

> It is … without doubt one of the three most popular faces available today.
> With this type face a typographer worthy of his salt may build type forms
> of exceeding beauty and dignity. It reflects great credit on Mr. Benton as a
> type designer and the American Type Founders Company as producer.[149]

Frazier agreed:

> The genius of its designer, Morris Benton, is reflected in every detail of this
> handsomest of Venetian faces. Smoother, more graceful and more stylish
> by far than the Golden type, the movement from the stiff, mechanical style
> toward interesting and legible forms is admirably represented by Cloister.[150]

A. Raymond Hopper included Cloister Oldstyle in a 1944 dissertation on "enduring" typefaces, stating, "It took Morris Benton of the American Type Founders, centuries

ABCDEFGHIJKL ABCDEFGHIJKL
MNOPQRSTUVW MNOPQRSTUVW
XYZabcdefghijkl XYZabcdefghijkl
mnopqrstuvwxyz mnopqrstuvwxyz
The quick brown fox jumped The quick brown fox jumped
over the lazy dog. & 12345678 over the lazy dog. & 12345678

18 *Point Cloister Old Style*   A.T.F.   18 *Point Cloister Lightface*   A.T.F.

Cloister Oldstyle   Cloister Lightface

after Jenson's day, to reveal the true charm of the original in his still popular—and probably always popular—Cloister Oldstyle."[151] The American typographer Joseph Blumenthal wrote that Cloister Oldstyle was "a first breakthrough in the availability of new typefaces based on historic originals,"[152] and printer and typefounder Paul Hayden Duensing called it "the first well done, close approximation to the Jenson roman of 1470."[153]

Stanley Hlasta explained that because Morris Benton, the perfectionist, wanted to be sure that a printer's use of different kinds of paper wouldn't distort Cloister Oldstyle's beauty, he designed an alternate version of the type. Cloister Lightface, 1924, was intended for use on the earlier soft, antique papers, which generally thickened a typeface upon printing. The original 1913 Cloister Oldstyle, on the other hand, was slightly heavier, designed instead for the hard paper finishes and improved printing conditions of the early 1900s. These smoother papers were very different from the paper used in Jenson's day.[154]

Author and typographer Paul A. Bennett, director of typography for 30 years for Mergenthaler Linotype, explained that for the design of Cloister Lightface, "A. T. F. instructions to Mr. Benton were 'to let Mr. Jenson have his own way.'"[155] Bennett felt that Benton's result was an admirable face: "Of the several recuttings of Jenson's celebrated roman, Cloister and Cloister Lightface are the most faithful renderings."[156] McGrew considered Cloister Lightface the most faithful representation of Jenson's original type,[157] and Watts called it "the finest body letter ever cast, but sales of the type hardly paid for cutting the matrices."[158] Morris Benton included Cloister Oldstyle and six variants in his 1936 list.

Two other famous revivals of the original Jenson roman face were made after William Morris's Golden types fell out of favor. The first, well before Benton's Cloister Oldstyle, was the proprietary type used at the Doves Press, founded in 1900 in Hammersmith, London, by T. J. Cobden-Sanderson and Emery Walker, both friends of William Morris. The punches for their Jenson-based types were cut in 1899, also by

They all had need, I as thou seest have none.
₵ How hast thou hunger then; Satan reply'd,
Tell me if Food were now before thee set,
Would'st thou not eat? Thereafter as I like
The giver, answer'd Jesus. Why should that
Cause thy refusal, said the subtle Fiend,
Hast thou not right to all Created things,
Owe not all Creatures by just right to thee
Duty and Service, nor to stay till bid,

The Doves type

E thinks vertue is another manner of thing,
and much more noble, than the inclina-
tions unto goodnesse which in us are ingen-
dered. Mindes well borne and directed by
themselves follow one same path, and in
their actions represent the same visage that
the vertuous doe. But vertue importeth and
soundeth somewhat, I wot not what, greater
and more active, than by an happy com-
plexion, gently and peaceably, to suffer it selfe to be led or drawne
to follow reason. He that through a naturall facilitie and genuine
mildnesse should neglect or contenme injuries received, should no
doubt performe a rare action and worthy commendation; but he who,

Montaigne

Was born in a cavern of these mountains.
Like the river in yonder valley, whose first
drops flow from some cliff that weeps in a
deep grotto, the first moments of my life
sped amidst the shadows of a secluded re-
treat, nor vexed its silence. As our mothers
draw near their term, they retire to the cav-
erns, and in the innermost recesses of the
wildest of them all, where the darkness is
most dense, they bring forth, uncomplaining, offspring as silent as
themselves. Their strength-giving milk enables us to endure with-

Centaur

LOISTER OLDSTYLE and Cloister Lightface are adaptations to twentieth century use of the celebrated roman type
design of Nicolas Jenson, first used by
him in his printing house in Venice in
1470. Jenson's design, cut by him in
one size only (approximately 16 point), has been acclaimed
by many authorities as the ideal roman type design. The
American Type Founders Company has conscientiously

Benton's Cloister Lightface

Edward Prince (who had cut the Golden types).[159] But, starting in 1913, Cobden-Sanderson secretly began to throw the punches, matrices, and finally more than a ton of the Doves type itself off the Hammersmith Bridge into the Thames River below, to prevent it from falling into Walker's hands after his death.

The other famous Jenson revival was Centaur, designed in the U.S. by Bruce Rogers. Punches from his first set of drawings based on Jenson's types were cut freehand near Boston in 1901 by John Cumming, but Rogers was unhappy with the outcome. This early version was called Montaigne. Rogers later reworked the design for the Metropolitan Museum of New York by simply enlarging Jenson's letters and drawing over them.

> When I made the Centaur type I enlarged Jenson's and wrote *over* the
> prints with a flat pen—just as rapidly as I could—then I selected the best
> (?) of my characters and touched them up with a brush and white—(no
> black) just about as much as a punch-cutter would do with a graver—and
> the type was cut from these patterns.[160]

This time Rogers asked Robert Wiebking of Chicago to cut the matrices using his matrix-engraving machine, and the work was completed in 1914.[161] The new type was first used in the Montague Press edition of *The Centaur*, a short story by Maurice de Guérin, translated from the original French by George B. Ives.

RIT Professor Herbert H. Johnson revealed the story of Centaur's influence on Cloister Lightface in his contribution to the 1998 book *American Proprietary Typefaces*. Apparently ATF attempted to purchase the Centaur matrices for casting on its own machines from Rogers, who was "no doubt willing to accept ATF's dollars, but he had already sold rights to the Metropolitan Museum of Art." ATF's failure to obtain the Centaur type then became the impetus for Benton to redesign Cloister Oldstyle and its italic. "The new Cloister Lightface and Italic," Johnson wrote, "designed in 1919 but not issued until 1924, was meant to fill a niche for a Centaur-like type in fine book work."[162]

> Juliet Shen prefers Centaur to Cloister Oldstyle because, as she wrote in 2006, Benton's Cloister Oldstyle, while showing his interpretive abilities in the refinement of serifs and terminals, suffers in the aggregate from a slightly too regularized stroke and baseline—the overall texture is a bit flat. It is an authentic revival when individual letterforms are examined, but the overall impression is less spirited than the original.

> Rogers seems to have grasped that the irregularities of the inked impression in Jenson's book were crucial to the charm of the typeface, for he went to pains to avoid having his drawings regularized in the cutting. His is a less faithful interpretation of Jenson, but the liberties taken resulted in a livelier typeface that better shares the spirit of the original.[163]

Morris Benton's Cloister Oldstyle was copied by Linotype, Intertype, and Monotype, "but not by Ludlow," McGrew noted, "which had its own distinctive version drawn by Ernst Detterer and Robert H. Middleton under the name Eusebius."[164]

Garamond, 1914–17

In 1914 Morris Benton began work on another classic face when he accepted Henry Lewis Bullen's suggestion to revive what they thought were the types of Claude Garamond, a 16th-century punch-cutter.[165] (Frank Denman explains in *The Shaping of Our Alphabet* that Garamont usually spelled his name with a 't' but that later it became "the fashion" to spell it "Garamond."[166] This chapter follows "the fashion.") The types that Benton used for his model were called the "Caracteres de l'Universite." Their punches and matrices had been discovered in 1845 at the Imprimerie Nationale in Paris, and after type was cast from them in the early 1900s they were erroneously identified as Garamond's.

Claude Garamond was born in about 1500 in France and became one of the first independent type designers there. Harry Carter wrote, "He was by trade a punchcutter and, no doubt, a matrix-maker too, not a printer."[167] In 1545 Garamond dabbled in publishing and established his own type foundry,[168] "the first in the world," according to Frazier, "which was not an adjunct of a printing plant."[169] At some point the French printer and typographer Geoffrey Tory gave Garamond a copy of *De Aetna* by Pietro Bembo, printed in 1495 using the big roman text type cut for Aldus Manutius by Francesco Griffo.[170] Garamond adapted Griffo's letters in a new cutting; later,

TERENTIANI

MAVRI NILIACAE SYENES PRAESI-
DIS, DE LITERIS, SYLLABIS, PEDIBVS ET
metris, tractatus infignis, fufpiciendus antiquitate eti=
am reuerenda, Nicolao Briffæo Montiuillario com=
mentatore & emendatore.

Garamond's original type

Les principaux poincts de la Foy contre les ministres
de la religion prétendue réformée, *par Mgr le cardinal de
Richelieu, in-folio, 1641;*

Plusieurs auteurs latins, un Novum Testamentum *en grec
& une* Biblia sacra, *tous deux in-folio & à la date de 1642;*

Conciliorum omnium generalium & provincialium
collectio regia,..... concinnata a P. Labbe, *in-folio, 1644.*

The "Caracteres de l'Universite," from the Impremerie Nationale

Garamond as released by ATF in 1919

Garamond and Garamond Italic, with T. M. Cleland's changes

Christopher Plantin used Garamond's type for his famous polyglot Bible. Garamond
died in poverty in 1561, and his punches and matrices were acquired by other type
founders. For example, the Egenolff-Berner type foundry of Frankfurt, Germany,
printed a type specimen in 1592 containing several fonts attributed to Garamond.[171]
It was generally presumed that other Garamond types became part of the collection of
the Imprimerie Nationale in Paris, and that these were the types that became known
as the Caracteres de l'Universite.

When Benton designed his Garamond he toned down the exaggerations of the Caracteres de l'Universite, "and as far as possible," Beatrice Warde wrote, avoided "'dazzle'
in the smaller sizes."[172] He shortened the descenders, increasing the typeface's legibility but also, unfortunately, making additional leading a necessity. Benton's ATF
revival was light and clean, with just a slight variation between thick and thin letter
strokes. It showed a shorter tail on the capital Q and a subdued italic lowercase *k* and
w, which had been rather exotic in their original versions.

Initially ATF did not publicize Benton's Garamond but, according to printing historian James Moran, "the fact that during 1916 and 1917 the firm was producing
a series of eminent merit leaked out and certain typographically conscious printers 'forced their orders on the Company,' to use Bullen's words, as each size was

12 POINT GARAMOND AND ITALIC. The body type faces shown on this and accompanying pages are some of the famous types of printing history. They cover a wide range of styles making easy the selection of the correct body type for any piece of printing. The lines have been made long enough to be of service in calculating copy space. *All the faces of each size have been grouped*

ATF Garamond

DIGNIFIED FOR
Broadsides, Booklets
and folders as well as

FINER BOOKS
in Garamont face

Display Heads

From ATF's 1921 booklet advertising Garamond type   Goudy's Garamont type

completed."[173] John Henry Nash of San Francisco was the first to request the type, in 14- and 18-point fonts. When his work with them became public, according to an eight-page ATF advertising pamphlet no doubt written by Bullen, "orders were forced upon the company by such other eminent printers as Bruce Rogers, Thomas M. Cleland, D. B. Updike, William E. Rudge, Edwin Grabhorn, and others."[174]

Benton designed Garamond Italic in 1918, the bold in 1920, and the bold italic in 1923. In 1922, T. M. Cleland added some swash characters and alternates to Garamond Italic. Henry Lewis Bullen noted in a 1923 article that Bruce Rogers was also responsible for some revisions to the face.[175] For example, Benton's original E, F, and L were considerably wider than those in ATF's subsequent Garamond Roman, and his original J did not extend below the baseline. Finally, in 1931, Benton designed Garamond Open. ATF Garamond became the U.S. standard for Garamond type. Hlasta claimed in 1950 that, "insofar as advertising faces are concerned, it is sufficient to say that this type is the pick of the crop for a versatile display face which may be used for most products."[176]

With Benton's Garamond revival he had once again started a trend. By 1921, Frederic Goudy had completed his Garamont type for Lanston Monotype, also based on the Caracteres de l'Universite. (His E, F, J, and L resembled Benton's original letters before they were revised.) Bullen was eager to have type critics compare Goudy's Garamont with Benton's Garamond, both modeled on the same original letters. Bullen of course favored Benton's work, but he allowed another opinion in an *Inland Printer* article he wrote in 1923: "Mr. [William A.] Kittredge says that Mr. Goudy's Garamond [*sic*] is better than Mr. Benton's Garamond." Bullen then pointed out that no matter which type won this contest, the ATF face had been in production 60 months before Goudy "decided to give his company a substitute,"[177] and thus ATF had started the Garamond craze in the U.S.

A 1926 article in the *Fleuron* by "Paul Beaujon" (Beatrice Warde's pseudonym) established the fact that the Caracteres de l'Universite were not Garamond types at all, but were the work of Jean Jannon, a Parisian from the early 1600s.[178] Jannon had been using Garamond types, but when he moved to Sedan (about 131 miles from Paris) in 1610, "he was unable to buy the needed types for his new undertaking, so he set out to create his own. The results [were] undoubtedly influenced by Garamond,"[179] but they were not Garamond's own.

The news that ATF's Garamond types were actually based on the types of Jean Jannon did not affect sales. On the contrary, the type became so popular that, besides the two Monotype versions already mentioned, Intertype copied it in 1927 and Mergenthaler Linotype in 1936. In 1924 the Stempel foundry in Germany produced a Garamond based on an actual Garamond type.[180] Linotype & Machinery of London also issued a type based on Garamond's original work that same year, designed by George W. Jones and called "Granjon" (one of Garamond's contemporaries). Other Garamond types followed.

Beatrice Warde wrote this about Benton's version:
> The design was copied in America after the war [World War I], but something was lost in the copying, naturally, and one might say fortunately; for "Garamond" emerged from Jersey City, U.S.A., with a chastened expression on its Gallic face, and began to look, in this soberer version, like a real book type.[181]

Like Cheltenham Bold Italic, Garamond Bold Italic was offered in 1934 on both a regular body and angle body for sizes 24 to 72 point. Morris Benton included all five of his Garamond types in his 1936 list of type designs.

Souvenir, 1914
Many people do not realize that the source for ITC's extremely popular Souvenir type was Morris Benton's Souvenir, released in 1914 in a single weight. Benton modeled this letter after "Schelter Antiqua," a 1905 German Art Nouveau type produced by the Schelter & Giesecke foundry in Leipzig. The Bitstream Digital Type Library

Nr. 17 293. 16 Punkt. 40 a 16 A ═ ¼ Satz etwa 6 kg

Bilder deutscher Städte

36 Point 6 A 10 a

MENDER

Nr. 17 294. 20 Punkt. 30 a 12 A ═ ¼ Satz etwa 7 kg

Moderne Gedichte

Straighten

Nr. 17 295. 24 Punkt. 24 a 10 A ═ ¼ Satz etwa 7 kg

Das Freie Wort

Nr. 17 296. 28 Punkt. 24 a 10 A ═ ¼ Satz etwa 9,2 kg

Sonnenbäder

30 Point 7 A 12 a

BRIGHTER

Nr. 17 297. 36 Punkt. 16 a 8 A ═ ¼ Satz etwa 12 kg

Gemeinde Neckerchief

Schelter Antiqua, from a late 1920s specimen book   Morris Benton's Souvenir

claims that "Morris Fuller Benton took the rounded half of the characters (g, s, v, w, y) almost without change, wholly redesigning the remainder, some of which have a chiseled appearance in the original."[182]

Souvenir is easily recognizable and somewhat odd. Perhaps due to its initial lack of sales, Benton did not draw any variants to the face. While his original revival of the Schelter type did not become popular, ITC licensed the face from ATF in the late 1960s and released ITC Souvenir for phototypesetting, re-drawn by type designer Edward Benguiat, in 1970. ITC Souvenir and its many variations subsequently became ubiquitous for book work and advertising in the 1970s and beyond, one of the few font families that even small printing shops were required to own. Souvenir became so popular that later it was cut on matrices in two weights with italics for the Linotype, by Matrotype in England. "This is one of very few instances of a phototype face being cut in metal," McGrew wrote.[183] Even ATF was prompted to reissue it in metal in 1972.

Souvenir elicits strong feelings from type aficionados. In the 1993 book *Types Best Remembered/Types Best Forgotten*, edited by Robert Norton, conflicting opinions of various typefaces are presented. Mark Batty, president of ITC until it was taken over by Agfa-Monotype and later president of the international typographic association ATypI, wrote in the *Types Best Remembered* section of the book that Souvenir was

> the very embodiment and representation of the most catholic zeitgeist of the middle 1970s onwards. And it is a quintessentially American typeface, with real solid character … [It] somehow communicates optimism, it is friendly, wholesome, and undemanding to the eye.[184]

However the *Types Best Forgotten* section of the book is replete with Souvenir entries. RIT Professor Frank Romano wrote, "There's nothing wrong with Souvenir that a complete re-design would not cure." Norton called it "A Terrible Typeface. What a bore." Peter Guy claimed that

> a more hideous rabble never straggled across a page … If this type had been cobbled together in a couple of hours under the influence of an emperor-sized hangover it would be bad enough. But this is a typeface saying "everyone must recognize me instantly. The layman may not know boring old Times from boring old Centaur or boring old Ehrhardt from boring old Baskerville but I am so different that everyone will recognize me." ANY author deserves better than Souvenir—even Barbara Cartland and I.[185]

French typographer and type designer Roger Excoffon used ITC Souvenir for his re-design of France's Income Tax Return forms in 1973. John Dreyfus wrote, "I have sometimes wondered whether he used the type named Souvenir (French for remember) so as to pique the conscience of typographically sophisticated French taxpayers."[186]

Morris Benton did not include Souvenir in his 1936 list of typefaces.

Baskerville, 1915

John Baskerville was born in 1706 in Worcestershire, England, and settled in Birmingham by the time he was 20, earning a living there at first by engraving tombstones and teaching handwriting, and later by the japanning (varnishing) trade.[187] In 1750 he began experimenting with type and printing, perhaps because in that year the *Universal Magazine* published an article entitled, "The Art of Cutting, Casting, and Preparing of Letter for Printing, with a neat Representation of a Letter-founder's Work-house." Baskerville hired John Handy to cut his punches, and his first type specimen was printed in 1754. He designed the type for his first book, a 1757 edition of Virgil's works, which was widely praised everywhere except in England.

After producing Milton's *Paradise Lost*, Baskerville's next ambition was to print the Book of Common Prayer and the Bible, and although he accomplished this goal (two Prayer Books were published at Cambridge in 1760, followed by a Bible at Cambridge and a New Testament set in his own Greek types at Oxford in 1763), he lost a great deal of money in the process and decided to sell his foundry and printing equipment. Without any acceptable offers, Baskerville regained some enthusiasm and then produced several other classic texts before he died in 1775.

Within the next few years his widow managed to sell a only few fonts of Baskerville's type, even though she was "willing to sell her whole printing equipment, with all punches, matrices, and everything pertaining to the typefoundry, besides the glazing machine and the receipt for printer's ink ."[188] She was finally able to sell everything, for

720 Ipſe, ſedens niveo candentis limine Phœbi,
  Dona recognoſcit populorum, aptatque ſuperbis
  Poſtibus: incedunt victæ longo ordine gentes,
  Quam variæ linguis, habitu tam veſtis, et armis.
  Hic Nomadum genus, et diſcinctos Mulciber Afros,
725 Hic Lelegas, Caraſque, ſagittiferoſque Gelonos
  Finxerat. Euphrates ibat jam mollior undis,
  Extremique hominum Morini, Rhenuſque bicornis,
  Indomitique Dahæ, et pontem indignatus Araxes.
    Talia, per clypeum Vulcani, dona Parentis

Baskerville's original type

Quouſque tandem abutêre, Catilina,
patientia noſtra? quamdiu nos etiam
furor iſte tuus eludet? quem ad finem
ſeſe effrenata jactabit audacia? nihil-
ne te nocturnum/præſidium palatii,
nihil urbis vigiliæ, nihil timor popu-

Joseph Fry & Sons' Baskerville Old Face, 1786

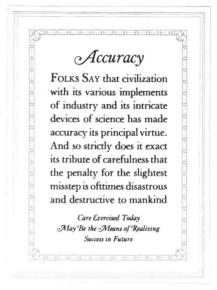

ATF's Baskerville Roman, and Baskerville Italic

less than half of Baskerville's initial offering price, to the Literary and Typographical Society, which apparently had only one member, Pierre-Augustin Caron de Beaumarchais, the French dramatist who wrote *The Barber of Seville* and *The Marriage of Figaro*. Baskerville's punches and matrices then began a bizarre odyssey, traced by the British type historian John Dreyfus in his essay *The Survival of Baskerville's Punches*.[189]

In the meantime, Isaac Moore had cut a copy of Baskerville's letterforms for the English type foundry Joseph Fry & Sons[190]; this "Baskerville Old Face" first appeared in a 1766 specimen sheet.[191] Some original matrices cut by Moore in 1795 eventually found their way to the Birmingham type foundry of Stephenson, Blake & Company, where Fry's Baskerville was reissued in 1910 in a full range of sizes.[192] According to Mac McGrew, ATF's version of Baskerville, Baskerville Roman, was produced from strikes (unfinished matrices) that had been brought to New York from Stephenson, Blake in 1915.[193] In 1915 Morris Benton designed ATF's Baskerville Italic, "with a few fancy capitals added."[194]

Fry's Baskerville type was not originally cut in the smaller sizes, but ATF made Baskerville Roman available in the full range of sizes, from 6 to 72 point, although most type shops only bought the display sizes. Watts listed Baskerville Roman as a type designed by Morris Benton, perhaps because Benton redrew the letters based on the images in the original strikes, and determined the extension/condensation variables on the engraving machine for the various sizes. Perhaps Benton also fitted the original unfinished matrices from England. But despite Watts's opinion that it was a Benton font, Morris Benton did not include Baskerville on his 1936 list of type designs.

The Baskerville types are graceful, open, and clear. The characters are round and wide, but thin, and therefore do not tolerate much abuse in hot metal form. Frazier wrote, "The hair-line elements and sharp-pointed serifs are more easily nicked than those of Caslon type, with which the uninitiated might readily confuse it, although it is a rounder, fuller face."[195] Harry Carter warned that Baskerville "is meant to be leaded: set solid it has a bad balance between vertical and horizontal spacing, but leading restores the equilibrium."[196]

Perhaps Morris Benton didn't include any members of the family on his 1936 list because ATF's revival of Fry's Baskerville did not catch on until many years after it was introduced, when national advertisers rediscovered the face and used it in several advertising campaigns.[197] ATF was the first American foundry to revive Baskerville, although other foundries and the composing machine manufacturers duly copied it. Linotype Baskerville, cut in 1926, was said to be based on Baskerville's original punches, which were still in existence.[198] These original punches were held by the Paris type foundry Deberny et Peignot until the early 1950s, when John Dreyfus persuaded Charles Peignot to donate them to the Cambridge University Press.

The demand for foundry Baskerville did not noticeably diminish until about 1948, and even then it remained a staple of ATF's dwindling inventory.

Goudy Bold, 1918
The story of this type and the nine-member family to which it belonged is told in Chapter 13. In 1983 Lawson and Provan wrote that Benton's Goudy Bold was "by far the most widely used of the series, and remains in daily use 65 years after its introduction."[199] However none of the members of the Goudy Bold family is included in Morris Benton's 1936 list.

Bulmer, 1926
Originally designed by William Martin in 1790 for the English printer William Bulmer, this typeface was used to print an edition of Shakespeare at Bulmer's Shakespeare Printing Office in London. Martin may have learned to cut punches in Baskerville's foundry in Birmingham, because his brother was the foreman of the printing office there.[200] Martin's design seemed to bridge the gap between the Baskerville and Bodoni types—it was more condensed and contrasty than Baskerville, but less mechanical and modern than Bodoni.

When Henry Lewis Bullen suggested that Martin's type become one of ATF's revivals, Morris Benton agreed.[201] Benton studied the books of Bulmer's press and decided to name the type after the printer rather than the original punch-cutter. Type historians disagree as to the exact date of Benton's work on Bulmer, but McGrew wrote, "Foundry records show that trial cuttings of the roman were made in 1925 and of the

Remote, unfriended, melancholy, slow,
Or by the lazy Scheld, or wandering Po;
Or onward, where the rude Carinthian boor
Against the houseless stranger shuts the door;
Or where Campania's plain forsaken lies,
A weary waste, expanding to the skies;
Where-e'er I roam, whatever realms to see,
My heart, untravell'd, fondly turns to thee:
Still to my Brother turns, with ceaseless pain,
And drags at each remove a lengthening chain.

William Martin's type, 1795

URS
OF PRE-EMINENT QUALITY

Dramatizing and heightening your love-
liness while subtly avoiding the obvious
and emphasizing the richness and good
taste that are the marks of distinction in
style and styling, furs by Curfelessi make
each wearing an unforgettable occasion,
and furnish a memorable climax to a
most truly distinguished social season.

Curfelessi
BOSTON

An ad set in Bulmer

MOUNTain scenery is the glory those
Bulmer Roman

MOUNTain scenery is the glory of those
Bulmer Italic

italic in 1926 with all sizes of each cut a year later."[202] In 1928 ATF issued Bulmer Roman, and it was immediately acclaimed. Bulmer Italic soon followed. Although the family consisted of only these two variants, Lawson noted that the type was "greatly admired by modern printers, and stands as one of Benton's most popular revivals."[203] In 1965, Dr. James Eckman rated Bulmer Roman and Italic "among the most distinguished text faces in use today,"[204] and Maurice Annenberg wrote in the 1970s that Benton's "Bulmer Roman and Italic have never been surpassed."[205] Hlasta called Bulmer "a regular face having few peculiarities."[206] The ascenders and descenders are long, the lower case g leans to the left, and the capital R has a curved tail.

Bulmer also became popular as a display type and later was made available for machine casting on the Monotype, and for line casting by Intertype. Bulmer was converted to film for early phototypesetting devices and several digital versions are available today. Morris Benton listed Bulmer and its accompanying italic as his typefaces.

Cambridge, Benton, or Whitehall, 1934

Benton designed a typeface in the early 1930s that sold for a few years and then was withdrawn[207] but has been discussed ad infinitum by Morris Benton enthusiasts. Its original name, "Cambridge," was changed to "Benton" on the cutting slips. Many years after it was withdrawn, ATF revived the type as "Whitehall." The type was Mac McGrew's favorite face for certain applications and the house type he chose for his Press of the Licorice Cat.[208] He called it "a modern interpretation of traditional types, combining refinement and legibility."[209] It suggests Baskerville, Caledonia, or Bulmer, McGrew wrote, but "several little details delight me—the almost calligraphic foot on

BENTON [48]
ATF 566, aka [36]
Whitehall

∾

ABCDEFGHIJKLMNO
PQRSTUVWXYZ&abcd
efghijklmnopqrstuvwxyz
$1234567890(.,-:;"!?)

Eight sizes seek good home

Like the beauty of old lace, the attractiveness of a type page depends upon a combination of many separate designs, each one beautiful in itself but without individual oddities to detract from the mass effect. Benton is the result of a long study of the best of the classical types. It retains many of the notable characteristics of both the Oldstyle and the Modern and produces a page which is readable and brilliant without being dazzling. This paragraph is 10 Point Benton.

Benton type, "in preparation," 1934

the d, for instance, and the way the crossbar of the e flows into the curve; these little things keep it from being severe."[210]

The first seven trial letters of the italic were cut in 36 point on November 20, 1931.[211] The following week the same letters were cut in 12 point, and a few years later, on June 28, 1934, 69 characters were cut in 12 point. The roman was first announced as "Benton" on page 9 of ATF's 1934 *Book of American Types*, where a paragraph set in 10 point appears with five other new types "in preparation." But the face with the name "Benton" never made it into an ATF specimen book as a completed product. "It was listed and shown in one line in the 1937 and 1939 Index of American Types, and included in the 1938 price list,"[212] McGrew wrote in 1985. But it was never again listed as "Benton."

Morris Benton retired from ATF in 1937, although for a time he remained a consultant to the company. Watts, in charge of ATF's type sales by 1948, became especially interested in the Bentons, and decided in 1953 that the type named after Morris Benton should be reissued under a new name. Watts explained:

> This face, designed by Morris Benton, he named "Cambridge." For some reason unknown to me, cutting of a companion italic for this face had been abandoned and "Benton" was never made for sale. When I decided that the type should be given a chance, in 1953, the name "Whitehall" was the result of a compromise to save moving tons of type to place it on stock shelves at the foundry and at sales branches. More than half of the ATF faces at that time were in the A, B, and C categories. "Whitehall" as a name placed it at the tail end of the alphabetical list, after Wedding Text.[213]

ALL KNIGHTS OF
An apprenticeship as
page and squire was

ATF's re-named Benton type, Whitehall

Richard Marder poses in 1984 with ATF types

Thus the only Morris Benton typeface that at one time indicated the identity of its designer was renamed. Alexander Lawson reiterated the story in a 1961 magazine article:

> ATF chose to call [the Benton type] Whitehall. The reason was quite simple. At the foundry, and in all the dealer locations in the various states, type is stored in inventory by alphabetical sequence. Thus it was decided to switch from a "B" to a "W," as fewer fonts would have to be shifted to make room for the new design.[214]

Given Morris Benton's persona at ATF, perhaps it is appropriate that none of his typefaces were named after him. The name "Whitehall" was taken from a New York telephone exchange.

Whitehall was shown in one-liners in the 1953, 1958, and 1966 ATF specimen books, and in full pages in the 1955 and 1961 books. But in a memo to dealers dated October 31, 1967, it was listed as one of the ATF faces to be discontinued.[215] It was never made into a machine-set face.

3. Gothics

In the 19th century, European type foundries began experimenting with letters that did not have serifs. Alexander Lawson called this development "the most radical typographical innovation since the invention of movable type itself." He continued:

> Before the early 1800s types were almost exclusively modeled on manuscript writing. The sans serif forms, however, had no historic precedent. Although some believe Roman coins inspired the sans serif, this can undoubtedly be discounted, as can the inscriptional sans serif lettering dating from the

BRIDGENORTH
Communicate

The first known example of an upper- and lowercase sans-serif type, from Thorowgood & Co.'s Fann Street Letter Foundry, 1837

fifteenth-century which was probably unknown to the nineteenth-century founders. More likely, the success of the Egyptian, or Antique, display letters led to experiments producing this ultimate simplicity in a printer's type.[216]

James Mosley, librarian of the St. Bride Printing Library in London from 1958 to 2000, wrote an essay about the origins of sans-serif typefaces in England, entitled *The Nymph and the Grot: The Revival of the Sanserif Letter.* While British type historians might not have been surprised at the discovery of a 1748 sans-serif inscription on a stone on the Stourhead estate in Wiltshire County, Mosley also found many 18th-century examples of hand-drawn sans serifs on maps, architectural renderings, medals, and commercial posters. These letterforms were reminiscent of the early Greek sans-serif letters that are chiseled into a fifth-century marble slab that is part of the Elgin Collection in the British Museum. "Sanserifs were to be found almost everywhere during the first decade of the nineteenth century—in the work of architects, sculptors, die-cutters for medals, and engravers on copper and wood," Mosley wrote. "They were everywhere, therefore, except among the products of the typefounders."[217] When sans-serif letters began appearing on hand-drawn signs in the streets of London, "this new style was startling enough to attract the attention of a lay public that was normally indifferent to the forms of letters."[218]

The first known sans-serif type for printing was a one-line entry of all-capital monotone letters in a British type specimen book from the foundry of William Caslon IV, circa 1816, labeled "Two Lines English Egyptian." The term "Egyptian" was being used by the makers of street signs to designate the sans-serif style, and the term "English" referred to what we now call a 14-point type size. Curiously, the term Egyptian was soon afterwards applied to "slab serif" types[219] (see the section on Egyptian types in this chapter).

The first example of an upper- and lowercase sans-serif printing type was produced by William Thorowgood at London's Fann Street Foundry in 1832 and called "Grotesque." Other British foundries began using various names for the style, such as Sans-serif, Sans-surryphs, Doric, and Gothic. German foundries adopted the Fann

These Letters

Are modeled after suggestions by General Chas. H. Taylor of the Boston Daily Globe. Attention is called to the remarkable clearness of the 6-point and 8-point sizes, and to the absence throughout the entire series of all close white spaces which tend to fill up in printing. A larger size, 96 point, is in preparation, to be ready at an early date

Globe Gothic Extended

Globe Gothic Condensed

Globe Gothic Extra Condensed

Globe Gothic Bold

Benton's Globe Gothic, 1904

ROSEBUSH
Glad 9 Peal

36 POINT   5 A $2 55   8 a $2 45 $5 00

BOLD SCARE
Master Reach

30 POINT   6 A $2 30   9 a $1 95 $4 25

PRODUCTIONS
Quick & Legible

Street Foundry's term, and in France the style became known as "Antique." The first type foundry in the U.S. to produce a sans-serif font of type was the Boston Type and Stereotype Foundry in 1837. According to Lawson, in "a typical demonstration of American independence,"[220] the Boston foundry called the type "gothic."

The term "gothic" in Europe referred to type based on styles from the very early days of printing (in other words, what later came to be called "blackletter" in the U.S.). The only similarity between the original "gothic" types and these new sans-serif types was their weight—they were bold and black. British typographers finally agreed on the term "sans serif" for the style, and in Germany it became known as "block." But in the U.S., ever since the Boston foundry's naming decision, 19th-century sans serifs have traditionally been called "gothics." Frazier maintained that "only the American name for the breed seems altogether unfit and inappropriate."[221]

Morris Benton became familiar with a wide range of gothic typefaces when he consolidated the types that ATF had inherited from the merger in 1892. His own gothic designs became very popular, and remain so to this day.

Globe Gothic, 1900

Benton began his design program of gothics in 1900 when he drew Globe Gothic, apparently "modeled after suggestions by General Chas. H. Taylor of the Boston *Daily Globe.*"[222] The annotated 1923 ATF *Specimen Book* credits Benton with designing three other Globe Gothics in the same year: condensed, extra condensed, and extended. However, Stevens L. Watts noted in a 1964 letter to Dr. James Eckman that Frederic Goudy designed Globe Gothic Extended 176 in 1905.[223]

Mystery surrounds the bold variation. It is somewhat jarring because although Globe Gothic is a sans-serif face, hints of serifs appear in Globe Gothic Bold. In *A Half Century of Type Design*, Frederic Goudy claims to have designed Globe Gothic Bold,[224] and the catalogue of the 1947 Donnelley exhibition repeats this statement. But Watts claimed that this was an error, and that Goudy's design was the aforementioned Globe Gothic Extended.[225] In his book Goudy makes no mention of the typeface he apparently did design. Because he was writing many years after the fact, it is possible that Goudy confused the names. D. J. R. Bruckner repeated this error in his 1990 book *Frederic Goudy*, claiming that Goudy thought of Globe Gothic Bold as "the least satisfactory (to me) of all my types."[226] McGrew felt that Globe Gothic Bold was "not at all characteristic of Goudy's work—nor of Benton's, for that matter."[227] According to Watts, Morris Benton designed Globe Gothic Bold and Globe Gothic Bold Italic in 1907 and 1908. But the bolds did not sell very well and were dropped from the 1923 *Specimen Book*.

None of the Globe Gothics are included on Benton's 1936 list.

Franklin Gothic, 1902

Morris Benton's other early gothics became popular almost immediately, and after a brief hiatus became classics in the gothic style. Of Benton's Alternate, Franklin, and News Gothic types, Alexander Lawson stated in 1961: "In retrospect, Benton evinced a positive clairvoyance in producing types which, a half century later, are among the top current faces."[228] McGrew felt that Benton's gothics from the early 1900s—Franklin, News and Lightline—"drove most of the older gothics into obsolescence."[229]

Franklin Gothic is a bold sans-serif, Benton's first important modernization of a 19th-century gothic typeface. Designed in 1902, it was named for Benjamin Franklin. Benton added condensed and extra condensed versions in 1906, italic in 1910, and condensed shaded in 1912. His original extended version was abandoned, but in 1952 ATF came out with a Franklin Gothic Wide, drawn by Bud (John L.) Renshaw.[230]

Franklin Gothic and Benton's first three variants were initially successful and remained so for many years. Franklin Gothic was ATF's 15th best-selling typeface in 1951, Franklin Gothic Extra Condensed was number 8, and Franklin Gothic Condensed was number 25.[231] A sales bulletin sent to ATF branches in June 1953 stated that "Four Franklin Gothics are best sellers,"[232] and in a 1982 edition of "Let's Talk Type" from his Press of the Licorice Cat, McGrew called it the "granddaddy" of American gothics.[233] McGrew later refined his nomenclature for his book *American Metal Typefaces in the Twentieth Century*, writing that Franklin Gothic "might well be called the patriarch of modern American gothics."[234] Juliet Shen described Franklin Gothic as "a rationalization of and measured improvement upon the plethora of nineteenth century gothics that Benton had inherited."[235] The original face is heavy,

Franklin Gothic

36 Point   4 A $2 65 7 a $2 55 $5 20

HERMETICAL
Grand Endowment

30 Point   5 A $2 20 8 a $2 05 $4 25

RIGHTEOUS MAN
Demand Contributions

24 Point   5 A $1 65 11 a $1 85 $3 50

PRINTERS DELIGHT
Founders of American Line
Elegant Spaced

18 Point   8 A $1 50 17 a $1 75 $3 25

MAGNIFICENT FEATURES
Designer Enormous Advertisement
Newspaper Letter Face

Benton's Franklin Gothic

HELLO

YOUR ATTENTION IS CALLED TO THIS NEW AND HANDSOME FACE FRANKLIN GOTHIC CONDENSED

Get on the Line

The careless printer who doesn't keep up with modern demands will be all alone, he will be left in the rear. The buying public is beginning to appreciate good work and demand the latest and best in type design

Franklin Gothic Condensed

Brass and Copper Thin Spaces make justification so easy that no printing office, large or small, can successfully attempt to do without them. These spaces are put up in special cases, made the size of the regular Wisconsin Quarter Cases, four of which just fit in a regular blank case. They

Franklin Gothic Extra Condensed

Entertained

Franklin Gothic Italic, non-kerning

with a subtle thick and thin contrast. It was copied by Monotype, Linotype, Intertype, and Ludlow.[236] ITC Franklin Gothic, drawn by Victor Caruso, was released in 1980. According to MyFonts.com, which lists 20 variants of the face, "Even today, Franklin Gothic remains one of the most widely used sans serif typefaces."[237]

Morris Benton's 1936 list of typeface designs included four members of the family: Franklin Gothic, Franklin Gothic Italic, Franklin Gothic Condensed, and Franklin Gothic Extra Condensed.

In 1964 the Museum of Modern Art in New York chose Morris Benton's original Franklin Gothic as the typeface for its new logo. Andrew Blum explained why in a 2003 *New York Times* article:

> Franklin Gothic No. 2 [is] one of the grandest and most familiar of American typefaces. Designed in 1902 by Morris Fuller Benton in Jersey City, Franklin is simultaneously muscular, with an imposing weight, and humanist, with letterforms reminiscent of the strokes of the calligrapher's pen rather than a mechanical compass. "Quite simply, it's a face that's modern with roots," Ivan Chermayeff, the designer who made the selection for the museum, recalled recently. "It has some character, and therefore some warmth about it, and some sense of the hand—i.e., the artist. All of which seemed to me to make a lot of sense for the Museum of Modern Art, which is not only looking to the future but also looking to the past."[238]

For 40 years the museum used Franklin Gothic, switching to a digital version when it became available. With its most recent major renovation (completed in 2004), the

---

The Museum of Modern Art's new typeface

question of its signature typeface came up again. Ed Pusz of the museum's Graphic Design Department asked the Toronto-based designer Bruce Mau "to explore a range of possibilities for the new building's signage—including rounder, more symmetrical typefaces." But Mau

> felt strongly that Franklin should be left alone. "Everybody gets tired of their own voice," Mr. Mau said from his studio in Toronto, "and so they want to change it. But I was like: 'Don't mess with it! It's an extraordinary landmark identity: don't throw the baby out with the bathwater.'"

> The museum's director, Glen Lowry, agreed. "We looked at all sorts of options, and said, 'You know, we don't need to go there.' Our self-image hasn't shifted so dramatically that our identity needs to be expressed in an utterly new way. We don't need to go from chintz to stripes."

> But Mr. Mau noticed that the Franklin the museum was using didn't seem to him like Franklin at all. Somewhere in the process of its evolution from Benton's original metal type to the readily available digital one it had lost some of its spirit, becoming "a hybrid digital soulless version," in Mr. Pusz's words. Metal type traditionally has slight variations between point sizes, to compensate for the properties of ink and differences in proportion. But digital versions of historic typefaces are often created from metal originals of a single point size—as was the case with the commercially available Franklin. It had been digitized from metal type of a small size, distending the proportions at its larger sizes. Once its defects were recognized, they became glaring: the letters were squat and paunchy, sapping all the elegance out of the white space between them. With some of the signage applications in the new building [the museum had been expanded in 1984] requiring type four feet tall, the small variations became "hideous," Mr. Pusz said.[239]

To solve the problem, the museum hired Matthew Carter to update its digital version of Franklin Gothic. Luckily, eight trays of ATF Franklin Gothic No. 2 had been found

BRAZIL AND OTHER COUNTR
It shows civilization at the
Alternate Gothic No. 1

REPRODUCED
Neat Pamphlet
News Gothic

BRAZIL AND OTHER CO
It shows civilization at a
Alternate Gothic No. 2

HANDSOME COVER
Beautiful Designing
News Gothic Condensed

BRAZIL AND OTHERS
It showed civilization
Alternate Gothic No. 3

GOLDEN HARVESTING BEGINS
Everybody Enjoying Prosperity
News Gothic Extra Condensed

in the museum's basement for Carter to work with. "Mr. Carter scanned printed samples from the trays," Blum explained, "and using a software program called Fontographer, began the long process of plotting the curve points for each letter—a task requiring the full extent of his long-learned craft." The outcome was subtle, but subtle details were the specialty of Morris Benton, and so it is fitting that they were just as important to MoMA. Blum wrote,

> You would have to look rather closely to see it. Extremely closely. In fact, someone could set the old logo and the new logo side by side and stare for some time before detecting even the slightest distinction. The folks who led the exhaustive makeover process couldn't be more pleased.[240]

Alternate Gothic, 1903

Continuing his work on modernizing the 19th-century gothic types, Benton designed three widths of Alternate Gothic in 1903 (No. 1, No. 2, and No. 3) to give typographers options for various layouts. A fourth version, Alternate Gothic Title No. 1, was later abandoned. Since Alternate Gothic's fate was similar to that of News Gothic, its story continues below.

News Gothic, 1908

In 1908 ATF introduced Morris Benton's News Gothic, essentially a lighter version of Franklin Gothic except for the Q. The slight thicks and thins of Franklin Gothic are missing in News Gothic, giving the face a slightly condensed look. Benton again designed three versions—condensed, extra condensed, and extra condensed title. Barbara Roethlein's 1912 type legibility study (sometimes called simply the Clark University Study) found that, of the 26 typefaces studied, News Gothic was the most

Lightline Gothic
Monotone Gothic
News Gothics
Alternate Gothics
Franklin Gothics
and Italic

HOLD EXHIBITION
Modernistic creation
awarded new honors
EXCEPTIONAL ABILITY
Coloratura soprano makes
very favorable impression

Novel Gothic

BANK GOTHIC LIGHT
18 Point No. 10 10 A
MECHANICS

BANK GOTHIC MEDIUM
18 Point No. 20 10 A
EXTENDING

BANK GOTHIC BOLD
18 Point No. 30 9 A
PRODUCED

BANK GOTHIC CONDENSED LIGHT
18 Point No. 40 13 A
MODERN HOUSE

BANK GOTHIC CONDENSED MEDIUM
18 Point No. 50 12 A
REGAL EMPIRES

BANK GOTHIC CONDENSED BOLD
18 Point No. 60 11 A
RIGHT DESIGN

Bank Gothic Light, Medium, and Bold; Bank Gothic Condensed Light, Medium, and Bold

legible. "If legibility is to be our sole criterion of excellence of type-face," the study stated, "News Gothic must be regarded as our nearest approximation to an ideal face, in so far as the present investigation is able to decide this question."[241]

News Gothic and its variations met with considerable commercial success, as did the Alternate Gothics. The two families weathered several decades of typographic change and were still popular in the 1960s. The 1953 ATF sales bulletin cited above remarked, "News Gothics and Alternate Gothics are standbys that always do a fine job."[242] They were copied by the machine composition companies, and ATF introduced two other versions of News Gothic after Morris Benton retired in 1948. Today the major digital type distributors offer both faces; for a few days in May 2007, almost 100 years after Morris Benton had designed it, Bitstream's digital version of News Gothic was number five on its in-house list of online bestsellers.[243] In 1995 type designer Tobias Frere-Jones studied Benton's drawings of News Gothic in the Smithsonian and began redrawing it for the Font Bureau. Cyrus Highsmith and the Font Bureau studio subsequently expanded this work into an extension and modernization of News Gothic in 128 variations (as of December 2008) of "Benton Sans."[244]

All three widths of Alternate Gothic were included on Benton's 1936 list, as well as three News Gothics: the roman, condensed, and extra condensed.

Other Early Gothics

Benton designed Monotone Gothic in 1907 as a wider version of News Gothic, and the following year introduced an all-capital version, Monotone Title. Benton's Lightline Gothic (1908) was a lighter version of News Gothic, with a slight change in the

ABCDEFGHIJK LMNOPQRSTUV WXYZ& $1234567890

Headline Gothic

M and Q. In 1951, Lightline Gothic was still number 71 on the ATF Merchandising Department's list of the foundry's 100 most important faces.[245] Benton's all-capital version, Lightline Title Gothic, came out in 1921. One-Tone Gothic, designed in 1912, was abandoned.

Of these gothics, Benton included just Lightline on his 1936 list, and, not surprisingly, since Benton had an excellent sense for these things, Lightline Gothic is still available from many different digital font vendors today.

Novel Gothic, 1928

Gothic types temporarily fell out of favor among advertising typographers with the advent of the Cheltenham family and the classic type revivals. But in 1928 Benton again began an outpouring of gothic types. The first was Novel Gothic, originated by Charles Herman Becker, a hand engraver in ATF's matrix-cutting department. Novel Gothic was unusual and modern, a bridge between the "Jazz Age" types of the 1920s and the gothics that followed. Maybe it was *too* novel—no variations were produced, and it did not appear in the 1934 specimen book. Morris Benton did not list it in his 1936 tally of types.

Bank Gothic, 1930

In 1930 Benton started designing another gothic type, and by 1933 the all-capital monotone Bank Gothic series included three weights and two widths: medium, light, and bold, and condensed medium, condensed light, and condensed bold. The type became popular for letterheads and legal documents. Bank Gothic Light was ATF's 24th bestseller in 1951,[246] and in December 2008, Bitstream's digital Bank Gothic ranked 18th on the company's list of on-line bestsellers.[247] All six versions of Bank Gothic are included in Benton's 1936 list of typefaces.

Later Gothics

Benton drew Agency Gothic in 1932, a narrower and more squarish all-capital font with alternates for the A and M. Agency Gothic Open, the only variant, follows the

ABCDEFGHIJKLMNOPQRSTUV

Raleigh Gothic Condensed

ADVERTISING ATTRACTIVE

Agency Gothic   Agency Gothic Open

same outline but adds a shadow. Agency FB, based on Agency Gothic, is a standard Microsoft font today. Benton also designed Raleigh Gothic Condensed in 1932, a very narrow, medium-weight, all-capital monotone type, which ATF offered in sizes from 72 to 144 point with alternate characters for A, K, M, N, and S. Poster Gothic followed in 1934—a continuation of Bank Gothic Condensed Medium into larger sizes (24 to 96 point). Two years later Benton's Headline Gothic was introduced, a bold all-capital typeface that became popular for newspapers.

Morris Benton included Agency Gothic and Agency Gothic Open on his 1936 list. They are both available digitally today.

4. Egyptian

The 1815 specimen book of the London typefounder Vincent Figgins shows three sizes of an all-capital font called "Antique."[248] It is a bold, monotone type with square serifs, that is, unbracketed serifs, in nearly the same weight as the main stroke. (Square serifs are also sometimes called "slab" serifs.) This style soon came to be known as "Egyptian."

Walter Tracy, for 30 years the manager of typographic development at English Linotype, wondered why this classification of type was called "Egyptian." Tracy found the writings of a Danish naval officer and artist named Frederick Norden (1708–1742), whose journals and drawings, published in the 1740s in England, inspired an interest in Egyptian antiquities there. The interest grew: Thomas Hope (1769–1831) decorated and furnished one room in his home on Duchess Street in the style of ancient Egypt; the London furniture maker George Smith imitated Hope's Egyptian-style pieces in some of the plates in his book *Designs for Household Furniture*; and the "Egyptian Hall" was built in 1812 "in the midst of the sober facades of Piccadilly."[249] Tracy linked this British fascination with ancient Egypt with the typeface that became popular during this period.

> It has been suggested that the use of the name "Egyptian" may have been influenced by a resemblance between the structures of the early heavy

MANKIND

ABCDEFGHIJKLMNOPQRSTUVW

Figgins's Antique type

Bracketed serif, unbracketed serif, square or slab serif, sans serif

slab-serif letter forms and ancient Egyptian buildings. Perhaps so, if we assume that the typefounders and their printer customers had the time and inclination to take an interest in ancient Egyptian architecture as depicted by Norden and others. It seems equally possible, though, that the founders, busy tradesmen in a competitive field, simply adopted terms that were currently fashionable, without concerning themselves as to whether the terms were apposite to the type designs they were introducing.[250]

All-capital Egyptian types became popular in Europe in the 1820s. By 1825 many had added lowercase letters, and as experimenting continued, the serifs began to show traces of slight bracketing (see illustration) with some contrast evident in the letters as well. By the 1850s Egyptian or square-serif types were generally available in several widths and weights.[251]

Tracy explained that "though all Egyptians are slab-serif, not all slab-serif faces are Egyptian." He defines an Egyptian type as "a face having unbracketed serifs as thick as the secondary strokes, which are themselves nearly as thick as the main strokes, or as thick as they can be."[252]

Stymie Bold, 1931

The Stymie family, according to Mac McGrew, was named after a term meaning to block an opponent's play on the putting green in a discarded rule of golf, "with the literal idea of blocking the flow of similar European square-serifs into America."[253] Stymie was ATF and Benton's answer to "Memphis," a 1930 geometric Egyptian slab-serif type designed by Rudolph Wolf for the Stempel Type Foundry in Germany. Stanley Hlasta called Stymie "a squared serif face derived from the Egyptian black letter."[254]

Stymie had a roundabout history. Two years after the Central Type Foundry in St. Louis was sold to ATF in 1892 as part of the terms of the original merger, the three sons of Carl Schraubstadter, one of the former foundry's owners, established a new St. Louis business, the Inland Type Foundry. (The three sons were William, Oswald,

Durability of Type and Machinery Essential
PRINTING MATERIAL SUPPLIED

An Egyptian type from London, circa 1921

GILLESPIE ABBOTT|CO.
drugs

Stymie

and Carl Jr. As noted in Chapter 5, William had operated a punch-cutting machine that pre-dated Benton's at his father's foundry.) In January 1910, the new foundry introduced one of its many financially successful typefaces, a square-serif font cut by William Schraubstadter called Litho Antique.[255] But by the end of the following year the Inland Type Foundry had been absorbed by ATF. The original Litho Antique matrices were preserved in ATF's vaults, and the face was reissued with a few Benton-drawn extra characters as Rockwell Antique in 1931. But almost immediately, McGrew noted, "Benton saw that something more was needed and redrew it as Stymie Bold in the same year."[256] He refined some characters, tightened the fit, and included the additional characters he had drawn for Rockwell Antique. (In the meantime, Rockwell Antique was immediately copied by Monotype and called Stymie Bold, which led to much confusion because ATF's Stymie Bold was slightly different.)

Stymie has a modern feel and is completely symmetric. Benton designed four weights, and by 1935 the Stymie family had eight members:

> Stymie Light
> Stymie Medium
> Stymie Bold
> Stymie Black
> Stymie Light Italic
> Stymie Medium Italic
> Stymie Bold Italic
> Stymie Black Italic

Stymie Bold Condensed, drawn in 1937 by Gerry Powell, was also added to the family.

To create an unusual headline option, Benton added nine alternate characters, this time with much longer ascenders or descenders, to the roman light, medium, and bold fonts. In the 1934 specimen book there appear to be 11 extra characters—the b and d were also meant to be printed upside-down as the p and q. This Stymie font with elongated ascenders and descenders was not easy to print, as McGrew explained,

STYMIE Light
STYMIE *Light Italic*
STYMIE Medium
STYMIE *Medium Italic*
STYMIE **Bold**
STYMIE ***Bold Italic***
STYMIE **Black**
STYMIE ***Black Italic***

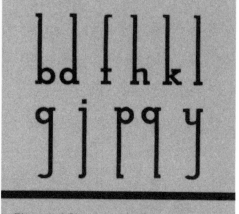

Elongated Characters for Stymie Bold may
be had in all sizes from 18 to 144 point.
Sold in sets or by the single character.

Benton's Stymie variations   Special Stymie characters

regarding his experience with 42-point Stymie Bold:

> The long characters are on 96 point body (cast from deeper mats than the 42
> point, incidentally), and it isn't too hard to add 54 points of space between the
> ascenders. But the descenders aren't cast to matching alignment, and have to be
> moved down about 5 points—except the inverted ones, which have to move
> down about 8 points. No wonder they were hardly used—too time-consuming![257]

Despite this drawback, Stymie became a classic face—six of the eight variants made
the ATF "Top 100" list in 1951, with Stymie Medium as Number 12. Monotype
copied all three weights, plus italics, and also extended the family. Sol Hess designed
Stymie Extrabold for Lanston Monotype, which also produced several condensed
versions. As of this writing in January 2009, Bitstream's digital Stymie is the company's fifth highest-selling online font.[258]

Some time after the first Stymie fonts were introduced, ATF decided to produce the
type in extra large sizes. "Stymie Compressed was cast in 288-point from drawings by
Wadsworth A. Parker, head of the ATF specimen department," McGrew wrote.

> This is believed to be the largest complete font ever cast in regular type
> molds. However, apparently there never was a 288-point mold. Instead,
> all characters are designed to cast the long way in smaller molds, from
> 30-point for the *I* to 144-point for the *W*, each 288 points "wide" … The
> cap *W* alone weighed about 2 pounds![259]

Several other ATF Stymie variations were designed after this, by Parker and perhaps
others. Four Stymie faces are included in Benton's 1936 list.

DRAMATIZE YOUR ME
Dramatize your message
by setting it effectively in

Benton's Tower

Tower, 1934

Morris Benton designed Tower in 1934, and the following year Monotype produced a similar font called Stymie Medium Condensed. The face is tall, slim, and strong. It has short descenders and longer ascenders, and the round lowercase letters are formed like rectangles with rounded corners. Benton designed Tower Bold in 1936, but it was abandoned in favor of Gerry Powell's Stymie Bold Condensed.[260] Nevertheless the parent design, Tower, is included on Benton's 1936 list.

5. Scripts

In his 1971 book *Printing Types: An Introduction*, Alexander Lawson wrote, "There are today a bewildering array of script types, yet almost none of them existed before 1930."[261] Benton's early script faces are an important exception, since he began drawing them early in his career. "Benton appears to have enjoyed designing scripts," Juliet Shen wrote. "Perhaps they gave him more opportunity than the romans and gothics to employ his freehand drawing skills."[262]

Typo Script, 1903

Probably the best-known American script up to the advent of phototypesetting was Benton's Typo Script (originally introduced as Tiffany Script), drawn in 1903. Typo Script remained an important face for many years, ranking as the fourth most popular ATF type on the 1951 sales list. Benton's 1903 Typo Script Extended became number 16 on the same list. He added Typo Slope (originally Tiffany Slope) and Typo Upright (originally Tiffany Upright) in 1905, and Typo Upright Bold and Typo Shaded in 1906. Typo Upright and many of the other "Typo" faces were unrelated to the scripts or to each other, except that all were designed to be used for stationery, invitations, and other social printing.[263] Benton designed Typo Roman Shaded in 1921 (although it was not released until 1924), and Typo Roman in 1926, both very loosely related to the original scripts, and both appearing further down the list of ATF's "Top 100" types in 1951. They are narrow, elegant faces with very tall ascenders.

Today several digital versions of Typo Upright are available. Benton included seven Typo designs in his 1936 listing of typefaces.

THE BENTONS

York Symphony Orchestra
Typo Script

Handwriting Expert
Typo Upright

Candidates Report
Typo Script Extended

Kentucky Tobaccos
Typo Shaded

Typo Roman

Metropolitan Securities Company

Independent Organization

Typo Roman Shaded

Beautiful Gowns

Finest Lace Embroidery

Reliable Customers

Metropolitan Securities Company

Independent Organization

Typo Roman and Typo Roman Shaded

Expecting Unusual Originality

Soliciting Brought Results

Benton's Adscript

Adscript, 1914

Script types were a bother to compositors because they were either cast on special angled type bodies or contained many fragile kerned letters and thin hairlines. Morris Benton tried to overcome these drawbacks with Adscript, a non-kerning type—the finishing strokes of the lowercase letters were designed to almost meet the initial thicker stroke of their neighbors. "This gives the connected effect of continuous script, with only a slight, almost unnoticeable break in some combinations, but avoids the joining of two delicate hairlines which causes problems in most traditional script designs," McGrew wrote.[264] Juliet Shen's study of Morris Benton's typefaces pays particular attention to Benton's relatively obscure Adscript type, calling it "the only one of the fifteen scripts in the 1923 specimen book that looks contemporary."[265]

Adscript's advantage as a "non-kerning font" is explained in the specimen book:

> Here is a series that appears to be a script, yet it is not exactly a script, for the letters are cast in a regular straight body and there are no kerns or overhanging characters; the letters do not join as in script type, and there are no hair-lines. Adscript is cast point set and the capitals and lower case of various sizes can be used together, something not practicable when using the regular script faces.[266]

Shen guessed that Morris Benton wrote this paragraph about Adscript: "It is likely that he came up with the technical brief himself, for the traditional, more inclined historical scripts were firmly entrenched in the public taste when Adscript was designed."[267]

French cursive handwriting from 1494

Civilité, cut by Robert Granjon for Christophe Plantin in 1557

The Civilite Series is a very beautiful rendering of a gothic cursive handwriting in vogue in the middle Sixteenth Century

American Type Founders Company

From an ATF specimen booklet featuring Civilité

Despite the advantage it gave to compositors, Adscript must not have been very successful since it did not appear in ATF's 1934 *Book of American Types* or on Morris Benton's 1936 list.

Civilité, 1924

Civilité is a fancy script face with historical significance. Morris Benton's 1922 drawings were based on Robert Granjon's cursive type of 1557, which imitated the semi-formal handwriting popular in France at the time. Granjon's type and variations of it were frequently used to print poetry and books of etiquette instruction for children. Erasmus wrote one of these books, *La Civilité Puerile*, which was printed in Lyons in 1558 and gave the type its name.[268] "Despite its complication and wealth of ligatures," Harry Carter wrote in 1954, Civilité "was made in four sizes and went on being used until late in the eighteenth century in France, the Low Countries, and to a less extent in England."[269]

The Dickinson Type Foundry of Boston produced a font of Civilité before it joined the ATF merger, but Benton's version became the only one known to most American printers.[270] Many of the lowercase letters are shown in two forms, the more flamboyant of which can be used at the beginning or end of a word. Ironically, according to Paul Hayden Duensing, "over the years, the more authentic forms of E H K d h l p and s have been eliminated and the more debased forms have survived—presumably because they were more "normal" or at least less exotic in design."[271]

The extreme height of the capitals and length of the descenders make it necessary to print foundry Civilité type in two impressions if the lines are close together—one impression for the even-numbered lines, and another for the odd. The larger letters

NO doubt this fact is often ignored or overlooked, but it is nevertheless true, that by having your account with a bank of very high standing you

Hobo

We hardly need suggest their appropriateness as gifts. Should you desire to give a present that will prove lasting, we can recall

Light Hobo

will thus overlap, simulating handwriting. Benton drew a second version of Civilité in 1924, but it was abandoned. He included and starred Civilité in his 1936 list, but Duensing calls both the ATF and Dickinson Type Foundry's versions "badly misconceived renderings, drawn by artists not conversant with the history and tradition of the Civilité heritage."[272]

The spelling using an accented e (é) was only given in the early showings of ATF's Civilité. McGrew wrote, "Some [American] printers call it *SI-vil-EET*, but an accented *e* in early specimens indicated the intended *si-VIL-i-TAY*."[273]

6. *Advertising Types*

Although the family treatment of roman types (their bold members, in particular) enabled newspaper typographers to meet their needs for headlines and ads, the demand for more interesting and commercially compelling display types continued to grow. As a result, years after the composing machines had taken over most text composition work, ATF continued to produce novelty and display types.

Hobo, 1912

Benton designed Hobo in 1910, ATF introduced it in 1912, and it was patented in 1915. As one of the first "Gee whiz! Look at me!" types,[274] Hobo was a radical departure from Benton's other early typefaces and type revivals. It is a sans-serif face with no straight lines and no descenders in the lower case. Benton designed two variants, Light Hobo and Hobo Shaded, but the latter was abandoned. McGrew's sources revealed this tidbit:

> One story says that it was drawn in the early 1900s and sent to the foundry
> without a name, which was not unusual, but that further work on it
> was continually pushed aside, until it became known as "that old hobo"
> because it hung around so long without results. More time elapsed before it
> was patented in 1915.[275]

Hobo first appeared in the 1912 ATF specimen book. It was called a failure by some critics, including Eugene Ettenberg, one of the original members of the Typophiles Club of New York,[276] but nevertheless it is still available today. The independent Internet typeface directory Identifont lists Hobo as one of the three "humorous" novelty designs that Morris Benton became known for. (The other two, for some unknown reason, are Stymie and Broadway.)[277] Benton included Hobo on his 1936 list.

Fine Musical Program
Freehand

NEW MODEL
Broadway

CLEVER Knight
Broadway Condensed

Freehand, 1917
Another Morris Benton novelty face was based on pen lettering. Its working title was "Quill,"[278] and McGrew claimed that it had "quite a bit of use." Today the complete set of cutting slips for Freehand is part of RIT's Cary Graphic Arts Collection.[279] Morris Benton was happy enough with this type to include it in his 1936 list.

Broadway, 1926
American typography went through a radical change in the late 1920s. It was the Jazz Age, a time of excess, and wild display types were all the rage. Most of them were geometric, sans serif, and lacking symmetry. According to Lawson, "This period was one of great confusion from the standpoint of typographic design."[280] The German Bauhaus school of thought was slowly being imported to the U.S., and the first attempts of American modernism were simply copies of European models. Typographic versions of the Bauhaus experiments were sans-serif types. Before the new style matured a profusion of bad types were manufactured. "A glance at the period 1929–31," Lawson wrote, "will indicate that advertisers believed the hard sell could be accomplished only with the combined use of bad types and bad design."[281] But Morris Benton seemed to understand the modernist climate. He had already designed Hobo, and several of his subsequent commercial display faces in the new style caught on with the American public. One of these was Broadway, which has been called the most representative type of the era.

ATF issued Benton's Broadway in 1928 as an all-capitals font. It is sans serif and very round, with extreme thicks and thins. The following year Benton designed a condensed version with a lower case. Two other Broadways, Numbers 2 and 3, were abandoned. In 1929 Monotype copied the original Broadway and added a lower case designed by Sol Hess. Another Monotype version was called Broadway Engraved. Oz Cooper, the type designer famous for his Cooper Black type, was asked to make rough sketches for a somewhat similar face, which was later named Boul Mich after Chicago's fashionable Michigan Boulevard.[282]

MUSICIAN Healthy Girls

Modernique   Louvaine Light

Steady Gilt Edge

Chic   Louvaine Bold

BIG ships Eagles

Parisian   Dynamic Medium

Broadway itself was the longest-lived of the host of other commercial types that were introduced during the same time. "Whenever a publication referring to the Jazz Age appears," Lawson and Provan wrote in 1983, "the chances are better than average that the display typography will feature Broadway."[283] Today the font is used to evoke the Roaring Twenties. Digital versions of Broadway are readily available. Morris Benton included both Broadway and Broadway Condensed in his 1936 list.

Other Benton Advertising Types

The demand for commercial types was at its highest in the late 1920s, and Benton responded by designing several advertising types: Modernique (1928), closely resembling Broadway, and the freely drawn Chic (1927) and Parisian (1928). McGrew called Parisian frivolous,[284] although it was the only one of the three to make it into ATF's 1934 specimen book and is still popular today. The Intertype version of Parisian became a standard face for printed stationery. Benton's sans-serif type Dynamic Medium (1928) made use of large triangles within many of the letters. It was not shown in the 1934 specimen book.

Louvaine, another of Benton's commercial types, was a 1929 adaptation of Bodoni. Its original working title was Modern Bodoni, and many of the characters are identical to their Bodoni counterparts. "Only the g and y are different," McGrew explained, "otherwise the distinction is in the more abrupt transition from thick to thin strokes in this series."[285] Benton expanded the Louvaine family to contain three weights each in roman and italic. In an advance showing of the series, ATF called it "vigorous, zestful and modern," but Louvaine didn't last long enough to be included in the 1934 specimen book.

Parisian is the only advertising typeface in this section that was included on Morris Benton's 1936 list.

7. *Miscellany*

Other Morris Benton typefaces may not have made it onto any known list of his type designs since ATF's records did not include such information. For example, John Murphy stated, "Incidentally, in his time Mr. Benton has created both Greek and Chinese types that received high praise for their accuracy and beauty, and he did not know either the Chinese or Greek language."[286] Perhaps Benton designed one of the Greek fonts that appeared in the 1900 or 1912 ATF specimen books. There is no reference to a Benton Greek font in Columbia University's annotated 1923 ATF *Specimen Book* because that specimen book contains no foreign-language fonts at all. After studying everything I could find about Morris Benton for years and finding no evidence for an ATF Chinese type, I concluded that Morris Benton must have been pulling Murphy's leg during their talks. Benton's grandson Laurence Gregg agreed with this explanation, recalling, "He liked to 'deadpan'—I remember that!"[287]

However, Theo Rehak revealed that Benton did cut some Chinese kanji matrices in the 1920s as a way of gauging the effectiveness of the matrix engravers that were to be sold to Japan,[288] since Chinese characters are used to write Japanese. Murphy may have been referring to the quality of these trial Chinese kanji matrices, since it is highly unlikely that ATF could have produced the thousands of characters in an entire Chinese "font" without leaving any record of that accomplishment. As for the Greek types, Bullen had observed in 1923 that "Some … foreign types are imported by the typefoundries for customers who want hieroglyphic, Coptic, Greek, Russian and Hebrew types, which can not be made profitably here, owing to the limited demand."[289]

Morris Benton also designed type ornaments. The Tabard Borders were patented in 1904 under the names of W. H. Bradley and M. F. Benton,[290] although they are not designated as Benton's work in the annotated 1923 ATF *Specimen Book*. However, at least 35 other type accessories and decorative borders are indicated there as having been designed by Benton, either alone or in collaboration with Clarence Marder. Twenty-two of these are fractions.

Chapter 14 Endnotes

1   Fred C. Williams, "Herman Zapf: Calligrapher, Typographer, Type Designer, Writer, Teacher, Lecturer," *Type & Press* 24 (Spring 1980): 1. Paraphrased from Zapf's *About Alphabets* (New York: The Typophiles, 1960), 71.

2   Paul Shaw, "On Type: The Century Family," *Fine Print* 7, no. 4 (October 1981): 141.

3   Maureen D. Hitchcock, *Benton Types: Typefaces Designed or Adapted by Morris Fuller Benton* (Rochester, N.Y.: The Press of the Good Mountain, 1978), 2.

4   Hand-annotated copy: American Type Founders Company, *Specimen Book and Catalogue, 1923* (Jersey City, N.J.: ATF Co., 1923), Book Arts Collection, Rare Book and Manuscript Library, Columbia University.

5   M. F. McGrew to Alexander Lawson, 5 April 1962; McGrew to Hitchcock, 9 April 1978.

6   Stevens L. Watts, "Some Type Series Originated or Restyled by Morris Fuller Benton," June 1965.

7   McGrew, "The Bentons, Father & Son," *Typographic i* 10, no. 1 (March 1978). Reprinted by the author, 1978, 2–3.

8   McGrew, *American Metal Typefaces of the Twentieth Century*, 2nd ed. (New Castle, Del.: Oak Knoll Press, 1993), 154.

9   Morris Fuller Benton to Harold Kathman, 23 April 1936.

10 Watts to David L. Ritter, 30 May 1965.

11 Ibid.

12 Lawson, "After 70 Years Century Typefaces Hold Their Own," *Inland Printer/American Lithographer* 154, no. 4 (January 1965): 47.

13 Watts to Ritter.

14 "'Scoreboard' Reveals Popularity Trends in Typefaces," *Inland Printer* 115, no. 3 (June 1945): 55.

15 McGrew, "The Bentons," 4.

16 McGrew, "Conversation on Whitehall" (Pittsburgh: Press of the Licorice Cat, 1969): 4.

17 Some good sources for this type of study are fontbureau.com, myfonts.com, identifont.com, paratype.com, faces.co.uk, and fonts.com. Since new digital fonts are continually being issued, it would be fruitless to attempt to compile a definitive list of Benton digital fonts. However, on December 9, 2008, I found 114 (of the 226) typefaces that Benton designed available digitally online. In most cases, types were available in many different digital versions.

18 Richard Marder, in discussion with the author, November 1984.

19 Barbara Elizabeth Roethlein, "The Relative Legibility of Different Faces of Printing Types," *American Journal of Psychology* 23, no. 1 (January 1912): 27.

20 Lawson, *Anatomy of a Typeface* (Boston: David R. Godine, 1990), 15.

21 McGrew, *American Metal*, 333.

22 Lawson and A. Provan, *100 Type Histories* (Arlington, Va.: National Composition Association, 1983), 1:58.

23 McGrew, "Engravers Old English Bold," *Let's Talk Type* (Pittsburgh: Press of the Licorice Cat, June 1985).

24 McGrew, *American Metal*, 95.

25 Morris Benton, U.S. Patent No. 37,235, November 15, 1904, for Cloister Black; U.S. Patent No. 37,234, November 15, 1904, for Flemish Black.

26 Lawson, *Anatomy*, 28.

27 Lawson and Provan, *Type Histories* 1:54.

28 Harry Carter, *A View of Early Typography Up To About 1600: The Lyell Lectures 1968* (Oxford: Clarendon Press, 1969), 45.

29 Ibid., 48.

30 *American Type Designers and Their Work*, exhibition catalog, Chicago: R. R. Donnelley, 1947, 7.

31 Lawson, "The Prolific Career of Morris Benton," *Printing Impressions* (April 1971): 77.

32 A. Raymond Hopper, "The Romance of Roycroft," *Inland Printer* 99, no. 3 (June 1937), 36.

33 Hand-annotated *Specimen Book*, Columbia University, 504.

34 Henry Lewis Bullen, "Linn Boyd Benton—The Man and His Work," *Inland Printer* 70, no. 1 (October 1922): 63; "Little Life Stories of Live Men Known to the Printers of America, Linn Boyd Benton: Typefounder, Inventor," *American Printer* 76, no. 5 (Mach 5, 1923): 34; McGrew, "The Bentons," 2.

35 "Two Men Whose Work Greatly Benefits All Typographers," *Inland Printer* 76, no. 3 (December 1925): 453.

36 Lawson, "'Rugged' Typefaces Are Latest Revival," *Inland Printer/American Lithographer* 155, no. 1 (April 1965): 64.

37 Hopper, "Romance," 35.

38 Lawson, "Rugged," 64.

39 Julius Leroy Frazier, *Type Lore: Popular Types of Today, Their Origin and Use* (Frazier, 1925), 85.

40 Lawson, "After 70 Years," 46.

41 Watts, "Century Roman and Century Oldstyle," to Dr. James Eckman, 14 October 1963 (copy).

42 American Type Founders Company, *Specimen Book of American Line Type Faces: American Point Line, Point Body and Point Set* (New York: ATF Co., 1903), 148–49, 247.

43 Henry Hillman, "The Types of a Quarter Century," *Inland Printer* 79, no. 5 (August 1927): 811.

44 McGrew, "The Bentons," 2.

45 Shaw, "Century," 142.

46 In *Designing with Type: A Basic Course in Typography*, rev. ed. (New York: Watson/Guptill Publications, 1992), James Craig called Century Expanded "an excellent example of a refined Egyptian typeface" (italics mine) because of its "thick slab serifs and thick main strokes with little contrast between the thicks and thins" (p. 64). A mere glance at the Century Expanded capitals will show that they do not fit Walter Tracy's definition of Egyptian type (see the section on Egyptian type in this chapter). Benton's true Egyptian types are Stymie and Tower.

47 McGrew, "The Bentons," 2.

48 Frazier, *Type Lore*, 85.

49 Watts, "Century Roman."

50 Lawson, "Anatomy of a Type: Century, Part 3," *Printing Impressions* 24, no. 8 (January 1982): 62.

51 Charles Bigelow, in discussion with the author, June 2007.

52 The Font Bureau, Inc., "Benton Modern," www.fontbureau.com/fonts/BentonModern (accessed April 23, 2008).

53 McGrew, *American Metal*, 77.

54 Font Bureau, "Century FB," http://www.fontbureau.com/fonts/CenturyFB (accessed April 23, 2008).

55 Ibid.

56 Font Bureau, "Bureau Roman," www.fontbureau.com/fonts/BureauRoman (accessed April 23, 2008).

57 McGrew, *American Metal*, 79.

58 Frazier, *Type Lore*, 87.

59 Watts, "Century Roman."

60 Adobe Type Library, "Century Old Style," *Typeface Notes*. To access this page, perform a search for Century Old Style at http://www.adobe.com/type

61 Font Bureau, "Bureau Roman."

62 McGrew, *American Metal*, 79.

63 Watts to Eckman, 28 September 1962 (copy).

64 Frederic W. Goudy, *Typologia: Studies in Type Design & Type Making* (Berkeley: University of California Press, 1940), 138.

65 John Allen Murphy, "Morris Benton, Part 2," *Inland Printer* 97, no. 1 (April 1936): 44.

66 Roethlein, "Legibility," 5.

67 Harold E. Burtt and Coryne Basch, "Legibility of Bodoni, Baskerville Roman, and Cheltenham Type Faces," *Journal of Applied Psychology* 7 (September 1923): 237.

68 Murphy, "Morris Benton, Part 2," 44.

69 "Report on the Influence of School-Books upon Eyesight," 2nd ed. (London: British Association for the Advancement of Science, 1913): 4.

70 Ibid., 21.

71 Ibid., 9.

72 Ibid., 12.

73 Lawson, "Century, Part 3," 63.

74 Morris Benton to N. J. Werner, 9 June 1936.

75 Shaw, "Century," 144.

76 American Type Founders Company, "The Industrial Educators of New Jersey, 1925 Luncheon" (program), Jersey City: ATF Co., 1925.

77 Frazier, *Type Lore*, 87.

78 Watts, "Century Roman."

79 Harry Carter, "Optical Scale in Type Founding," *Typography* 4 (Autumn 1937): 4.

80 McGrew, "The Bentons," 4.

81 Lawson, "After 70 years," 46–47.

82 Ibid., 47.

83 J. I. Biegeleisen, *Art Directors' Workbook of Type Faces* (New York: Arco Publishing Co., 1976), 66.

84 Juliet Shen, "Searching for Morris Fuller Benton: Discovering the Designer through his Typefaces" (MS thesis, University of Reading, 2006): 43.

85 Burtt and Basch, "Legibility," 245.

86 Frazier, *Type Lore*, 93.

87 Ibid., 90.

88 Watts, "'Chelt' Really Got Around," *Printing* 81, no. 5 (May 1957): 78.

89 Eckman to Ritter, 11 May 1965.

90 Watts, "'Chelt' Really," 78.

91 Murphy, "Morris Benton, Part 2," 42.

92   McGrew, *American Metal*, 85.

93   Lawson, "Anatomy of a Type: Cheltenham," *Printing Impressions* 13, no. 10 (March 1971): 55.

94   Frazier, *Type Lore*, 91.

95   Murphy, "Morris Benton, Part 2," 44.

96   Lawson, "Cheltenham," 55.

97   Bullen, "What the Typefounders Have Done," *Inland Printer* 79, no. 5 (August 1927): 763.

98   Lawson, "Cheltenham," 54. It was common for American compositors to dispense with "the niceties of literary pronunciation, as in their rendering of *bourgeois*, the old term for 9 point, always 'burjoys.'" (Lawson, *Anatomy*, 253.)

99   Benton to Kathman.

100   Lawson, "Cheltenham," 55.

101   Frazier, *Type Lore*, 89.

102   Lawson, "Cheltenham," 55; Watts, "'Chelt' Really," 79.

103   Benjamin P. Duffield, "An Appreciation for Cheltenham," *American Bulletin*, 2nd series, no. 14 (December 1915): 7.

104   Murphy, "Morris Benton, Part 2," 43.

105   Lawson, "Cheltenham," 54.

106   Frazier, *Type Lore*, 95.

107   Stanley C. Hlasta, *Printing Types & How to Use Them* (Pittsburgh: Carnegie Press, 1950), 217.

108   Lawson and Provan, *Type Histories*, 1:50.

109   Bigelow, discussion.

110   ATF Co., *Book of American Types: ATF Standard Faces* (Jersey City, N.J.: ATF Sales Corp., 1934), 8.

111   Fonts.com Website, "ITC Cheltenham/Tactile," http://www.fonts.com/AboutFonts/Articles/TypeTradingCards/ITC+Cheltenham+and+Tactile.htm (accessed April 23, 2008).

112   "The Clearface Family, Optically Correct in Design," *American Bulletin*, new series, no. 3 (July 1910): 7.

113   Shen, "Searching," 31.

114   McGrew, *American Metal*, 93.

115   Shen, "Searching," 27.

116   Shen, "Searching," 35.

117   Lawson and Provan, *100 Type Histories*, 1:52.

118   Joseph Blumenthal, *Art of the Printed Book*, (New York: Pierpont Morgan Library, 1973): 39.

119   Lawson, *Anatomy*, 202.

120   Blumenthal, *Art*, 28.

121   Bigelow and Jonathan Seybold, "Technology and the Aesthetics of Type," *Seybold Report* 10, no. 24 (August 24, 1981): 7.

122   Hopper, "What Are 'Enduring' Type Faces?" *Inland Printer* 113, no. 1 (April 1944): 31.

123   Lawson, "Prolific," 77.

124   McGrew, *American Metal*, 39.

125   Bullen, "Bodoni, Benjamin Franklin, and Bodoni's Grandson," *American Bulletin* 2, no. 5 (April/May 1912): 1–2.

126   Anon. [Henry Lewis Bullen] to Kent D. Currie, 29 April 1927 (copy for M.F. Benton), 1.

127   Ibid.

128 Bullen, "Observations on Type Designs and Type Designers and Their Press Agents," *Inland Printer* 71, no. 6 (September 1923): 833.

129 Watts to Ritter.

130 Hlasta, *Printing Types*, 138.

131 "Bodoni," *Inland Printer* 104, no. 3 (December 1939): 53–57.

132 Frazier, *Type Lore*, 71.

133 "Narrative of Cloister Oldstyle, Cloister Oldstyle Italic and Cloister Title," *American Bulletin* 3, no.4 (April 1914): 4.

134 Frazier, *Type Lore*, 35.

135 Hlasta, *Printing Types*, 33.

136 Lawson, *Anatomy*, 49.

137 According to McGrew's *American Metal Typefaces*, Jenson Oldstyle was designed by J. W. Phinney of the Dickinson Type Foundry (ATF); Barnhardt Brothers and Spindler introduced Mazarin; and Kelmscott was produced by the Inland Type Foundry.

138 Paul Hayden Duensing, "On Type: Twentieth-Century Contributions to the Jensonian Model," *Fine Print* 16, no. 2 (Summer 1990): 70.

139 Frazier, *Type Lore*, 37.

140 Bullen, *Nicolas Jenson, Printer of Venice* (San Francisco: John Henry Nash, 1926), 7.

141 Linn Boyd Benton, "Inventions of Linn Boyd Benton," to David Gustafson (Carnegie Institute of Technology), 30 June 1932, for inclusion in the United Typothetae of America's *Who's Who in Printing in the United States*, 2.

142 Bullen, "Observations," 833.

143 Murphy, "Morris Benton, Part 2," 43.

144 Ibid.

145 McGrew, "Conversation on Whitehall," 4.

146 Lawson, "Morris Fuller Benton Deserves More Than Obscurity," *Inland Printer/American Lithographer* 148, no. 1 (October 1961): 80–81.

147 "Obituaries: Philip B. Meggs," *Graphis* 349 (January/February 2004), 146.

148 Philip B. Meggs, "American Type Founders Specimen Book and Catalogue 1923," *Print* 48, no. 1 (January/February 1994): 85.

149 Hillman, "Types of a Quarter Century," 811.

150 Frazier, *Type Lore*, 38.

151 Hopper, "Enduring," 30.

152 Blumenthal, *Art*, 28.

153 Duensing, "Jensonian Model," 70.

154 Hlasta, *Printing Types*, 36.

155 Paul A. Bennett, "On Recognizing the Type Faces," *Dolphin* 2 (1935): 19.

156 Ibid., 18.

157 McGrew, *American Metal*, 95.

158 Watts to Ritter.

159 Marianne Tidcombe, *The Doves Press* (London and New Castle, Del.: The British Library and Oak Knoll Press, 2002), 22.

160 Lawson, *Anatomy*, 67.

161 Lawson, *Anatomy*, 64–69.

162 Herbert H. Johnson, "On the Montaigne and Centaur Types of Bruce Rogers," in *American Proprietary Typefaces*, ed. David Pankow (New York: American Printing History Association, 1998), 52.

163 Shen, "Searching," 39.

164 McGrew to the author, 3 October 1986.

165 David Walker Mallison, "Henry Lewis Bullen and the Typographic Library and Museum of the American Type Founders Company," (Ph.D. diss., Columbia University, 1976), 222.

166 Frank Denman, *The Shaping of Our Alphabet: A Study of Changing Type Styles* (New York: Alfred A. Knopf, 1955), 71.

167 Carter, *View*, 84.

168 Paul Beaujon [Beatrice Warde], "The 'Garamond' Types: A Study of XVI and XVII Century Sources," *Fleuron* 5 (1926): 137; Neil MacMillan, *An A-Z of Type Designers* (New Haven, Conn.: Yale University Press, 2006), 89.

169 Frazier, *Type Lore*, 43–44.

170 Nicolas Barker, "The Aldine Roman in Paris, 1530–1534," *Library*, 5th series, vol. 29, no. 1 (March 1974): 11.

171 Lawson, *Anatomy*, 134.

172 Beaujon, "Garamond Types," 170.

173 James Moran, *Stanley Morison: His Typographic Achievement* (New York: Visual Communication Books, 1971), 28.

174 ATF Co., "Claude Garamond: The First Type Founder and His Types" (Jersey City, N.J.: ATF Co., 1921), 5.

175 Bullen, "Observations," 834.

176 Hlasta, *Printing Types*, 233.

177 Bullen, "Observations," 834.

178 Beaujon, "Garamond Types," 131–179.

179 McGrew, "Garamond: The Typeface & The Designers," *Typographic i*. Reprinted by the author, n.d., 2.

180 Lawson, *Anatomy*, 139.

181 Beaujon, "Garamond Types," 131.

182 MyFonts.com, "ITC Souvenir," http://www.myfonts.com/fonts/bitstream/itc-souvenir/ (accessed April 23, 2008).

183 McGrew, *American Metal*, 285.

184 Robert Norton, ed., *A Collection of Observations on Types Best Remembered by Various People Charitably Disposed to an Expatriate Editor/A Collection of Observations on Types Best Forgotten by Various People Uncharitably Disposed to All Sorts of Different Things* (London: Parsimony Press, 1993), unpaginated.

185 Ibid.

186 John Dreyfus, "The Speed and Grace of Roger Excoffon," *U&lc* Online Issue: Other Articles, http://www.itcfonts.com/Ulc/OtherArticles/Excoffon.htm (accessed April 23, 2008).

187 Dreyfus, *The Survival of Baskerville's Punches* (Cambridge: University Printer, 1949), 1.

188 Ibid., 7.

189 In addition to the 1949 edition (footnote #187), the essay is also found in John Dreyfus, *Into Print: Selected Writings on Printing History, Typography and Book Production* (Boston: David R. Godine, 1995).

190 McGrew, *American Metal*, 27.

191 Lawson, *Anatomy*, 194.

192 McGrew to the author, 3 October 1986.

193 McGrew, *American Metal*, 27.

194 Watts, "Typorhythmics," *Pastime Printer* (March 1957): 8.

195 Frazier, *Type Lore*, 103.

196 Carter, "Optical Scale," 4.

197 Lawson, "More Than Obscurity," 81.

198 McGrew, *American Metal*, 27.

199 Lawson and Provan, *100 Type Histories*, 1:98.

200 Lawson, "Anatomy of a Type: Bulmer," *Printing Impressions* 15, no. 3 (August 1972): 44.

201 Linn Boyd Benton, "Inventions," 5.

202 McGrew, *American Metal*, 55.

203 Lawson, "More than Obscurity," 81.

204 Eckman, *Heritage of the Printer*, vol. 1 (Philadelphia: North American Publishing Co., 1965), 114.

205 Maurice Annenberg, *Type Foundries of America and their Catalogs*, 2nd ed. (New Castle, Del.: Oak Knoll Press, 1994), 64.

206 Hlasta, *Printing Types*, 109.

207 McGrew, "Benton … or Whitehall," *It's a Small World* 26 (1980): 33.

208 McGrew, "BENTON ATF 566, aka Whitehall," *Let's Talk Type* (Pittsburgh: Press of the Licorice Cat, September 1997): 4.

209 McGrew, "Benton, ATF, 566" type specimen card (Pittsburgh: Press of the Licorice Cat, n.d.).

210 McGrew, "Conversation on Whitehall," 3.

211 Francis X. Simpson, "Record of Matrices Cut at the ATF Co., 1896–1944" (copy), courtesy of Dr. James Eckman.

212 McGrew to the author, 29 June 1985.

213 Watts to Ritter.

214 Laswon, "Prolific," 77.

215 McGrew to the author, 29 June 1985.

216 Lawson, *Printing Types: An Introduction* (Boston: Beacon Press, 1971), 97.

217 James Mosley, *The Nymph and the Grot: The Revival of the Sanserif Letter* (London: Friends of the St. Bride Printing Library, 1999), 10.

218 Ibid., 38.

219 Lawson, *Printing Types*, 93

220 Ibid., 97.

221 Frazier, *Type Lore*, 18.

222 ATF Co., *Specimen Book of American Line Type Faces: American Point Line, Point Body and Point Set* (New York: ATF Co., 1904), 40b.

223 Watts to Eckman, 11 March 1964.

224 Frederic Goudy, *A Half-Century of Type Design & Typography, 1895–1945* (New York: Typophiles, 1946), 66.

225 Watts to Eckman, 11 March 1964.

226 D. J. R. Bruckner, *Frederic Goudy* (New York: Harry N. Abrams Inc., 1990), 123.

227 McGrew, *American Metal*, 153.

228 Lawson, "More than Obscurity," 80.

229 McGrew, "Gothics Reconsidered," *Let's Talk Type* (Pittsburgh: Press of the Licorice Cat, October 1982): 3.

230 McGrew, *American Metal*, 143.

231 D. Mirocco to Don Neale, 4 March 1952, in Watts, "Notebook of Stevens Lewis Watts, 1895–1966," n.d., Typographic Library Manuscripts, Rare Book and Manuscript Library, Columbia University.

232 Watts to Ritter.

233 McGrew, "Gothics Reconsidered," 1.

234 McGrew, *American Metal*, 143.

235 Shen, "Searching," 23.

236 McGrew, *American Metal*, 143.

237 MyFonts.Com, Inc., "ITC Franklin Gothic," http://www.myfonts.com/fonts/linotype/itc-franklin-gothic/ (accessed April 23, 2008).

238 Andrew Blum, "The Modern's Other Renovation," *New York Times*, Arts & Leisure (September 21, 2003), http://www.andrewblum.net/typepad/2003/09/the_moderns_oth.html (accessed 23 April 2008).

239 Ibid.

240 Ibid.

241 Roethlein, "Relative Legibility," 29.

242 Watts to Ritter.

243 *Para*Type, "Bitstream Bestsellers," http://www.paratype.com/store/bestsellers.asp?foundry=Bitstream (accessed May 2008). Because this site is updated daily, it no longer reflects News Gothic's fifth place ranking.

244 Font Bureau, "Benton Sans," http://www.fontbureau.com/fonts/BentonSans (accessed December 11, 2008).

245 Mirocco to Neale.

246 "Little Life Stories of Live Men Known to the Printers of America: Linn Boyd Benton, Typefounder, Inventor," *American Printer* 76, no. 5 (March 1923): 34.

247 *Para*Type, "Bitstream Bestsellers," http://www.paratype.com/store/bestsellers.asp?foundry=Bitstream (accessed December 11, 2008).

248 Vincent Figgins, *Type Specimens, 1801 and 1815, Reproduced in Facsimile* (London: Printing Historical Society, 1967), 205, 207.

249 Walter Tracy, "Why Egyptian?" *Printing History* 31/32, vol. 16, nos. 1 & 2 (1994): 4.

250 Ibid., 6.

251 Lawson, *Printing Types*, 93.

252 Tracy, "Why Egyptian?" 6.

253 McGrew, *Let's Talk Type* (Pittsburgh: Press of the Licorice Cat, June 1982): 3.

254 Hlasta, *Printing Types*, 287.

255 Eckman, "The Inland Type Foundry, 1894–1911," *Printing & Graphic Arts* (*PaGA*) 8, no. 2 (June 1960): 41.

256 McGrew, *American Metal*, 271.

257 McGrew, *Let's Talk*, June 1982, 2.

258 *Para*Type, "Bitstream Bestsellers," http://www.paratype.com/store/bestsellers.asp?foundry=Bitstream (accessed January 5, 2009).

259 McGrew, *American Metal*, 299.

260 Hitchcock, *Benton Types*.

261 Lawson, *Printing Types*, 110.

262 Shen, "Searching," 45.

263 McGrew, *American Metal*, 319.

264 McGrew, *American Metal*, 5.

265 Shen, "Searching," 47.

266 ATF Co., *Specimen Book and Catalogue* (Jersey City, N.J.: ATF Co., 1923), 416.

267 Shen, "Searching," 47.

268 Duensing, "On Type: A New Civilité," *Fine Print* 11, no. 1 (January 1985): 35.

269 Carter, "Letter Design & Typecutting," *Journal of the Royal Society of Arts* 102, no. 4935 (October, 1954): 886.

270 Duensing, "Civilité," 35.

271 Ibid, 36.

272 Ibid.

273 McGrew, "Civilite" type specimen card (Pittsburgh: Press of the Licorice Cat, n.d.).

274 Lawson and Provan, *Type Histories*, 2:14.

275 McGrew, *American Metal*, 181.

276 Eugene M. Ettenberg, *Types for Books and Advertising* (New York: D. Van Nostrand Co., Inc., 1947), 24.

277 Identifont, "Morris Fuller Benton (1872–1948)," http://www.identifont.com/show?16W (accessed April 23, 2008).

278 McGrew, *American Metal*, 145.

279 These cutting slips were donated to RIT by Theo Rehak of the Dale Guild type foundry in Howell, N.J.

280 Lawson, "Young Typographers Are Going Back to Design of 'Roaring Twenties,'" *Inland Printer/ American Lithographer* 152, no. 6 (March 1964): 70.

281 Ibid.

282 McGrew to the author, 3 October 1986; McArthur, Richard N., "On Cooper Type Faces … With Some Digressions," in *The Book of Oz Cooper: An Appreciation of Oswald Bruce Cooper* (Chicago: Society of Typographic Arts, 1949), 97.

283 Lawson and Provan, *Type Histories*, 1:36.

284 McGrew, *American Metal*, 245.

285 McGrew, *American Metal*, 205.

286 Murphy, "Morris Benton, Part 3," *Inland Printer* 97, no. 2 (May 1936), 71.

287 Laurence Gregg, handwritten note on 2006 version of ms.

288 Theo Rehak, telephone conversation with the author, 23 January 2006.

289 Bullen, "Observations," 834.

290 Morris Benton and Will Bradley, Tabard Borders, U.S. Patent No. 37,072, August 9, 1904.

The Later Plainfield Years

About the time that Morris Benton's great Century Schoolbook type was making its debut, he endured a personal tragedy that must have contributed to his reticence. On St. Patrick's Day, March 17, 1920, with his two daughters in college and his parents still thriving, Morris's wife, Ethel, died suddenly of an infection after an operation. She was only 42 years old, and her death was a shock to the family. "I was rather amazed how my father kept producing," Caroline said, "despite the fact that he had [a] crisis at home. He kept going at the plant, and produced a lot. For a little while, he was terrifically lonely and terrifically unhappy."[1] Later Morris shared his thoughts with Caroline. She remembered him saying that "life divided itself up into compartments, and they didn't necessarily follow through, they cut off ... He just felt that one [had] ended, and he was very, I wouldn't say that he was philosophical, but he did accept that the facts were the facts. He had to make a new life."[2]

Morris began looking for a summer cottage, which he previously had felt that he couldn't afford, and bought one in Beaver Lake, New Jersey. About three years later, on February 28, 1923, Morris married Katrina Ten Eyck Wheeler, his second cousin on his father's side of the family and the daughter of Stoughton Rawley Wheeler, a surgeon of East Bloomfield, New York.[3] She was 31 at the time, 20 years younger than Morris. Katrina was intelligent and dedicated to Morris, and significantly taller, with a big voice. They moved out of the big white house in Plainfield to an apartment about half a block away and remained there for seven years.

Katrina Ten Eyck Wheeler Benton   Morris and Katrina at Beaver Lake, circa 1930

Morris Fuller Benton, 1922   Linn Boyd Benton, 1923

Linn Boyd Benton's Last Ten Years

During the 1920s, Morris's health suffered again with the onset of serious stomach ulcers. His father was getting older and the added pressures at ATF also took their toll. Linn Boyd Benton "would come into the factory and all hell would break loose—everything had to be just so," Caroline explained. "That's the trouble when you work 'til you're 88, you know, somebody has to help you. And you know who did it."[4] But, Caroline stressed, Morris remained "very patient with his father, and very sweet."

To other observers, Boyd's advancing age only made him more affable. In 1922, when he was 78 years old, Henry Lewis Bullen wrote,

> Mr. Benton outdoes his youthful years in humor and geniality. An observant man, he has accumulated a great fund of genial anecdotes. With a clean life, based upon absolute probity, he commands the admiration and respect of all his associates. He has as ardent an interest now in every detail of typefounding

as ever he had when confronting its most difficult problems in earlier years. He permits nothing to interfere with a most punctual attention to his duties, though these are largely self-imposed. His vocation knows no avocation.[5]

An anonymous author in the *American Printer* described Linn Boyd Benton in 1923 as "one of those men, quietly doing their day's work, who have a tremendous influence on the American printing industry."[6] He was characterized elsewhere as an extremely modest man, which was perhaps why he was "so little known among those men whose pleasure and livelihood are dependent upon the graphic arts."[7] He was respected by his peers, modest, reserved, and yet, according to Bullen, "much loved by those he admits to an intimacy." His character was beyond reproach, and "in his thought and the expression of his thought he [was] as accurate and precise as his own machines."[8]

Linn Boyd Benton's friends were at ATF and his social life revolved around the company. He did not have the same interest in hobbies, sports, and the outdoors that his son had, so he put off thoughts of retirement even though his eyesight continued to deteriorate. He knew all the conductors, brakemen, and regular passengers on the train he took to work every day, and loved to read or tell jokes to pass the time. "When he couldn't read anymore," Caroline said, "he always carried a couple of humorous magazines in his pocket, and he'd hand one to the man he was riding with and ask, 'Any good stories in here?'"

His visual problems and eventual near blindness may have been due to macular degeneration. Both of his granddaughters, Elizabeth and Caroline, also lost their eyesight when they were older. Elizabeth called her condition a "bleeding of the retina,"[9] and Caroline had the same symptoms. Elizabeth's daughter Kit suffers from macular degeneration today.

In 1930, when Boyd was 86 years old, the *Plainfield Courier-News* published an article calling him the "Edison of the Typographic Industry." Without giving further details, it reported that he had been awarded a patent "for an important improvement in the larger printing types used in newspaper headings."[10] On September 9 of the same year, his wife Jessie died at the age of 84. Boyd missed her greatly. Caroline remembered, "He would stand at the dining room table and bring his fist down, saying, 'Damnable! I've lost my little doll!'"

After Morris's mother died, he and Katrina moved back into the house on Crescent Ave. to be with Boyd, who continued working for almost two more years. Elizabeth's daughter Kit remembered visiting her grandfather and great-grandfather there. "As a 4 year old I was there at Christmas [1931]," Kit wrote. "Either grandpa Morris or great grandpa dressed up as Santa Claus and came down the stairs. I was so scared I hid under the player piano."[11]

Linn Boyd Benton's final portrait

Linn Boyd Benton retired from his position as manager of ATF's general manufacturing department on July 1, 1932. He became ill about a week later and died on July 15 of a cerebral hemorrhage. Lengthy obituaries appeared in the *Plainfield Courier-News* and the *American Printer*. The *Inland Printer* published the following testament:

> In recognition of the benefits showered upon the industry through the genius of this great figure, some of whose achievements are here recorded, the seat of honor, as it were, in this issue is given over to his most recent portrait. Turn to the frontispiece … study the kindly, intelligent features, recognize that he worked to benefit you—even after years of practical blindness—until past eighty-eight, and remember him as one of the truly great in the industry's march of progress.
>
> —The Editor[12]

The minutes of the ATF director's meeting for October 14, 1932, included this statement:

> RESOLVED: That the Directors of the American Type Founders Company place upon record their sorrow and deep sense of loss to themselves personally and to the Company in the death of LINN BOYD BENTON, who has been a member of the Board of Directors since its first organization in 1892, a period of forty years.
>
> Devoting his great natural genius of invention *exclusively* for the advantage of this Company from the time, forty years ago, he became a Director of the Company, and Manager of its General Manufacturing Department, Mr. Benton's inventions revolutionized the typefounding art and craft, and placed the Company in a position of leadership, to the great advantage of

Morris Benton and the Benton Hardness Tester From the July 1935 *Printing* magazine

the Company and the printing industry which it serves. These benefits have been, from the beginning, of incalculable value. These benefits will continue as long as the indispensable art of typography survives.

Those engaged in the arts of typography throughout the world have acknowledged Mr. Benton's genius, and the resulting benefits. This Company has benefited by his prestige. No other man connected with the Company has served it more valuably than our late departed friend.

As a Man Mr. Benton endeared himself to us by his modesty, his delightful humor, and his probity in all matters, intellectual and material. He was ever faithful to his conscience and also to this Company and the Board of Directors, who were conscious of the honor of being associated with so great and fine a Man.

The Directors respectfully present this appreciation of the Man and his character and genius to his Family in profound sympathy with their grief.[13]

Morris Benton's Last Years

The following year ATF filed for voluntary bankruptcy under Thomas Roy Jones. Immediately afterwards, the company was forced to decrease its debt instead of honoring its contracts. It sold the Jersey City plant and moved to Elizabeth, New Jersey, in 1935; in the process, many of Linn Boyd Benton's possessions were "not intelligently cared for."[14] Morris Benton remained at ATF for another five difficult years after his father's death.

Despite the company's financial woes, his picture, along with the "Benton Hardness Tester" for metal type, appeared on the cover of the July 1935 *Printing* magazine. There is no indication in the magazine as to who invented the device; the sole inside reference to the Bentons in the issue was on page 33, an advertisement for ATF foundry type and its "characteristic hardness," measured by the Benton Hardness Tester:

> Not the least interesting of the many ingenious machines employed in controlling the quality of ATF Foundry Type is the Benton Hardness Tester, the only machine of its kind in the world.

> Those familiar with the achievements and traditions of the Benton family will recognize in the photograph on the front cover, Mr. Morris Benton, son of the late Linn Boyd Benton, and for years head of the Designing and Engraving Departments of the American Type Founders.[15]

In 1936 the *Inland Printer* published John Murphy's three-part article about Morris Benton, and the following year, at the age of 65, Benton retired as ATF's chief type designer. Judging from an August 8, 1937, letter to Ben Lewis from "Benton's Shack, Beaver Lake, N.J.," Benton apparently planned to maintain few contacts with the firm, since he wrote: "I have definitely retired from business and am no longer connected with the A.T.F."[16] About a year later Morris asked by letter for a copy of the 1923 *Specimen Book*, and the following day E. G. Williams replied:

> Your letter of May 23 has just been received and I was glad to hear from you. I had a search made of the cabinets in your old office for a copy of the 1923 Specimen Book but none was found. The few copies that we have around here are in constant use and no one feels that he wants to relinquish his copy. However, I am going to make further inquiries and if I am at all successful in obtaining a copy I shall be glad to forward it to you.[17]

While the situation at ATF remained bleak, Morris Benton apparently maintained his interest in type. He wrote a detailed letter about the process of nickel facing an engraved matrix in 1942, including a formula and instructions, to William Kelly of Westfield, New Jersey, presumably the same man who had invented the Kelly Press.[18] He told his granddaughter Kit that Century Schoolbook "was his pride and joy. He was so proud because it was so legible," she said.[19]

In 1939, after Jessie and Linn Boyd Benton had been dead for several years, Morris and Katrina sold the Crescent Avenue "White Elephant" and bought a house on Long Hill Road in Millington, New Jersey, about six miles from Plainfield. Their new house included a large landscaped area on a slope and a pastoral view on three sides. Morris loved it—it was the one home he could truly call his own.

Morris Benton with his wife Katrina (far left), his daughter Caroline, and granddaughters Barbara and Kit (Elizabeth's daughters), circa 1936

Morris Benton at Beaver Lake

Morris and Katrina admire their first home-grown potato, 1941

Like his father, Morris offered political advice to his family, cautioning Caroline to vote for Wendell Wilkie, not Roosevelt, in the 1940 presidential election. "I am *firmly & completely* convinced that another four years of FDR will be the finish of the U.S.," he wrote.[20] Just before World War II Morris bought a convertible, "which he kept in immaculate condition"[21] and enjoyed driving with the top down to the cottage on Beaver Lake. For several summers, Kit alternated with her sister Barbara in spending a month with her grandfather. Kit remembered:

> At Beaver Lake he would stand on the diving board with a huge straw hat on his head, his hands at his sides, and dive. He would come up with the hat on his head and his hands still at his sides. He taught me how to swim, row the boat, and paddle the old canoe. He rowed next to me when I swam a mile across Beaver Lake and back. We read books and talked about his favorite authors, and discussed music we heard on the radio (and the player piano). He made up problems for me when I told him I took calculus, but he never showed any disappointment when I couldn't come up with answers.[22]

Morris was at some point advised that his recurrent ulcers required treatment and possibly surgery, but he resisted exposing himself to the same risk that had taken his first wife. In 1944 he wrote to Caroline, "The doctor says there is nothing the matter with me; but the multitude of complications of the present times gets my goat easier than it would twenty years ago."[23] He also smoked heavily, and Caroline felt that in his earlier life, if he hadn't had an ulcer he probably would have had lung cancer. Morris started to shrink as he got older; one day, upon seeing his granddaughter Kit, he said, "You must be wrong about your height. I'm taller than you."[24]

Morris became ill in the late spring of 1948; around the same time, Caroline and her two children came to New Jersey for a visit. From his bed he delighted in hearing the children outside singing some Gilbert and Sullivan songs they had learned for a play. Morris died of an embolism after a brief illness, on June 30, 1948, in All Souls Hospital in Morristown, New Jersey, at the age of 75. Brief obituaries appeared in the *New York Times* and the *Inland Printer* and, in each case, dwelled for a precious sentence or two on his father's importance to the type founding industry.

Chapter 15 Endnotes

1   Caroline Benton Gregg, in discussion with Theo Rehak, Racine, Wisconsin, July 1987.

2   Gregg, in discussion with the author, Milwaukee, March 20, 1984.

3   "Benton, Morris Fuller," 15 January 1951, typewritten, for the *National Cyclopedia of American Biography* (New York: James T. White and Company), 4.

4   Gregg, in discussion with the author.

5   Henry Lewis Bullen, "Linn Boyd Benton—The Man and His Work," *Inland Printer* 70, no. 1 (October 1922): 64.

6   "Little Life Stories of Live Men Known to the Printers of America. Linn Boyd Benton: Typefounder, Inventor," *American Printer* 77, no. 5 (March 5, 1923): 34.

7   "Achievements of Linn Boyd Benton Vital to Industry's Progress," *Inland Printer* 89, no. 5 (August 1932): 53.

8   Quadrat [Henry Lewis Bullen], "Discursions of a Retired Printer, No. VII," *Inland Printer* 38, no. 4 (January 1907): 520.

9   Elizabeth Benton Swain, in discussion with Theo Rehak, Hingham, Massachusetts, October 13, 1987.

10 "Hails Linn Boyd Benton's Type Inventions as One of Greatest of Present Era," *Plainfield* (N.J.) *Courier-News*, October 9, 1930.

11 Caroline Swain ("Kit") Clayton, "My Memories," April 2007, 1–2.

12 "Achievements," *Inland Printer*, 53.

13 Resolution recorded in the minutes of the American Type Founders Company board meeting, 14 October 1932.

14 Theo Rehak, *Practical Typecasting* (New Castle, Del.: Oak Knoll Books, 1993), 115.

15 *Printing*, July 1935: cover, 33.

16 Morris Benton to Ben Lewis, 8 August 1937.

17 E. G. Williams to Morris Benton, 24 May 1938.

18 Morris Benton to William M. Kelly, 13 March 1942.

19 Clayton, in discussion with the author, April 2007.

20 Morris Benton to Carolibus [Caroline Benton Gregg], Millington, New Jersey, 16 October 1940, 3.

21 Clayton, "Memories," 2.

22 Ibid., 3.

23 Benton to Carolibus, 15 November 1944, 3.

24 Clayton, discussion.

The Benton Legacy

THE EASE WITH WHICH we can choose a typeface today from a plethora of options to fit a particular need is something we may take for granted, but it is possible only because of the tremendous amount of labor and ingenuity that came before. Almost every literate person today benefits from the legacy of Linn Boyd Benton and Morris Fuller Benton, but due to the nature of their work and to their own reticence, this legacy has for the most part remained hidden.

Most books written before 1990 about the history of type omitted the Bentons altogether, some lamented that they were being ignored, and the rest devoted perhaps a few sentences to them, glossing over years of hard work and success. For example, Ruari McLean summarized Linn Boyd Benton's accomplishments in one sentence in his 1980 book *The Thames and Hudson Manual of Typography* : "Type continued to be cast, and composed, by hand until the American Linn Boyd Benton's invention of the punchcutting machine in 1884 made the Monotype and Linotype composition systems feasible."[1]

Warren Chappell complained about Benton's "zeal for standardization" in *A Short History of the Printed Word* (1970): "The shop convenience and economic advantage of [Benton's] 'improvements' were bought at high cost to individual letter forms and the effect of the type on the page."[2]

Chappell did not mention Benton's system of expanding and condensing letters in the book, or even how his engraving machine was a necessary component of the Linotype and Monotype systems, which he described in detail.

Not much was written about Morris Benton, either. "Sufficient credit has not been given to Morris Benton," J. L. Frazier wrote in *Type Lore* in 1925, "who has never sought or been thrust into the limelight, despite his great service to printers."[3] In 1982, William Ovink called the younger Benton "the engineer who had a far greater share in type design than our mainly artist-oriented histories of type production suggest."[4]

While some early 20th century typographers considered type design to be an art form, certainly the Bentons did not regard themselves as artists. They expected type to express profound ideas but remain the servant of those ideas, and they felt that in text matter, a typeface's own particular beauty should not intrude upon the reader. "When the printed page conveys information to the reader, without attracting attention to itself," Linn Boyd Benton wrote in 1906, "it is ideal." But he also realized that type for advertising had different requirements: "The design for a display type is often made to attract attention, not only to itself, but to what it proclaims, by its boldness and beauty and sometimes even by its ugliness."[5]

In an address before the British Typographer's Guild in London in 1932, Beatrice Warde paraphrased Benton's first statement above, saying that typography should be invisible, like a crystal goblet, "because everything about it is calculated to reveal rather than to hide the beautiful thing which it was meant to contain."[6] Her metaphor became famous in typographic circles. "Printing demands a humility of mind," she went on, "for the lack of which many of the fine arts are even now floundering in self-conscious and maudlin experiments. There is nothing simple or dull in achieving the transparent page. Vulgar ostentation is twice as easy as discipline."[7]

Warde's crystal goblet metaphor may have been inspired by a 1929 essay on type design by the British typographer Harry Carter, in which he compared the amateur type designer to one who followed more traditional practices. Carter suggested that printing was a supremely conservative art, "concealing technical revolutions under an appearance of unruffled continuity."[8]

> After all, the art of the type-designer is a comparatively humble one. His business is very largely not to obtrude himself needlessly between the writer and the reader. All moral qualities are irrelevant to aesthetic considerations, but if there is one that is not amiss if it makes itself felt in the design of a fount of type it is dislike of pretentiousness—a very negative quality. The danger of amateur influence upon printing is too great an attention to the objective excellences of the page. The craft-revival, instinct as it was with moral and social doctrine, is a new wine very little of which can safely be poured into the printer's old bottle, and one may expect to find the best work in type-design from one who has not drunk very deeply of it.[9]

The Bentons would have agreed with Carter and Warde. While father and son were largely responsible for a revolution in the way type was made, they were also plain-spoken, hard-working, highly disciplined, and even secretive Protestant Americans with a quiet, unassuming way of going about their lives. "They were interested in their work," Morris's daughter Elizabeth said. "They weren't looking for publicity."[10]

CENTURY NOVA

On September 22, 1964, more than 200 art directors, graphic artists, typographers, printers, trade press editors, and graphic arts educators attended an event at the Milwaukee Hilton Inn to which they had been invited by the Art Directors Club of Milwaukee. During the evening program ATF introduced a new foundry type, Century Nova, designed by a free-lance lettering artist in Milwaukee named Charles Hughes, who had studied ATF's earliest Century typefaces: the original Century Roman, cut by Linn Boyd Benton in 1895 for Theodore Low De Vinne's *Century Magazine*, and the revised version of the type that Linn Boyd and his son Morris had designed together in 1900, Century Expanded. Hughes had never designed a metal typeface before, and said, "To me, Century Nova has been primarily an education."[11]

Morris Benton's daughter Caroline was invited to attend the event and later wrote about it to her family. "I was introduced right and left as the daughter of Morris Benton. The newspaper article played up Linn Boyd, because of his Milwaukee ties, but *Morris* was the one they all wanted to talk to me about."[12] For the remainder of the letter, she referred to her father as "Morrie."

The evening's printed program explained that Linn Boyd Benton had originally lived and worked in Milwaukee, and that his son was born there, so Milwaukee was the logical setting for this first showing of the new type. "When Morris Benton died in 1948," it went on, "the Century Expanded which had been introduced a half-century previously was known and used extensively in every part of the globe and either imitated or pirated in many of them. Century Nova is thus a posthumous tribute to the Bentons, father and son."[13]

The following month, Emil J. Klumpp, then sales manager of ATF's type division, wrote to Caroline to thank her for her participation as guest of honor at the festivities. In his letter he reiterated the importance of her father and grandfather to the world of type:

> The Bentons' places as greats in history are already established, and their influence continuously guides us to adding lustre to their fame. The Benton heritage is a daily used keystone in ATF's progress as well as in printers [*sic*] shops all over the world. As long as men keep histories, none will be complete or meaningful without acknowledging the imprint of the Bentons.[14]

Dr. James Eckman (r.), type historian, chats with Mrs. Carol Benton Gregg, daughter of Morris Fuller Benton, at premiere of new ATF Century Nova typeface. Listening in are (l. to r.) Robert Blanchard of the Journal of Commercial Art; Emil Klumpp, ATF director of type design; Harry Verploegh of Frederick Ryder Co., Chicago typesetting firm, and Charles E. Hughes, designer of the Century Nova typeface.

But just six years earlier, in 1958, the Advertising Typographers Association of America, Inc., had published an article in *Type Talks* entitled "Typography's Forgotten Man: Morris Fuller Benton."[15] And in October 1961, the *Inland Printer/American Lithographer* ran an essay by Alexander Lawson entitled "Morris Fuller Benton Deserves More Than Obscurity," explaining that Benton was not well known, certainly not as well as the other type designers of his day, because he had "submitted his talents to the needs of a commercial type foundry."[16] Perhaps someone at ATF read Lawson's 1961 article and decided to commission a new Century typeface as a reaction to it.

Charles Hughes modeled Century Nova after the 1900 Benton father and son collaboration, Century Expanded.[17] This would not have been the choice of Steve Watts, who had been in charge of ATF type sales and the production of new typefaces from 1947 until his retirement in 1955. About a year after Lawson's article was published, Watts made some notes about ATF's Century type family for Dr. James Eckman, the type enthusiast from Rochester, Minnesota. In his memo Watts admitted that he had never liked Century Expanded. "For my money, the De Vinne Century Roman was rosin-to-the-bow [i.e., as necessary as rosin is to a violinist]. Wish the mats were still available."[18]

The publicity that accompanied Century Nova's debut led to several additional trade magazine articles about Morris Benton and the Century family. For example Dr. Eckman, who also attended the program in Milwaukee, wrote an article for the November 1964 *Printer's Digest* entitled, "The Immortal Century Type Face and The Bentons, Father and Son."[19] But soon after, references to the Bentons in printing-related publications became scarce.

Bon Voyage to Henry Lewis Bullen

ABCDEFGHIJKLMNOPQRSTUVWXYZ
abcdefghijklmnopqrstuvwxyzffifflfffifl
1234567890$¢£%?!.,;""""----··*()[]&
Century Nova

In the 1970s, RIT printing students Maureen Hitchcock and David Ritter worked on separate projects gathering information about Morris Benton. *U&lc* (Upper & lower case) magazine published an article about Morris Benton in 1984.[20] Several years after I completed my original master's thesis on the Bentons in 1986, some edited extracts from it appeared as an article in the American Printing History Association (APHA) journal, *Printing History*,[21] and books on typography began to include whole chapters about the Bentons.

For example, Simon Loxley's *Type: The Secret Life of Letters* (2005), includes a not entirely accurate chapter about the Bentons. Loxley calls Linn Boyd Benton "a skilful punch-cutter,"[22] although there is no evidence that Benton ever cut a punch by hand. Loxley maintains that Linn Boyd was "a smothering force in his son's life,"[23] an unfortunate conclusion that doesn't reflect Morris's rich family life, two happy marriages, highly successful career, and innately laconic nature. Also, in a 1923 photograph reprinted in the chapter (see above),[24] Loxley incorrectly identifies Joseph F. Gillick as Frederic Warde. Morris Benton is the fourth from the left, with his hand on the shoulder of a man Loxley erroneously identifies as Linn Boyd Benton, who appears in the back row on the far right. The seated man may be Wadsworth A. Parker, head of ATF's Specimen Department.[25] He was at the event, he had collaborated with Morris on several typefaces, and he must have been friendly with the Benton family since Caroline referred to him as "Waddy."

More significant than these misunderstandings is the recent renewed interest in Morris Benton's typefaces. In 2004 the Ascender Corporation, a Chicago font development company, did a survey of the fonts used on the front pages of 97 U.S. newspapers.[26] Both display and text typefaces were included, so in most cases more than one type family was counted per front page. In the rank order listing of the most popular newspaper typefaces from the survey, Morris Benton's Franklin Gothic was fourth on the list; Century Old Style was ranked eighth; "Benton Gothic," derived from News Gothic, was 15th; "Benton Modern," derived from ATF's Century Expanded, was 18th; "Bureau Roman," based on Morris Benton's Century Old Style, was ranked 26th; and "Century" was 27th. The most popular typeface family overall was the Poynter Gothic series.[27] In designing Poynter Gothic Text, "Tobias Frere-Jones began with [Morris Benton's] 4-point ATF Franklin Gothic drawings, modifying proportions to mix with Poynter Oldstyle & Benton Gothic, and adjusting ends of curved strokes 'C G S a c e r s' to suit news printing conditions,"[28] so the Poynter Gothic series is also essentially a Benton-derived design.

"I think it is safe to say," Charles Bigelow wrote, "that Benton's designs constitute 7 of the top 29 news faces in this study."[29] Because the survey was restricted to types used on newspaper front pages, it left out the small faces used for classified ads and stock listings. One common typeface used for these purposes is Poynter Agate, based on Benton's drawings of the small sizes of sans-serifs. These drawings are now housed in the Smithsonian's type collection.

A Tribute

The Bentons weren't required to promote themselves as freelance inventors and independent type designers must do, so they were able, for the most part, to side-step writing about their work. Fortunately what they did write was carefully guarded by family members and in a few instances was published.

Linn Boyd Benton wrote columns for and letters to his Milwaukee type foundry's publication, *The North-Western*. He enjoyed composing humorous asides and pontificating on various topics in this venue, but left his writing unsigned. He also wrote a technical chapter on how type was made for *The Building of a Book*, published in 1906, but most of his subsequent orations were confined to the audiences of his family and colleagues at ATF. Luckily, two weeks before he died, on his last day at ATF, Linn Boyd Benton completed a three-page summary of his patents and filled out a form about his working life. What the senior Benton loved was a good joke, and although he realized the significance of his inventions, he was humble about his work and accomplishments.

With a keen, dead-pan sense of humor, Morris Benton was a fiercely private person who was apparently most happy in the company of his family. He and Ethel exchanged letters for nearly five years before they married, and many years later he gathered information about his family history and wrote several pages of it for his children. Near the end of his life, when he was asked to write something about his father, grandfather, and himself for the Little Falls, New York, Public Library, Morris replied[30] with direct, lengthy quotations from the series of articles that John Allen Murphy had written about him for the *Inland Printer* magazine in 1936—never mind that Murphy had complained about getting Morris to talk, stating that he was "one of the most difficult men to interview I have ever talked to—and I have interviewed thousands in my time."[31]

Morris's reserved personality complemented that of his more outgoing father. It had to, because they worked side by side at ATF and lived in the same house as adults for more than 30 years. The stories of a youthful Morris climbing into a tree for an outdoor family portrait, of the older Morris keeping silent in his Halloween costume so as not to be found out, of interviewer Murphy struggling to get him to talk about himself, and of his patience with his aging father, reveal a self-possessed man who did not look to others for validation. Immediately after Ethel died in 1920, his output slowed considerably (according to Columbia's annotated 1923 *Specimen Book*, the only type he designed in 1920 was Garamond Bold in July), but by the end of 1922 he had already worked on ten other faces.[32]

The story of the lives and work of Linn Boyd and Morris Fuller Benton recalls a time in American history when men quietly worked at developing and improving mechanical technologies which, they must have believed, would continue evolving incrementally into the foreseeable future. As they performed manual mathematical calculations, slowly and deliberately, to engineer the machines and workflows that would produce metal types faster and more precisely than previous methods had done, little did they realize that their mechanical world would someday be transformed by a digital one, when volumes of type would be set by computers performing billions of calculations in just seconds. And even less did they suspect that those calculations would result in the instantaneous rendering in print and on electronic displays of the very letter designs that they had created with their mechanical devices and their untiring dedication to the science and art of typographic communication. Given their progressive attitudes and dedication to continuous technological improvement, the Bentons would undoubtedly be thrilled by what has happened in the years since they worked at the forefront of the industry.

Chapter 16 Endnotes

1   Ruari McLean, *The Thames and Hudson Manual of Typography* (London: Thames and Hudson, Ltd., 1980), 24.

2   Warren Chappell, *A Short History of the Printed Word* (New York: Alfred A. Knopf, 1970), 201.

3   J. L. Frazier, *Type Lore* (Chicago: Frazier, 1925), 105.

4   William Ovink, in "On Type: Eric Gill's Perpetua Type," by James Mosley, *Fine Print* 8, no. 3 (July 1982): 90.

5   Linn Boyd Benton, "The Making of Type," in *The Building of a Book*, ed. Frederick H. Hitchcock (New York: Grafton Press, 1906), 32.

6   Beatrice Warde, *The Crystal Goblet: Sixteen Essays on Typography*, ed. Henry Jacob (Cleveland and New York: World Publishing Co., 1956), 11.

7   Ibid., 17.

8   Harry Carter, "Observations on Modern Type Design," *Gutenberg-Gesellschaft Jahrbuch*, 1929: 297.

9   Ibid., 302.

10   Elizabeth Benton Swain, in discussion with Theo Rehak, Hingham, Massachusetts, October 13, 1987.

11   "ATF Unveils New Century Type Face In Historic Site," *Printing News*, October 17, 1964, 25.

12   Caroline Benton Gregg to her extended family, n.d. [1964].

13   Art Directors Club of Milwaukee, "Century Nova" pamphlet, September 1964, 1.

14   Emil J. Klumpp to Mrs. Gordon C. Gregg, 1 October 1964.

15   "Typography's Forgotten Man: Morris Fuller Benton," *Type Talks*, May/June 1958, 11–12.

16   Alexander Lawson, "Morris Fuller Benton Deserves More Than Obscurity," *Inland Printer/American Lithographer* 148, no. 1 (October 1962): 80.

17   "ATF Unveils," *Printing News*, 25.

18   Stevens L. Watts, "Notes for Dr. James Eckman," 28 September 1962.

19   Eckman, "The Immortal Century Type Face and the Bentons, Father and Son," *Printer's Digest*, November 1964, 4–6.

20   Alan Haley, "Typographic Milestones: Morris Fuller Benton," *U&lc*, September 1983, 16–19.

21   Patricia A. Cost, "Linn Boyd Benton, Morris Fuller Benton, and Typemaking at ATF," *Printing History* 31/32, vol. 16, nos. 1 & 2 (1994): 27–44.

22   Simon Loxley, "American Spring: Creating the Modern Age," in *Type: The Secret History of Letters* (London, New York: I. B. Tauris, 2005), 70.

23   Ibid., 74.

24   Ibid., 73.

25   McGrew, *American Metal*, 299.

26   Bill Davis, "Fonts on the Front Page—A Study of Typefaces on the Front Pages of America's Top Newspapers" (Elk Grove Village, Ill.: Ascender Corporation, 19 November 2004), http://www.ascendercorp.com/pr/pr2004_11_09.html (accessed April 23, 2008).

27   Ibid., 5.

28   Font Bureau, "Poynter Gothic Text," http://www.fontbureau.com/fonts/PoynterGothicText (accessed January 8, 2009).

29   Charles Bigelow, email message to the author, 16 January 2007.

30   Morris Fuller Benton to Loomis Burrell, 25 May 1948.

31   John Allen Murphy, "Morris Benton, Part 2," *Inland Printer* 97, no. 1 (April 1936): 42.

32   Maureen D. Hitchcock, *Benton Types: Typefaces Designed or Adapted by Morris Fuller Benton* (Rochester, N.Y.: Press of the Good Mountain, 1978).

A Software Engineer Admires Benton's Optical Scaling System

by Raph Levien, with comments by Theo Rehak

At Google, Inc., Raph Levien is a software engineer who also works on spam prevention. He has designed digital type, including the monospaced design Inconsolata, and is finishing his Ph.D. dissertation at U.C. Berkeley on mathematical techniques for designing curves in computer graphics. He wrote the following two essays for this book in 2007, without ever having seen a Benton engraving machine; Theo Rehak, who owns and operates two Benton engraving machines, commented on Levien's second essay.

The history of printing technology is a continuing story of automating tasks that formerly took intensive labor. Movable type, the Benton pantograph engraver, the Monotype and Linotype composing machines, and, in the 20th century, photo and digital typesetting each saved a huge amount of time compared with the previous technology, but each also incorporated a different set of tradeoffs to balance aesthetic quality and cost. The Benton pantograph engraving machine is a particularly interesting instance of this general pattern, for several reasons. To achieve the automated production of many sizes of type from a single master, while retaining quality comparable to the hand-cut punches that preceded it, the combination of ingenious mechanical engineering and a deep understanding of the aesthetic appearance of printed type was required. In short, the Bentons solved a problem that still bedevils the production of digital type. Unfortunately, the details of their solution were more or less lost as the world moved past metal type to phototypesetting. A strong argument can be made for reviving their techniques in digital form, just as revivals of classic Benton designs comprise an essential part of any modern type library. In fact, one could maintain that the currently available non-optically-scaled versions of the Benton designs are pale imitations, rather than true revivals.

The central issue addressed by the Bentons is now generally known as "optical scaling." In high-quality printing, the small sizes of type are not simply photographic reductions of the larger sizes. Rather, they are heavier, lower in contrast (the ratio between thick and thin strokes), generally slightly wider, and more generously spaced. Very small sizes also have a larger x-height, which means shorter ascenders and descenders. Conversely, large sizes appear more refined and have higher contrast compared with photographic enlargements of smaller sizes. In the days before the Benton engraving machine, achieving optical scaling required no special technology. Rather, as each size of "punch" was separately cut by hand, the punch cutter made the necessary adjustments as a matter of course. Rather, the significant challenge was making the various sizes consistent, or at least harmonious.

With the advent of the Benton matrix engraver, these issues were reversed. From a single design (embodied in a "pattern plate"), the various sizes were automatically consistent, but, without some additional adjustments, lacked optical scaling. To make both small and large type from a single design would have yielded small type that was thin and spindly, large type that was heavy and crude, or both. The Bentons realized that they must solve this problem to produce type of a quality sufficient to compete.

It is possible today to analyze and reconstruct the techniques used by the Bentons, based on contemporary descriptions of the machines, cutting slips and other documentation from ATF's type production operations, and careful scanning of printed results. This analysis reveals a set of algorithms, implemented by the Bentons using steam-powered mechanical devices, but almost equally applicable to digital computers today. These algorithms, if properly implemented and applied, would yield results superior to most digital typography produced today, while requiring significantly less labor and expertise than competitive solutions for optical scaling. Thus, the work of the Bentons over one hundred years ago still has much to teach us today.

Levien: The Benton engraving machine serves as a strong example of a familiar pattern in the history of industrial technology. It replaced the very finicky and labor-intensive process of striking a punch into a matrix with an efficient, repeatable manufacturing process. Quality matrices could, for the first time, be produced in quantity.

Rehak: I would add, such quality matrices were made in perfect, exact, continuity, something unattainable from a human punch-cutter where there are always variations, however slight.

Levien: But there is another way to view the Benton engraver. It was also a sophisticated, special-purpose "analog computer," encoding *algorithms* for type design, particularly optical scaling, into the workings of its machinery. Let us see what we can learn of the nature of those algorithms from what we know of the machine. The two main algorithms were *anamorphic scaling* and *stroke offset.* Anamorphic scaling expands or condenses the body of the type at the same time as producing different sizes. Of course, one of the huge economic impacts of the engraving machine was the production of a full array of matrices across a range of sizes, as opposed to the old way, which required cutting a separate punch for each size of type.

Rehak: Certain body sizes have subtle but seriously restrictive values, as to available space and fitting proportions, which necessitate special patterns sometimes.

Levien: Benton understood that hand-cut punches were not exact photographic replicas across the size range, as if made by simply changing the focal length of a zoom lens. Rather, there is a systematic trend that small types are wider (more extended) and large sizes are comparatively narrower. To be sure, it's a subtle effect, but enough to make the small sizes more readable, and the larger ones more refined in appearance. Benton wanted to preserve this subtlety, rather than bow to the natural tendency of the technology to dictate the shapes of the resulting fonts just because it was more convenient to build a machine that did simple scaling only.

Rehak: Benton said that the "normal" viewing size for the average human eye was about 1/2 inch in height when reading. He fixed this as his standard height parallel (approx 36 to 40 points in actual height). Below this size the character required "expansion," a fattening and reducing of the height parallel. Above it the eye required "condensation," a thinning and increase of the height parallel. Remember, he confined his outcomes specifically to the range of sizes of foundry cast printing type: from 3-point to 144-point bodies.

Levien: The basic scaling action of the engraving machine was fairly straightfor-
            ward. The shape of the letter (its *outline,* really, in modern terms) was
            encoded in the movement of a *lever arm,* fixed at the top of the device and
            guided at the bottom by the operator tracing the *pattern,* an intaglio out-
            line of the letter for matrix cutting, roughly three inches tall.

Rehak: Since the Benton engraving machine was originally conceived as a punch-
            cutting device, it utilized wrong-reading raised patterns to which it cut a
            periphery outline. Next came right-reading patterns for cutting electro-
            models on blank quads of cast type. By 1903, both Bentons realized
            that new matrices could be cut directly into prepared planchets of free-
            machining brass, and in so doing did away with all the previous technics,
            streamlining matrix production. Because of the ratios involved, Benton
            found that the standard height parallel for the Benton engraving machine
            was a constant 3.59 inch. (Along the way, the Benton engraving machine
            just happened to save the Linotype machine, by providing a reliable source
            for new punches with which to strike Linotype replacement matrices with
            accuracy and efficiency.)
                    The Benton engraving machine does not have a simple lever arm.
            If it did, it would never accomplish what it does with any success. The
            relative motion "floats" through a series of interacting lever assemblies
            that orbit through each other. The precise action of each component has
            never been deciphered properly or clearly, engineering-wise. My machinist
            refused to be responsible if asked to disassemble the cutting head, quite
            rightly fearing that he could never get it accurately re-assembled, based on
            the scant references and terse instructions as supplied in the original patent
            application and drawings.

Levien: A simple version of the engraving machine, not capable of anamorphic
            scaling, would transfer the motion of the lever arm to the relative motion
            of the engraving tool (housed in the quill assembly) and the matrix being
            engraved (the work). Because the work was so much smaller than a high-
            speed steam-powered drill and didn't contain any moving parts, it was
            the work that moved, while the engraving tool remained stationary. Such
            a machine would have been a significant advance, allowing near-perfect
            reproductions of the pattern plate at different sizes, as if by photography.
            But the ingenuity of Linn Boyd Benton did not stop there.

Rehak: Good point on Mr. Levien's part. We know what the components do, but
            not their spatial relationships or adjustments. Quite simply no one except
            Benton ever took them apart, or if they did dare, ever put them right again.

Levien: To accomplish anamorphic scaling, Benton used a clever system of gimbals to decompose the motion of the lever into left-right and up-down components. This decomposition is essentially the same insight that Rene Descartes introduced in his invention of orthogonal coordinates, which did so much to open geometry to mathematical analysis. Thus, if the lever traces a pure circle in the pattern plate, then the motion of one gimbal describes a sine curve, and the other a cosine.

Rehak: Exactly so.

Levien: But decomposing the motion of the lever arm into two one-dimensional movements opened another possibility. The sampling of the motion of the lever could occur at two different heights. Thus, one motion would be amplified with respect to the other. Recombining these motions into the total relative motion of the quill and work, the resulting curve is an ellipse rather than a circle. If the left-right motion is sampled at a lower height of the lever arm than the up-down, then it is of higher amplitude, and the resulting ellipse is wider than a circle. Conversely, if it is sampled higher up on the lever arm, then the resulting ellipse is narrower.

            The adjustment to the width of the character was specified as a height value for the sampling of the horizontal motion, expressed as a distance higher (in the case of narrowing) or lower (in the case of widening) than the reference for the horizontal motion.

Rehak: True, but Benton himself referred to the calibration of such finessing as "controlling a distortion." This he understood to be an interaction between functions of the partial orbits of the gimbal device which was based on the "normal" coordinate's affectation and the dimensional increment of the Anglo-American *pica* (.1660 inch), comprised of 12 Anglo-American points. His machines and all their devices are based, designed, and machined on this increment of measure.

Levien: **Stroke offset**
            The relative wideness of a letter is not the only significant difference for smaller type when compared with larger. The nature of the line making the letter is also different. Strokes in smaller sizes are relatively *bolder* and also lower in *stroke contrast* than those in larger sizes. Both of these variations contribute to readability in lower sizes. A 72-point Bodoni letter has beautifully refined hairlines, but if that were to be simply photographically reduced by a factor of 12, the resulting hairline would be nearly invisible.

Benton automated these changes to the letter outline by building a form of *stroke offset* into the engraving process. Mathematically, stroke offset can be seen as drawing the outline with a pen of nonzero radius. When drawing a circle of radius R, say, with a pen of radius r, then the outer edge describes a circle of radius $R + r$. Similarly, when tracing both sides of the outline of a line of width w, the resulting line width is $w + 2r$. Note that this mathematical equation captures the effects both of making strokes bolder and reducing the contrast between thick and thin strokes.

Today, these kinds of adjustments to the outline of the letter would be achieved by a *stroke offset* algorithm, one that is notoriously tricky to implement using digital techniques such as Bezier curves. In fact, new algorithms for stroke offset continue to be published.

Rehak: Benton was a "black-and-white" kind of guy. The imprecise nature of deriving values and real dimensions within a chaotic regime of factors, such as the Bezier curves mentioned by Mr. Levien, would have annoyed him. Benton would not have tolerated an ethereal world of imprecision. Perhaps Bezier curves, holograms, and the Kirlian image would have fascinated him, but most likely he would have rejected them as valuable tools within his environment of precise methods and outcomes.

Levien: Benton's approach to stroke offset made use of the fact that the engraving tool had a nonzero radius. For example, if the tool was 1 mil (0.001 inch) in diameter, then the outline engraved into the work was equivalent to the outline traced by the lever arm (and anamorphically scaled) with an added pen radius of 1/2 mil.

Rehak: Without imposing a constant and definite value of the "normal" setting as a point of constant reference, the Benton system would descend into chaos. When cutting designs into matrices, many different paths and dimensions can lead to the same dimension of cutting. What Benton did was to regularize the procedure and make it reliable.

Levien: The Benton method could both add and remove stroke weight when transferring the outline of a letter from the pattern plate to the work. The lever arm ended, not in a sharp needle, but in a peg with nonzero radius, called the "follower." If the follower was the same diameter as the engraving tool (in units relative to the design), then the stroke weight engraved into the work was the same as the design on the pattern plate. If the tool was larger (again, in the same relative units), then the outline was heavier. If however the follower was larger, then the stroke weight engraved into the work was less than the design on the pattern plate.

Cutting slips for Freehand, sizes 8 and 48, showing the differences in followers used for different point sizes

Rough engraving

This balancing-offset approach also helps solve a tricky and important engineering problem. Engraving an entire matrix, especially a large one, with a tiny quill around 1 mil (0.001 inch) in diameter, would not be practical. It would take a very long time to cut, and the wear on the tool would be significant.

Rehak: Yes, well expressed.

Levien: The actual process of engraving a matrix instead used three passes with three different cutting quills. The first one was large and cut a large outline, and the next two cut sufficiently finer detail, with more precision. Once the bulk of the metal was cut away with the first quill, the actual amount of metal to be removed with the smaller quills was manageable.

As a manufacturing process, the technique of using multiple passes, each refining the outline, was ingenious. As an algorithm, it is of less interest, because the outline of the final resulting matrix is the same as if it had (impractically) all been cut with the finest quill. Perhaps, though, this method is strong praise for Benton's engineering talents: the practical goal of more efficient cutting was accomplished without in any way sacrificing the precision of the result.

Corners

The above discussion of the changes to the outline is in terms of strokes in general. Along the length of a stroke, if the follower and quill were of the same (relative) size, the outline cut into the metal was exactly the same as on the pattern plate. Corners are different, though. A rotating quill cannot cut an exact square corner into the work. At best, it can cut a rounded corner, with the radius equal to the radius of the finest cutting quill.

Rehak: There are no precisely acute angles or "corners" in the real world. There is always, no matter how minute, a radius at the junction between two lines.

Levien: Some font designs (perennial Benton favorites Souvenir and Hobo come to mind) contain no sharp corners, only rounded ones, so this is not an issue. Others, such as the Bodoni series and the surprisingly modern Franklin Gothic family, appear to have quite sharp corners indeed. Only when examining the printed page under high magnification is the lack of sharp corners visible at all. The precision of the Benton engraving machine, with its 1/2 mil cutting radius typical of the finest quill, was renowned in its day, and commands respect even by the standards of today's printing processes. A 1/2 mil rounded corner is equivalent to laser imaging of approximately

2,000 dpi, well above the capability of office printers and competitive with high-end prepress imagesetters.

Making significant changes to stroke weight when transferring outlines from the pattern plate to the final matrix would present challenges to the production of sharp corners, even if the cutting quill was infinitely fine. It is in the nature of the stroke offset algorithm that outside corners will become rounded when strokes are thickened (while sharpening the radius of inside corners), and the converse is true when strokes are thinned, as is the case for producing large sizes. Fortunately, the amount of change to the stroke weight is relatively subtle, so the appearance of sharp corners is not greatly impacted. And, in this case, a clever *use* of the machinery ensures the best results.

A careful study of the ATF cutting slips (and summary information contained in ATF's Day Book) reveals that the pattern plates for most fonts were drawn for a particular design size. When cutting actual matrices at this particular size, all adjustments were at zero—no expansion or condensation, and no increase or decrease in stroke weight. Typically, this nominal design size was in the *middle* of the useful range for that font. Thus, the softness of outer corners at small sizes is balanced with the softness of inner corners at large sizes, and, in all cases, the loss of sharpness is worse for the extreme sizes than the (more common) sizes in the middle of the range.

From the fact that ATF paid such careful attention to minimizing the loss of sharpness at corners, we can infer that the *intent* was to achieve as much sharpness as possible. In modern digital techniques, it is typical to encode corners explicitly, so that they remain sharp corners even after the application of stroke offset (either positive or negative)—it need not be constrained to use a perfectly circular "pen" across the entire outline, corners and smooth sections alike. If the Bentons were still alive and using digital production techniques, it is reasonable to expect that they would make use of this digital capability, which could only be approximated (no matter how impressively) using the steam-powered analog computational techniques available at the time.

Yet, if the goal is fanatical accuracy when producing historical revivals of the classic ATF typefaces, a very reasonable approach is to apply two stroke offset operations to the outline as it appeared on the pattern plate— an inset corresponding to the radius of the follower, followed by a weight gain operation corresponding to the radius of the quill. The data representing these parameters (as well as the expansion or condensation) is available in the ATF Day Book. Future historians, and type enthusiasts interested in historically accurate ATF revivals, will greatly appreciate efforts made now to conserve that information.

A few words on spacing

While the computational techniques for automatically adjusting outlines for optical sizing in Benton's day are impressive, an equally important facet of the final printed pages is the marvelously even color of printed text, a consequence of the fanatical attention paid by ATF to good spacing. Pages from the classic, grand ATF specimen books easily rival modern, digitally produced type, with their unlimited tables of kern pairs. Indeed, it would be fair to say that many modern digital type designers use these huge kern tables as a crutch to make up for less careful "fit" of the letters themselves within their side bearings.

Spacing also plays an essential role in proper optical scaling. At small sizes, letters need more space so they don't jumble together in the visual field. At large sizes, gaps between letters need to be avoided, otherwise letters fail to relate to each other, especially as regards the shapes of the white spaces between letters.

Analytically minded students of typography would do well to study the spacing of ATF fonts. The quality of the results, in context with the extreme limitations of the technology, suggests a deep knowledge of how to space type well.

Rehak: By spacing characters I assume Mr. Levien is referring to the orientation of the design on the body and in interaction with a specific character's fellow characters in composition. [That is correct.] The fitting of ATF fonts was accomplished by trial and error in "silly proofs" done in the matrix department by the fitter. Adjustments were made even beyond the eighth or tenth proof trials before being approved for production casting. In practice as well as theory, every character of the font must interact properly with all the rest of the characters in the font.

Levien: **Conclusion**

The genius of the Bentons is many-fold:

- The invention of an entirely new manufacturing process for engraving matrices.
- The development of algorithms for adjusting the outlines of letters to improve their quality beyond what simple photographic scaling could achieve.
- The careful choosing of parameters for these algorithms, as well as parameters for spacing, to optimize quality.
- The design of new, innovative, practical, and beautiful letterforms, ideally suited to make best use of all this technology.

In the history of printing, newer, more automated technology invariably replaces older, vastly more labor-intensive craft. Almost always, the economic pressure to save the cost of labor conflicts with a loss of quality. Then, as the new technology gains market share, the demand for quality pushes development on the high end, and finally that technology becomes mainstream.

The digital typography industry is following exactly this pattern when it comes to proper optical scaling – it is becoming common in high end offerings such as Adobe's Garamond Premier Pro, drawn by Robert Slimbach, but mass-market applications, even those as high profile and cutting-edge as Microsoft's ClearType font suite, still do not incorporate true optical scaling.

The Bentons, by focusing on quality from the beginning, and bringing their considerable ingenuity and design skills to the task, broke that mold. Their type was in every way a match for the quality of the hand-cut punch process they displaced, and in some ways superior. With luck, the inevitable future waves of technology that will continue to transform the way people create type will follow the example of the Bentons. And designers, technical workers, and analytically minded historians still have much to learn from their work.

Morris Benton's Typefaces

There is no official ATF list of Morris Benton's typefaces. This list was generated from the following sources, the first four of which are discussed in Chapter 14:

1   The anonymously annotated 1923 ATF specimen book at Columbia University, with dates (ATF).

2   The 1936 "partial list of my designs," by Morris Benton (MFB). The typefaces that were starred on Benton's list are also starred here, after the checkmark under his initials.

3   The 1965 list compiled by Stevens L. Watts, with dates and ATF serial number (SLW). Maureen Delaney Hitchcock explained in *Benton Types* that Watts was manager of type sales at ATF from 1947 to 1955. She wrote in her introduction that "his attributions ... seem to have been derived from matrix department files, his dates evidently referring to the production of Benton's types rather than to their design."

4   The 1993 book *American Metal Typefaces of the Twentieth Century*, by Mac McGrew (McG). In the few cases where Steve Watts did not give an ATF series number, McGrew's ATF series number is noted. I have included McGrew's design (not production) dates. Some typefaces had no dates in McGrew's book, although they had been dated in McGrew's 1978 article "The Bentons, Father & Son." Where the 1978 and 1993 McGrew dates conflicted, the 1993 information is presented. Benton typefaces that are illustrated in McGrew's *American Metal Typefaces* are indicated.

5   "A Cursory Census of ATF Matrices, Sold at the Auction of August 24, 1993," compiled by Gregory J. Walters, who attended the auction. His census was updated for this book in January 2009.

	Name of Type	ATF	MFB	SLW	McG	ATF #	Dates
	Acquitaine *see* Phenix						SLW: 1935
1	Adscript	√		√	√	2	ATF: April 1914
							SLW: 1916, non-kerning
							McG: 1914†
2	Agency Gothic		√	√	√	578	SLW: 1933
							McG: 1932†
3	Agency Gothic Open		√	√	√	580	SLW: 1934
							McG: designed 1932,
							issued 1934†
4	Alternate Gothic No. 1	√	√	√	√	6	ATF: May 1903
							SLW: 1906
							McG: 1903‡
5	Alternate Gothic No. 2	√	√	√	√	7	ATF: May 1903
							SLW: 1906
							McG: 1903‡
6	Alternate Gothic No. 3	√	√	√	√	8	ATF: February 1903
							SLW: 1906
							McG: 1903†
	Alternate Gothic Title No. 1						SLW: 1906
7	American Backslant		√	√	√	586	SLW: 1934
							McG: designed 1933,
							issued 1935†
8	American Caslon	√			√	458	ATF: 1922
							McG: 1919‡
9	American Caslon Italic	√			√	471	ATF: 1922
							McG: 1919†
10	American Text		√	√	√	567	SLW: 1932
							McG: 1932†
11	Announcement Roman	√			√	456	ATF: September 1916
							McG: designed 1916,
							issued 1918†

† Illustrated in *American Metal Typefaces of the Twentieth Century* as an ATF font.

‡ Illustrated as a Monotype font.

Comments	Matrices sold at ATF auction
SLW: "name changed to Phenix"	
McG: "Sizes under 36-point were added in 1935."	
	24 pt. to Rich Hopkins
abandoned	
ATF: "Inland New Caslon except figures and descenders by MFB" McG: same as the Inland Type Foundry's 1905 New Caslon but with "long descenders, oldstyle figures, and italic swash characters"	18 pt. to Howard Bratter; 36 pt. to Greg Walters; (long descenders & OS numbers only) 30, 42, 48 pt. to Greg Walters
ATF: "Inland New Caslon Italic except figures and descenders by MFB" McG: "in 18 point and larger … Italic [is a copy] of Caslon Bold"	6, 8, 10, 12, 14, 18 pt. to Howard Bratter; 24, 30, 36, 42, 48, 60, 72 pt. to Greg Walters
SLW: "devoid of curved strokes"	
ATF: "Adapted from engravings by MFB"	6, 8, 10, 12, 14, 18, 24, 30, 36, 48 pt. to Greg Walters; 14/18, 18 pt. to Howard Bratter

	Name of Type	ATF	MFB	SLW	McG	ATF #	Dates
12	Announcement Italic	√			√	452	ATF: April 1916 McG: designed 1916, issued 1918†
13	Antique Shaded	√	√	√	√	12	ATF: September 1910 SLW: 1911 McG: designed 1910, issued 1913‡
14	Bank Gothic Light		√	√	√	532	SLW: 1932 McG: 1930†
15	Bank Gothic Medium		√	√	√	533	SLW: 1932 McG: 1930†
16	Bank Gothic Bold		√	√	√	534	SLW: 1932 McG: 1930†
17	Bank Gothic Condensed Light		√	√	√	574	SLW: 1933 McG: 1930–33†
18	Bank Gothic Condensed Medium		√	√	√	575	SLW: 1933 McG: 1930–33†
19	Bank Gothic Condensed Bold		√	√	√	576	SLW: 1933 McG: 1930–33†
20	Baskerville Roman			√		15	SLW: 1915
21	Baskerville Italic	√		√	√	16	ATF: 1915 SLW: 1915 McG: 1915†
22	Benton (Whitehall)		√*	√	√	566	SLW: 1934 McG: designed 1930, released 1934†
23	Bodoni	√	√*	√	√	22	ATF: February 1909 SLW: 1909 McG: 1910‡
24	Bodoni Italic	√	√*	√	√	23	ATF: March 1910 SLW: 1909 McG: 1910–11†
25	Bodoni Bold	√	√*	√	√	24	ATF: May 1911 SLW: 1912 McG: 1910–11‡
	Bodoni Bold Condensed			√			SLW: 1933

† ATF ‡ Monotype

† ATF ‡ Monotype

Comments	Matrices sold at ATF auction
ATF: "Adapted from engravings by MFB"	6, 8, 10, 12, 14, 18, 24, 30, 36 pt. to Greg Walters
McG: "cut on a new shading machine invented by the designer's father"	
	No. 20 capitals and points, 18 pt. to Howard Bratter
SLW: "after Fry Foundry version"	Steve Heaver; 14 pt. to Rich Hopkins
	8, 10, 14, 16, 18 pt. to Rich Hopkins
SLW: "renamed Whitehall" McG: designed under the name Cambridge, released as Benton, reintroduced in 1953 as Whitehall	
	72 pt. to Peter Kruty; for Newark Evening News: 96, 120 pt. to Cary Collection at RIT
abandoned	

	Name of Type	ATF	MFB	SLW	McG	ATF #	Dates
26	Bodoni Bold Italic	√	√*	√	√	25	ATF: April 1911 SLW: 1913 McG: 1910–11‡
27	Bodoni Bold Shaded	√		√	√	26	ATF: August 1912 SLW: 1913 McG: 1912†
28	Bodoni Book	√	√*	√	√	27	ATF: August 1910 SLW: 1911 McG: 1910–11‡
	Bodoni Book Expanded			√			SLW: 1924
29	Bodoni Book Italic	√	√*	√	√	28	ATF: April 1911 SLW: 1911 McG: 1910–11†
	Bodoni, Card *see* Card Bodoni						
	Bodoni, Engravers *see* Engravers Bodoni						
30	Bodoni Open	√	√	√	√	544	SLW: 1925 McG: designed 1918†
	Bodoni Open, Engravers *see* Engravers Bodoni Open						
31	Bodoni Shaded Initials	√		√		none	ATF: undated SLW: 1914
	Bodoni, Ultra *see* Ultra Bodoni						
32	Bold Antique	√		√	√	29	ATF: June 1904 SLW: 1904 McG: designed 1904, issued 1905†
	Bold Antique Italic			√			SLW: 1904
33	Bold Antique Condensed	√		√	√	30	ATF: December 1906 SLW: 1908 McG: designed 1906, issued 1908–09‡
	Bold Antique Extra Condensed			√			SLW: 1912
	Book Title			√			SLW: 1926

† ATF   ‡ Monotype

Comments	Matrices sold at ATF auction
	12/18 pt. to Howard Bratter
abandoned	
McG: "discontinued after a time and reintroduced in 1930."	10, 12, 14, 18, 24, 30, 36, 48 pt. to Greg Walters
SLW: "renamed Whitin Black" McG: "About 1963 these faces were reissued as Whitin Black …"	
abandoned	
McG: "… and Whitin Black Condensed	
abandoned	
abandoned	

	Name of Type	ATF	MFB	SLW	McG	ATF #	Dates
34	Broadway		√*	√	√	506	SLW: 1926 McG: designed 1927, issued 1928‡
35	Broadway Condensed		√	√	√	529	SLW: 1929 McG: 1929†
	Broadway Nos. 2 and 3			√			SLW: 1928
36	Bulfinch Oldstyle	√			√	41	ATF: 1903 McG: 1903†
37	Bulletin Typewriter		√			491	McG: issued 1933†
38	Bulmer Roman		√*	√	√	497	SLW: 1926 McG: designed as early as 1923†
39	Bulmer Italic		√*	√	√	498	SLW: 1927 McG: designed as early as 1923†
	Cambridge *see* Benton (Whitehall)						
	Cambridge Italic			√	√		SLW: 1934 McG: no date
40	Canterbury		√	√	√	508	SLW: 1928 McG: designed 1920, issued 1926†
41	Card Bodoni			√	√	43	SLW: 1915 McG: 1912–16†
42	Card Bodoni Bold			√	√	443	SLW: 1917 McG: 1912–16
43	Card Litho	√		√	√	44	ATF: 1917 SLW: 1917 McG: 1917
44	Card Light Litho	√		√	√	45	ATF: 1917 SLW: 1917 McG: 1917
45	Card Mercantile *see also* Mercantile				√	46	McG: two sizes only, 1901†

† ATF   ‡ Monotype

Comments	Matrices sold at ATF auction
abandoned	
ATF: partly McG: designed by William Martin Johnson, adjustments made by MFB	
Only MFB lists this as one of his designs	
McG: Adapted by MFB from a type cut in about 1790 by William Martin for William Bulmer's Shakespeare Press in London	6, 8, 10, 12, 14, 18, 24, 30, 36, 42, 48 pt. to Fritz Klinke; (owned but not purchased at the auction) 48 pt. (incomplete), Cary Collection at RIT
	6, 8, 10, 12, 14, 18, 24, 30, 36, 42, 48 pt. to Fritz Klinke
SLW: abandoned McG: designed, pattern plates and trial castings made, but never completed	
ATF: "Inland" McG: The title series of the Inland Foundry's Litho Roman, modified by MFB	
ATF: "Inland" McG: The title series of the Inland Foundry's Litho Roman, modified by MFB	
A redesign by MFB of the two smallest sizes of the Dickinson Type Foundry's Mercantile Extended, which appeared to be a duplicate of Extended No. 3 of Stevens, Shanks in England.	

	Name of Type	ATF	MFB	SLW	McG	ATF #	Dates
46	Card Roman			√	√	488	SLW: 1925 McG: designed 1921, issued 1925†
	Caslon, American *see* American Caslon						
	Caslon Initials	√					ATF: undated
	Castile			√			SLW: 1931
47	Century Bold (companion to Century Expanded)	√	√*	√	√	55	ATF: December 1904 SLW: 1906 McG: designed 1904, issued 1905‡
48	Century Bold Condensed	√	√	√	√	56	ATF: February 1908 SLW: 1909 McG: designed 1906, issued 1909†
49	Century Bold Condensed Title			√			SLW: 1924
50	Century Bold Extended	√		√	√	57	ATF: April 1909 SLW: 1910 McG: designed 1906, issued 1910‡
51	Century Bold Italic (companion to Century Expanded)	√	√*	√	√	58	ATF: February 1905 SLW: 1906 McG: designed 1904, issued 1905†
52	Century Catalogue	√	√	√	√	444	ATF: February 1914 SLW: 1922 McG: 1917†
53	Century Catalogue Italic		√	√	√	468	SLW: 1922 McG: undated†
54	Century Expanded	√	√*	√	√	59	ATF: 1900 SLW: 1900 McG: 1900‡
55	Century Expanded Italic	√	√*	√	√	60	ATF: 1900 SLW: 1900 McG: 1900 (implied)†

† ATF   ‡ Monotype

Comments	Matrices sold at ATF auction
abandoned	
abandoned	
SLW: "reproduces design for Baskerville Italic, with plain capitals and slightly different face sizes" McG: "cut from the patterns for Baskerville Italic"	
SLW: "with Linn Boyd Benton"	
SLW: "with L. B. Benton"	

	Name of Type	ATF	MFB	SLW	McG	ATF #	Dates
56	Century Oldstyle	√	√*	√	√	61	ATF: May 1906 SLW: 1906 McG: designed 1906, 　　issued 1908–09‡
57	Century Oldstyle Italic	√	√*	√	√	62	ATF: September 1906 SLW: 1906 McG: undated†
58	Century Oldstyle Bold	√	√	√	√	63	ATF: May 1909 SLW: 1910 McG: 1909†
59	Century Oldstyle Bold Italic	√		√	√	64	ATF: November 1906 [?] SLW: 1910 McG: 1910†
60	Century Oldstyle Bold Condensed	√		√	√	65	ATF: August 1910 SLW: 1916 McG: designed 1911, 　　issued 1915†
61	Century Schoolbook	√	√*	√	√	454	ATF: November 1919 SLW: 1920 McG: designed 1917–19, 　　issued 1918–21‡
62	Century Schoolbook Italic	√	√*	√	√	465	ATF: November 1919 SLW: 1920 McG: designed 1917–19, 　　issued 1918–21‡
63	Century Schoolbook Bold		√	√	√	479	SLW: 1924 McG: designed 1919, 　　cut 1923†
64	Cheltenham Bold	√	√*	√	√	67	ATF: 1904 SLW: 1904 McG: 1904‡
	Cheltenham Bold Black Outline			√			SLW: 1913
65	Cheltenham Bold Condensed	√	√	√	√	68	ATF: 1905 SLW: 1905 McG: 1904‡

† ATF   ‡ Monotype

Comments	Matrices sold at ATF auction
McG: Linotype font also shown.	
abandoned	

	Name of Type	ATF	MFB	SLW	McG	ATF #	Dates
66	Cheltenham Bold Condensed Italic	√	√	√	√	69	ATF: 1906 SLW: 1905 McG: 1905‡
	Cheltenham Bold Condensed Shaded			√			SLW: 1915
67	Cheltenham Bold Extra Condensed	√	√	√	√	70	ATF: 1906 SLW: 1906 McG: 1906‡
68	Cheltenham Bold Extra Condensed Title			√		71	SLW: 1907
69	Cheltenham Bold Extended	√	√	√	√	72	ATF: 1906 SLW: 1906 McG: 1906†/‡
	Cheltenham Bold Initials		√				SLW: 1912
70	Cheltenham Bold Italic	√	√*	√	√	73	ATF: 1904 SLW: 1905 McG: 1905‡
71	Cheltenham Bold Italic Shaded	√		√	√	74	ATF: June 1912 SLW: 1915 McG: 1912†
72	Cheltenham Bold Outline			√	√	75	SLW: 1905 McG: 1905†/‡
73	Cheltenham Bold Shaded	√		√	√	76	ATF: January 1912 SLW: 1913 McG: 1912‡
	Cheltenham Bold Slope			√			SLW: 1905
74	Cheltenham Extrabold	√		√	√	77	ATF: 1911 SLW: 1911 McG: 1910†
75	Cheltenham Extrabold Shaded	√		√	√	78	ATF: September 1912 SLW: 1914 McG: 1912†
76	Cheltenham Inline	√		√	√	79	ATF: 1907 SLW: 1907 McG: 1907†

† ATF   ‡ Monotype

abandoned

abandoned

SLW: formerly named Cheltenham Bold Slope

McG: "in the original foundry version it is cut
from the same patterns as Bold so they will register for two-color work"

renamed Cheltenham Bold Italic

42 pt. to Greg Walters

	Name of Type	ATF	MFB	SLW	McG	ATF #	Dates
77	Cheltenham Inline Extended	√		√	√	80	ATF: 1907 SLW: 1907 McG: 1907†
78	Cheltenham Inline Extra Condensed	√		√	√	81	ATF: 1907 SLW: 1907 McG: 1907†
79	Cheltenham Medium	√	√	√	√	83	ATF: April 1909 SLW: 1910 McG: 1909†
80	Cheltenham Medium Italic	√	√	√	√	84	ATF: April 1909 SLW: 1910 McG: 1910†
81	Cheltenham Medium Condensed	√		√	√	85	ATF: April 1913 SLW: 1914 McG: 1913
82	Cheltenham Medium Expanded	√		√	√	86	ATF: February 1913 SLW: 1914 McG: 1913†
83	Cheltenham Monotone		√				SLW: 1907
84	Cheltenham Oldstyle Condensed	√		√	√	88	ATF: March 1909 SLW: 1910 McG: 1909‡
	Cheltenham Rimmed			√			SLW: 1907
85	Cheltenham Wide	√	√	√	√	89	ATF: before 1907 SLW: 1905 McG: 1905‡
86	Chic			√	√	514	SLW: 1927 McG: designed 1927, issued 1928†
87	Civilité	√	√*	√	√	482	ATF: September 1922 SLW: 1923 McG: designed 1922, cut 1923–24†
	Civilité No. 2			√			SLW: 1924
88	Clearface	√		√	√	91	ATF: November 1907 SLW: 1907 McG: 1906 through 1911†

† ATF   ‡ Monotype

Comments	Matrices sold at ATF auction
	36, 48, 60, 72 (caps only) pt. to Greg Walters
McG: Linotype font shown	
abandoned	
abandoned	
ATF: "caps same as Cheltenham O.S." McG: "identical with Cheltenham Oldstyle except for the lowercase"	
	to Steve Heaver
abandoned	
ATF: "MFB (& L.B.B. advisor)" McG: "with his father, Linn B. Benton, as advisor"	

	Name of Type	ATF	MFB	SLW	McG	ATF #	Dates
89	Clearface Bold	√		√	√	92	ATF: November 1905 SLW: 1908 McG: designed 1905, cut 1906†
90	Clearface Bold Italic	√		√	√	93	ATF: June 1906 SLW: 1908 McG: 1906 through 1911†
91	Clearface Gothic	√		√	√	94	ATF: September 1908 SLW: 1909 McG: designed 1908, cut 1910†
92	Clearface Heavy	√		√	√	95	ATF: December 1909 SLW: 1909 McG: 1906 through 1911†
93	Clearface Heavy Italic	√		√	√	96	ATF: January 1910 SLW: 1909 McG: 1906 through 1911†
94	Clearface Italic	√		√	√	97	ATF: November 1907 SLW: 1908 McG: 1906 through 1911†
95	Cloister Black	√	√*	√	√	98	ATF: before 1903 SLW: 1904 McG: 1904‡
96	Cloister Oldstyle	√	√*	√	√	102	ATF: January 1913 SLW: 1913 McG: designed 1913, issued 1914†
97	Cloister Bold	√	√*	√	√	99	ATF: October 1913 SLW: 1913 McG: designed 1913, cut 1915‡
98	Cloister Bold Italic	√	√*	√	√	100	ATF: February 1915 SLW: 1915 McG: cut 1915‡

† ATF   ‡ Monotype

Comments	Matrices sold at ATF auction
ATF: "MFB (L.B.B. advisor)"	
ATF: "MFB (L.B.B. advisor)"	
McG: non-kerning	
ATF: "MFB (& L.B.B. advisor)"	
ATF: "The actual design was conceived by Mr. J.W. Phinney." SLW: "with Joseph W. Phinney" McG: "Its design is generally credited to Joseph W. Phinney, of ATF's Boston foundry, but some authorities give some or all of the credit to Morris Benton."	6, 8, 14, 18, 24, 30, 36, 42, 48, 60, 72 pt. to Cary Collection at RIT; 18 pt. to Howard Bratter
The parent face of the following Benton Cloister types.	6, 8, 10, 14, 18, 24, 30, 36, 42, 48, 60, 72 pt. to Rich Hopkins
	6, 8, 10, 12, 14, 18, 24, 30, 36, 42, 48, 60, 72 pt. to Rich Hopkins
	6, 8, 10, 12, 14, 18, 24, 30, 36, 42, 48, 60, 72 pt. to Rich Hopkins

	Name of Type	ATF	MFB	SLW	McG	ATF #	Dates
99	Cloister Bold Condensed	√		√	√	451	ATF: May 1915 SLW: 1919 McG: designed 1915, cut 1917†
100	Cloister Bold Title			√	√	101	SLW: 1915 McG: cut 1914–15
101	Cloister Cursive	√		√	√	478	ATF: June 1922 SLW: 1922 McG: cut 1922†
102	Cloister Cursive Handtooled			√	√	493	SLW: 1923 McG: designed 1923, completed 1926†
103	Cloister (Oldstyle) Italic	√	√*	√	√	103	ATF: April 1913 SLW: 1913 McG: issued 1914
104	Cloister Lightface		√	√	√	486	SLW: 1924 McG: designed 1919, cut 1924†
105	Cloister Lightface Italic		√	√	√	490	SLW: 1924 McG: cut 1925†
106	Cloister Title			√	√	104	SLW: 1915 McG: cut 1914–15†
107	Commercial Script				√	107	McG: designed 1906, cut 1908†
108	Copperplate Gothic Shaded	√			√	136	ATF: September 1912 McG: designed 1912†
109	Cromwell	√		√	√	138	ATF: October 1913 SLW: 1916 McG: designed 1913, issued 1916†
110	Cushing Antique	√		√	√	140	ATF: May 1902 SLW: 1905 McG: designed 1902, cut 1905
	Cushing Antique Italic			√			SLW: 1907

† ATF ‡ Monotype

Comments	Matrices sold at ATF auction
McG: comparable to Cloister Title (but not shown)	8, 10, 12, 14, 18, 24, 30, 36, 42, 48 pt. to Rich Hopkins
ATF: "MFB (caps) L. case same as Cloister O.S. Italic" McG: "It has the same lowercase and figures as Cloister Italic, but a more freely designed set of capitals."	6, 8, 10, 12, 14, 16, 18, 24, 30, 36, 42, 48, 60, 72 pt. to Rich Hopkins
SLW: "with Charles H. Becker" McG: "designed by Benton and Charles H. Becker"	12, 14, 18, 24, 30, 36, 42, 48, 60, 72 pt. to Rich Hopkins
	(with swash) 6, 8, 10, 14, 18, 24, 30, 36, 42, 48, 60, 72 pt. to Rich Hopkins
	6, 8, 10, 14, 18, 24, 30, 36, 42, 48 (incomplete) pt. to Rich Hopkins
	8, 10, 14, 18, 24, 36, 42, 48 pt. to Rich Hopkins
McG: "shows the essential J and Q revisions"	8, 10, 12, 14, 18, 24, 30, 36, 42, 48 pt. to Rich Hopkins
ATF: "Caps same as Cloister O.S." McG: "It uses the same capitals as Cloister"	
SLW: "design suggested by J. S. Cushing" McG: Ludlow font shown.	
abandoned	

	Name of Type	ATF	MFB	SLW	McG	ATF #	Dates
	Cushing Roman *see* Norwood Roman			√			SLW: 1906
112	Della Robbia Light	√		√	√	445	ATF: October 1913 SLW: 1918 McG: 1913, some sources say 1918†
113	Dynamic Medium			√	√	535	SLW: 1928 McG: designed 1928, issued 1930†
114	Eagle Bold		√	√	√	581	SLW: 1934 McG: 1933†
115	Engravers Bodoni		√*	√	√	501	SLW: 1926, introduced 1933 McG: designed 1926, issued 1933†
	Engravers Bodoni Open			√			SLW: 1926
116	Engravers Old English	√			√	148	ATF: before 1903 McG: 1901†
117	Engravers Old English Bold	√		√	√	149	ATF: December 1907 SLW: 1907 McG: 1910‡
118	Engravers Shaded	√	√	√	√	151	ATF: December 1906 SLW: 1906 McG: about 1906†
119	Engravers Text			√	√	541	SLW: 1930 McG: 1930†
120	Franklin Gothic	√	√*	√	√	162	ATF: June 1902 SLW: 1905 McG: 1902‡
121	Franklin Gothic Condensed	√	√*	√	√	163	ATF: October 1905 SLW: 1906 McG: 1906‡
122	Franklin Gothic Condensed Shaded	√		√	√	164	ATF: October 1912 SLW: 1914 McG: 1912†

† ATF   ‡ Monotype

Comments	Matrices sold at ATF auction
renamed Norwood Roman	
SLW: "after design by T. M. Cleland"	
McG: inspired by the National Recovery Administration's 1933 emblem	
abandoned	
ATF: "Cowan and MFB" McG: Designed "by Morris Benton and another person identified by ATF only as Cowan, but has also been ascribed to Joseph W. Phinney."	(Boston): 6, 8, 10, 12, 14, 18 pt. to Kingsley, then to Kevin Auer, then to Howard Bratter; (Boston): 24 (incomplete), 30, 36, 42, 48, 60, 72 pt. to Greg Walters; 30 pt. to Dan Solo
	72 (incomplete) pt. to Greg Walters

	Name of Type	ATF	MFB	SLW	McG	ATF #	Dates
	Franklin Gothic Extended			√			SLW: 1906
123	Franklin Gothic Extra Condensed	√	√*	√	√	165	ATF: October 1906 SLW: 1906 McG: 1906†
124	Franklin Gothic Italic	√	√*	√	√	166	ATF: October 1910 SLW: 1913 McG: 1910†
125	Freehand	√	√*	√	√	464	ATF: September 1917 SLW: 1919 McG: 1917†
126	Gallia		√			502	McG: 1927‡
127	Garamond	√	√*	√	√	459	ATF: October 1917 SLW: 1917 McG: designed 1917, issued 1919†
128	Garamond Bold	√	√*	√	√	474	ATF: July 1920 SLW: 1920 McG: 1920‡
129	Garamond Bold Italic		√*	√	√	489	SLW: 1923 McG: 1923‡
130	Garamond Italic	√	√	√	√	460	ATF: May 1918 SLW: 1918 McG: issued 1919†
131	Garamond Open		√	√ .	√	557	SLW: 1931 McG: 1931†
132	Globe Gothic	√			√	172	ATF: about 1900 McG: about 1900‡
133	Globe Gothic Bold			√	√	173	SLW: 1907 McG: 1907
134	Globe Gothic Bold Italic			√	√	174	SLW: 1908 McG: 1908
135	Globe Gothic Condensed	√			√	175	ATF: about 1900 McG: about 1900†
136	Globe Gothic Extended	√			√	176	ATF: about 1900 McG: about 1900
137	Globe Gothic Extra Condensed	√			√	177	ATF: about 1900 McG: about 1900‡

† ATF   ‡ Monotype

Comments	Matrices sold at ATF auction
abandoned	
SLW: "non-kerning"	
McG: attributed to Wadsworth A. Parker	
McG: redesigned and additional characters by T. M. Cleland added in 1922	to Dan Carr; capitals and points 10/18 pt. to Howard Bratter
SLW: "with T. M. Cleland" McG: redesigned and additional characters by T. M. Cleland added in 1922	to Dan Carr
	to Dan Carr
McG: illustrated but not attributed to ATF, Monotype, or any other source	
McG: illustrated but not attributed to ATF, Monotype, or any other source	
McG: illustrated but not attributed to ATF, Monotype, or any other source	

	Name of Type	ATF	MFB	SLW	McG	ATF #	Dates
138	Goudy Bold	√		√	√	446	ATF: June 1916 SLW: 1918 McG: 1916
139	Goudy Bold Italic	√		√	√	464	ATF: April 1919 SLW: 1920 McG: 1919†/‡
140	Goudy Catalogue	√		√	√	457	ATF: July 1919 SLW: 1921 McG: 1919†
141	Goudy Catalogue Italic			√	√	470	SLW: 1921 McG: 1921†
142	Goudy Extrabold			√	√	494	SLW: 1927 McG: 1927†
143	Goudy Extrabold Italic			√	√	496	SLW: 1927 McG: 1927†
144	Goudy Handtooled	√		√	√	475	ATF: about January 1922 SLW: 1922 McG: 1922
145	Goudy Handtooled Italic	√		√	√	476	ATF: about January 1922 SLW: 1922 McG: 1922
146	Goudy Title			√	√	180	SLW: 1918 McG: 1918†
147	Gravure		√	√	√	505	SLW: 1927 McG: 1927†
148	Greeting Monotone			√	√	504	SLW: 1927 McG: 1927†
	Grolier			√			SLW: 1934
149	Headline Gothic			√	√	650	SLW: 1936 McG: 1936†

† ATF   ‡ Monotype

Comments	Matrices sold at ATF auction
SLW: "after basic design by F. W. Goudy" McG: illustrated but not attributed to ATF, Monotype or any other source	
	6, 8, 10, 12, 14, 18, 24, 30, 36, 42, 48, 60, 72 pt. to Greg Walters
ATF: [attributed to Charles H.] "Becker" SLW: "with Wadsworth A. Parker" (handwritten on ms.) McG: "has been credited to Charles H. Becker by some authorities, and to Morris Benton and Wadsworth A. Parker by others." Illustrated but not attributed to ATF, Monotype or any other source.	10, 12, 14, 18, 24, 30, 36, 42, 48, 60, 72, 84, 96, 120 pt. to Greg Walters
ATF: attributed as above SLW: attributed as above McG: attributed as above	10, 12, 14, 18, 24, 30, 36, 42, 48, 60, 72 pt. to Greg Walters
	6#1, 6#2, 6#3, 8#1, 8#2, 10, 12, 14, 18, 24, 30, 36, 42 pt. to Pat Taylor; then to Greg Walters
	24, 30, 36, 42, 48, 60, 72 pt. to Greg Walters; 14 pt. to Kingsley, then to Kevin Auer, then to Howard Bratter
	10, 12, 14, 18 pt. to Howard Bratter
abandoned	

	Name of Type	ATF	MFB	SLW	McG	ATF #	Dates
150	Hobo	√	√*	√	√	193	ATF: June 1910
							SLW: 1910, issued 1912,
							patented 1915
							McG: issued 1910†
	Hobo, Light *see* Light Hobo						
	Hobo Shaded			√			SLW: 1914
151	Invitation	√	√	√	√	157	ATF: April 1917
							SLW: 1917
							McG: 1917†
152	Invitation Shaded	√	√	√	√	217	ATF: September 1914
							SLW: 1914
							McG: 1916†
153	Light Hobo	√		√	√	447	ATF: June 1915
							SLW: 1917
							McG: issued 1915†
154	Light Oldstyle			√	√	225	SLW: 1916
							McG: 1916†
155	Lightline Gothic	√	√*	√	√	222	ATF: December 1908
							SLW: 1908
							McG: 1908†
156	Lightline Title Gothic			√	√	480	SLW: 1921
							McG: 1921
	Lincoln			√			SLW: 1935
157	Lithograph Shaded	√			√	315	ATF: 1914
							McG: 1914†
158	Louvaine Light			√	√	519	SLW: 1929
							McG: 1928†
159	Louvaine Light Italic			√	√	520	SLW: 1929
							McG: 1928†
160	Louvaine Medium			√	√	521	SLW: 1929
							McG: 1928†
161	Louvaine Medium Italic			√	√	522	SLW: 1929
							McG: 1928†
162	Louvaine Bold			√	√	523	SLW: 1929
							McG: 1928†

† ATF   ‡ Monotype

abandoned

McG: "ATF says it originated with Inland Type
Foundry"

abandoned

ATF: "MFB and W. F. Capitan"
McG: "same design as Engravers Shaded, except
for the unusual shading which is heavier at top"

McG: "[The series] is an adaptation of Bodoni …
and many of the characters are identical."

	Name of Type	ATF	MFB	SLW	McG	ATF #	Dates
163	Louvaine Bold Italic			√	√	524	SLW: 1929
							McG: 1928†
	Mercantile *see also* Card Mercantile	√					ATF: before 1903
164	Miehle Extra Condensed	√		√	√	326	ATF: October 1905
							SLW: 1906
							McG: 1906†
165	Miehle Extra Condensed Title	√		√		327	ATF: undated
							SLW: 1907
166	Modernique			√	√	517	SLW: 1928
							McG: 1928†
167	Monotone Gothic	√		√	√	329	ATF: September 1907
							SLW: 1907
							McG: 1907†
168	Monotone Title			√	√	330	SLW: 1908
							McG: undated
169	Motto	√		√	√	447	ATF: October 1915
							SLW: 1915
							McG: 1915†
170	News Gothic	√	√*	√	√	338	ATF: April 1908
							SLW: 1908
							McG: 1908†
171	News Gothic Condensed	√	√*	√	√	339	ATF: April 1908
							SLW: 1908
							McG: 1908‡
172	News Gothic Extra Condensed	√	√*	√	√	340	ATF: April 1908
							SLW: 1908
							McG: 1908†
173	News Gothic Extra Condensed Title	√		√		341	ATF: undated
							SLW: 1908
174	Norwood Roman	√		√	√	431	ATF: May 1906
							SLW: 1906
							McG: 1906†
175	Novel Gothic			√	√	512	SLW: 1928
							McG: 1928†
	One-tone Gothic			√			SLW: 1912

† ATF ‡ Monotype

Comments	Matrices sold at ATF auction
ATF: "Dickinson Fdry, 3 smallest sizes"	
	8, 12, 14, 18, 24, 30, 36 pt. to Greg Walters
ATF: "Monotone" [*sic*, for "MFB"]	
	8, 8/18, 10, 10/18, 12, 14, 14/18, 18, 30, 36, 42 pt. to Howard Bratter
	14/18 pt. to Howard Bratter
SLW: "design suggested by J. S. Cushing" McG: "renamed for Cushing's Norwood Press Co. in Norwood, Massachusetts"	
SLW: "with Charles Herman Becker" McG: "originated by Charles H. Becker, a hand- engraver in the matrix cutting department of ATF"	
abandoned	

	Name of Type	ATF	MFB	SLW	McG	ATF #	Dates
176	Othello		√	√	√	594	SLW: 1934
							McG: 1934†
177	Packard				√	348	McG: 1913†
178	Packard Bold	√		√	√	453	ATF: November 1916
							SLW: 1917
							McG: 1916†
179	Paramount		√	√	√	536	SLW: 1930
							McG: 1930†
180	Parisian		√*	√	√	513	SLW: 1928
							McG: 1928†
181	Pen Print Open			√	√	466	SLW: 1921
							McG: 1921†
182	Phenix			√	√	651	SLW: 1935
							McG: 1935†
183	Piranesi Bold			√	√	569	SLW: 1933
							McG: 1933†
184	Piranesi Bold Italic			√	√	570	SLW: 1931
							McG: 1931†
185	Piranesi Bold Italic Plain Caps			√		572	SLW: 1932
							McG: †
186	Piranesi Italic			√	√	526	SLW: 1930
							McG: 1930†
187	Piranesi Italic Plain Caps			√		1974	SLW: 1930
							McG: †
188	Poster Gothic			√	√	592	SLW: 1934
							McG: 1934†

† ATF ‡ Monotype

Comments	Matrices sold at ATF auction
SLW: "revision of 1884 Central Type Foundry face"	
McG: "ATF's adaptation of a distinctive style of lettering done by Oswald Cooper … Packard Bold followed in 1916. The latter is credited to Morris Benton, again closely following Cooper's original lettering, and it is quite likely that Benton did the actual adaptation of the first face also."	
SLW: "with Oswald Cooper" McG: see above	
McG: "basically a heavier companion to Rivoli"	6, 8, 10, 12, 14, 18, 24, 30, 36, 42, 48, 60, 72 pt. to Cary Collection at RIT
	14/18, 18 pt. to Howard Bratter
McG: "It is the same founder's and designer's News Gothic Extra Condensed, with several characters redesigned in the 'round' fashion of the time."	24, 30, 36, 48, 60, 72 pt. to Greg Walters
SLW: "after basic design by W. T. Sniffin"	6, 8, 10, 12, 14, 18, 24, 30, 36, 42, 48, 60, 72 pt. to Cary Collection at RIT
McG: "Plain Caps (Charles Sikorski)"	
	30, 36, 42 pt. to Greg Walters
McG: "There seems to be no apparent explanation for the high series number of Piranesi Italic Plain Caps, but that is how it appears in ATF literature."	
McG: "It is essentially a continuation into larger sizes of Bank Gothic Condensed Medium, but is more closely fitted, as a large face should be."	

	Name of Type	ATF	MFB	SLW	McG	ATF #	Dates
189	Raleigh Gothic Condensed			√	√	564	SLW: 1934 McG: 1932†
	Rialto			√			SLW: 1930
190	Rockwell Antique			√	√	312	SLW: 1931 McG: issued 1931‡
191	Roycroft	√			√	371	ATF: about 1898 McG: designed about 1898, cut 1900†
192	Rugged Roman	√		√	√	375	ATF: September 1904 SLW: 1912 McG: designed 1909–11, patented 1915, first showing 1917†
193	Schoolbook Oldstyle		√*	√	√	484	SLW: 1924 McG: about 1924†
194	Shadow		√	√	√	589	SLW: 1934 McG: designed 1934, issued 1935†
195	Souvenir	√		√	√	449	ATF: September 1914 SLW: 1915 McG: 1914†
196	Sterling	√			√	461	ATF: May or June 1917 McG: 1917†
197	Sterling Cursive	√			√	473	ATF: May or June 1919 McG: 1919†
198	Stymie Black			√	√	598	SLW: 1935 McG: 1935†
199	Stymie Black Italic			√	√	599	SLW: 1935 McG: undated†
200	Stymie Bold		√	√	√	551	SLW: 1931 McG: 1931†
201	Stymie Bold Italic		√	√	√	561	SLW: 1933 McG: a bit later (than 1931)†

† ATF   ‡ Monotype

Comments	Matrices sold at ATF auction
	144 pt. to Greg Walters
abandoned	
SLW: "revision of Inland Litho Antique" McG: "Morris Benton of ATF added several characters to the old Inland face, matrices of which were then in ATF's vaults."	
ATF: "MFB (partly)" McG: "has been credited to Lewis Buddy, a former [*Saturday Evening*] *Post* artist and letterer"	
	6, 8, 10, 12, 14, 18, 24, 30, 36, 42, 48, 60, 72 pt. to Dave Peat
	6, 8, 10, 12, 14, 18, 24, 36 (inc.), 48 pt. to Dave Peat
	6, 8, 10, 12, 14, 18 pt. to Howard Bratter; 24 (inc.), 30, 36 pt. to Greg Walters
	6, 8, 10, 12, 14, 18 pt. to Howard Bratter; 24, 30, 36, 42, 48 pt. to Greg Walters
McG: "a redesign of Rockwell Antique ... which in turn was a reissue of Litho Antique, introduced by Inland Type Foundry in 1910."	
	6, 8, 10, 12, 14, 16/18, 18 pt. to Howard Bratter; 24, 30, 36, 42, 48, 60 pt. to Greg Walters

	Name of Type	ATF	MFB	SLW	McG	ATF #	Dates
202	Stymie Light		√	√	√	553	SLW: 1931
							McG: 1931†
203	Stymie Light Italic		√	√	√	554	SLW: 1932
							McG: 1931†
204	Stymie Medium			√	√	552	SLW: 1931
							McG: 1931†
205	Stymie Medium Italic			√	√	555	SLW: 1932
							McG: 1931†
206	Thermo 100 Series (also called Thermotype)			√	√	548	SLW: 1931
							McG: 1931†
207	Thermo 200 Series			√	√	549	SLW: 1931
							McG: 1931
208	Thermo 300 Series			√	√	550	SLW: 1931
							McG: 1931
209	Tower		√*	√	√	587	SLW: 1934
							McG: 1934†
	Tower Bold			√	√		SLW: 1936
							McG: 1936
	Two-tone Italic			√			SLW: 1930
210	Typo Roman		√	√	√	509	SLW: 1926
							McG: 1926†
211	Typo Roman Shaded	√	√	√	√	481	ATF: July 1921
							SLW: 1924
							McG: designed 1921, issued 1924†
212	Typo Script	√	√*		√	399	ATF: September 1903
							McG: designed and cut 1902†
213	Typo Script Extended	√	√*		√	400	ATF: September 1903
							McG: designed and cut 1902†
214	Typo Shaded	√	√*	√	√	401	ATF: April 1906
							SLW: 1906
							McG: 1906†
215	Typo Slope	√			√	402	ATF: 1905
							McG: 1905†

† ATF ‡ Monotype

Comments	Matrices sold at ATF auction
	(with long ascenders/descenders) 84/72 pt. to Howard Bratter
	(long ascenders/descenders only) 12/30, 24/54, 30/60, 36/84, 42/96, 48/108, 60/120, 72/144 pt. to Greg Walters
	6, 8, 10, 12, 14, 18 pt. to Howard Bratter; 24, 30, 36, 42, 48, 60, 72 pt. to Greg Walters
McG: Thermotype Series 100-200-300 is shown as one specimen.	
	6 pt. to Howard Bratter
	6 pt. to Howard Bratter
SLW: "abandoned in favor of Stymie Bold Condensed"	
abandoned	
	18 pt. to Howard Bratter
ATF: "adapted from engravings"	
McG: originally called Tiffany Script	48, 60 pt. to Bowne & Co.; 60 (inc.) pt. to Greg Walters
McG: originally Tiffany Script Extended	(lower case only) 14, 18, 24, 30, 36, 48, 60 pt. to Greg Walters
McG: originally Tiffany Shaded	14, 18, 24#1, 24#2, 30, 48 pt. to Greg Walters
McG: Originally Tiffany Slope	12, 14, 18, 24#1, 24#2, 30, 36, 48 pt. to Greg Walters

	Name of Type	ATF	MFB	SLW	McG	ATF #	Dates
216	Typo Upright	√	√*	√	√	404	ATF: November 1905 SLW: 1905 McG: 1905†
217	Typo Upright Bold	√	√*	√	√	405	ATF: January 1906 SLW: 1911 McG: designed 1906†
218	Ultra Bodoni		√*	√	√	518	SLW: 1929 McG: designed 1928‡
219	Ultra Bodoni Condensed			√	√	562	SLW: 1930 McG: 1930†
220	Ultra Bodoni Extra Condensed		√*	√	√	573	SLW: 1933 McG: 1933†
221	Ultra Bodoni Italic		√*	√	√	516	SLW: 1928 McG: 1928‡
222	Venetian	√		√	√	408	ATF: April 1911 SLW: 1913 McG: designed about 1911†
223	Venetian Bold	√		√	√	450	ATF: October 1913 SLW: 1917 McG: about 1913†
224	Venetian Italic	√		√	√	409	ATF: December 1911 SLW: 1913 McG: designed about 1911†
225	Wedding Text	√	√*	√	√	414	ATF: about 1901 SLW: 1907; see additional comment McG: cut 1901†
226	Wedding Text Shaded	√		√	√	415	ATF: August 1913 SLW: 1916 McG: cut about 1913
	Whitehall *see* Benton						
	Whitin Black *see* Bold Antique						

† ATF   ‡ Monotype

Comments	Matrices sold at ATF auction
McG: originally Tiffany Upright	12, 14, 18, 24#1, 24#2, 30, 36, 48 pt. to Greg Walters
	12, 14, 18, 24#1, 24#2, 30, 36, 48, 60 pt. to Greg Walters
SLW: "type metal originals, 90 characters in 12 point size were cut in 1901" McG: "the face was hailed as new in 1907 and again in 1909."	8, 10, 18#1, 18#2, 24#1, 36 pt. to Greg Walters; 6, 24 pt. to Bowne & Co.

Credits

Books, magazines, archives and ephemera collections cited are part of the Cary Graphic Arts Collection at RIT unless otherwise indicated. Multiple illustrations on one page are listed in clockwise order.

CHAPTER 1

p. 1, 2 Cary Graphic Arts Collection, photos by Frank Cost.

p. 3 Photo by Frank Cost; Rudolf Koch and Fritz Kredel, "On Punch Cutting & Wood Cutting," *Colophon* 10 (1932); Fritz Kredel for Paul Koch's "The Making of Printing Types," *Dolphin* 1 (1933): 30, plate 2; ibid., 36.

p. 5 Rudolf Koch, *The Typefoundry in Silhouette: A Portfolio of Twenty-Five Silhouettes* (Offenbach, Germany: Klingspor Bros. Type Foundry, 1918); "The Making of Printing Types," 47.

p. 6 "Type Making," *Chicago Specimen* 9, no. 4 (October 1875): 4, courtesy of the Book Arts Collection, Rare Book and Manuscript Library, Columbia University.

p. 7 Theodore Lowe De Vinne, *The Practice of Typography: A Treatise on the Processes of Type-Making, the Point System, the Names, Sizes, Styles and Practices of Plain Printing Types* (New York: The Century Co., 1900), 45–46; ATF ephemera, uncatalogued.

p. 8 Photos by Frank Cost.

p. 9 "The Making of Printing Types," 52; *Histoire de l'Invention de l'Imprimerie par Les Monuments* (Paris: Imprimerie Rue de Verneuil, No. 4, June 1840), 12.

p. 10 Theodore Lowe De Vinne, *The Practice of Typography: A Treatise on the Processes of Type-Making, the Point System, the Names, Sizes, Styles and Practices of Plain Printing Types* (New York: The Century Co., 1900), 23; Daniel Berkeley Updike, *Printing Types: Their History, Forms and Use*, vol. 1 (Cambridge, Mass.: Harvard University Press, 1922), 21.

p. 12 Photo by Frank Cost; Lucien Alphonse Legros and John Cameron Grant, *Typographical Printing-Surfaces: The Technology and Mechanism of their Production* (London, New York: Longmans, Green and Co., 1916), 79; Cary Collection.

p. 13 Photo by Frank Cost; Rudolf Koch, *The Typefoundry in Silhouette*; ATF/Kingsley Archives; ATF ephemera.

p. 15 Carl Schraubstadter Jr., "Electrotype Matrices," *Inland Printer* 4, no. 6 (March 1887): 382.

CHAPTER 2

p. 23 Courtesy of Caroline Benton Gregg, rephotographed by Henry Weiland.

p. 24 Courtesy of Caroline Benton Gregg.

p. 25 Courtesy of Laurence Gregg.

p. 27, 28, 29 Courtesy of Laurence Gregg; middle photo on p. 27 by T. H. Powe, Milwaukee.

CHAPTER 3

p. 38 Courtesy of Laurence Gregg.

p. 39 Line image courtesy of James Eckman, MD; American Type Founders Co., *Portable Book of Specimens from The Benton & Waldo Foundry Operated by American Type Founders Company, Pantentees and Manufacturers of Benton's Self Spacing Type* (Milwaukee, New York: ATF Co., ca. 1893), courtesy of Laurence Gregg.

p. 41 All examples from the *Portable Book of Specimens*.

Chapter 4

p. 44 Cary Graphic Arts Collection, photo by Frank Cost.

p. 46 Quadrat [Henry Lewis Bullen], "Discursions of a Retired Printer, No. VII," *Inland Printer* 38, no. 4 (January 1907): 520.

p. 48 U.S. Patent No. 290,201, http://patft.uspto.gov (browser plug-in required to access full image); *Typographic Specimens: Benton's Self Spacing Type* (Milwaukee, St. Paul: Benton, Waldo & Co., ca. 1884), back cover, courtesy of Laurence Gregg; "Benton's Punch Engraving Machine," Benton-Waldo Type Foundry, Milwaukee, Wis., U.S.A. (pamphlet), n.d., back cover, courtesy of Laurence Gregg; *Portable Book of Specimens*, 4; *Typographic Specimens: Benton's Self Spacing Type*, 8.

p. 49 *Typographic Specimens: Benton's Self Spacing Type*, 1.

p. 50 *Typographic Specimens: Benton's Self Spacing Type*, 12, 14; *Portable Book of Specimens*, 32.

p. 51 *Typographic Specimens: Benton's Self Spacing Type*, 1.

Chapter 5

p. 58 U.S. Patent No. 332,990, http://patft.uspto.gov; Theodore Lowe De Vinne, *The Practice of Typography: A Treatise on the Processes of Type-Making, the Point System, the Names, Sizes, Styles and Practices of Plain Printing Types* (New York: The Century Co., 1900), 349.

p. 63 Henry Lewis Bullen, "Origin and Development of the Linotype Machine, Part II," *Inland Printer* 72, no. 6 (March 1924): 936; Bullen, "Origin and Development of the Linotype Machine, Part I," *Inland Printer* 72, no. 5 (February 1924): 769.

p. 66 Bullen, "Origin and Development … Part II," 937.

p. 68 "Benton's Punch Engraving Machine," Benton-Waldo Type Foundry, Milwaukee, Wis., U.S.A. (pamphlet), n.d., cover, courtesy of Laurence Gregg; photo by Morris Benton, courtesy of Laurence Gregg.

p. 71 U.S. Patent No. 809,548, http://patft.uspto.gov

p. 72 Lucien Alphonse Legros and John Cameron Grant, *Typographical Printing-Surfaces: The Technology and Mechanism of Their Production* (London, New York:

Longmans, Green and Co., 1916), facing p. 204; ibid., facing p. 205.

Chapter 6

p. 82 Quadrat [Henry Lewis Bullen], "Discursions of a Retired Printer, No. VII." *Inland Printer* 38, no. 4 (January 1907): 515–16.

p. 84 *Specimen Book* (New York, Nos. 32–34 Lafayette Place: Publisher's Printing Company, 1898), 4, courtesy of Typographic Library Manuscripts, Rare Book and Manuscript Library, Columbia University; "New President of the American Type Founders Company," *Inland Printer* 27, no. 1 (April 1901): 99.

Chapter 7

p. 90 Edward L. Wilson, "Finding Pharaoh," *Century* 34, no. 1 (May 1887): 3; Theodore Lowe De Vinne, "The Century's Printer on the Century's Type," *Century* 51, no. 5 (March 1896): 795; American Type Founders Co., *Desk Book of Type Specimens, Borders, Ornaments, Brass Rules and Cuts* (New York: ATF Co., 1900), 34.

Chapter 8

p. 94 Hand-written message on stationery from the North-Western Type Foundry, Office of Benton, Gove & Co., Milwaukee, November 7, 1877, courtesy of Typographic Library Manuscripts, Rare Book and Manuscript Library, Columbia University; U.S. Patent No. 326,009, http://patft.uspto.gov

p. 95 Courtesy of Laurence Gregg, photo by Frank Cost.

p. 98 Original copy of U.S. Patent No. 790,172 courtesy of Theo Rehak.

Chapter 9

p. 105 Jacobus de Voragine, *The Golden Legend* (Hammersmith, London: Kelmscott Press, 1892), 105.

p. 106 Henry Lewis Johnson, "Bon Voyage to Henry Lewis Bullen," *Inland Printer* 72, no. 4 (January 1924): 640; courtesy of Caroline Benton Gregg, rephotographed by Henry Weiland; ibid.

p. 108 Fournier, le jeune [Pierre Simon], *Manual Typographique, Utile Aux Gens de Letters* ..., Tome II (Paris: Chez l'Auteur, 1767), 42– 49.

p. 110 Original copy of U.S. Patent No. 720,314 courtesy of Theo Rehak.

p. 112 *Printing* 59, no. 7 (July 1935), cover, courtesy of Laurence Gregg.

CHAPTER 10

p. 118 Photo by Frank Cost; micrograph by Sheila Donnelley.

p. 121 W. J. Kaup, "Modern Automatic Type Making Methods," *American Machinist* 32 (December 16, 1909): 1042, courtesy of Typographic Book Collection, Rare Book and Manuscript Library, Columbia University.

p. 122 "Modern Automatic," 1042; photo by Morris Benton, courtesy of Laurence Gregg.

p. 123 Courtesy of Theo Rehak; ATF/Kingsley Archives, photo by Dmitri Kessel, published in "Design and Manufacture of Foundry Type," *American Printer* 127, no. 5 (November 1948): 37; photo by Frank Cost.

p. 124 Photo by Patricia Cost.

p. 125 Ibid.; ATF Co., *American Specimen Book of Type Styles, Complete Catalogue of Printing Machinery and Printing Supplies* (Jersey City, N.J.: ATF Co., 1912), ix; ATF/Kingsley Archives; "Modern Automatic," 1043.

p. 126 Dale Guild Type Foundry, Howell, N.J., photos by Roger Cost.

p. 127 Ibid.; next three photos from ATF/Kingsley Archives.

p. 128 Legros and Grant, *Typographical Printing-Surfaces*, 203; "Modern Automatic," 1044.

p. 129 Photo by Frank Cost.

p. 130 Courtesy of Theo Rehak; ATF/Kingsley Archives.

p. 131 ATF/Kingsley Archives (both images).

p. 135 ATF Co., *Specimen Book and Catalogue, 1923*, 52.

p. 137 Courtesy of Theo Rehak.

p. 138 ATF/Kingsley Archives (both images).

p. 139 Joseph Blumenthal, "The Fitting of Type," *Dolphin* 2 (1935), 71; ATF/Kingsley Archives.

p. 141 Both images at Dale Guild Type Foundry website, as of November 2010: www.daleguild.com/Bentons_Gauge.html

p. 142 Henry Lewis Bullen, "The Effect of the Composing Machines Upon the Typefounding Industry," *Inland Printer* 73, no. 4 (July 1924): 596; ATF/Kingsley Archives.
p. 143 ATF/Kingsley Archives; ATF Co., *American Specimen Book of Type Styles* (1912), xi; photos by Frank Cost.

CHAPTER 11

p. 148 Courtesy of Laurence Gregg; next three courtesy of Caroline Benton Gregg, rephotographed by Henry Weiland.

p. 150 Courtesy of Caroline Benton Gregg, rephotographed by Henry Weiland.

p. 151 Courtesy of Laurence Gregg; next two courtesy of Caroline Benton Gregg, rephotographed by Henry Weiland.

p. 152 Courtesy of Laurence Gregg.

p. 153 Courtesy of Caroline Benton Gregg.

p. 154 Courtesy of Laurence Gregg.

CHAPTER 12

p. 158 ATF Co., *Specimen Book and Catalogue, 1923* (Jersey City, N.J.: ATF Co., 1923), 4; ATF Co., Engineering Department, *American Cut-Cost System of Printing Plant Equipment* (Elizabeth, N.J.: ATF Co., ca. 1926), 4, ATF ephemera.

p. 159 Photo by Frank Cost.

p. 161 Courtesy of Caroline Benton Gregg; *American Cut-Cost System*, cover.

p. 162 *American Cut-Cost System*, 11; ibid., 3.

p. 163 Ibid., 5; ATF Co., *The Kelly Press* (Elizabeth, N.J.: ATF Co., Kelly Press Division, 1927), 8, ATF ephemera.

p.164 Henry Lewis Bullen, "Robert Wickham Nelson: An Intimate History," *Inland Printer* 77, no. 6 (September 1926): opp. 905; "American Type Company's New President," *American Printer* 85, no. 6 (December 1927): 88.

CHAPTER 13

p. 176 American Type Founders Company, *Specimen Book and Catalogue, 1923* (Jersey City, N.J.: ATF Co., 1923), 45; ibid., 46.

p. 178 Goudy photo archives.

Chapter 14: p. 190 ATF Co., *American Specimen Book of Type Styles* (1912), 800; loose specimen sheet, ATF ephemera.

p. 191 Cary Collection digital image database; next two, Cary Collection artifacts; type specimens: ATF Co., *American Line Type Book, Borders, Ornaments, Price List, Printing Material and Machinery* (Jersey City, N.J.: ATF Co., 1906), 125 and 122.

p. 192 A. Raymond Hopper, "The Romance of Roycroft," *Inland Printer* 99, no. 3 (June 1937): 36; ATF Co., *The Rugged Roycroft* (Boston: The Company [ca. 1902]).

p. 194 Theodore Lowe De Vinne, "The Century's Printer on the Century's Type," *Century Magazine* 51, no. 5 (March 1896): 795; ATF Co., *Specimen Book of American Line Type Faces: American Point Line, Point Body and Point Set* (New York: ATF Co. [1904]), 247.

p. 196 ATF Co., *American Specimen Book of Type Styles* (1912), 233; ATF Co., *Specimen Book and Catalogue, 1923*, 539.

p. 200 ATF Co., *Specimen Book and Catalogue, 1923*, 571; next three, "ATF Section H Type Specimens" ATF ephemera.

p. 201 J. L. Frazier, *Type Lore: Popular Types of Today, Their Origin and Use* (Chicago: published by the author, 1925), 93.

p. 203 ATF Co., *American Line Type Faces* [1904], 15.

p. 204 ATF Co., *American Specimen Book of Type Styles* (1912), 225.

p. 206 ATF Co., *Book of American Types: ATF Standard Faces* (Elizabeth, N.J.: ATF Sales Corp., 1934), 8; ATF Co., *Specimen Book and Catalogue, 1923*, 218; ATF Co., *American Specimen Book of Type Styles* (1912), 283.

p. 207 ATF Co., *American Specimen Book of Type Styles* (1912), 286; ibid., 312; ibid., 294.

p. 209 Giambattista Bodoni, *Manuale Tipografico del cavaliere Giambattista Bodoni, Vol. 1* (Parma: Presso la Vedova, 1818), 97; ATF Co., *American Specimen Book of Type Styles* (1912), 379.

p. 211 "ATF Section i Type Specimens," ATF ephemera.

p. 212 Gellius Aulus, *Noctus Atticae* (Venice: Nicolas Jenson, 1472), 28; ATF Co., *Specimen Book and Catalogue, 1923*, 66; Jacobus de Voragine, *The Golden Legend* (Hammersmith, London: Kelmscott Press, 1892), 245.

p. 215 Paul A. Bennett, "On Recognizing the Type Faces," *Dolphin* 2 (1935): 19.

p. 216 John Milton, *Paradise Regain'd* (Hammersmith, London: Doves Press, 1905), 41 (leaf); Michel de Montaigne, *Essays* (Cambridge, Mass.: Riverside Press, 1902–04), 97 (leaf); ATF Co., *Book of American Types* (1934), 78; Maurice de Guérin, *The Centaur* (Montague, Mass.: Montague Press, 1915), 1.

p. 218 Terentianus Maurus, *De Literis, Syllabis, Pedibus et Metris* (Paris: Simon de Colines, 1531), title page; M.F. McGrew, specimen card for Garamond (Pittsburgh: Press of the Licorice Cat, n.d.); ATF Co., *Specimen Book and Catalogue, 1923*, 18–19; Arthur Christian, *Débuts de L'Imprimerie en France: L'Imprimerie Nationale: L'Hôtel de Rohan* (Paris: Imprimerie Nationale, 1905), 75.

p. 219 ATF ephemera; ATF Co., *Book of American Types* (1934), 196; Lanston Monotype Machine Company, *Specimens of Monotype Type Faces, Borders, Ornaments, Rules* (Philadelphia, Lanston Monotype, ca. 1967).

p. 221 *Gedrängte Schriftenprobe* (Leipzig: J.G. Schelter & Giesecke, [1927]), 71, courtesy of Charles Bigelow; ATF Co., *Specimen Book and Catalogue, 1923*, 452.

p. 223 Virgil, Publii Virgilii Maronis Bucolica, Georgica, et Aeneis (Birmingham: John Baskerville, 1757), 314; ATF Co., *Specimen Book and Catalog, 1923*, 237; Joseph Fry and Sons, *A Specimen of Printing Types, by Joseph Fry and Sons, Letter-Founders to the Prince of Wales* (London: Joseph Fry and Sons, 1786), 10.

---

p. 225 Oliver Goldsmith, *Poems by Goldsmith and Parnell* (London: Bulmer, 1795), 3; George Trenholm, *ATF Style Book on Bulmer* (Elizabeth, N.J.: ATF Co., ca. 1938), 3, ATF ephemera; specimen sheet, ATF ephemera.

p. 226 M.F. McGrew, "BENTON ATF 566, aka Whitehall," *Let's Talk Type*, September 1997 (Pittsburgh: Press of the Licorice Cat): 1; ATF Co., *Book of American Types* (1934), 9.

p. 227 "ATF Section H Type Specimens," ATF ephemera; photo by Patricia Cost.

p. 228 *Thorowgood & Co.'s Specimen of Printing Types* (London: Fann Street Letter Foundry, [1837]).

p. 229 ATF Co., *Specimen Book of American Line Type Faces* [1904], 40b; ibid.; Globe Gothic Extended: ATF Co., *American Line Type Book* (1906), 185; Globe Gothic Condensed: ibid., 193; Globe Gothic Extra Condensed: ibid., 197; Globe Gothic Bold: ATF Co., *American Specimen Book of Type Styles* (1912), 775.

p. 231 ATF Co., *American Line Type Book* (1906), 357; ATF Co., *American Specimen Book of Type Styles* (1912), 742; ibid., 746; ATF Co., *Specimen Book and Catalogue, 1923*, 465.

p. 232 Photo by Roger Cost.

p. 233 Alternate Gothics 1, 2 and 3: "ATF Section A Type Specimens," ATF ephemera; three News Gothics: ATF Co., *Specimen Book and Catalogue, 1923*, 472–74.

p. 234 ATF Co., *Type Specimens Supplement 1* (n.d.), 8, ATF ephemera; ATF Co., *Modern Type Styles* (n.d.), 7, ATF ephemera; ATF Co., *Book of American Types* (1934), 140–141.

p. 235 "ATF Section B Type Specimens," 9, ATF ephemera.

p. 236 ATF Co., *Book of American Types* (1934), 166; ibid., 164; ibid., 165.

p. 237 *Specimens of Printing Types, by Vincent Figgins, Letter-Founder* (West Street, West Smithfield, London: Vincent Figgins, 1821); Philip Gaskell, "A Nomenclature for the Letter-forms of Roman Type," *Library*, 5th ser., vol. 29, no. 1, (March 1974): 50.

p. 238 *Printing Type Specimens, Comprising a Large Variety of Book and Jobbing Faces, Borders and Ornaments* (Edinburgh, London: Miller & Richard, [1921]), 117; "ATF Stymie Bold and Bold Italic" (specimen sheet, n.d.), ATF ephemera.

p. 239 "ATF Stymie Bold and Bold Italic" (specimen sheet, n.d.), ATF ephemera; ibid.

p. 240 ATF Co., *A Supplement to the Book of American Types* (Elizabeth, N.J.: ATF Sales Corp., 1941), 27.

p. 241 Typo Script and Typo Script Extended: ATF Co., "Script and Semiscript Faces" (specimen pamphlet, n.d.), A3, ATF ephemera; Typo Upright and Typo Shaded: ATF Co., "Popular Script and Semi-Script Type Faces" (specimen pamphlet, n.d.), 6 and 8, ATF ephemera; Benton's Adscript: ATF Co., *Specimen Book and Catalogue, 1923*, 416; Typo Roman and Typo Roman Shaded: ATF Co., *Book of American Types* (1934), 134.

p. 242 Cary Collection digital image database; Mauritius Sabbe and Marius Audin, *Die Civilité-Schriften des Robert Granjon ...* (Vienna: Bibliotheca Typographica, 1929), plate 1; ATF Co., "Advance Showing: The New Civilite Type Series" (specimen pamphlet, n.d.), ATF ephemera.

p. 243 ATF Co., *Specimen Book and Catalogue, 1923*, 275–76.

p. 244 ATF Co., *Book of American Types* (1934), 153; ATF Co., "Calendar Silhouettes" (specimen pamphlet, n.d.), ATF ephemera; ATF Co., *Book of American Types* (1934), 159.

p. 245 Modernique: ATF Co., "Modern Type Styles" (specimen pamphlet, n.d.), ATF ephemera; Louvaine Light and Bold: "An Advance Showing of the Louvaine Types" (specimen pamphlet, n.d.), ATF ephemera; Dynamic Medium: "Advance Proof of Dynamic Medium" (specimen pamphlet, 1930), ATF ephemera; Parisian: ATF Co., "Advertising Agencies Recommend Unusual Type Faces, Because They Attract Attention" (specimen pamphlet, 1930), ATF ephemera; Chic: ATF Co., "Modern Type Styles."

CHAPTER 15

p. 258 Courtesy of Caroline Benton Gregg, rephotographed by Henry Weiland.

p. 260 *Inland Printer* 89, no. 5 (August 1932): 24.

p. 261 Courtesy of Laurence Gregg; "The Only Machine of Its Kind in the World," *Printing* 59, no. 7 (July 1935): 33, courtesy of Laurence Gregg.

p. 263 Courtesy of Caroline Benton Gregg, rephotographed by Henry Weiland.

Chapter 16

p. 270 "Century Nova, New Typeface, Shown at Premiere in Milwaukee," *Inland Printer/American Lithographer* 154, no. 2 (November 1964): 112.

p. 271 S. H. Horgan, "Henry L. Bullen in Europe," *Inland Printer* 72, no. 4 (January 1924): 642; Century Nova specimen pamphlet, ATF ephemera.

Appendix A

p. 283 Courtesy of Theo Rehak.

Selected Bibliography

"Achievements of Linn Boyd Benton Vital to Industry's Progress." *Inland Printer* 89, no. 5 (August 1932): 53–54.

"American Type Company's New President." *American Printer* 85, no. 6 (December 1927): 88.

American Type Designers and their Type Faces on Exhibit, September 29 to October 30, 1948. Chicago: Lakeside Press (R. R. Donnelley), for American Institute of Graphic Arts (AIGA), 1948.

"American Type Designers Exhibit Turns Up Some Not-So-Widely-Known Styles." *Inland Printer* 121, no. 3 (June 1948): 51–52.

American Type Founders Company. *A Desk Book of Printing Types.* Boston: American Type Founders Co., 1898.

———.*American Bulletin*, 1910–17. Graphic Arts Collection, Rare Book and Manuscript Library, Columbia University.

———.*American Line Type Book, Borders, Ornaments, Price List, Printing Material and Machinery.* Jersey City, N.J.: ATF Co., 1906.

———.*American Specimen Book of Type Styles, Complete Catalogue of Printing Machinery and Printing Supplies.* Jersey City, N.J.: ATF Co., 1912.

———. *Book of American Types: ATF Standard Faces.* Elizabeth, N.J.: ATF Sales Corp., 1934.

———. *Claude Garamond: The First Type Founder and His Types.* Jersey City, N.J.: ATF Co., 1921.

———. *Desk Book of Type Specimens, Borders, Ornaments, Brass Rules and Cuts.* [New York]: ATF Co., 1900. (Cover title: *Desk Book of Type and Printing Material, 1900, American Type Founders' Co., San Francisco*)

———. *The Kelly Press.* Elizabeth, N.J.: Kelly Press Division, ATF Co., 1927.

———. *Portable Book of Specimens from The Benton & Waldo Foundry Operated by American Type Founders Company, Pantentees and Manufacturers of Benton's Self Spacing Type.* Milwaukee, New York: ATF Co., n.d., ca. 1893. (Cover title: *Type: Benton-Waldo Type Foundry, Milwaukee, Wis.*)

———. *Specimen Book and Catalogue, 1923.* Jersey City, N.J.: ATF Co., 1923.

———. *Specimen Book and Catalogue, 1923.* Jersey City, N.J.: ATF Co., 1923. Hand-annotated copy, Book Arts Collection, Rare Book and Manuscript Library, Columbia University.

———. *Specimen Book of American Line Type Faces: American Point Line, Point Body and Point Set.* New York: ATF Co., 1904.

———. *Specimens of Printing Types.* Philadelphia: American Type Founders Company, 1898. (Cover title: *Specimen Book of Type*)

———. *A Supplement to the Book of American Types.* Elizabeth, N.J.: ATF Sales Corp., 1941.

——— Engineering Department. *Engineering Applied to Composing Rooms for Increased Production: American Cut-Cost System of Printing Plant Equipment.* Elizabeth, N.J.: ATF Co., n.d., ca. 1926.

"American Typefounders' Company." *Inland Printer* 10, no. 2 (November 1892): 150–151.

Annenberg, Maurice. *Type Foundries of America and their Catalogs.* 2nd ed. New Castle, Del.: Oak Knoll Press, 1994.

Art Directors Club of Milwaukee. "Century Nova" (pamphlet). September 1964.

Ascender Corporation. *See* Davis, Bill.

"ATF Unveils New Century Type Face in Historic Site." *Printing News*, October 17, 1964.

Avis, F. C. *Edward Philip Prince: Type Punchcutter.* London: Glenview Press Ltd., 1967.

Barker, Nicolas. "The Aldine Roman in Paris, 1530–1534." *Library*, 5th ser., vol. 29, no. 1 (March 1974): 5–20.

Beaujon, Paul [Beatrice Warde]. "The 'Garamond' Types: A Study of XVI and XVII Century Sources." *Fleuron* 5 (1926): 131–179.

Bennett, Paul A. "On Recognizing the Type Faces." *Dolphin* 2 (1935): 11–59.

"Benton, Charles Swan." Biographical Directory of the United States Congress. http://bioguide.congress.gov/scripts/biodisplay.pl?index=B000394

Benton, Linn Boyd. "The Making of Type." In *The Building of a Book*, ed. Frederick H. Hitchcock, 31–40. New York: Grafton Press, 1906.

"Benton, Nathaniel Seley." The Political Graveyard: Index to Politicians. http://politicalgraveyard.com.

Benton, Waldo & Co. *Typographic Specimens: Benton's Self Spacing Type.* Milwaukee, St. Paul: Benton, Waldo & Co., n.d., ca. 1884.

Biegeleisen, J. I. *Art Directors' Workbook of Type Faces.* New York: Arco Publishing Co., 1976.

Bigelow, Charles. Introductory remark to "On Type: The Century Family" by Paul Shaw. *Fine Print* 7, no. 4 (October 1981): 141.

———. "On Type: Form, Pattern, & Texture in the Typographic Image." *Fine Print* 15, no. 2 (April 1989): 75–82.

———, and Donald Day. "Digital Typography." *Scientific American* 249, no. 2 (August 1983): 106–119.

———, and Jonathan Seybold. "Technology and the Aesthetics of Type." *Seybold Report* 10, no. 24 (August 24, 1981): 24–3 to 24–16.

Blum, Andrew. "The Modern's Other Renovation." Design, *New York Times*, September 21, 2003. http://www.andrewblum.net/typepad/2003/09/the_moderns_oth.html.

Blumenthal, Joseph. *Art of the Printed Book*. New York: Pierpont Morgan Library, 1973.

———. "The Fitting of Type." *Dolphin* 2 (1935): 71–81.

"Bodoni." *Inland Printer* 104, no. 3 (December 1939): 53–57.

Bruckner, D. J. R. *Frederic Goudy*. New York: Harry N. Abrams, Inc., 1990.

Bruce Jr., David. *History of Typefounding in the United States*. Edited by James Eckman. New York: The Typophiles, 1981.

Bryant, Benjamin F., ed. *Memoirs of La Crosse County from earliest historical times down to the present with special chapters on various subjects, including each of the different towns, and a genealogical and biographical record of representative families in the county, prepared from data obtained from original sources of information.* Madison, Wisconsin: Western Historical Association, 1907. http://murphylibrary.uwlax.edu/digital/lacrosse/BryantMemoirs/02480248. htm.

Bucsko, Mike. "Obituary: M.F. 'Mac' McGrew / Foremost Authority on Metal Typefaces, Worked at Ketchum." *Pittsburgh Post-Gazette*, March 4, 2007. http://www.postgazette.com/pg/07063/766709-122.stm.

Bullen, Henry Lewis. "Bodoni, Benjamin Franklin and Bodoni's Grandson." *American Bulletin* 2, no. 5 (April/May 1912): 1–2.

———. "A Composite Showing of Goudy Types." Elizabeth, N.J.: ATF Co., 1927.

———. "The Creators of the New Era in Typefounding." *Inland Printer* 73, no. 5 (August 1924): 761–764.

———. "The Effect of the Composing Machines Upon the Typefounding Industry." *Inland Printer* 73, no. 4 (July 1924): 595–597.

———. "John Marder: A Benefactor of Printers." *Inland Printer* 62, no. 4 (January 1919): 446.

———. "Linn Boyd Benton – The Man and His Work." *Inland Printer* 70, no. 1 (October 1922): 60–64.

———. *Nicolas Jenson, Printer of Venice: His Famous Type Designs and Some Comment upon the Printing Types of Earlier Printers.* San Francisco: John Henry Nash, 1926.

———. "Observations on Type Designs and Type Designers and Their Press Agents." *Inland Printer* 71, no. 6 (September 1923): 833–835.

———. "Origin and Development of the Linotype Machine, Part I." *Inland Printer* 72, no. 5 (February 1924): 769–771.

———. "Origin and Development of the Linotype Machine, Part II." *Inland Printer* 72, no. 6 (March 1924): 936–938.

———. "Robert Wickham Nelson: An Intimate History." *Inland Printer* 77, no. 6 (September 1926): 905–909.

———. "What the Typefounders Have Done." *Inland Printer* 79, no. 5 (August 1927): 762–763.

———. "Why a Typographic Library?" *American Bulletin*, new ser., no. 2 (June 1910): 7.

———. *See also* Quadrat.

Burtt, Harold E., and Coryne Basch. "Legibility of Bodoni, Baskerville Roman, and Cheltenham Type Faces." *Journal of Applied Psychology* 7 (September 1923): 237–245.

Carter, Harry G., *A View of Early Typography Up To About 1600: The Lyell Lectures 1968.* Oxford: Clarendon Press, 1969.

———, ed. *Fournier on Typefounding: The Text of the Manuel Typographique (1764–1766).* New York: Burt Franklin, 1973.

———. "Letter Design and Typecutting." *Journal of the Royal Society of Arts* 102, no. 4935 (October 1, 1954): 878–895.

———. "Observations on Modern Type Design." *Gutenberg-Gesellschaft Jahrbuch*, 1929, 297–302.

———. "Optical Scale in Type Founding." *Typography* 4 (Autumn 1937): 2–6. Reprinted in *Printing Historical Society Bulletin* 13 (September 1984): 144–148. Page references are to the 1937 edition.

——— and George Buday "Stereotyping by Joseph Athias: The Evidence of Nicholas Kis." *Quaerendo* 5, no. 4 (October 1975): 312–320.

"Century Nova, New Typeface, Shown at Premiere in Milwaukee." *Inland Printer/ American Lithographer* 154, no. 2 (November 1964): 112.

Chappell, Warren. *A Short History of the Printed Word.* New York: Alfred A. Knopf, 1970.

"The Clearface Family, Optically Correct in Design." *American Bulletin*, new ser., no. 3 (July 1910): 6–7.

Coggeshall, Howard W. "The Designer." *Typographer*, Spring 1960, 19–24.

Cost, Patricia A. "Linn Boyd Benton, Morris Fuller Benton, and Typemaking at ATF." *Printing History* 31/32, vol. 16, nos. 1 & 2 (1994): 27–44.

Crook, Stephen Glenn. "The Contributions of R. Hunter Middleton to Typeface Design and Printing in America." M.S. diss., University of Chicago, 1980.

"Crowell-Collier Adopts a Type Developed by London *Times*," *Inland Printer* 111, no. 6 (September 1943): 51–52.

Davis, Bill. "Fonts on the Front Page—A Study of Typefaces on the Front Pages of America's Top Newspapers." Elk Grove Village, Illinois: Ascender Corporation, November 19, 2004. http://www.ascendercorp.com/pr/pr2004_11_09.html.

"Deaths in the Trade: Linn Boyd Benton." *American Printer* 95, no. 2 (August 1932): 52.

Denman, Frank. *The Shaping of Our Alphabet.* New York: Alfred A. Knopf, 1955.

"Design and Manufacture of Foundry Type." *American Printer* 127, no. 5 (November 1948): 36–38.

De Vinne Press. *Types of the De Vinne Press.* New York: Theodore L. De Vinne & Co., 1907.

De Vinne, Theodore Lowe. "The Century's Printer on the Century's Type." *Century Magazine* 51, no. 5 (March 1896): 794–796.

———. *The Practice of Typography: A Treatise on the Processes of Type-Making, the Point System, the Names, Sizes, Styles and Practices of Plain Printing Types.* New York: The Century Co., 1900.

Dreyfus, John. *Into Print: Selected Writings on Printing History, Typography and Book Production.* Boston: David R. Godine, 1995.

———. "The Speed and Grace of Roger Excoffon." *U&lc* Online Issue: Other Articles, n.d. http://www.itcfonts.com/Ulc/OtherArticles/Excoffon.htm.

———. *The Survival of Baskerville's Punches.* Cambridge, England: University Printer for Friends in Printing & Publishing, Christmas 1949.

———. *The Work of Jan van Krimpen.* London: Sylvan Press, 1952.

Drost, Henk. "Punch Cutting Demonstration." *Visible Language* 19, no. 1 (Winter 1985): 99–105.

Duensing, Paul Hayden. "On Type: A New Civilité." *Fine Print* 11, no. 1 (January 1985): 35–41.

———. "On Type: Twentieth-Century Contributions to the Jensonian Model." *Fine Print* 16, no. 2 (Summer 1990): 69–71.

———. "The Punchcutter in the Tower of Babel." *Fine Print* 12, no. 1 (January 1986): 6–10.

Duffield, Benjamin P. "An Appreciation of the Cheltenham Family." *American Bulletin* 2nd ser., no. 14 (December 1915): 6–7.

Dwiggins, William Addison. *WAD to RR: A Letter about Designing Type.* Cambridge, Massachusetts: Harvard College Library, 1940.

Eckman, James R. "The Chicago Type Foundry of Marder, Luse & Co., 1863–1892." *Printing & Graphic Arts (PaGA)* 7, no. 3 (September 1959): 69–83.

———. *The Collectanea Typographica of Henry Lewis Bullen, 1857–1938, in The Inland Printer, 1918–1924 and 1928–1931.* Rochester, Minnesota: The Doomsday Press, 1960.

———. *The Heritage of the Printer*, vol. 1. Philadelphia: North American Publishing Company, 1965.

———. "The Heritage of the Printer. Taps for the Old Trooper: Steve L. Watts." *Printing Impressions* 9, no. 2 (July 1966): 19.

———. "The Heritage of the Printer. The Many Talents of Steven L. Watts." *Printing Impressions* 6, no. 9 (February 1964): 7–8.

———. The Immortal Century Type Face and the Bentons, Father and Son." *Printer's Digest* (November 1964): 4–6.

———. "The Inland Type Foundry, 1894–1911." *Printing & Graphic Arts* (*PaGA*) 8, no. 2 (June 1960): 31–46.

———. "The Story of an Historic Typeface—Century and the Bentons." *Industrial Arts Methods* 3, no. 12 (December 1964): 22–24.

Ettenberg, Eugene M. "American Type Designers and Their Work: an R. R. Donnelley Exhibition." *American Printer* 126, no. 5 (May 1948): 17–22.

———. *Type for Books and Advertising*. New York: D. Van Nostrand Co., Inc., 1947.

Fabian, Nicholas. "The History of the American Point System." Nicholas Fabian, 1997. http://cg.scs.carleton.ca/~luc/fabian-point.html.

Figgins, Vincent. *Type Specimens, 1801 and 1815, Reproduced in Facsimile*. London: Printing Historical Society, 1967.

"Frank M. Gove," obituary. *Typographic Advisor* 28 (Fall 1882): 774.

Frazier, Julius Leroy. *Type Lore: Popular Types of Today, Their Origin and Use*. Chicago: Frazier, 1925.

Gaskell, Philip. *A New Introduction to Bibliography*. New York and Oxford: Oxford University Press, 1972.

———. "A Nomenclature for the Letter-forms of Roman Type." *Library*, 5th ser., vol. 29, no. 1, (March 1974): 42–51.

Goudy, Frederic W. *Elements of Lettering.* New York: Mitchell Kennerley, 1922.

———. "The Goudy Method." *Typographer's Digest* 27 (Spring 1969): 8–11.

———. *A Half-Century of Type Design Typography, 1895–1945,* vol. 1. New York: The Typophiles, 1946.

———. "Type Design: A Homily." *Ars Typographica* 1, no. 4 (Autumn 1934): 3–27.

———. "Type Designs: Old and New." *Ars Typographica* 1, no. 1 (Spring 1918): 38–40.

———. *Typologia: Studies in Type Design & Type Making.* Berkeley: University of California Press, 1940.

Gress, Edmund G. "N. J. Werner and the Designers of Typefaces." *American Printer* 94, no. 5 (May 1932): 52–53.

"Hails Linn Boyd Benton's Type Invention As One Of Greatest Of Present Era." Plainfield, N.J. *Courier-News*, Thursday, October 9, 1930.

Haley, Alan. "Typographic Milestones: Morris Fuller Benton." *U&lc* 10, no. 3 (September 1983): 16–19.

———. "Typographic Milestones: Frederic W. Goudy." *U&lc* 11, no. 2 (August 1984): 20–23.

Harris, Elizabeth. "ATF & the Smithsonian Institution." *Type & Press* 78 (Fall 1993): 1

———. Introduction to *The Biography of Ottmar Mergenthaler.* Edited by Carl Schlesinger. New Castle, Del.: Oak Knoll Press, 1989.

Hartz, S. L. "An Approach to Type Designing." *Penrose Annual* 52 (1958): 39–42.

Heir, Martin. "The Evolution of American Typography." *Inland Printer* 79, no. 5 (August 1927): 769–772.

Hillman, Harry. "The Types of a Quarter Century." *Inland Printer* 79, no. 5 (August 1927): 811–817.

Histoire de L'Invention de L'Imprimerie par les Monuments. Paris: L'Imprimerie Rue de Verneuil, No. 4, June 1840.

Hitchcock, Maureen Delaney. *Benton Types: Typefaces Designed or Adapted by Morris Fuller Benton*. Rochester, N.Y.: Press of the Good Mountain, 1978.

Hlasta, Stanley C. *Printing Types & How to Use Them*. Pittsburgh: Carnegie Press, 1950.

Hopkins, Richard L. *Origin of the American Point System*. Terra Alta, Virginia: Hill & Dale Private Press, 1976.

Hopper, A. Raymond. "Fitting: A Vital Step in the Perfection of a Type Face." *Inland Printer* 119, no. 1 (April 1947): 50–52.

———. "The Romance of Roycroft." *Inland Printer* 99, no. 3 (June 1937): 35–36.

———. "What Are 'Enduring' Type Faces?" *Inland Printer* 113, no. 1 (April 1944): 30–31.

Horgan, S. H. "Henry L. Bullen in Europe." *Inland Printer* 72, no. 4 (January 1924): 642–643.

"How Frederic W. Goudy Cuts a Type Face." *American Printer* 106, no. 5 (May 1938): 20–21.

Huey, Edmund Burke. *The Psychology and Pedagogy of Reading*. Cambridge, Massachusetts: The M.I.T. Press, 1968. First published in 1908 by The Macmillan Company.

———. *The Development of Printers' Mechanical Typesetting Methods, 1822–1925*. Charlottesville: University Press of Virginia, 1973.

Huss, Richard E. *The Printer's Composition Matrix*. New Castle, Del.: Oak Knoll Books, 1985.

"It's a Quiz." *Inland Printer* 115, no. 3 (June 1945): 48, 72.

Jaspert, W. Pincus, W. Turner Berry, and A. F. Johnson. *The Encyclopedia of Type Faces*. 4th ed. Poole, Dorset, UK: Blandford Press, 1983.

"John Marder Passes Away." *Inland Printer* 62, no. 3 (December 1918): 331.

Johnson, Henry Lewis. "Bon Voyage to Henry Lewis Bullen." *Inland Printer* 72, no. 4 (January 1924): 640–642.

Johnson, Herbert H. "On the Montaigne and Centaur Types of Bruce Rogers." In *American Proprietary Typefaces*, ed. David Pankow, 42–56. New York: American Printing History Association, 1998.

Johnson, Peter. "How Alameda Changed the World (for Printers)." *Alameda Sun* 5, no. (16 February 16, 2006): 9.

Johnston, Alastair. *Alphabets to Order: The Literature of Nineteenth-Century Typefounders' Specimens*. London and New Castle, Del.: The British Library and Oak Knoll Press, 2000.

Jones, Thomas Roy. *Printing in America—and ATF*. New York: Newcomen Society of England, American Branch, 1948.

Karch, R. Randolph. "It's a Quiz." *Inland Printer* 122, no. 2 (October 1948): 55, 46.

Kaup, W.J. "Modern Automatic Type Making Methods." *American Machinist* 32 (December 16, 1909): 1042–1046. Typographic Book Collection, Rare Book and Manuscript Library, Columbia University.

Koch, Paul. "The Making of Printing Types." *Dolphin* 1 (1933): 24–57.

Koch, Rudolf. *The Typefoundry in Silhouette: A Portfolio of Twenty-Five Silhouettes*. Offenbach, Germany: Klingspor Bros. Type Foundry, 1918.

―――― and Fritz Kredel. "On Punch Cutting & Wood Cutting." *Colophon* 10 (1932): no pagination.

"Lamented Dead: Colonel Charles S. Benton." La Crosse, Wis. newspaper, May 5, 1882. Cooney Room, Arphaxed Loomis Notebook, Book E, 99, Little Falls (N.Y.) Historical Society.

Lawson, Alexander. "After 70 Years Century Typefaces Hold Their Own." *Inland Printer/American Lithographer* 154, no. 4 (January 1965): 46–47.

――――."Anatomy of a Type: Bembo." *Printing Impressions* 14, no. 2 (July 1971): 54–55.

――――."Anatomy of a Type: Bulmer." *Printing Impressions* 15, no. 3 (August 1972): 44–45.

———. "Anatomy of a Type: Century, Part 1." *Printing Impressions* 24, no. 5 (October 1981): 42–43.

———. "Anatomy of a Type: Century, Part 2." *Printing Impressions* 24, no. 7 (December 1981): 40.

———. "Anatomy of a Type: Century, Part 3." *Printing Impressions* 24, no. 8 (January 1982): 62–63.

———. "Anatomy of a Type: Cheltenham." *Printing Impressions* 13, no. 10 (March 1971): 54–55.

———. *Anatomy of a Typeface*. Boston: David R. Godine, 1990.

———. "Morris Fuller Benton Deserves More Than Obscurity." *Inland Printer/American Lithographer* 148, no. 1 (October 1961): 80–81.

———. *Printing Types: An Introduction*. Boston: Beacon Press, 1971.

———. "The Prolific Career of Morris Benton." *Printing Impressions* 13, no. 11 (April 1971): 76–77.

———. "'Rugged' Typefaces Are Latest Revival." *Inland Printer/American Lithographer* 155, no. 1 (April 1965): 64–65.

———, ed. *Typographer's Digest* 27 (Spring 1969) – Frederic W. Goudy issue.

———. "Young Designers Are Going Back to Design of 'Roaring Twenties.'" *Inland Printer/American Lithographer* 152, no. 6 (March 1964): 70–71.

———, and Archie Provan. *100 Type Histories*, 2 vols. Arlington, Va.: National Composition Association, 1983.

"L. B. Benton." *Inland Printer* 11, no. 3 (June 1893), 237-38.

Lee, Jennifer B. "The Exhibition." In *The American Type Founders Company Collection*. New York: Rare Book and Manuscript Library, Columbia University, 2002, 22–71. Concurrently published in *Printing History* 43/44, vol. 22, nos. 1 & 2 (2002): 22–71.

Legros, Lucien Alphonse, and John Cameron Grant. *Typographical Printing-Surfaces: The Technology and Mechanism of Their Production.* London, New York: Longmans, Green and Co., 1916.

Lewis, John, and John Brinkley. *Graphic Design.* London: Routledge & Kegan Paul, 1954.

"Linn Boyd Benton, 'Edison of Typographic Industry,' Is Dead at His Home Here." Plainfield, N.J. *Courier-News,* July 16, 1932, 1, 6.

"Little Life Stories of Live Men Known to the Printers of America. Linn Boyd Benton: Typefounder, Inventor." *American Printer* 76, no. 5 (March 5, 1923): 34.

Loxley, Simon. "American Spring: Creating the Modern Age," in *Type: The Secret History of Letters.* London, New York: I. B. Tauris, 2005, 68–78.

Loy, William E. "Designers and Engravers of Type, No. XI: Gustav F. Schroeder." *Inland Printer* 22, no. 3 (December 1898): 338.

———. "Typefounders and Typefounding in America, No. XVII: Edward Miller." *Inland Printer* 28, no. 4 (January 1902): 584.

MacKaye, Milton. "Profiles: Glorifier of the Alphabet." *New Yorker,* January 14, 1933, 20–24.

MacMillan, Neil. *An A–Z of Type Designers.* New Haven, Conn.: Yale University Press, 2006.

Mallison, David Walker. "Henry Lewis Bullen and the Typographic Library and Museum of the American Type Founders Company." Ph.D. diss., Columbia University, 1976.

Man, John. *Gutenberg: How One Man Remade the World with Words.* New York: John Wiley & Sons, Inc., 2002.

McArthur, Richard N. "On Cooper Type Faces … With Some Digressions." In *The Book of Oz Cooper: An Appreciation of Oswald Bruce Cooper*, 71–124. Chicago: Society of Typographic Arts, 1949.

McGrew, M.F. *American Metal Typefaces of the Twentieth Century.* 2nd ed. New Castle, Del.: Oak Knoll Books, 1993.

———. "BENTON ATF 566, aka Whitehall." *Let's Talk Type*, September 1997 (Pittsburgh: Press of the Licorice Cat): 1–4.

———. "Benton…or Whitehall." *It's a Small World* 26 (1980): 33.

———. "The Bentons, Father & Son." *Typographic i* 10, no. 1 (March 1978): 2–5. Reprinted by the author, 1978.

———. "Conversation on Whitehall." Pittsburgh: Press of the Licorice Cat, October 1969.

———. "Frederic W. Goudy: Master Type Designer." *Typographic i* (September 1978). Reprinted by the author, 1978.

———. "Garamond: The Typeface & the Designers." *Typographic i* (n.d.). Reprinted by the author, n.d.

———. "Gothics Reconsidered." *Let's Talk Type*, October 1982 (Pittsburgh: Press of the Licorice Cat): 1–4.

———. *Let's Talk Type*, June 1982 (Pittsburgh: Press of the Licorice Cat): 1–4.

———. "My Quest for Morris Benton." Pittsburgh: Press of the Licorice Cat, September 1978.

McLean, Ruari. *The Thames and Husdon Manual of Typography*. London: Thames and Hudson, Ltd., 1980.

McMurtrie, Douglas. *Type Design, An Essay on American Type Design in the Twentieth Century*. Pelham, New York: Bridgman Publishers, 1927.

Meggs, Philip B. "American Type Founders Specimen Book and Catalogue 1923." *Print* 48, no. 1 (January/February 1994): 78–85, 119.

Middleton, R. Hunter. *Chicago Letter Founding*. Chicago: Black Cat Press, 1937.

Moran, James. *Stanley Morison: His Typographic Achievement*. New York: Visual Communication Books, 1971.

Morison, Stanley. "Towards an Ideal Italic." *Fleuron* 5 (1926): 93–129.

"Morris F. Benton," obituary. *New York Times*, July 1, 1948, 26.

"Morris Fuller Benton," obituary. *Inland Printer* 121, no. 5 (August 1948): 72.

Mosley, James. "A Bodoni Museum in Parma." *Linotype Matrix* 34 (December 1960): 6–7.

———. *The Nymph and the Grot: The Revival of the Sanserif Letter.* London: Friends of the St. Bride Printing Library, 1999.

———. "On Type: Eric Gill's Perpetua Type." *Fine Print* 8, no. 3 (July 1982): 90–95.

Murphy, John Allen. "Morris Benton – Type Designer-Executive." *Inland Printer* 96, no. 6 (March 1936): 33–36.

———. "Morris Benton, Part 2." *Inland Printer* 97, no. 1 (April 1936): 42–44.

———. "Morris Benton, Part 3." *Inland Printer* 97, no. 2 (May 1936): 69–71.

"Narrative of Cloister, Cloister Oldstyle Italic and Cloister Title." *American Bulletin* 3, no. 2 (April 1914): 4.

Nelson, Stan. "Mould Making, Matrix Fitting, and Hand Casting." *Visible Language* 19, no. 1 (Winter 1985): 106–120.

———. "On Type: Cutting Anglo-Saxon Sorts." *Fine Print* 12, no. 4 (October 1986): 228–29.

"A New Leader in Our Industry." *Inland Printer* 78, no. 1 (October 1926): 111.

"New President of the American Type Founders Company." *Inland Printer* 27, no. 1 (April 1901): 99.

The North-Western. Milwaukee: Benton, Waldo & Co. Several issues from 1876–1892.

Norton, Robert, ed. *A Collection of Observations on Types Best Remembered by Various People Charitably Disposed to an Expatriate Editor/A Collection of Observations on Types Best Forgotten by Various People Uncharitably Disposed to All Sorts of Different Things.* London: Parsimony Press, 1993.

"Of Interest to the Craft." *Inland Printer* 3, no. 12 (September 1886): 788–789.

"The Only Machine of Its Kind in the World." *Printing* 59, no. 7 (July 1935): 33.

Ono, Takashi, tr. Yahoo! Japan. "ものが語る産業の歴史" [The Industrial History that a Thing Recites]. Department of Engineering, Chiba University, n.d. http://www.chiba-u.ac.jp/message/prs/koho118/tokushu07.htm.

"Origin of Point-Set Type." *Inland Printer* 38, no. 6 (March 1907): 852–853.

Ovink, G. W. "Back to Humanism in Type Design." *Penrose Annual* 50 (1956): 69–72.

———. "From Fournier to Metric, and from Lead to Film." *Quaerendo* 9, no. 4 (Autumn 1974): 283–307.

Pankow, David. "The Rise and Fall of ATF." Delivered at ATypI Congress, San Francisco, September 1994; *Printing History* 43/44, vol. 22, nos. 1 & 2 (2002): 3–14.

Parker, Mike. "Early Typefounders' Moulds at the Plantin–Moretus Museum." *Library* 5th ser., vol. 29, no. 1 (March 1974): 93–102.

Porritt, Edward. "Trade Unionism and the Evolution of the Typesetting Machine." *Journal of Political Economy* 2, no. 2 (March 1894): 292–297.

"The Printers' Library and Museum." *American Bulletin*, April 1915, 4.

Pye, Alfred. "Typefounding, No. I," *Inland Printer* 3, no. 1 (October 1885): 29–30.

———. "Typefounding, No. II," *Inland Printer* 3, no. 2 (November 1885): 84–85.

———. "Typefounding, No. III," *Inland Printer* 3, no. 3 (December 1885): 143–144.

———. "Typefounding, No. IV," *Inland Printer* 3, no. 4 (January 1886): 203–204.

———. "Typefounding, No. V," *Inland Printer* 3, no. 5 (February 1886): 258–259.

Quadrat [Henry Lewis Bullen]. "Discursions of a Retired Printer, No. VI." *Inland Printer* 38, no. 3 (December 1906): 353–358.

———. "Discursions of a Retired Printer, No. VII." *Inland Printer* 38, no. 4 (January 1907): 513–521.

———. "Discursions of a Retired Printer, No. VIII." *Inland Printer* 38, no. 5 (February 1907): 673–680.

———. "Discursions of a Retired Printer, No. IX." *Inland Printer* 38, no. 6 (March 1907): 856–862.

———. "Discursions of a Retired Printer, No. XII," *Inland Printer* 39, no. 4 (July 1907): 513–517.

Rehak, Theo. *The Fall of ATF.* Privately printed, 2004.

———. *Practical Typecasting.* New Castle, Del.: Oak Knoll Books, 1993.

———. "Seizing Ordered Chaos: A Serious Attempt at Reproducing Gutenberg's B-42 Types, Part 2." Dale Guild Type Foundry website. http://www.daleguild. com/B-42_Story_02.html.

Rice, Roy. "Matrix Making at the Oxford University Press, Part II." Atlanta: Recalcitrant Press, 1982. http://personal.lig.bellsouth.net/r/_/r_rice2/mmoup/Text1.htm.

Roethlein, Barbara Elizabeth. "The Relative Legibility of Different Faces of Printing Types." *American Journal of Psychology* 23, no. 1 (January 1912): 1–36.

Rogers, Bruce. *The Centaur Types.* Chicago: October House, 1949.

Rollins, Carl Purlington. Introduction to "American Type Designers and Their Work." An exhibition catalog. Chicago: R. R. Donnelley, 1947.

Romano, Frank. *Machine Writing and Typesetting.* Salem, N.H.: Graphic Arts Marketing Association, 1986.

Rosen, Ben. *Type and Typography: The Designer's Type Book.* New York: Van Nostrand Reinhold Co., 1976.

Rumble, Walker A., "A Time of Giants: Speed Composition in Nineteenth-Century America," *Printing History* 28, vol. 14, no. 2 (1992): 14–21.

Ruppel, Aloys. Introduction to *The 500th Anniversary Pictorial Census of the Gutenberg Bible*, by Don Cleveland Norman. Chicago: Coverdale Press, 1961.

Sawada, Yoshihiko, tr. Yahoo! Japan. "It is Photocomposition Style of Handwriting and Digital Style of Handwriting (11)." Japan Association of Graphic Arts Technology, n.d. http://www.jagat.or.jp/story_memo_view.asp?StoryID=7745 (accessed April 10, 2008).

Schlesinger, Carl, ed. *The Biography of Ottmar Mergenthaler.* New Castle, Del.: Oak Knoll Press, 1989.

Schraubstadter, Carl Jr. "Electrotype Matrices." *Inland Printer* 4, no. 6 (March 1887): 382.

"Scoreboard Reveals Popularity Trends in Type Faces." *Inland Printer* 115, no. 3 (June 1945): 55.

"Self-Spacing Type." *Inland Printer* 4, no. 3 (December 1886): 180.

Shaw, Paul. "On Type: The Century Face," *Fine Print* 7, no. 4 (October 1981): 141–44.

"Show Type Design Exhibit." *Inland Printer* 122, no. 2 (October 1948): 77.

Siegfried, Laurance B. "Ninth Annual Frederic W. Goudy Distinguished Lecture in Typography." Rochester, N.Y.: Press of the Good Mountain, 1977.

"Sketches and Impressions of an American Printer." *American Printer* 76, no. 9 (May 5, 1923): 33–34.

Southall, Richard. *Printer's Type in the Twentieth Century.* London and New Castle, Del.: British Library and Oak Knoll Press, 2005.

Spencer, Herbert. *The Visible Word.* London: Royal College of Art, 1968.

Standard, Paul. "Goudy at Seventy." *Penrose Annual* 38 (1936): 58–59.

Tidcombe, Marianne. *The Doves Press.* London and New Castle, Del.: British Library and Oak Knoll Press, 2002.

Trenholm, George F. *ATF Style Book on Bulmer.* Elizabeth, N.J.: American Type Founders Co., n.d., ca. 1938.

"Two Men Whose Work Greatly Benefits All Typographers." *Inland Printer* 76, no. 3 (December 1925): 453.

"Type Face Premiere Honors Designer Here." *Milwaukee Journal*, September 18, 1964, Business section, 1.

"Type Making." *Chicago Specimen* 9, no. 4 (October 1875): 3–4. Book Arts Collection, Rare Book and Manuscript Library, Columbia University.

"Typographic Scoreboard." *Inland Printer* 103, no. 6 (September 1939): 69.

"Typography's Forgotten Man: Morris Fuller Benton." *Type Talks* 100 (May/June 1958): 11–12.

Updike, Daniel Berkeley. *Printing Types: Their History, Forms and Use*, vol. 1 & 2. Cambridge, Mass.: Harvard University Press, 1922.

Vervliet, H. D. L. *Sixteenth-Century Printing Types of the Low Countries.* Amsterdam: Menno Hertzberger & Co., 1968.

Vollrath, Francis R. "Goudy Oldstyle: An Appreciation." *American Bulletin*, 2nd ser., no. 17 (January 1917), 10–11.

Warde, Beatrice. *The Crystal Goblet: Sixteen Essays on Typography*. Edited by Henry Jacob. Cleveland and New York: World Publishing Co., 1956.

———. "Cutting Types for the Machines: A Layman's Account." *Dolphin* 2 (1935): 60–70.

———. *See also* Beaujon, Paul.

"Watts Had A Career Just As Colorful As It Was Typographic." *Printing News*, June 4, 1966, 7–8.

Watts, S. L. "'Chelt' Really Got Around." *Printing* 81, no. 5 (May 1957): 78–79, 114.

———. "A Tribute to the Memory of Henry Lewis Bullen and His Work." Lecture, Heritage of the Graphic Arts series, New York City, March 30, 1966. Reprinted (n.d.) by the Privateer Press, Warren County, Va.: 13.

———. "Typorythmics: A Pastime Celebration." *Pastime Printer* 4 (March 1957): 8.

Way, W. Irving. "Theodore L. De Vinne, the Scholar Printer." *Inland Printer* 23, no. 1 (April 1899): 33–37.

Werner, N. J. "Saint Louis' Place on the Type Founders' Map." *Inland Printer* 79, no. 5 (August 1927): 764–766.

———. "St. Louis in Type-Founding History." *Share Your Knowledge Review* 22, no. 3 (January 1941): 21–24.

———. "Wiebking Created Popular Face in Chicago, Friend Discloses." *Inland Printer* 90, no. 2 (November 1932): 71–73.

Williams, Fred C., ed. "American Type Founders in Bankruptcy!" *Type & Press* 77 (Summer 1993): 1–3.

———. "Herman Zapf: Calligrapher, Typographer, Type Designer, Writer, Teacher, Lecturer." *Type & Press* 24 (Spring 1980): 1–2.

———. "The Issue of Several Sizes of Type on One Body!" *Type & Press* 68 (Spring 1991): 1–2.

———. "The Lost Art of Cutting Type Punches." *Type & Press* 82 (Fall 1994): 1–2.

———. "The Rise and Fall of the Kelly Press." *Type & Press* 44 (Spring 1985): 1–2.

———. "Theodore De Vinne's Type of the Century." *Type & Press* 49 (Summer 1986): 1–2.

Zapf, Hermann. *About Alphabets*. New York: The Typophiles, 1960.

Index

Fergusson, James, 44
Fine Print (magazine), 121
Fink, William E., 172
Flemish Black, 190, *191*
Fleuron (journal), 52
The Font Bureau, Inc., 195–197, 247*n17*
Fournier, Pierre Simon, 1, 4, *43*, 44, 45, 107
Franklin Gothic, 180, *230–233*
Franklin Type & Stereotype Foundry (Cincinnati), 36, 81
Frazier, J.L., 176, 194, 201, 204, 211, 212, 217, 268
Freehand, *130,* 136, 244, 283
Frere-Jones, Tobias, 195, 234, 272

Gallia, 186
Gally, Merritt, 62
Garamond, Claude, 217
Garamond type, 106, 217–220
Garamont, 105, 219–220
Gaunt, Sidney, 172
Gill, Eric, 171
Gillick, Joseph F., 164, *164,* 271
Ginn and Company, 197, 198
Globe Gothic, 229–230
Golden type, *212,* 213
Goodhue, Bertrand Grosvenor, 109, 118, 171, 200–202
Gorton engraving machine, 123
Gothics, 227–236
Goudy Bold, 171, 175, *176,* 177, 205, 224
Goudy, Frederic W., 59, 106–107, 117–118, 119, 121, 134, 171, 172, 173–180, 197, 219–220, 229–230
Goudy Old Style, 171, 175–178
Goudy type family, 175–178, 187
Gove, Frank M., 37, 40
Grabhorn, Edwin, 219
Granjon, Robert, 242
Grant, John Cameron, 1
Great Chicago Fire (1871), 44
Great Depression, 164, 165
Gregan, William Charles, 60, *73,* 173
Gregg, Laurence, 24, *31n39,* 246
Griffith, C.H., 172
Griffo, Francesco, 217
Grotesque, 228
Guérin, Maurice de, 216
Gutenberg, Johannes, 1, 8, 11, 190
Guy, Peter, 222

Hagar Type Foundry (New York), 36
Hahl, August, 61, 62
Hahl, Louis, 61
Hall, Caroline Bottum, 27
Hammer, Victor, 172
Handy, John, 222
Harris, Elizabeth, 61, 65
Hartz, S.L., 4
Hartzell Machine Works (Philadelphia), 129
Hasbrouck, Philip Bevier, 28
Hawks, Nelson Crocker, 44–46
Haynes, Elwood, 111
H.C. Hansen Type Foundry (Boston), 36, 81
Headline Gothic, 236
Hess, Sol, 172, 195, 239, 244
Highsmith, Cyrus, 197, 234
Hillman, Harry, 214
Hitchcock, Maureen Delaney, 185, 186, 271
Hlasta, Stanley, 205, 210, 215, 219, 225, 237
Hobo, 243
Holmes, Kris, 207
Hooper, Wilson & Co. Type Foundry (Baltimore), 81
Hope, Thomas, 236
Hopkins, Richard L., 45
Hopper, A. Raymond, 118, 139, 192, 193, 208, 214
Hubbard, Elbert, 192
Huey, Edmund Burke, 88
Hughes, Charles, 269, *270*
Huss, Richard, 60

Illinois Type Founding Co. (Chicago), 36
Imprimerie Nationale (Paris), 217, 218
Industrial Educators of New Jersey, 199
Inland Printer (magazine), 5, 194, 220
   band machine, 62
   on Benton's perfectionism, 37
   Cheltenham type family, 109
   composing machines, 70
   on early American Type Founders Company, 83
   electrotype process for matrices, 15, 59
   fitting, in type making, 139
   on foundries' discounting practices, 79, 80
   Linn Boyd Benton, 67, 97
   Linotype machine, 64
   Morris Fuller Benton, 113, 262
   on Nelson's views, 104
   punch-cutting machine, 60–61
   Roycroft type, 192
   on self-spacing type, 49, 51–52

Colophon

Printed and bound by
Thomson Shore,
Dexter, Michigan
on Nature's Natural paper

Composed in Monotype's
digital version of Bulmer type,
originally designed about 1790
by William Martin
for the London Shakespeare Printing Office
of William Bulmer

Morris Benton revived Martin's type
for the American Type Founders Company,
and ATF Bulmer was issued in 1928

This book is made possible,
in part, by support from the
Bower Family Publication Fund at RIT

Designed by Marnie Soom
Cary Graphic Arts Press
Rochester, New York

green
press
INITIATIVE

RIT Press is committed to preserving ancient forests and natural resources. We elected to print this title on 30% post consumer recycled paper, processed chlorine free. As a result, for this printing, we have saved:

6 Trees (40' tall and 6-8" diameter)
2 Million BTUs of Total Energy
617 Pounds of Greenhouse Gases
2,973 Gallons of Wastewater
181 Pounds of Solid Waste

RIT Press made this paper choice because our printer, Thomson-Shore, Inc., is a member of Green Press Initiative, a nonprofit program dedicated to supporting authors, publishers, and suppliers in their efforts to reduce their use of fiber obtained from endangered forests.

For more information, visit www.greenpressinitiative.org

Environmental impact estimates were made using the Environmental Defense Paper Calculator. For more information visit: www.papercalculator.org.